BLACK NATIONALISM

ALIVE AND WELL

FREDERICK MONDERSON

SUMON PUBLISHERS

SuMon Publishers
PO Box 160586
Brooklyn, New York 11216

fredsegypt.com@fredsegypt.com
sumonpublishers.com@sumonpublishers.com
blackfolksbooks.com@blackfolksbooks.com
blackegyptbooks.com@blackegyptbooks.com

Copyright Frederick Monderson/SuMon Publishers, 2014. All Rights Reserved.

No part of this book may be reproduced, stored in a retrieval system, or transmitted by any means without the written permission of the author.

ISBN –1610230094
LCCN – 2010941482

Dr. Fred Monderson presenting a lecture at a "Book Party" to mark the release of his book entitled, "*The Holy Land: African Americans in Kemet/Egypt.*"

ABOUT THE AUTHOR

Frederick Monderson is a retired college professor and school teacher who taught African History in the City University of New York and American History and Government in the New York public schools. He has written nearly 1000 articles in the New York Black Press, *Daily Challenge*, *Afro Times* and *New American* newspapers. In this venture, Monderson lends his expertise as a historian, Egyptologist, journalist and author of several books including *Michael Jackson: The Last Dance*; *50 on Point*; *Barack Obama: Ready, Fit to Lead*; *Barack Obama: Master of Washington D.C.*; *Obama: Master and Commander*; *Sonny Carson: The Final Triumph (5 volumes)*; and on ancient Egypt - *Eternal House: The Egyptian Tomb*; *Ladies in the House*; *Seven Letters to Mike Tyson on Egyptian Temples*; *10 Poems Praising Great Blacks for Mike Tyson*; *Research Essays on Ancient Egypt*; *Temple of Karnak: The Majestic Architecture of Ancient Kemet*; *Where are the Kamite Kings?*; *Abydos and Osiris*; *Temple of Luxor*; *Medinet Habu: Mortuary Temple of Rameses III*; *The Quintessential Book on Ancient Egypt: "Holy Land" (*A Travel Novel on Egypt); *An Egyptian Resurrection*; *Hatshepsut's Temple at Deir el Bahari*; *The Majesty of Egyptian Gods and Temples* (a book of Egyptian Poems); *Intrigue Through Time (A Novel)*; *Egypt Essays on Ancient Kemet*; *The Ramesseum: Mortuary Temple of Rameses II*; *The Colonnade: Then and Now*; *Reflections on Ancient Kemet*; *Grassroots View of Ancient Egypt*; *Glory of the Ancestors: 19 Letters to O.J. Simpson on Ancient African History*; and *Celebrating Dr. Ben-Jochannan*. A student of the esteemed Dr. Yosef ben-Jochannan, Dr. Monderson conducts tours to Egypt.

For Tour information, Please contact Orleane Brooks-Williams at Nostrand Travel, 730 Nostrand Avenue, Brooklyn, New York 11216. Phone Number 718-756-5300. **Next Tour of Egypt** is **July 11-July 25, 2014**.

Black Nationalism. "Old Glory" in Red, White and Blue.

Black Nationalism. Elombe Brath's "Tribute to Gil Noble" in Harlem, on successfully hosting **LIKE IT IS** for 30 years on TV.

Black Nationalism. On the steps of City Hall, supporters gather to press for street naming for Brooklyn legend Sonny Carson.

Black Nationalism. Reverend Herbert Daughtry at the podium backed by Councilwoman Darlene Mealy, Imam Mohammed, Charles Barron, Al Vann, Conrad Mohammed and a host of others who truly believed Sonny Carson deserved the street naming honor.

Black Nationalism. Amiri Baraka (Leroy Jones) among members of the audience at Temple University's Forum following the 2008 Presidential Elections.

Black Nationalism. Councilmember Charles Barron and State Assemblyman Karim Camara join others to rename Linden Park, "Sonny Abubadika Park."

BLACK NATIONALISM ALIVE AND WELL

TABLE OF CONTENTS

1. INTRODUCTION — 49
2. WHO'S BETRAYING US TODAY? — 77
3. BEN CARSON, SERIOUSLY? — 91
4. SONNY CARSON: BORN VISIONARY — 112
5. REFLECTIONS ON RACE IN AMERICA 2008 — 124
6. HARRIET TUBMAN: LIVE FREE OR DIE! — 145
7. A. PHILIP RANDOLPH'S MARCH ON WASHINGTON, DC IN 1941 — 158
8. MARCUS GARVEY AND BLACK NATIONALISM — 177
9. MARCUS GARVEY AND THE UNIA — 192
10. HAVE WE FORGOTTEN SONNY CARSON? — 207
11. MARJORIE MATTHEWS: HEALTH CARE ADVOCATE EXTRAORDINAIRE! — 214
12. A BLACK AGENDA — 219
13. CEMOTAP, RON DANIELS AND HAITI — 229
14. WASHINGTON AVENUE NAMED FOR MARY GLOVER PINKETT — 238
15. REV. AL SHARPTON: THE NEXT LEVEL AND EARNED ASCENT — 244
16. THE BOOK OF ESSAYS ON ANCIENT KEMET, THE COLONNADE, AND ARCHITECTURAL FRAGMENTS FROM HERE AND THERE — 256
17. DICK GREGORY: CALLUS ON MY SOUL — 274
18. DICK GREGORY AT CEMOTAP — 280

FREDERICK MONDERSON

19.	JAMES BROWN: A PERSONAL VIEW	285
20.	PERSPECTIVES ON SONNY (AB) CARSON	294
21.	GEORGE SIMMONDS: UNSUNG HERO	309
22.	DR. YOSEF A.A. BEN-JOCHANNAN	311
23.	PRAISE FOR DR. BEN	338
24.	THE GOLDEN AGE OF WEST AFRICA	353
25.	CENTRAL BROOKLYN FAMILY HEALTH NETWORK 2009 LEGISLATIVE BREAKFAST	365
26.	SONNY CARSON: "TORCH STILL BURNING"	375
27.	SENMUT	379
28.	HANIBAL OF CARTHAGE	385
29.	MOHAMMED ALI	393
30.	SAMORI TOURE: "BLACK NAPOLEON OF THE SUDAN"	396
31.	RACE: FROM DUBOIS TO OBAMA	399
32.	BLACK MEN IN CHAINS, REVISITED	403
33.	NARMER/MENES	410
34.	ROSA PARKS	416
35.	BLACK SOLIDARITY DAY: HISTORY AND VISION	419
36.	BLACK SOLIDARITY DAY ACTIVITIES	428
37.	UNITED AFRICAN MOVEMENT	437
38.	LIKE IT IS AND IMPERIALISM	441
39.	MILLIONS MORE MOVEMENT: I Was There!	489
40.	GREED IS GOOD	504
41.	THE ROAD AHEAD	525
42.	BLACK NATIONALISM: ALIVE AND WELL	537

BLACK NATIONALISM ALIVE AND WELL

43.	WHO WERE THE ANCIENT EGYPTIANS?	542
44.	CELEBRATING DR. IVAN VAN SERTIMA	607
45.	BLACK SPENDING HABITS	623
46.	HEAVEN IN AN UPROAR	637
47.	DR. JOHN HENRIK CLARKE	653
48.	MAJOR OWENS: A REFLECTION	668
49.	SURPRISE: THEY'RE DISRESPECTING THE PRESIDENT	675
50.	PRESIDENT OBAMA'S MANDELA ADDRESS	681
51.	"SOUTHERN SHERIFFS"	691
52.	MR. MANDELA'S LONG WALK	698
53.	BOB LAW'S TRIBUTE TO MANDELA	724
54.	KWANZAA AT CEMOTAP	739
55.	DR. KARENGA ON KWANZAA	749

PHOTOGRAPH CAPTIONS

Black Nationalism 1. The First Fruits of the Kwanza Festival sits on the Kwanza Flag of Green, Red and Black.

Black Nationalism 1a. Jitu Weusi, iconic nationalist, educator, community leader, theorist, family man and friend, will forever remain in our hearts.

Black Nationalism 2. How Beautiful the People look among icons Jesse Jackson in the center and other fighters for freedom.

Black Nationalism 3. Angela Davis, educator, activist and Nationalist who befriended George Jackson is honored by the Bed-Stuy community in this mural.

FREDERICK MONDERSON

Black Nationalism 4. Mural on side of a building at Church Avenue and Rogers Avenue depicting the tri-parte – Slave Castle in West Africa, "The Door of No Return," and the waiting and packed slave ship.

Black Nationalism 5. A Playground for America's first martyred patriot, Crispus Attucks, the epitome of Black Nationalism!

Black Nationalism 5a. "Master Teacher," Dr. Leonard James, Professor Emeritus, New York City Technical College, CUNY.

Black Nationalism 6. Rainbow **PUSH** Coalition says "Eliminate Student Loan Debt" and people want "Jobs Now!"

Black Nationalism 6a. Veteran activist Jitu Weusi and his brother Job Mashiriki share a joyful moment.

Black Nationalism 7. Elk Street renamed the "African Burial Ground Way," in Lower Manhattan.

Black Nationalism 8. Erik and two friends at the "March on Washington," 8-24-2013.

Black Nationalism 8a. Jitu Weusi and son Kojo help provide "Security" at the Million Woman March in Philadelphia.

Black Nationalism 8b. Jitu Weusi and Dr. Fred Monderson share a moment together at this affair for Sonny Carson.

Black Nationalism 9. "Sacred Space," the African Burial Ground!

Black Nationalism 9a. Sonny Carson, accompanied by Prof. Patterson (left) and Prof James Smalls (right) and anther, conducts a tour of a church basement that was a station of the Underground Railroad.

Black Nationalism 9b Prof. James Smalls speaks at the Institutional Church on Adelphi Street, Brooklyn, on the significance of the "Bones of the Runaway Samuel Carson" on way to Ghana for internment as a site of African American pilgrimage.

Black Nationalism 10. Erik Monderson among the Brothers who gathered to celebrate the 50th Anniversary of the March on Washington, 2013.

BLACK NATIONALISM
ALIVE AND WELL

Black Nationalism 11. Erik posing with the "Empowered" poster of the National Urban League.

Black Nationalism 12. Leading the charge, among the Ladies, who have been so instrumental in the struggles to free African people.

Black Nationalism 13. Among the leaders of the parade at the "50th Anniversary of the March on Washington, for Jobs and Freedom."

Black Nationalism 14. Voting Equals Democracy is a way to empower Blacks who hold the "balance of power" as Malcolm said!

Black Nationalism 15. … And "Children Shall Lead Them!"

Black Nationalism 16. Yes, "Failure is not an Option" is a message very apropos to any struggle.

Black Nationalism 17. Dr. John Henrik Clarke, long a light and Black Nationalist theorist, no longer with us but whose spirit lives on in Clarke House in Harlem beside his beautiful wife, Sister Sybil Williams-Clarke and their escorts.

Black Nationalism 18. On the mural wall of Amun-Ra, depictions of Bob Marley, Dr. Erik Williams, Malcolm X, Marcus Garvey, Kwame Nkrumah, Toussaint L'Ouverture, and Haile Selaisse as well as Harriet Tubman and Maurice Bishop.

Black Nationalism 19. Dr. Yosef ben-Jochannan pictured on the same above mural with the famous quote from the *Papyrus of Hunefer* indicating the "Origin of the ancient Egyptians."

Black Nationalism 20. One of "Our Fathers," Dr. John Henrik Clarke, who himself did "A Long and Mighty Walk."

Black Nationalism 21. "Two Great Ones," Manhattan Borough President Percy Sutton and Mayor David Dinkins. Two Harlem and New York political icons; Sutton did much for Harlem and the Black cause, while Dinkins did a great deal for the Borough of Manhattan and the City of New York.

FREDERICK MONDERSON

Black Nationalism 22. Radio Legend, Gary Byrd, creator of the **GBE** (Gary Byrd Experience) "Global Black Experience."

Black Nationalism 23. Dr. John Henrik Clarke on the same Brooklyn mural stating an unmistakable fact: "The role of history is to tell a people what they have been, where they have been, what they are, where they are, where they still must go, and what they still must be!"

Black Nationalism 24. Black Power in its classic sense with (from left to right), Charlie Rangel, David Dinkins, Bertrand Aristide, Jesse Jackson and Major Owens.

Black Nationalism 25. Rev. Charles Norris, Sr., Pastor of Bethesda Missionary Baptist Church of Jamaica Avenue in Queens was tremendously incensed in the statement: "Have you seen what they are doing to my President Barack Obama!"

Black Nationalism 26. The "Sons of Africa" buried in the historic "African Burial Ground" in Foley Square, Lower Manhattan.

Black Nationalism 27. Dr. James McIntosh and Sister Betty Dobson, Co-founders and Co-Chairs of **CEMOTAP** (Committee to Eliminate Media Offensive to African People).

Black Nationalism 28. The African family, shackled and on the auction block, as depicted on the mural!

Black Nationalism 29. Many facets of the mural depicting issues in the Black experience.

Black Nationalism 30. Description of factors related to the **Underground Railroad** in which "Runaways" were assisted in their flight from slavery.

Black Nationalism 31. Samori Marksman, Radio Personality of Station **WBAI**.

Black Nationalism 32. Professor James Blake, who is always on point on Black History.

Black Nationalism 33. Locations in the Bronx and Brooklyn where "Stations on the Underground Railroad" were located.

BLACK NATIONALISM
ALIVE AND WELL

Black Nationalism 34. More locations of "Stations of the Underground Railroad" in Manhattan, Queens and Staten Island.

Black Nationalism 34a. Harriet Tubman, Liberator, Intelligence Agent and Humanitarian.

Black Nationalism 35. There is a message in the man's attire.

Black Nationalism 35a. Dr. Leonard James and the young men he schooled.

Black Nationalism 36. Sojourner Truth Social Reformer, Orator and humanitarian.

Black Nationalism 37. Frederick Douglass - Publisher, Orator, Author and American Statesman.

Black Nationalism 38. Dr. James McCune Smith, Doctor and Author.

Black Nationalism 39. The Brothers, Arthur and Lewis Tappan, Entrepreneurs and Reformers.

Black Nationalism 40. Ministers Reverend Henry Ward Beecher and Henry Highland Garnett.

Black Nationalism 40a. Ms. Pusey, Education activist, "folk heroine" and resident of Brooklyn, New York.

Black Nationalism 41. Sonny Carson admires the poster-bill for his Biography-movie, **The Education of Sonny Carson**.

Black Nationalism 42. Marjorie Matthews, education, health care and social activist beside an associate.

Black Nationalism 43. Wearing the lion skin, Ptah stands with scepter and ankh with the Sphinx and Pyramid at his rear, the beetle, ankh and obelisk represented beside the emblem of Sankofa, "Return to Fetch it!"

Black Nationalism 43a. Mother showing the young the many roads that diverge from the straight and narrow!

FREDERICK MONDERSON

Black Nationalism 44.   Dr. Leonard Jeffries makes a point at an event following the death of Sonny Carson.

Black Nationalism 45.   Prof. James Black, a lucid mind, full of information on Black History.

Black Nationalism 45. Jitu Weusi speaks at an affair honoring Sonny Carson shortly after his passing.

Black Nationalism 45a. Very young Erik Monderson poses with Jitu Weusi.

Black Nationalism 46.   Ma'at wearing her emblematic feather headdress with outstretched arms stands for truth, righteousness and justice.

Black Nationalism 47.   Map of the Nile, the Red Sea and flora of the landscape.

Black Nationalism 48. At Akbar's funeral, Sonny Carson in yellow hat (center) is surrounded by several others including George Murden (left) and former Brooklyn Deputy-Borough President Ms. Jeanette Gadsen (facing).

Black Nationalism 49.   Robert Matthews, former Chairman of Community Board 8 in Brooklyn.

Black Nationalism 50.   Black American Leaders on wall behind the happy lady, as seen from her smiling face.

Black Nationalism 51.   Black Lady II. Judge Phillips asks, "Black Man, which one are you?"

Black Nationalism 51a.   Gil Noble at the podium to introduce **CEMOTAP's** Guest Speaker – Dick Gregory in 2005.

Black Nationalism 51b. African people saying hello as is customary in their friendly frame of mind.

Black Nationalism 52.   Dr. Adelaide Sanford makes a point at affair honoring Sonny Carson after "he passed" to join the ancestors.

Black Nationalism 53.   Dr. James McIntosh shows off the newest issue of the **Freedom Fighters Journal**.

Black Nationalism 54.   The artist Sapp in hat to the right and working his paint palette has produced this masterpiece on Sly's

BLACK NATIONALISM
ALIVE AND WELL

Trophy Shop wall that is no longer on display but preserved in this writer's effort.

Black Nationalism 55. One of the many mythical scenes of early Africa painted by the artist Sapp.

Black Nationalism 56. Ossie Davis, actor, activist and beloved husband is flanked by two righteous brothers.

Black Nationalism 57. Hawking the **Amsterdam News** is Brother Abdul Haqq, while the Journalist Playtel Benjamin, "The Sword of Obama," purchases a copy.

Black Nationalism 58. An Expression explaining how fighting systems came about by various peoples.

Black Nationalism 59. Another explanation of how fighting systems came about.

Black Nationalism 60. Image of President Barack Obama serving his first term.

Black Nationalism 61. Slave Theater I is a veritable storehouse of remarkable wisdom.

Black Nationalism 62. Sign carried in the 2010 "Rally on the Mall."

Black Nationalism 63. The names are yours for the taking.

Black Nationalism 64. It took "Marbles" for this guy to wear this shirt at the 2010 "Rally on the Mall."

Black Nationalism 64a. While Dr. James McIntosh, Co-Chair of **CEMOTAP** and **BEPAA** speaks about Malcolm X at **Clarke House**, Black Panther and Nationalist Shepherd listens attentively.

Black Nationalism 65. The Judge oftentimes told the truth!

Black Nationalism 66. Dr. Fred Monderson and on board a Felucca on the Nile River.

FREDERICK MONDERSON

Black Nationalism 67. Activist icon Jitu Weusi on the "Protest Circuit" fighting for the best in Education.

Black Nationalism 68. The power of reading is the message of this mural.

Black Nationalism 68a. Delegates to the "All-Caribbean People's Conference" in Barbados, August 1, 2010

Black Nationalism 69. Again, the "Old Master" is at it again.

Black Nationalism 70. New York City Councilman Jumane Williams at the Martin Luther King celebration.

Black Nationalism 71. Here the message takes a religious bent.

Black Nationalism 72. Little Black Angels sure are cute.

Black Nationalism 72a. Mother Africa doing her thing painting a wonderful environment.

Black Nationalism 73. The belief is this fellow is lost!

Black Nationalism 74. Congressman Harold Forde and Erik Monderson at Sharpton's tribute to Dr. M.L. King.

Black Nationalism 75. Jim Butler, union leader and fierce fighter for his constituencies.

Black Nationalism 76. Reverend Al Sharpton poses with two Black "heavyweights."

Black Nationalism 77. Question is, "Who is the Real Black man?" He asks and answers his own question!

Black Nationalism 78. This is a really cute one!

Black Nationalism 79. New York State Governor David Patterson.

Black Nationalism 79a. Marcus Garvey, Mohammed Ali and Stevie Wonder are featured in this mural on Sly's Wall in Brooklyn.

Black Nationalism 80. A. Philip Randolph, activist, labor leader and President of Sleeping Car Porters of America.

Black Nationalism 81. The Big contradiction! "May the Good Lord Have Mercy!"

BLACK NATIONALISM
ALIVE AND WELL

Black Nationalism 82. Congressman Charlie Rangel hugs young Erik Monderson at Sharpton's affair for Dr. King.

Black Nationalism 83. Laugh, laugh, laugh!

Black Nationalism 84. People praying for President Obama outside the White House.

Black Nationalism 84a. Two beautiful ladies on a visit to Clarke House in Harlem to hear Dr. Leonard Jeffries speak on Malcolm X.

Black Nationalism 85. Well, read the message.

Black Nationalism 86. This image is subject to interpretation.

Black Nationalism 86b. The Honorable Minister Louis Farrakhan, Leader, The Nation of Islam!

Black Nationalism 86a. Delegate at the Podium at the All Caribbean People's Conference in Barbados in 2010.

Black Nationalism 87. Barack Obama and the winning galvanizing "Yes We Can" logo.

Black Nationalism 88. Amiri Baraka, Poet Laureate of New Jersey and nationalist extraordinaire

Black Nationalism 89. "Washing an Ethiopian White?"

Black Nationalism 90. Amiri Baraka (Leroy Jones), extraordinary revolutionary poet and one-time Poet Laureate of New Jersey, his home state.

Black Nationalism 91. Rev. Jesse Jackson with Judge Bruce ("Cut 'em Loose Bruce") Wright.

Black Nationalism 92. Judge Philips calls this, "No further Division of Black Men."

Black Nationalism 93. Go Rilla Commandments and their Purpose.

Black Nationalism 94. A Compatriot from struggles at and with **National Action Network**.

FREDERICK MONDERSON

Black Nationalism 95. The Messenger, Elijah Mohammed, founder of the Black Muslims of America.

Black Nationalist 95a. Longtime Black Nationalist Brother in the audience at Clarke House to hear about Malcolm X.

Black Nationalism 96. The "Lion in Brooklyn!"

Black Nationalism 96a. New York City Councilman Jumane Williams with Erik Monderson at the 2013 "March on Washington."

Black Nationalism 97. Erik Monderson shakes hands with two New York State Senators, John Sampson and Erik Adams.

Black Nationalism 97a. "Mother" in her numerous varieties.

Black Nationalism 97b. Enduring mother's love for a child!

Black Nationalism 98. Education Icon Jitu Weusi and State Assemblywoman Inez Baron on the Firing Line protesting Mayor Bloomberg's choice of Chancellor for the City of New York's Board of Education.

Black Nationalism 98a. Barry Campbell and members of his organization, **Veterans Quality of Life** (The Forgotten Ones) that helps veterans get various forms of benefits.

Black Nationalist 98b. Celebrated author, columnist and Harlemite Herb Boyd offers wisdom on the Life and Times of Malcolm X at Clarke House in Harlem.

Black Nationalism 99. Gentleman holds photograph of Judge John Phillips, founder and proprietor of the Slave Theater I and II in Brooklyn, whose powerful "Images decorated Mon's living room!"

Black Nationalism 100. Beauty - Physical and Botanical, "Kiss the Rose!"

Black Nationalism 101. Oh, that sweet angel called **MOTHER**!

Black Nationalism 102. Michele and Barack Obama dolls surround that of Abraham Lincoln.

Black Nationalism 103. This message is about freedom of worship!

BLACK NATIONALISM
ALIVE AND WELL

Black Nationalism 103a. Barry Campbell leads his contingent down Fifth Avenue at the 2013 Veterans Day parade in Manhattan.

Black Nationalism 104. Reversing the process of enslavement!

Black Nationalism 104a. Following Sonny Carson's death, singers and dancers from Ghana came to pay tribute and so the Brothers did the **PUSH Ceremony** with the youngest Brother there!

Black Nationalism 105. Sonny Carson accompanied by two Brothers as the poster bill for the movie **The Education of Sonny Carson** stands over their shoulders.

Black Nationalism 106. Sonny Carson's *The Final Triumph* in 4 volumes.

Black Nationalism 107. The "Man" and "Master" Judge John L. Phillips, responsible for the murals of the two movie houses, "The Slave Theater I and II."

Black Nationalism 108. Mr. Caldwell, President of the **77th Precinct Council** shakes hands with Erik Monderson.

Black Nationalism 108a. The Brothers doing **PUSH**!

Black Nationalism 109. Marjorie Matthews, extraordinary education, health care and community activist.

Black Nationalism 110. His Imperial Majesty, Haile Selassie I.

Black Nationalism 110a. Dr. Leonard Jeffries speaks at **Clarke House** on Malcolm X but delves into how things are getting better in Africa and does so by the use of illustrations.

Black Nationalism 111. Collage of "The Prophet Marcus Moziah Garvey." May he live forever!

Black Nationalism 112. Senator Erik Adams shakes hands with Erik Monderson at Sharpton's Affair.

Black Nationalism 113. Malcolm X will live forever!

FREDERICK MONDERSON

Black Nationalism 113a. Members of "**The Brotherhood**," Ofori Payton (left); Diallo, Bishop Shivers (second from right); Atiim Ferguson and the Bishop's son who presents Sonny Carson "Holding Forth the Light."

Black Nationalism 114. In Haiti, Connie Lesold of Crown Heights, Brooklyn, and Madame Marie Rene, **Founder and Chancellor of the University of the Haitian Academy** (First in New York and then in Haiti,) sandwich **Sister** who was the sole survivor of a convent demolished during the Earthquake.

Black Nationalism 115. Much loved by all Americans, President John Fitzgerald Kennedy!

Black Nationalism 116. The Presidential Palace in Haiti after the Earthquake that wrecked havoc on that poor island.

Black Nationalism 117. President Lynden Johnson, successor who established continuity of President Kennedy's "Great Society Program" which brought to fruition the **1964 Civil Rights Act** and the **1965 Voting Rights Act**.

Black Nationalism 118. President Bertrand Aristide of Haiti who erected this memorial to the **Haitian Constitution of 1801** in homage to Toussaint L'Ouverture (1743-1803).

Black Nationalism 119. The National Cathedral in Haiti after the earthquake that was so devastating.

Black Nationalism 120. President Bertrand Aristide and friends in New York.

Black Nationalism 121. Heroes of the Haitian Revolution are enshrined in statue.

Black Nationalism 122. The People and their Liberators in Haiti.

Black Nationalism 123. Marcus Garvey among other art expressions.

Black Nationalism 124. Washington Avenue, a street, dedicated to Mary Pinkett.

BLACK NATIONALISM
ALIVE AND WELL

Black Nationalism 125. Image of Marcus Garvey as portrayed by Ron Bob Semple.

Black Nationalism 126. Logo of Al Sharpton's "Keepers of the Dream 2011."

Black Nationalism 127. Dr. Roscoe Lee Brown (right) and an associate, both members of "Tuskegee Airmen," famous fighters during World War II.

Black Nationalism 128. Toussaint L'Ouverture, Haitian Liberator.

Black Nationalism 129. Charles Finch III, in Washington, DC, commenting on the significance of the election of Barack Obama as President.

Black Nationalism 130. Reverend Al Sharpton, "AB" "Abubadika" Sonny Carson and Reverend Wyatt Tee Walker at **National Action Network** headquarters.

Black Nationalism 131. Ladies and Gents of all hues.

Black Nationalism 132. The "Young Al Sharpton" listens attentively to concerns of "The People."

Black Nationalism 133. "The Savior!" In his true self! Look at both, but closely at the picture to the left!

Black Nationalism 134. New York State Governor David Patterson embraces Erik Monderson at Al Sharpton's "Keepers of the Dream 2011" affair.

Black Nationalism 135. Commerce Secretary in the Clinton Administration, Ron Brown, killed in an aircraft crash.

Black Nationalism 136. Great Americans, George Washington, Abraham Lincoln and another great but unknown Black Man.

Black Nationalism 137. Harry Belafonte, "Quintessential Black Activist" with a youngster.

Black Nationalism 138. "Our Father" Marcus Moziah Garvey (1887-1940).

FREDERICK MONDERSON

Black Nationalism 139. All the powerful Black "movers and shakers" are shown in this mural.

Black Nationalism 140. Replica sample of a Slave Castle on the Coast of West Africa that held the "**Door of No Return**" through which millions of Africans passed on way to New World enslavement.

Black Nationalism 141. Celebrants gather for a January 1st Religious Ceremony at a Batey in San Juan de la Maguanas in Dominican Republic.

Black Nationalism 142. The Monster and the "Dragon," Bruce Lee.

Black Nationalism 143. Councilman Charles Barron and his wife, Inez Barron, a "Power Couple," who go all out for the people!

Black Nationalism 144. If you recall, Putney Swope reminded us, "The Drums carry a message all need to hear!"

Black Nationalism 145. Quintessential Black Nationalist!

Black Nationalism 146. Dick Gregory, "distance runner" some have labeled "The Bear Hunter," who sure knows his facts!

Black Nationalism 147. Perennial and Quintessential Nationalist, Sister Viola Plummer of the **December 12th Movement**.

Black Nationalism 148. The continent of Africa under assault!

Black Nationalism 149. Image of Dr. Martin Luther King, Jr. in that memorable pose associated with his "I Have a Dream" speech at the 1963 March on Washington.

Black Nationalism 150. The entrance of a school named for the Haitian Liberator Toussaint L'Ouverture; and, entrance to Medgar Evers College for the Civil Rights advocate killed for registering people to vote.

Black Nationalism 150a. Sonny Carson in a relaxed and pensive mood.

Black Nationalism 151. Egyptian Ankhs in bow-tie.

BLACK NATIONALISM
ALIVE AND WELL

Black Nationalism 152. "If you don't stand for something you will fall for anything." This Brother certainly stands for many things and he should be celebrated and commemorated.

Black Nationalism 153. Queen Mother Moore on the road and in company of wonderful people.

Black Nationalism 153a. Jitu Weusi (left); Sonny Carson, Atiim Ferguson; and Joshua (right); on way to attend the Malcolm X Parade in Bushwick, Brooklyn.

Black Nationalism 154. The High School on Fulton Street in Bedford-Stuyvesant in Brooklyn, where Nelson Mandela visited and which will be renamed for the South African icon.

Black Nationalism 154a. Jitu Weusi, another Brother, Angela Weusi, Sonny Carson and George Murden at the **African Street Festival** on Boys and Girls High School grounds.

Black Nationalism 154b. Cherise Maloney speaks to an attentive Sonny Carson on Boys and Girls grounds.

Black Nationalism 154c. Cherise Maloney, George Murden and Sonny Carson who greets an admirer.

Black Nationalism 154d. Michael Hooper of **Roots Revisited** and Legendary Basketball Coach Mr. George Murden.

Black Nationalism 155. Here's a historic intersection in Brooklyn where Harriet Ross Tubman Avenue meets Malcolm Boulevard. It is interesting that Sonny Carson played an important part in naming these two streets.

Black Nationalism 156. Sonny Carson examines and discusses the bones of his ancestor Samuel Carson, **The Runaway**, with Atiim Ferguson and others in attendance.

Black Nationalism 156a. Flying the Colors!

Black Nationalism 156b. Prof. James Smalls (left), an unnamed "Brother," Sonny Carson and Mzee Mora (right).

Black Nationalism 156c. The Caption contains the message.

FREDERICK MONDERSON

Black Nationalism 157. Close-up of the street name of the Super-Nationalist, Malcolm X.

Black Nationalism 157a. The Legendary Malcolm Little turned Malik El-Hajj Shabazz, Malcolm X.

Black Nationalism 158. Sonny Carson (left), Atiim Ferguson (center) and James (Chief) Parker (right), "The Brotherhood."

Black Nationalist 158a. Senator Montgomery, Sonny Carson and Omowale Clay, testify at the Medgar Evers Congressional Hearing on Police Brutality convened by Congressman John Conyers and a Congressional delegation.

Black Nationalism 158b. Congressmen John Conyers (left), Major Owens (right) and Coleman (center) comprising the male members of the Congressional Delegation holding hearings on Police Brutality in New York City especially.

Black Nationalism 158c. John Conyers and other members of the Congressional Delegation conducting "Hearings" on "NYC Police Brutality," which is a national trend.

Black Nationalism 158d. At his funeral parade banner extols Sonny (Abubadika) Carson as the Founder of the **Committee to Honor Black Heroes**.

Black Nationalism 158e. Mother Jordan and son walk behind Dr. Delores Blakeley in the funeral parade for Sonny Carson.

Black Nationalism 158f. At the start of the funeral parade beside New York Technical College near the Brooklyn Bridge, Councilman Charles Barron, Abdul Haqq, Rev. Herbert Daughtry and Reverend Mother Jordan and her son.

Black Nationalism 158g. The funeral parade works its way down Fulton Street towards the Bedford Stuyvesant community.

Black Nationalism 159. The school Sonny Carson was instrumental in naming for Malcolm X, El Hajj Malik el Shabazz.

Black Nationalism 159a. Lumumba Carson, son of famed activist Sonny Carson.

BLACK NATIONALISM
ALIVE AND WELL

Black Nationalism 160. Professor Kelson Maynard steadfastedly at what he does best, preparing for the next lecture, as a classroom teacher.

Black Nationalism 160a. At the funeral and flanked by Ali Lamont and Rasheed Allah, "Pops" holds high the impending street name of Harriet Tubman Avenue.

Black Nationalism 160b. The funeral parade finally arrives at **Restoration Plaza** where Sonny Carson "Held Court!"

Black Nationalism 160c. Dr. Segun Shabaka and John Branch, founder of the **African Poetry Theater** in New York.

Black Nationalism 161.   The famed Malcolm X, El Hajj Malik Shabazz, "More than just a man," an extraordinary leader and visionary.

Black Nationalism 162.   Prof. George Simmonds embraces young Fred Monderson on a visit to Middle School 61, Gladstone Atwell in Brooklyn.

Black Nationalism 162a. Rev. Charles Norris, Sr., "Spiritual Father" of the **CEMOTAP** Movement and Pastor Emeritus of Bethesda Missionary Baptist Church.

Black Nationalism 163.   Dr. Josef ben-Jochannan, elder nationalist, author, lecturer and early self-publishing promoter.

Black Nationalism 164.   At the "Tribute to Prof. George Simmonds" at the Victoria 5 Theater in Harlem, "Young" Fred Monderson sat at the feet of his heroes.

Black Nationalism 164.   At the "Tribute to Prof. George Simmonds" at the Victoria 5 Theater in Harlem, "Young" Fred Monderson sat at the feet of his heroes, with Dr. Ben in light suit.

Black Nationalism 165.   Dr. Yosef ben-Jochannan delivers a Lecture with a number of his Self-published works in background.

Black Nationalism 166.   Sister Dr. Betty Shabazz, wife of Malcolm X, who always said, "Find the Good and Praise it!"

Black Nationalism 166a.   Celebrating **KWANZAA** in New York.

FREDERICK MONDERSON

Black Nationalism 167. Dr. Fred Monderson sits beside his mentor and friend, Dr. Yosef ben-Jochannan, at a Harlem lecture.

Black Nationalism 168. Honorable Robert "Sonny" Carson, venerated activist, always insisted young people "Stay in School."

Black Nationalism 168a. Sonny Carson and his son Lumumba Carson at the funeral for **Allah U Akbar**.

Black Nationalism 169. Another view of Dr. Ben-Jochannan delivering a lecture at the Dempsey Center in Harlem.

Black Nationalism 169a. **Allah U Akbar**, whose funeral drew some important persons, is shown on horseback.

Black Nationalism 169b. Sonny Carson, Atiim Ferguson and Mr. Wright, in tearful moment, came to pay respects to Akbar.

Black Nationalism 169c. Richard Green of the **Youth Collective** came to pay his respects to Akbar.

Black Nationalism 170. The revered Reverend Dr. Martin Luther King, Jr. (1929-1968).

Black Nationalism 170a. Attorney Carl Thomas is interviewed for a local program.

Black Nationalism 170b. "In the Name of Allah U Akbar."

Black Nationalism 171. Dr. Yosef ben-Jochannan sits beside a friend with young Senator David Patterson, who will later become Lieutenant and then Governor of New York State, in light coat, standing in rear.

Black Nationalism 171a. Cherise Maloney sits, admiring the **PUSH** Ceremony.

Black Nationalism 172. The highly respected and admired South African icon and freedom fighter who spent 27-years in prison to finally dismantle apartheid and whose autobiography was entitled "A Long Walk to Freedom."

Black Nationalism 173. Dr. Leonard Jeffries, Prof. James Smalls and Dr. Lewis, the Ophthalmologist from Harlem who address a gathering at PS 258 in Brooklyn.

BLACK NATIONALISM ALIVE AND WELL

Black Nationalism 173a. Rev. Al Sharpton and Carl Thomas sit and listen attentively to testimony at the Congressional Hearings on Police Brutality.

Black Nationalism 173b. Attorney Carl Thomas gives testimony to the Congressional delegation on Police Brutality.

Black Nationalism 173c. Its Ron Daniels' turn to give testimony.

Black Nationalism 173d. Members of the audience expressing their cases at the Congressional Hearing on Police Brutality (top); while others sit silently, with Connie Lesold (center) and Marlene Sanders beside her, as events unfold.

Black Nationalism 173e. Families expressing their grief to the Congressional Delegation about their loss due to violence.

Black Nationalism 174. Musical legend Bob Marley featured in this mural in the Bed-Stuy area of Brooklyn.

Black Nationalism 175. "Young" Fred Monderson, student of Dr. ben-Jochannan and more importantly, Dr. Leonard James.

Black Nationalism 176. Sign indicating the **African Burial Ground National Monument** served by the National Parks Service of the U.S. Department of the Interior.

Black Nationalism 177. Sankofa International Academy is one of those institutions Bob Law insisted we support financially and otherwise for the good work they do in educating our youth.

Black Nationalis178. Entrance to **The Ancestral Chamber** or **The Well**, a sort of **Door of No Return**! Interesting, but Sonny Carson created **The Door of Return** by repatriating his ancestor, **The Runaway**, Samuel Carson, to Ghana to create a site of pilgrimage for African Americans seeking their ancestral roots in Africa.

Black Nationalism 179. The engraved message on the wall of the **Ancestral Chamber** says it all!

FREDERICK MONDERSON

Black Nationalism 180. Entrance into **The Well** showing continents, symbolisms and names and dates of African buried therein.

Black Nationalism 181. View from within **Circle of the Diaspora** or **The well** where the following engraved symbolism recounts the religious and philosophical belief systems, not simply of Africans, but of other people also.

Black Nationalism 182. Circle of the Diaspora – Close-up evidence of the map of Africa and the West carved in the floor of the Memorial.

Black Nationalism 183. **ANKH** - "Egyptian Symbol of Life!"

Black Nationalism 184. **LATIN CROSS** - "Christian Faith."

Black Nationalism 185. **TANIT** - "Islamic Faith."

Black Nationalism 186. **GYE NYAME** - "Supremacy of God."

Black Nationalism 187. **LEGBA** - "Guardian of the Crossroads."

Black Nationalism 188. Fred Monderson pets the brown bear.

Black Nationalism 189. **BARON** - "Male Cemetery Guardian."

Black Nationalism 190. Cherise Maloney and Clive Monderson sandwich Dr. Fred Monderson of Brooklyn, New York.

Black Nationalism 191. **MANMAN BRIGITTE** - "Female Cemetery Guardian."

Black Nationalism 192. **YOWA** – "Continuity of Human Life."

Black Nationalism 193. **MEDICINE WHEEL** - "Native American Circle of Life."

Black Nationalism 193a. Brother Herman and Mrs. Ferguson, quintessential nationalists.

BLACK NATIONALISM ALIVE AND WELL

Black Nationalism 194. **NKISI SARABANDA** - "Signature of the Spirit."

Black Nationalism 195. **NSOROMMA** - "Guardianship."

Black Nationalism 196. View of Deir el Bahari temple from the north showing the two ramps and three colonnades.

Black Nationalism 197. **ASASE YE DURU** - "Divinity of Mother Earth."

Black Nationalism 198. Image of the Tomb of Vizier Nespakashuty, 26th Dynasty.

Black Nationalism 199. **FUNTUNFUNEEU ENKYEMFUNEFU** - "Unity in Diversity."

Black Nationalism 200. **HYE WON HYE** - "Imperishability and Endurance."

Black Nationalism 201. **MATE MASIE** - "Wisdom and Prudence."

Black Nationalism 202. **AKOMA NTOSO** - "Understanding."

Black Nationalism 203. **DWENNIMMEN** – "Humility and Strength."

Black Nationalism 204. Tomb of Vizier Nespakashuty, 26th Dynasty, on the slopes of the North Assasif beside the Deir el Bahari amphitheater.

Black Nationalism 205. **DENKYEM** - "Adaptability."

Black Nationalism 206. **AKOMA** - "Endurance."

Black Nationalism 207. **NSIBIDI SYMBOL** - "Love and Unity."

Black Nationalism 208. **The African Burial Ground Way** at Elk Street in Lower Manhattan.

Black Nationalism 209. **CHI WARA** – "Symbol of the Spirit of the African Burial Ground" in Foley Square.

FREDERICK MONDERSON

Black Nationalism 210   The Thurgood Marshall U.S. Courthouse in honor of the Honorable Supreme Court Justice.

Black Nationalism 211.   The African Burial Ground, "A Place of Remembrance."

Black Nationalism 212.   Mural showing the **Circle of Diaspora**, **Ancestral Chamber** and **Ancestral Reinterment Ground**.

Black Nationalism 213.   Part of the activist demonstrations held in 1992 when the site of the African Burial Ground was first discovered.

Black Nationalism 213a.   The message is clear!

Black Nationalism 214.   The Last and most Terrible Ordeal of the Soul of the Scribe Ani.

Black Nationalism 215.   Ani, Vindicated in the Day of his Judgment, Comes Before Osiris.

Black Nationalism 216.   Evidence of "Sacred Traditions" in the "Sacred Space" and efforts surrounding the fight to preserve the site.

Black Nationalism 217.   Burial scene showing no more than 12 persons the legal amount permitted to attend a funeral.

Black Nationalism 218.   Step-Pyramid of Zoser at Sakkara, forerunner of all its kind.

Black Nationalism 219.   The most famous of all the Pyramids of Egypt, the "Crowning Triad of the Gizeh Plateau."

Black Nationalism 220.   "Sacred Tradition," "Sacred Ground."

Black Nationalism 220a.   Dr. Jeffries gestures with a map showing distortion in representation in relation to the size of Africa.

Black Nationalism 221.   Africans in Early New York!

Black Nationalism 222.   Notice the white guy wears a shoe but the Black does not!

Black Nationalism 223.   Poster for the naming of Linden Park for Sonny Carson.

BLACK NATIONALISM
ALIVE AND WELL

Black Nationalism 223a. At the Elombe Brath sponsored Harlem event celebrating 30-years of "**Like It Is**," Atiim Ferguson, *Daily Challenge* Publisher Tom Watkins, Sonny Carson and Gil Noble.

Black Nationalism 223b. Sonny Carson relaxes with his Chief of Staff Atiim Ferguson (right) and Security Detail of Rasheed Allah (right) and James (Chief) Parker at rear.

Black Nationalism 223c. Sonny Carson meets Congressman Charlie Rangel.

Black Nationalism 224.   Changing Landscape in New York City.

Black Nationalism 225.   Dr. Fred Monderson was on hand for the naming of Linden Park, **Sonny Abubadika Carson Park**.

Black Nationalism 225a. Councilwoman Una Clarke (seated), as Rev. Calvin Butts and Gil Noble introduces Dr. Benjamin Chavis to Mrs. Gil Noble.

Black Nationalism 226. Changing landscape obscures the past!

Black Nationalism 227.   Sonny Carson as "The Bringer of the Light!"

Black Nationalism 227a. Jitu Weusi greets Gil Noble thanking him for 30-years of Television journalist service to the Black Community.

Black Nationalism 228.   Message of the **Chi Wara**!

Black Nationalism 228a. Rev. Calvin Butts, Pastor of Abyssinian Baptist Church in Harlem, sits between Councilwoman Una Clarke and Mrs. Gil Noble.

Black Nationalism 229.   Lorenzo Pace's Message of the **Chi Wara** Dedication!

FREDERICK MONDERSON

Black Nationalism 229a. Red, Black and Green on the Great Lawn, listening to the Minister Farrakhan at the Million Family March.

Black Nationalism 230. Self Portrait of the artist Sapp who left public evidence of his work in Bed-Stuy and Crown Heights that has subsequently deteriorated by force of the weather and graffiti. Fortunately this writer has preserved some aspects of his creativity.

Black Nationalism 231. Mural created by the Artist Sapp.

Black Nationalism 232. Chancellor of the University of the Haitian Academy, Madame Marie Rene and Connie Lesold on the institution's grounds in Haiti.

Black Nationalism 233. The Group including Dr. Leonard Monroe in Egypt.

Black Nationalism 234. "Moms Mabley" and cartoon characters created by the Artist Sapp.

Black Nationalism 235. Keisha and "Chief" Bryce Green in embrace.

Black Nationalism 235a. Dr. Fred Monderson poses with Dr. Maulana and Mrs. Karenga, founder of **Kwanzaa** and the **Nguzu Saba**.

Black Nationalism 236. Marcus Garvey, Mohammed Ali and Stevie Wonder, Black American heroic figures.

Black Nationalism 237. A panoramic view of the mural created by the Artist Sapp on the wall of **Syl's Trophies** on Nostrand Avenue in Brooklyn which has now disappeared. This shows that history not preserved does not exist!

Black Nationalism 238. As Cherise Maloney stands beside Brooklyn Icon Jitu Weusi in a relaxed mood, Basir Mchawi gives a report at the **African Street Festival** held at Boys and Girls High School, soon to be renamed for Nelson Mandela.

Black Nationalism 239. Journalist Euline Innis beside photographer Lem Peterkin, at an affair held in the Sankofa Academy School on Fulton Street in Brooklyn, New York.

BLACK NATIONALISM
ALIVE AND WELL

Black Nationalism 240. Not only did the Artist Sapp have a sense of humor but he was able to show people and animals interacting in joyful moments.

Black Nationalism 241. Remarkable evidence of "Blacks Killing Black," a national phenomenon, but in this case these are actually people who died in the neighborhood. Notice on the left from top to bottom, the names of the three Richardson Brothers, Earl, Keith and Mark Richardson.

Black Nationalism 242. On a trip to Albany to advocate for Health Care, Dr. Fred Monderson stands beside "Read" poster featuring Senator Ruth Hassell-Thompson for New York's Libraries.

Black Nationalism 243. Mr. Sapp tried to show African lifestyle in the Congo at 25,000 B.C.

Black Nationalism 244. Sporting his "Million Woman March" shirt, Dr. Fred Monderson supports Jeannette Gadsen for Brooklyn Boro President.

Black Nationalism 245. The "Brother" who coined the term "Black Power!" was Stokely Carmichael (Kwame Ture).

Black Nationalism 246. Dr. Fred Monderson stands beside a poster featuring his heroes, "Scholar Warriors," Dr. Leonard Jeffries, Prof. Scobie, Dr. John H. Clarke, Dr. Ben-Jochannan and Prof. James Smalls.

Black Nationalism 247. "Righteousness Exalteth a Nation" is a Colored Motto for "Freedom's Journal," the first Black newspaper in the nation.

Black Nationalism 248. The Anti-Slavery Record feature showing Frederick Douglass making his confession: "I prayed for twenty years but received no answer until I prayed with my legs."

Black Nationalism 249. Samuel Ringgold Ward's statement is very apropos, "In New York I saw more of the foolishness, wickedness, and at the same time invincibility, of American Negro-hate, than I ever saw elsewhere."

FREDERICK MONDERSON

Black Nationalism 250. Graphic evidence of hatred for the Black man.

Black Nationalism 251. Evidence of the **Underground Railroad** in New York City.

Black Nationalism 252. Dr. James McIntosh welcomes Dr. Jack Felder to the podium at **CEMOTAP**.

Black Nationalism 253. The Churches supporting **Underground Railroad** in the Bronx and Brooklyn.

Black Nationalism 254. More evidence of churches and locations supporting the **Underground Railroad** in Brooklyn, New York.

Black Nationalism 255. Locations supporting the **Underground Railroad** in Manhattan.

Black Nationalism 256. Dr. Fred Monderson and Erik beside Dr. James McIntosh (left) and Sister Betty Dobson (right), Co-Chairs of **CEMOTAP**.

Black Nationalism 257. More locations supporting the **Underground Railroad** in lower Manhattan and in Queens and Staten Island.

Black Nationalism 258. Tracing the routes of the Underground Railroad in the Bronx and Queens.

Black Nationalism 258a. Dr. James McIntosh, John, and Malcolm Z's daughter Alisha. Notice Malcolm X and Dr. King in the photo on the wall.

Black Nationalism 259. Even more on the **Underground Railroad** in Manhattan and Brooklyn.

Black Nationalism 260. Erik Monderson in audience to see Senator Barack Obama at Al Sharpton's affair. That's Jeffrey Davis of **Stop the Violence** in brown suit at the rear.

Black Nationalism 261. **Underground Railroad** and **Abolition** sites in New York City.

BLACK NATIONALISM
ALIVE AND WELL

Black Nationalism 261a. NYC Councilman Jumane Williams and Erik Monderson at the 50th Anniversary March on Washington; and Dr. Norman Nyg-a-Qi and Sister, Professor Joycelynne Loncke, Members of the **Guyana Branch of the Pan African Movement** at 25th Biennial Conference August, 2013.

Black Nationalism 262. Frederick Douglass (1818-1895) - Publisher, Orator, Author and American Statesman.

Black Nationalism 263. Harriet Tubman (c. 1820-1913) - Liberator, Intelligence Agent and Humanitarian.

Black Nationalism 264. Sojourner Truth (c. 1797-1883) - Social Reformer, Orator and Humanitarian.

Black Nationalism 265. Rev. Henry Highland Garnet (1815-1882) - Minister and social activist.

Black Nationalism 266. Michael Hooper (left), Cherise Maloney (center) and Dr. Fred Monderson (right) at the **African Street Festival**.

Black Nationalism 267. Rufus King (1755-1827) - Attorney, Politician and Diplomat (left); and, David Ruggles (1810-1849) - Printer, Publisher and Journalist (right).

Black Nationalism 268. Rev. Henry Ward Beecher (1813-1887) - Minister (left); and George Bourne (1780-1845) - Organizer and Journalist (right).

Black Nationalism 269. Erik Monderson in process of "Knocking Out" Dr. James McIntosh in his headquarters at **CEMOTAP**.

Black Nationalism 270. Arthur Tappan (1876-1865) - Entrepreneur and Reformer (left); and, Lewis Tappan (1788-1873) Entrepreneur and Reformer (right).

Black Nationalism 270a. Dr. Yosef ben-Jochannan sits beside Mrs. Gil Noble (center) while Sister Sybil Williams-Clarke sits beside Mr. Gil Noble (right).

FREDERICK MONDERSON

Black Nationalism 271. Rev. James McCune Smith (1913-1865) - Doctor and Author (left); and, John B. Russwurm (1799-1851) - Newspaper Publisher and Abolitionist (right).

Black Nationalism 272. The Abolitionist Wall.

Black Nationalism 273. National Culture Shame (Center). Political Poster of PNC defaced by supporters of the PPP/Civic Party after they won the National Elections in Guyana. Use of Black paint signifies that Black is Evil.

Black Nationalism 273a. Dr. and Mrs. Lewis, the Ophthalmologist of Harlem were in attendance at Gil Noble's tribute.

Black Nationalism 274. Dr. James McIntosh addresses the audience at **CEMOTAP** with Dr. Felder and Betty Dobson in attendance at his rear.

Black Nationalism 274a. Elombe Brath, Chairman of the **Patrice Lumumba Coalition** and sponsor of the "Tribute to Gil Noble."

Black Nationalism 274b. Drs. James McIntosh and Leonard Jeffries at the Podium in **Clarke House** in Harlem.

Black Nationalism 274c. Sonny Carson makes a point standing before the revered Red, Black and Green!

Black Nationalism 275. Publisher Milton Allimadi at **CEMOTAP**.

Black Nationalism 276. Political poster defacement by supporters of the winners of the National Elections. The board stands in front of the **National Culture Center**. Use of Black paint signifies that "Black is Evil."

Black Nationalism 277. Radio personality Gary Byrd poses with Erik Monderson at Sharpton's affair for Dr. King.

Black Nationalism 278. Close-up of political poster of PNCR-1G defaced in front of the **National Culture Center** by supporters of the PPP/Civic party that won the election. Black paint signifies evil.

BLACK NATIONALISM ALIVE AND WELL

Black Nationalism 278a. Prolific writer and activist, James Baldwin.

Black Nationalism 279. Political Poster of PNC defaced at prominent junction of Airport Highway intersection with West Ruimveldt. Again, Black paint signifies that "Blacks are Evil."

Black Nationalism 280. Dr. Fred Monderson on a mission to Haiti after the Earthquake.

Black Nationalism 280a. Harlem's Tribute to Harriet Tubman, leader, revolutionary and **Underground Railroad Conductor**.

Black Nationalism 280b. Heroes of the **Haitian Revolution** and the nation's Independence.

Black Nationalism 280c. Rev. Al Sharpton and Stevie Wonder.

Black Nationalism 280d. Teddy Cubia at work in Middle School.

Black Nationalism 280e. Dave Clarke, Middle School Assistant Principal, as "Hannibal" for Budweiser African Series.

Black Nationalism 281. The flag of Red, Black and Green with 50 stars for fifty African countries.

Black Nationalism 282. City Councilman Al Vann and education activist Jitu Weusi stand with a young man to receive an award for exemplary citizenship. Note Jitu's cameras.

Black Nationalism 282a. The Funeral Cortege of Sonny Carson makes its way down Fulton Street as seen in Caribbean Newspaper.

Black Nationalism 282b. Atiim Ferguson, Sonny Carson's Chief of Staff, in a very pensive mood at Sonny's funeral.

Black Nationalism 283. Urban art produced by young people and decorating a wall in Downtown Brooklyn.

Black Nationalism 283a. Mitch Penn, Kashida Maloney hugging Cherise Maloney and Santana Payton with others outside

FREDERICK MONDERSON

the Institutional Church on Adelphi Street awaiting the "Bones of Samuel Carson on way to Ghana.

Black Nationalism 284.   Sister Betty Dobson, Co-Chair of **CEMOTAP** at the Podium with Dr. James McIntosh listening on attentively.

Black Nationalism 285.   New York City Mayor David Dinkins presents an award to a well deserving citizen.

Black Nationalism 286.   Frederick Douglass, the great orator, abolitionist and freedom-fighter who escaped from slavery and founded the North Star newspaper.

Black Nationalism 287.   Urban art decorating a wall in downtown Brooklyn.

Black Nationalism 287a. Sonny Carson (center in glasses), Prof. Patterson, Funeral Director Gafney, Bishop Shivers and others including Ofori Payton in shorts waiting on the **Bones of the Runaway Samuel Carson** on way to Ghana to a site of pilgrimage.

Black Nationalism 288.   Erik Monderson working out as a Brown Belt in Karate.

Black Nationalism 289.   Urban art created by youths and adorning a wall in downtown Brooklyn.

Black Nationalism 289a. Mitch Penn (backing camera), Ofori Payton, Sonny Carson, Prof. Patterson, James Smalls, Santana Ofori, "Chief Barkim Parker" (partly hidden) and other ladies outside Institutional Church on Adelphi Street.

Black Nationalism 290.   Urban art created by young people and adorning a wall in downtown Brooklyn.

Black Nationalism 290a.   Bringing out the **Bones of Samuel Carson** from Institutional Church on Adelphi Street.

Black Nationalism 291.   Amon-ra enthroned among other gods in a chapel at Medinet Habu, no longer open to visitors.

Black Nationalism 292.   With Moon God Khonsu at his rear and in his shrine (uraei overhead), enthroned Amon-Ra in

BLACK NATIONALISM
ALIVE AND WELL

plumes or feathers offers the curved sword to Rameses III who in turn presents the symbol of eternity to the god.

Black Nationalism 293.   At the Temple of Edfu Horus, with Isis aboard, spears his evil uncle Seth in the war for the Osirian succession.

Black Nationalism 294.   In his temple to Osiris at Abydos, Seti I offers a platter to enthroned Isis.

Black Nationalism 295.   At the Temple of Isis at Philae, now on Agilka Island, enthroned Nephthys receives a gift from Pharaoh.

Black Nationalism 296.   The Khepre beetle, in his most colorful form, performing the function of pushing the sun across the sky.

Black Nationalism 297.   One of the two "Eyes of Horus."

Black Nationalism 298.   Another of the "Eyes of Horus' this time with a little variation in subliminal message.

Black Nationalism 299.   Another more colorful depiction of the Khepre beetle doing his function of pushing the sun across the horizon.

Black Nationalism 300.   Still another colorful depiction of the Khepre beetle.

Black Nationalism 301.   The "Great Cackler" or "Great Goose," an earthly manifestation of Amon-Ra, Theban great god!

Black Nationalism 302.   Still another colorful depiction of "The Great Cackler," one of many manifestation of the Theban deity Amon-Ra.

Black Nationalism 303.   Still another colorful depiction of "The Great Cackler," Theban deity of the Middle and New Kingdoms.

Black Nationalism 304. Yet another colorful ceramic depiction of the "Great Goose" or "Cackler," a manifestation of Amon-Ra, Theban deity.

FREDERICK MONDERSON

Black Nationalism 305. The peregrine falcon, a manifestation of Horus of Edfu, who defeated his wicked uncle Seth and succeeded the throne of his murdered father Osiris, who reigns as "Judge of the Dead or the Underworld."

Black Nationalism 306. Another version of Horus of Edfu, son of Isis and Osiris.

Black Nationalism 307. Yet another colorful representation of Horus of Edfu.

Black Nationalism 308. Still another more colorful representation of Horus of Edfu.

Black Nationalism 309. Yet another manifestation, "The Ram," of Amon-Ra, Theban deity.

Black Nationalism 310. Anubis, Egyptian "God of the Dead," who embalms the deceased and guards the way to the sepulchral chamber.

Black Nationalism 311. Uraeus, protector of Pharaoh, wearing horns and sun-disk.

Black Nationalism 312. Majestic and colorful bird in flight.

Black Nationalism 313. Another version of the colorful bird in flight.

Black Nationalism 314. Four colorful amphora vases used for storage.

Black Nationalism 315. This time, three amphora vessels made of ceramic.

Black Nationalism 316. Colorful uraei sporting sun-disk alongside feather symbol.

Black Nationalism 317. Beautiful hieroglyphic symbolism.

Black Nationalism 318. Two pyramids over water contained in a basket with handle.

Black Nationalism 319. Urban art by young people.

Black Nationalism 320. Ankh within the Sun-disk atop a pyramid.

BLACK NATIONALISM
ALIVE AND WELL

Black Nationalism 321. Dr. Fred Monderson (left) sits beside Dr. Runoko Rashidi.

Black Nationalism 321a. Prof. Jocelyn Loncke, Chairperson of the **Guyana Branch of the Pan-African Movement**, announces opening of the **Dr. Fred Monderson Reading Room and Library at the Ethiopian Society** in Georgetown, Guyana.

Black Nationalism 321b. Brooklyn District Attorney Thompson poses with Civil Rights icon John Lewis at Congressman Major Owens' funeral at First Baptist Church in Crown Heights, Brooklyn.

Black Nationalism 322. Black Veterans who served.

Black Nationalism 323. Mzee Moya, "the Brother from **The East**" (left); Michael Hooper of "**Roots Revisited**" (right).

Black Nationalism 323a. "Abubaca," longtime Black Nationalist, Community Activist and confidant of Sonny Carson.

Black Nationalism 324. Efforts and experiences of Our People "Span the Brooklyn Bridge."

Black Nationalism 325. That "Frederick Douglass is my ancestor" is a very good refrain!

Black Nationalism 326. Restoration, in the heart of Bed-Stuy, where Sonny Carson "Held Court" with **The Committee to Honor Black Heroes** and gave us **Marcus Garvey** and **Malcolm X Boulevards** and **Harriet Tubman Avenue**, the **Malcolm X School**, and was very instrumental in forcing the naming of a school for **Toussaint L'Ouverture**.

Black Nationalism 327. Jitu Weusi sits surrounded by Councilwoman Una Clarke (right), Assemblyman Al Vann (Center) and a friend, Preston Wilcox (right).

Black Nationalism 328. To shake the hand of a great actor as Ossie Davis (right) and stand beside Gordon Parks (left) is indeed a tremendous honor for Melvin Van Pebbles.

FREDERICK MONDERSON

Black Nationalism 329.   Urban art and poetry decorate this wall.

Black Nationalism 330.   Revered nationalist Jim Cuffe sits in his chair flanked by Atiim Ferguson and Ofori Payton, partially obscured.

Black Nationalism 331.   Let the good times roll!

Black Nationalism 332.   City Councilwoman Una Clarke and her daughter Councilwoman, later Congresswoman, Yvette Clarke who is flanked by Kwame, brother of Rasheed Allah, and El Hombe Brath with unidentified others.

Black Nationalism 333.   Evidently, Spanish men of distinction.

Black Nationalism 334.   Frederick Douglass and Marcus Garvey, outstanding African nationalists, influential in the 19th and 20th Centuries.

Black Nationalism 334a.   Newspaper publisher Milton Allimadi sits in quiet contemplation at one of many Forums defending Blacks.

Black Nationalism 335.   Ali Lamont (left) of **The Committee to Honor Black Heroes**, founded by Sonny Carson, and Assemblyman, later Councilman Al Vann (right) at his side.

Black Nationalism 336.   Without question, two serious brothers, Ishmael Reed and Rone Neal, committed to the cause of African Liberation!

Black Nationalism 337.   Cherise Maloney (left); George Murden (center); and Jitu Weusi (right); attend the **African Street Festival** at Boys and Girls High School, soon to be named in honor of the South African leader Nelson Mandela.

Black Nationalism 338.   Harry Belafonte (left) and associates entertaining during the "March on Washington in 1963."

Black Nationalism 339.   Carlos Walton, Dean of Students at MS 61, a sister teacher and Mr. Gerald Joshua, "been everywhere" and now passed on to "Ancestor Glory."

BLACK NATIONALISM
ALIVE AND WELL

Black Nationalism 339a. Kwame Ture (Stokely Carmichael), the quintessential Black Nationalist (left); and Dr. Carlos Russell, founder of **Black Solidarity Day** (right).

Black Nationalism 340. Rudy Giuliani, later Mayor of New York City, interviews Rosa Parks.

Black Nationalism 341. Justice Thurgood Marshall and Nationalist Malcolm X.

Black Nationalism 342. Attorney Johnny Cochran appearing at Rev. Sharpton's **National Action Network** (at the Madison Avenue location) where he spoke on behalf of Abner Louima (seated left) after Officer Volpe had assaulted him with a plunger.

Black Nationalism 343. Sitting beside Queen Mother Moore, Rosa Parks receives a Citation of Honor.

Black Nationalism 343a. In Stan Kinnard's candidacy for state Assemblyman, Sonny Carson, Al Sharpton and Michael Hardy came out to campaign for him.

Black Nationalism 344. Shirley Chisholm (left); and Harriet Tubman (right); stalwarts of African uplift.

Black Nationalism 345. "Coach" George Murden escorts Cherise Maloney as Jitu Weusi stops for a quiet conversation and his wife Angela Weusi looks towards the stage at the African Street Festival.

Black Nationalism 346. Rev. Al Sharpton introduces Senator Barack Obama (with black hair) when he visited **National Action Network** in 2008 as he campaigned to become President of the United States.

Black Nationalism 347. Senator Obama responds while Rev. Sharpton listens attentively from his seat.

Black Nationalism 347a. At the African Street Festival at Boys and Girls High School, Prof James Smalls makes nice with Cherise Maloney while Sonny Carson and a friend mugs for the photo.

FREDERICK MONDERSON

Black Nationalism 348.   Isaac Hayes, entertained often regarded as "The Black Moses" (left); and Bernie Mac, actor and comedian (right); both deceased.

Black Nationalism 349.   Revs. Jesse Jackson and Al Sharpton, his mentee, at the "Million Man March" in Washington, DC, 1995.

Black Nationalism 349a. Rev. Al Sharpton introduces Senator Barack Obama during his campaign for the Presidency.

Black Nationalism 350.   Minister Louis Farrakhan (organizer of the "Million Man March," October 16, 1995) (left); and DC Mayor Marion Barry (right); among throngs at the "Million Man March."

Black Nationalism 351. Minister Clemson Brown, photographer and Black History archivist.

Black Nationalism 352.   Notorious "Biggie Smalls" (left); and TuPac Shakur (right).

Black Nationalism 353.   Rev. Jesse Jackson shakes hands with Dr. Roscoe Lee Brown, famed "Tuskegee Airman."

Black Nationalism 353a. Stan Kinnard brings out "heavyweights" to support his candidacy for Assemblyman.

Black Nationalism 354.   Dr. Benjamin Chavis (center); Dr. Delores Blakeley ("**Queen Mother of the Slave Trade**") (left); Prof. James Blake in glasses at rear, and Minister Conrad Mohammed, etc.

Black Nationalism 355.   Haitian President Bertrand Aristide receives an award in the Oval Room at the World Trade Center.

Black Nationalism 356.   Sonny Carson is flanked by Reverends Al Sharpton (left); and Wyatt Tee Walker (right); President and Chairmen of the **National Action Network**.

Black Nationalism 357.   Comedian and actor Redd Foxx (left); and singer and entertainer James Brown (right).

BLACK NATIONALISM
ALIVE AND WELL

Black Nationalism 358. Dr. Leonard Jeffries makes a point at a Black United Front Celebration as he upholds Prof. Amos N. Wilson's book *Blueprint for Black Power*.

Black Nationalism 359. Richard Pryor - actor, entertainer and comedian.

Black Nationalism 360. Amiri Baraka (Leroy Jones) (left); beside a very distinguished Brother Max Roach (right).

Black Nationalism 361. Revolutionary Huey Newton (left); and singer and entertainer Bob Marley (right).

Black Nationalism 361a. At the Podium Gary Byrd extols Dr. John Clarke as Dr. Adelaide Sanford awaits her turn to give that electrifying speech and J.D. Livingston is there watching their backs!

Black Nationalism 362. The "Iron Pipeline" that is killing our young people!

Black Nationalism 363. Judge Bruce Wright, often called "Cut em Loose Bruce" because of his leniency in interpreting the law on bail.

Black Nationalism 364. Sonny Carson (right); Bishop Smallwood (second from left); Professor Patterson in light suit, in the Brooklyn Navy Yard discussing disposition of the "Bones of the Runaway Samuel Carson."

Black Nationalism 365. Supreme Court Judge Thurgood Marshall (left); and lawyer, scholar, activist Paul Robeson (right).

Black Nationalism 366. "Old Boys High School" in Bed-Stuy, Brooklyn.

Black Nationalism 367. "We the People;" and "How would you want to be remembered?"

Black Nationalism 368. Former Congresswoman Shirley Chisholm (on yellow horse) leads a woman's charge as a catalyst for change!

Black Nationalism 369. Two beautiful and powerful freedom fighters, Myrlie Evers and Coretta Scott King, wives of Medgar Evers and Dr. Martin Luther King.

FREDERICK MONDERSON

Black Nationalism 370. Young people facing choices, "Piece or Peace!"

Black Nationalism 371. Showing Respect for our Community!

Black Nationalism 372. Congressman Major Owens greeting young people whom he has often expressed great confidence in.

Black Nationalism 373. Albert Vann (left); and Major Owens (right); receiving awards.

Black Nationalism 373a. Major Owens is surrounded by Senator Velmanette Montgomery (left); and Sonny Carson, with Omowale Clay in light suit at right, as he explains why the Congressional Hearings were needed because of the rampant police killings in New York, with no accountability and no recourse for the community.

Black Nationalism 374. A Tuskegee Airman in a boastful moment!

Black Nationalism 375. Harriet Tubman as her image is preserved in the Museum of African American History in Washington, DC.

Black Nationalism 376. Congressman Major Owens (left); in a joyous mood and about to introduce the architect of "The Algebra Project," Robert Moses (right).

Black Nationalism 377. Two beautiful stalwarts for the cause!

Black Nationalism 378. Close-up of the architect of "The Algebra Project," Robert Moses.

Black Nationalism 379. Erik Monderson with camera on the Capital Building grounds.

Black Nationalism 380. The "Mountain of Despair" from which the "Stone of Hope" has been hewn.

Black Nationalism 381. Dr. King's "Stone of Hope" hewn from the "Mountain of Despair."

BLACK NATIONALISM
ALIVE AND WELL

Black Nationalism 382. A small shrine of farewell prepared for Nelson Mandela outside the Apollo Theater in Harlem.

Black Nationalism 383. What shall it be, Peace, respect, love or guns?

Black Nationalism 384. Dorothy Height, President of the **National Council of Negro Women**, in full and regal splendor.

Black Nationalism 385. Personal expression of sympathy beside the small shrine erected to pay tribute to Nelson Mandela outside the Apollo Theater in Harlem.

Black Nationalism 386. Rosa parks, "Queen of Civil Rights Protest," in a pensive mood.

Black Nationalism 387. The "First Black Boro President of Brooklyn" Abdul Hafiz, formerly Minister Kevin Mohammed.

Black Nationalism 388. Grandma and the Youth. We must talk to them.

Black Nationalism 389. "The Iron Pipeline" is killing our young!

Black Nationalism 390. Gun Shows require No ID to purchase firearms.

Black Nationalism 391. City Councilwoman and now State Assemblywoman, Annette Robinson (right) receives an award.

Black Nationalism 392. Forked tongues of the Devil and much more.

Black Nationalism 393. Attorney and Black Panther freedom fighter Malik Zulu Shabazz holds *The New Black Panther* newspaper announcing the "Million Man March Strikes Black!"

Black Nationalism 394. The role of Grandparents is crucial in influencing young people and being there for them.

Black Nationalism 395. Brooklyn Pride involves Community and is courageous, full of respect, truly full of family love, honor, honesty and relishes in culture.

FREDERICK MONDERSON

Black Nationalism 396.   Nelson Mandela as he exits the plane on his first visit to the United States invited by David Dinkins, Mayor of New York City, where his first stop was Brooklyn, Fulton Street, Boys and Girls High School, which will be renamed in his honor!

Black Nationalism 397.   Good advice: "Never Give Up on Yourself."

Black Nationalism 398.   Will Allen, ready in service to the people!

Black Nationalism 399.   Mr. Mandela gives his famous salute!

Black Nationalism 400.   A beautiful couple in aid of the cause of our people!

Black Nationalism 401.   Mr. Mandela being introduced to various guests at an affair.

Black Nationalism 402.   Another great warrior for the cause!

Black Nationalism 403.   Rev. Timothy Mitchell, "Can I get an Amen!" on that.

Black Nationalism 404.   Mural at Maggie Walker Middle School in Brooklyn, where several members of this writer's family received a quality education, in praise of Public Schools.

Black Nationalism 405.   We all need to be reminded, Children are our future!

Black Nationalism 406.   The Steps to Success!

Black Nationalism 406a. The ongoing struggle between "**Mother Africa**" and forces of oppression constantly seeking to divide to conquer Africans at home and in the Diaspora.

Black Nationalism 407.   Reverend Daughtry and Charles Barron at the **House of the Lord Church**.

Black Nationalism 408.   Reverend Herbert Daughtry, Pastor of **The House of the Lord Church** on Atlantic Avenue in Brooklyn.

BLACK NATIONALISM ALIVE AND WELL

Black Nationalism 409. Council Member Charles Barron and his wife Assemblywoman Inez Barron, with an unknown person (left).

Black Nationalism 410. A quintessential Black Nationalist, Dr. Marimba Ani, formerly of Hunter College of the City University of New York.

Black Nationalism 411. Xavier Bost lays it all out for Mr. Mandela.

Black Nationalism 412. Mr. Bob Law addresses his audience in Tribute to Nelson Mandela.

Black Nationalism 413. Mr. Law shares a humorous moment in Tribute to Nelson Mandela.

Black Nationalism 414. Craig Crawford creates sweet horn music for Mr. Mandela.

Black Nationalism 415. Xavier Bost sings one of her two songs, "A Hero Lies in You."

Black Nationalism 416. Dr. Jeffries stands tall in explaining Mandela's role in African liberation.

Black Nationalism 417. Dr. Leonard Jeffries makes a point in his Tribute to Nelson Mandela.

Black Nationalism 418. The message is clear! **DC STATEHOOD NOW!**

Black Nationalism 419. The Black Institute. Org.

Black Nationalism 419a. Dr. Michael Erik Dyson at Rev. Al Sharpton's 2014 Convention.

Black Nationalism 419b. The "Fireman" Hodari, who mastered the craft of "Eating Fire" and practiced on many an occasion.

Black Nationalism 419c. Kwaku, Santina and Adwoa Payton and Santina's brother Kofi Brown in white shirt and sunglasses at the International African Arts Festival.

FREDERICK MONDERSON

Black Nationalism 420.   Erik Monderson walks with the Children at the 50th Anniversary March on Washington.

Black Nationalism 420a. Portrait of Rev. Al Sharpton unveiled at the 2014 **National Action Network** Convention.

Black Nationalism 421.   Rev. Charles Norris of Bethesda Missionary Baptist Church and "Spiritual" head of **CEMOTAP** among the audience.

Black Nationalism 422.   **CEMOTAP** and, Betty Dopson and Dr. James McIntosh display the **Kwanzaa** symbol while paving the way and keeping alive the tradition.

Black Nationalism 423.   Prof. James Blake and Sister Betty Dopson, clearly in a joyous festive mood.

Black Nationalism 424.   Dr. James McIntosh, Co-Founder and Co-Chairman of **CEMOTAP**, clearly "fighting the good fight," with results.

Black Nationalism 425.   An African Dancer and Sister Dopson among the children!

Black Nationalism 426.   Another African Dancer beside Sister Dopson and Dr. McIntosh.

Black Nationalism 427.   Rev. Charles Norris and a family attending.

Black Nationalism 428.   The Drummer Naim Blake and Prof. James Blake.

Black Nationalism 429.   Brother Vincent Emanuel, very much a **Pan-African Black Nationalist** who can boast of being very much African and been part of many struggles on part of African Liberation.

Black Nationalism 430.   On a wall, **Kwanzaa** book advertising.

Black Nationalism 430a.   The **Kwanzaa** Candles backed by the "First Fruits of the Festival."

Black Nationalism 431.   Dr. Maulana Karenga sits beside his wife awaiting his turn on the Dais.

BLACK NATIONALISM ALIVE AND WELL

Black Nationalism 432. African dancers doing their thing in the cultural show before Dr. Karenga spoke.

Black Nationalism 433. Luis Daniel, one of the young people attending the **Kwanzaa** show in which Dr. Karenga delivered his outstanding lecture on this important festive day.

Black Nationalism 434. Dr. Segun Shabaka introduces Dr. Karenga.

Black Nationalism 435. Part of the entertainment on this **Kwanzaa** day!

Black Nationalism 436. Before the **Kwanzaa** flag, a saxophonist gives his all for this significant cultural festival.

Black Nationalism 437. Dr. Karenga sits beside his wife on the Dais before the Black Nationalist **Kwanzaa** flag of Green, Red and Black.

Black Nationalism 437a. Mteteaji O. Mlimwengu (A.K.A. "Wakili") with the Red, Black and Green on Black Solidarity Day in Brooklyn.

Black Nationalism 438. A mother who brought her daughter to the Unveiling of the new US Postage Stamp in honor of Congresswoman Shirley Chisholm, a fighter for justice and equality.

Black Nationalism 438a. Brooklyn Boro President Eric Adams speaks on behalf of Shirley Chisholm in her role paving the way for many including this former NYC Police Captain and State Senator to become the leader of the Boro.

Black Nationalism 438b. Legendary TV Newscaster Bill McCreary, Boro President Eric Adams and Assistant Post Master General who unveiled the stamp in honor of Shirley Chisholm.

Black Nationalism 438c. Rev. Al Sharpton spoke on behalf of Ms. Chisholm praising her influence on him as a young activist.

Black Nationalism 438d. Congresswoman Yvette Clarke spoke on the influence and impact of Shirley Chisholm on furthering an agenda that championed women, children, jobs, end to poverty

FREDERICK MONDERSON

and how this fighter for justice paved the way for both herself and mother Una Clarke who became a New York City Councilwoman.

Black Nationalism 438e. Before the unveiling! All are gathered in anticipation!

Black Nationalism 438f. The Unveiling of **Black Heritage US Postal Service Stamp** in honor of Congresswoman Shirley Chisholm.

Black Nationalism 438g. Councilwoman Darlene Mealy, Councilman Robert Cornegy, Boro President Eric Adams, Councilwoman Inez Baron, the Postmaster General, the MC for the program, Rev. Al Sharpton, Congresswoman Yvette Clarke and Congressman Charlie Rangel.

Black Nationalism 438h. Time to reflect, Caucus and look to the future with a serious eye on the past!

Black Nationalism 438i. Shirley Chisholm, "Catalyst for Change" gets her due recognition; for it is said, if the **United States Postal Service** recognizes your work and value then it's a significant honor; but more importantly it represents recognition of a tremendous life of service undergirded by integrity, daring, intellectuality and an unwavering commitment to aid and speak for people, without a voice or power, across a wide spectrum of the nation who benefitted tremendously from the Congresswoman's unselfish efforts.

Black Nationalism 1. The "First Fruits of the Kwanza Festival" sits on the Kwanza Flag of Green, Red and Black.

BLACK NATIONALISM ALIVE AND WELL

"MOUNTAIN OF A MAN"
By
Dr. Fred Monderson

Jitu Weusi, "Mountain of a Man," born Les Campbell, we mourn your passing but we rejoice for your presence and lasting contributions and we honor you as we have honored Malcolm X, Martin Luther King, Jr., Marcus Garvey, Rosa Parks and Sonny Carson your revered Brother in Struggle! Quintessential leader who would not accept the "thirty pieces of silver," who could not be bribed, you stood tall and firm as a resolute fighter for justice and social upliftment of Black African people, irrespective! You made your presence felt in many an arena. Educational activist, social critic and strategist confronting life's many challenges, your contributions to your people's march of progress earned you the "living legend" award and because of your vision, our people will not perish!

Black Nationalism 1a. Jitu Weusi, iconic nationalist, educator, community leader, theorist, family man and friend, will forever remain in our hearts.

FREDERICK MONDERSON

Indomitable spirit, leader in education, man of unbounded integrity and insightful thinking, we honor you because you fought the good fight, you kept the faith, and in this you were a perpetual light of social conscience. Creative genius of "**The East**" who innovated the African Street Festival among many creations, your place among revered ancestors assured, the pantheon of Black Champions now have a new star! Brooklyn Icon, from "**The East**" to **Attica** and **Ocean-Hill-Brownsville Decentralization** to the **Franklin Avenue Shuttle** struggle, and from the public school classroom to the college campus and back to the public school as administrator making a difference, your unmatched contributions for educational excellence and social justice are too numerous to mention. With the desire for quality education as watchword and hallmark of your work of upliftment, educator, activist, headmaster, advocate, administrator, your efforts established the highest standards for intellectual development of our youth.

Guiding light, visionary with clear sightedness, the influence of your classroom educational activities matched the brilliance of the brightest day, inspiring many to develop skills to achieve success. Resolute nationalist, Pan-African stalwart, your aspirations for your people's progress were seldom surpassed; and your equally untiring efforts as member of the "**Bones Committee**" helped assure Samuel Carson, "**The Runaway**," successful passage for internment in Ghana, West Africa, opening the "**Door of Return**." Master organizer, unquestionably in education and in Black Solidarity Day activism, politics and jazz organization, your name resounds as an effective and successful strategist of exceptional note. Son of Brooklyn, man of integrity, fortitude and resilience, allow us to clone your image, persona and strategic thinking abilities as an effective tool in our ongoing struggle for social, political and economic empowerment in advancement of our people.

BLACK NATIONALISM ALIVE AND WELL

Man of action and boundless vision, though sorrowful at your passing, we celebrate your creative spirit with sweet melodic sounds similarly played by the **Jazz Consortium** you orchestrated; forever memories of you will be remembered through the African Street Festival, a contribution of immense proportions. Revered leader, man of many seasons, it is our especial hope, your memory, image and name will forever be a part of the history of struggle to uplift all people, particularly Black people. We also hope the children will remember you because we honor you as father, husband, tactician and community leader earned in your unrelenting struggle to advance our cause and make Brooklyn a better place for them and all other residents.

Brother we salute you, we praise you, we honor you, and we thank you for a lengthy, constructive and successful life of meaningful service to the Brooklyn Community and African people worldwide. We are grateful you inspired us to persevere in the manner of Jitu Weusi's Way of integrity, stability and constructive service. This is the name Claver Place, the place of your origins, should be named, for your life has been an effective beacon that reflected the highest illumination, standards and aspirations of the Borough of Brooklyn and the best example of Black manhood. Companion at the Million Women March in Philadelphia, we are saddened you never lived to see the 50th Anniversary of the "**March on Washington**" but you would have been proud and active in concern for the safety and security of "The People."

1. INTRODUCTION

Black Nationalism: Alive and Well does not mean Black people are sitting around in treasonous gatherings and plotting to overthrow the US government; nor does it mean we are praying for this nation to become a failed state, even though some have argued the nucleus of world racism is centered in this country. Nevertheless,

FREDERICK MONDERSON

Black Nationalism does mean; first, as Marcus Garvey instructed, we could be critical and patriotic Americans and still proactively advocate for Africa and Africans worldwide as all other ethnic groups have done in aid of their people and place of cultural origin. However, and most important, as we stand today, **Black Nationalism** does mean that African-Americans have risen to a high level of historical, spiritual, and psychological consciousness being capable of decoding all forms of anti-Blackness.

Black Nationalism 2. How Beautiful the People look among icons Jesse Jackson in the center and other fighters for freedom.

BLACK NATIONALISM
ALIVE AND WELL

Black Nationalism 3. Angela Davis, educator, activist and Nationalist who befriended George Jackson, is honored by the Bed-Stuy community in this mural.

FREDERICK MONDERSON

Black Nationalism 4. Mural on side of a building at Church Avenue and Rogers Avenue depicting the tri-parte – Slave Castle in West Africa, "**The Door of No Return**," and the waiting and packed slave ship.

That is, we have progressed tremendously beyond the brutish stage foundation "patriots" had consigned us through legislative fiat, for when in 1662 the law decreed "enslaved Africans and their descendants thenceforth would be considered sub-human and chattel in perpetuity." In many respects, nearly four centuries later, such mindsets still pervade among some of the American citizenry. Important, it's generally agreed, you cannot keep a man in the gutter without muddying yourself! Thus, the slave trade, slavery and the behavior of racial hatred and prejudice perpetuated by and in the West, have created a pathological mindset in the European/American

BLACK NATIONALISM
ALIVE AND WELL

psyche that even after shedding the physical brutality associated with the resulting behaviors, has maintained a suspicion about the Black man that has proved even more dangerous for the inherent implications. As such, it is clearly evident Blacks have become more astutely aware of the forces arrayed against the religious, spiritual and moral significance they are and intend to become with the help of God, their strength, their redeemer.

Black Nationalism 5. A Playground for America's first martyred patriot, Crispus Attucks, the epitome of Black Nationalism!

FREDERICK MONDERSON

Black Nationalism 5a. "Master Teacher," Dr. Leonard James, Professor Emeritus, New York City Technical College, CUNY.

Nevertheless, as Dr. Maulana has insisted in his Kwanza message, "It is our destiny to bring good into the world!" An early example showed, faith intervened to buttress destiny, when Richard Allen was humiliated while on his knees at St. George Episcopalian Methodist Church. He firmly believed that God was with him in that admonition to do good, and thus his tenacity and the congregation provided the strength and spiritual grounding that made the difference in their destiny and their desire to praise the Almighty. In fact, God sent two souls to strengthen their faith and resolve in sowing the seeds of goodness. So much so, Mr. Allen would later write regarding the founding of the African Methodist Episcopalian Church, "I hope the names of Dr. Benjamin Rush and Robert Ralston will never be forgotten among us. They were the first two gentlemen

BLACK NATIONALISM
ALIVE AND WELL

who espoused the cause of the oppressed, and aided us in building the House of the Lord for the poor Africans to worship in. Here was the beginning and rise of the first African church in America."

That is, after the philosophic and practical realities of American foundation politics and religion, the spiritual notion of the "Father of God and the Brotherhood of Man" was seriously questioned.

However, the attitude and behavior demonstrated at the Church of St. George in those early decades of the 19th Century were not unique for many Christian whites felt uncomfortable worshipping with Blacks. Nearly some two centuries later, there are some Christians who still profess and manifest such un-Christian behavior. Yet, from that time to today, Blacks have evolved a high moral and spiritual mindset regarding such practices and, in fact, in many cases, are the ones who hold most high the tenets of the Christian faith evolved in the many strategies and tactics created for their survival and work for good.

FREDERICK MONDERSON

Black Nationalism 6. Rainbow **PUSH** Coalition says "Eliminate Student Loan Debt" and people want "Jobs Now!"

Black Nationalism 6a. Veteran activist Jitu Weusi and his brother Job Mashiriki share a joyful moment.

BLACK NATIONALISM
ALIVE AND WELL

This dynamic of the entire relationship is underscored in an interesting work entitled **Black Nationalism in America**, Edited by John Bracey, Jr., August Meier and Elliott Rudwick (New York: Bobbs-Merrill, 1970) that points to a whole slew of Black nationalistic strategies created and employed in the enslaved African's repertoire designed to combat the inhuman experiences from the nation's foundation to the Civil Rights struggle and beyond. These behaviors, characterized essentially by racial solidarity, were necessary because most Africans were victims of the same treatment whether of ethnicity, color, African-ness. Such dynamics evolved in what the authors characterized as cultural nationalism, religious nationalism, economic nationalism, black political nationalism, emigrationism, territorial separatism, and finally Pan-Africanism; all manifesting in more than a century of struggle towards promises of the Civil Rights movement and finally demands for Black Power and the cohesive consciousness such workings generated and unleashed. In this, the authors have defined "Black Nationalism" as "A body of thoughts, attitudes, and actions ranging from the simplest expressions of ethnocentrism and racial solidarity to the comprehensive and sophisticated ideologies of Pan-Negroism or Pan-Africanism. Between these extremes lie many varieties of black nationalism, varying degrees of intensity." Yet still, like all groups of people and ethnicities, Africans recognize we have our own "bad apples" and must work to reform them, praying they may come to see the misguided nature of their behaviors.

Nonetheless, it's recognized, the evolution of such practices were in response to the times and behaviors visited upon the hapless Africans. That is to say, in the continuum of the nation's growth, Africans have been victimized by legislative fiat and unconscionable and brutal human behavior; yet despite these practicalities the sons and daughters of the victims have fought to defend this nation in every one of America's wars, "Learning the ways of the White man!" Thus, the historical record is replete with evidence that from its early years African-Americans suffered unspeakable horrors of slavery; bore the inscrutably painful lashes scarring their backs and

FREDERICK MONDERSON

souls; and profoundly suffered the emasculating humiliation of the masters' wanton and malicious indignities visited upon African women and families whose legal status was never seriously considered, despite the promises of the **Declaration of Independence** and **Constitution of the United States**.

Black Nationalism 7. Elk Street renamed the "African Burial Ground Way," in Lower Manhattan.

First and foremost, a definition of the terms as defined by the authors is as follows. **Cultural Nationalism** argues that Black have a culture and lifestyle distinct and different from all other groups. Nonetheless, "Mild forms of cultural nationalism assert the superiority of Afro-American culture - usually on moral and aesthetic grounds - to Western civilization." In this regard, "Programmatic or institutional manifestations of cultural nationalism include the development of a body of social-science literature - history, philosophy, political science, and the like - written from the Afro-American point of view; the unearthing and publicizing of all the past glories of the race; the development of a distinct Afro-American literature, art, music; the formation of appropriate vehicles for the transmission of Afro-American culture - newspapers, journals, theaters, artistic workshops, musical groups; the assertion of a distinct life-style and world view in such ways as assuming

BLACK NATIONALISM
ALIVE AND WELL

African or Arabic names, wearing African clothes, and speaking African languages."

Black Nationalism 8. Erik and two friends at the "March on Washington," 8-24-2013.

Given that Blacks are a fundamentally spiritual people, **Religious Nationalism** has been expressed in various modalities. In that case, the naturalistic argument held, "Blacks should establish and run churches of their own, for their own people; that God, or Jesus, or both were black (the "Black Messiah" theme); that Afro-Americans are the chosen people. Religious nationalism has also taken non-Christian forms, as can be seen in such twentieth-century groups as the Nation of Islam, the Moorish Science Temple, the several varieties of Black Jews and the Yoruba Temple. A milder expression of religious nationalist feeling is manifested in the recent formation of Black Caucuses within the major Christian denominations. In Chicago in 1968 Black Catholic Priests conducted a 'Black Unity Mass' to the beat of conga drums; they wore vestments of colorful African cloth and shared the altar with, among others, a Baptist preacher."

FREDERICK MONDERSON

Economic Nationalism has been practiced through a number of strategies whether by educated or lay persons. For the mere implementation, some such actions have been labeled bourgeois. However, this article states, "Slightly to the left of the bourgeois nationalist are those who contend that formation of producer and consumer cooperatives is necessary. Further to the left are black nationalist socialists who feel that abolition of private property is a prerequisite for the liberation of the Negro people. (Such socialists should be distinguished from black integrationalists like A. Philip Randolph and Bayard Rustin.) At the opposite extreme are those who call for the reinstatement of preindustrial communalism. Black nationalist socialists tend to coincide with revolutionary nationalists who apply Marxian theory to the experience of Afro-Americans, whereas those who favor preindustrial African economic forms tend also to be militant cultural nationalists. Negro capitalists tend to be bourgeois in their political outlooks as well."

In view of slavery conditions and recognizing the potency of the ballot in American society, the quest for the vote marks the beginning of **Political Nationalism**. This is why so much effort has been expended to disfranchise Blacks especially in the pre and post-Reconstruction era and as late as today. Nevertheless, and in contrast, however, "Black Nationalism at its mildest is bourgeois reformism, a view which assumes that the United States is politically pluralistic and that liberal values concerning democracy and the political process are operative. Programmatic examples of such a view are the slating and supporting of Negro candidates for political office; the drive for Black political and administrative control of local and county areas where Negroes predominate; and the formation of all-black political parties. In contrast, **Revolutionary Black Nationalism** views the overthrow of existing political and economic institutions as a prerequisite for the liberation of Black Americans, and does not exclude the use of violence."

BLACK NATIONALISM
ALIVE AND WELL

Black Nationalism 8a. Jitu Weusi and son Kojo help provide "Security" at the Million Woman March in Philadelphia.

Recognizing that land is the basis of all forms of independence and control of one's destiny, and that equality in this society would be hard to come by, **Territorial Separatism** seemed the answer. To this end, "Territorial separatists advocated the establishment of all-black towns, especially in the South and Southwest, all-black states, or a black nation comprising several states. Recent and milder forms of territorial separatism are often linked to the concept of political pluralism and advocacy of 'Black control of the Black community.'"

FREDERICK MONDERSON

Black Nationalism 8b. Jitu Weusi and Dr. Fred Monderson share a moment together at this affair for Sonny Carson.

Emigrationism was a significant feature of early **Black Nationalism** and since many persons believed Blacks could not really be free and equal in America, they preferred to emigrate to Africa. Other areas such as South America and the Caribbean were also considered. However, there was much ambivalence in the movement because many prominent Blacks did not trust the leading proponent, the **African Colonization Society**. Ostensibly to Christianize and better Africa and stamp out the Slave Trade, its true purpose was to rid America of Blacks! While the Boston Quaker Paul Cuffe favored colonization for African upliftment, a letter to him from Prince Sanders, Thomas Jarvis and Perry Locke reinforced this idea. Nevertheless, he cooperated with the African Colonization Society. Bracey, et al (1970: 39-40) writes: "Cuffe corresponded with the founders of the African Colonization Society but the majority of articulate Negroes were hostile to the organization. They suspected - and many of the Society's supporters openly said, - that its object was to rid the country of free Blacks whom they regarded as a threat to the system of slavery.... Like [James] Forten, Richard

BLACK NATIONALISM
ALIVE AND WELL

Allen was a vigorous enemy of the **American Colonization Society**, but another founder of the American Methodist Episcopalian Church, Daniel Coker of Baltimore was not."

Black Nationalism 9. "Sacred Space," the African Burial Ground!

For much of the 19th and 20th Centuries, **Pan-Negroism** or **Pan-Africanism** has been an aspiration and quest of the African American. This has manifested in a number of ways through conferences to create strategies focusing on forces arrayed against Africa and African people, in theoretical or practical return to Africa efforts, and in cultural association through clothing, language, trade connections and religious expression. However, according to Bracey, et al, both **Pan-Negroism** and **Pan-Africanism** "foster the belief that people of African descent throughout the world have common cultural characteristics and share common problems as a result of their African origins, the similarity of their political oppression and economic exploitation by Western civilization, and the persistence and virulence of racist theories, attitudes, and behavior characterizing Western contact with people of African descent." In this regard, "Afro-American advocates of Pan-Negroism historically assumed that Afro-Americans would provide the leadership for any worldwide movement. Only recently, with the political independence of African nations, have Afro-Americans

FREDERICK MONDERSON

conceded that Africans themselves might form the vanguard in the liberation of all peoples of African descent."

All this, notwithstanding, the historical record is replete with events that fostered Nationalist sentiments among African Americans despite the contradictions posed to DuBois' "Dual Personality" concept. Mr. DuBois characterized this duality as "One ever feels his two-ness - an American, a Negro; two souls, two thoughts, two un-reconciled strivings; two warring ideals in one dark body, whose dogged strength alone keeps it from being torn asunder." As such, and for example, when the "founding fathers" compromised with the Constitution in 1787, they elevated the Black man to 3/5 of a person. Next, Eli Whitney's sinister invention buried him further with demands created by the "Cotton Gin" in 1793. That same year, 1793, **Fugitive Slave Laws** were instituted to curb runaways and empower slave catchers. Notwithstanding, and thanks to the work of British abolitionists, whose government outlawed the Slave Trade in 1807, America followed suit the next year in 1808. This essentially unenforced American prohibition gave birth to "Slave Farms" in the "Deep South" that visited a new and more horrible experience on "Black women forced to manufacture children" to expand the masters' financial coffers. While today we view trucks plying the highway with merchandise, in those days, in the resulting "horror movie" which was real, the slave farms sent forth coffles of hapless souls on way to be sold at slave marts. As all this transpired, Daniel Vesey, Gabriel Prosser and Nat Turner, honorable Black men, inspired by the Bible and the tenets of the Age of Revolution: American - "We hold these truths to be self evident that all men are created equal;" French *"Liberte, Franernite, Egalite;"* Haitian "United We Stand;" and thoughts and actions of Latin American patriots as Bolivar expressed the same ideals; all such revolts sought to liberate their enslaved and down-trodden brethren. Importantly, however, in case of the Africans, Herbert Aptheker documented some 200 Black rebellions in the Americas, all of which were betrayed by Blacks who "ran to tell Massa!" That Judas Iscariot syndrome is so very prevalent today it has forced President Obama to enquire, "You too Brutus?" The problem is, there are so many of

BLACK NATIONALISM
ALIVE AND WELL

these folks, either committed to betrayal or are misguided in choosing to follow persons whose ultimate thoughts and behaviors are questionable!

Black Nationalism 9a. Sonny Carson, accompanied by Prof. Patterson (left) and Prof James Smalls (right) and anther, conducts a tour of a church basement that was a station of the Underground Railroad.

Black Nationalism 9b. Prof. James Smalls speaks at the Institutional Church on Adelphi Street, Brooklyn, on the significance of the "Bones of the Runaway Samuel Carson" on way to Ghana for internment as a site of African American pilgrimage.

FREDERICK MONDERSON

As the Industrial Revolution developed in America after 1815 and the profit motive escalated, the work of abolitionists quickly became absolutely necessary. A decade later in 1826, in "An Address Delivered Before the General Colored Association of Boston," David Walker gave credit to these abolitionists whom he labels, "the great, the good, and the godlike Granville Sharpe, Wilberforce, Lundy, and the truly patriotic and lamented Mr. Ashmun, late Colonial Agent of Liberia, who, with a zeal which was only equaled by the goodness of his heart, has lost his life in our cause, and a host of others too numerous to mention: a number of private gentlemen too, who, though they say little, are nevertheless, busily engaged for good." Such humanitarianism proved tremendously helpful in advancing the cause of African freedom.

Nevertheless and so much so, Bracey, et al (1970: xxi) states: "In the context of worsening conditions and declining status the first clear tendencies toward Black Nationalism in America developed." This is at a time when both black and white were convinced despite how Blacks loved this land; they would never be full citizens and enjoy the benefits of its fruits. Then again, while some opposed leaving, others like Daniel Coker wrote "My heart cleaves to Africa" and Abraham Camp "We would rather be gone," were some prevailing sentiments. Yet, while some could leave, millions were tied to the land, to the plantation and exposed to all that life in those times entailed, the overseer, "day clean to last light," the brutality, and the whip, the disrespect of the family structure, divide to rule, etc.

To remedy this travesty a number of conventions were held from 1830s until the pre-Civil War years, designed "To use collective group action to achieve freedom for the slave, recognition of the constitutional rights of the freedman, and integration and assimilation of black men in the American social order." However, while preaching "the ideology of racial unity, self-help, and cooperation, the notion that colored people would have to accomplish their own advancement rather than depend on the whites," abolitionist Frederick Douglass expressed the view prevalent in many minds, as he spoke at Rochester on the 4th of July. He stated, "I am not included within the pale of this glorious

BLACK NATIONALISM
ALIVE AND WELL

anniversary! Your high independence only reveals the immeasurable distance between us ... the rich inheritance of justice, liberty, prosperity, and independence bequeathed by your fathers is shared by you, not by me.... This Fourth of July is yours, not mine. You may rejoice, I must mourn...." At the 1848 Convention in Rochester, New York he again stated the case: "We are the most oppressed people in the world. In the Southern States of this Union, we are held as slaves. All over that wide region our paths are marked with blood. Our backs are yet scarred by the lash, and our souls are yet dark under the pall of slavery. Our sisters are sold for purposes of pollution, and our brethren are sold in the market, with beasts of burden. Shut up in the prison-house of bondage - denied all rights, and deprived of all privileges, we are blotted from the pages of human existence, and placed beyond the limits of human regard. DEATH, moral DEATH, has palsied our souls in that quarter, and we are a murdered people." It was recognized, though the North was "free," there were instances in which it mirrored the South.

Black Nationalism 10. Erik Monderson among the Brothers who gathered to celebrate the 50th Anniversary of the "March on Washington," 2013.

FREDERICK MONDERSON

Notwithstanding these factors, Frederick Douglass often preached to free Blacks, "We are one people - one in general complexion, one in a common degradation, one in popular estimation. - As one rises all must rise, and as one falls all must fall. Having now, our feet on the rock of freedom, we must drag our brethren from the slimy depths of slavery, ignorance, and ruin. Every one of us should be ashamed to consider himself free, while his brother is a slave. The wrongs of our brethren, should be our constant theme. There should be no time too precious, no calling too holy, no place too sacred to make room for this cause. We should not only feel it to be the cause of humanity, but the cause of Christianity, and fit work for men and angels."

Showing a high level of abolitionist maturity and with one goal in mind, he insisted that his brothers "Never refuse to act with a white society or institution because it is white, or a black one, because it is black; but act with all men without distinction of color. By so acting, we shall find many opportunities for removing prejudices and establishing the rights of all men. - We say avail yourselves of white institutions, not because they are white, but because they afford a more convenient means of improvement."

Further, in a manner he seemed to foretell Booker T. Washington mission at Tuskegee Institute and his statement at the 1895 Atlanta Convention, Douglass insisted, "Try to get your sons into mechanical trades; press them into the blacksmith's shop, the machine shop, the joiner's shop, the wheelwright's shop, the cooper's shop, and the tailor's shop."

Nonetheless, Douglass was also quick to recognize while whites were in the anti-slavery movement, it was principally up to Blacks to learn the-ins-and outs of this form of activism and be prominent on the front lines. For, while some prominent Black traveled abroad and preached against the evils of slavery, he did insist they needed to be home! As such, and in the interest of Black Solidarity, he insisted, "If we rise, we must rise together; if we fall, we must fall together. We want such men as Ward, and Garnet, and Crummell, at home. They must come and help us. We know, by experience, that it is very

BLACK NATIONALISM
ALIVE AND WELL

pleasant to be where one can inhale a pure atmosphere, and lift up the voice against oppression, wafted as it were to the skies, upon the gratulations of the sympathizing multitude, but 'anyone can perform an agreeable duty.' Come home, then, brethren, and help us perform the 'disagreeable duty,' of telling the truth, the whole truth, though its promulgation makes enemies of 'our best friends;' come with an invincible determination to bring your mighty energies to bear upon the redemption of our race, and our whole race, from every species of oppression, irrespective of the form it may assume, or the source whence it may emanate."

Thus, at mid-century the ferocious nature, brutality and inhumanity of the institution of slavery reinforced by **Black Codes** and **Fugitive Slave Laws** forced the great one, Abraham Lincoln, to recognize and declare, "A house divided against itself cannot stand!" It's as if Republican enmity today is foretelling this repeat of history, since their conservative behavior, history and legacy is evident. When Dred Scott stood up to be free he was slapped down, the African suffered a major setback. Notwithstanding, Africans rose and are still standing! Evidence indicates, men will give their all to preserve an old way of life and though visionaries produced the Civil War Amendments, blind and conservative hatred produced the Ku Klux Klan and Knights of the White Camelia that unleashed unimaginary terror against the now freed African trying to readjust after centuries of inhumane behavior perpetrated against him by men who profess to be Christians. Rather than perish, this realization forced the Black man to come together to develop self-preservation strategies, whether economic, cultural, religious, or educational, as the most viable survival mechanisms in an environment fed by racial hatred because of skin color.

FREDERICK MONDERSON

Black Nationalism 11. Erik posing with the "Empowered" poster of the National Urban League.

BLACK NATIONALISM
ALIVE AND WELL

Black Nationalism 12. Leading the charge, among the Ladies, who have been so instrumental in the struggles to free African people.

Despite the advances Blacks have made toward realizing "Dr. King's Dream," today in view of current discrimination, racial profiling, scarcity of jobs, coupled with low standards of educational achievement, preponderance of medical ailments in the Black community, viz., diabetes, heart attacks, strokes, hypertension, AIDS and other sexually transmitted diseases, all "wounded" resulting in low self-esteem; from the Pre-Civil War years to now a general belief has held, "Black men must band together and help themselves." They must perennially remain vigilant, pool their finances and wisely spend their hard earned dollars, and enlighten, respect and support each other. While Frederick Douglass has insisted "Power concedes nothing without a struggle," we must still operate as if Jim Crow, Separate and Unequal treatment, lynching, denial of the fundamental guarantees of the Constitution are behaviors manifested in the past, but they are still being practiced. They have simply changed their *modus operandi*. Yet, "Still we rise!" After the numerous attempts to eradicate the soul and

FREDERICK MONDERSON

aspirations of the Black man, we were propelled to see Barack Obama twice elected President of the United States, as we showed the significance of the black vote, recognized the increase in Black earning potential and the potency of educational accomplishments that create endless possibilities. And again, "Still We Rise!" We rise despite the many and continuously emerging challenges!"

We rise through intellectual and social consciousness to rebut the insidious and spiteful assertions of a Ben Carson whose opposition to President Obama Affordable Care Act, designed to provide health care for millions of Americans who lack such consideration, has been unfortunate. Such pronouncements have tarnished his image among persons in the medical profession and those who looked up to him as a Black man with an extraordinary gift. So Black Nationalism has come a long way and must remain vigilant in wake of the many threats and disrespect to the first Black President Barack Obama, victimization in shopping while Black, killing of Blacks by police and even misguided Blacks out there "Doing the Man's Work!"

While in Pre-Civil War days Blacks considered the use of violence to destroy slavery and in Post Civil War terrorism, such was a viable strategy. Nevertheless, many recognize such an approach is not tenable today. The alternatives, however, are just as potent. Just as the cultural revolution of the Harlem Renaissance generated great pride among Blacks who were fed poetry, literature, music, sculpture and painting, and other creative expressions, economic nationalism and proper harnessing of political power has been and is always an effective strategy once used wisely.

During slavery, skilled and unskilled Blacks were hired out, worked extra and saved their pittances to eventually purchase their freedom and that of their families. In the Post-Civil War era when the government reneged on the "40 Acres and a Mule" promise, despite the trickery and inequity of "Share cropping" tenant farming, industrious Blacks, especially in the South, were able to purchase and hold land and property. In lean years, on these properties, Kitchen Gardens helped supplement meager wages. Through the

BLACK NATIONALISM
ALIVE AND WELL

lynchings, riots, burning of thriving Black communities, Black voters became disillusioned with Republican insensitivity and looked to the promise of the Democratic Party's "New Deal." Notwithstanding, in the Post World War II era and in face of blatant and proactive racism and injustice, Rosa Parks and the heroes and heroines of her age instituted and maintained a prolonged economic boycott of the Montgomery Alabama Bus System and the overall climate of that city, thus serving as an effective tool to redress systemic inequality nationwide. The problem is that this strategy is not employed sufficient today even though it is often touted as a formidable example.

Black Nationalism 13. Among the leaders of the parade at the "50th Anniversary of the March on Washington, for Jobs and Freedom."

The Radio personality, perennially active, Bob Law is now promoting an economic boycott strategy across the country. At first he concentrated on the "preponderance of fast food joints" in the Black Community whose substandard foods play a substantial role in Black Community health problems. The operators of such chains and independents alike, he pointed out, not only do not hire Blacks but remove their profits without reinvesting in any substantive projects

FREDERICK MONDERSON

on behalf of the communities in which they operate. Now with the nationwide profiling and disrespect of Black shoppers, these initiatives have become the wind propelling his sails. Yet, among Blacks a lot of work still needs to be done. On the radio recently, Mr. Law told of some Blacks who went shopping with legal tender, hundred dollar bills, but the stores would not accept their flashing greens. They left, deposited the money on someone else's debit card account and came back to make their purchases from the same store nevertheless. This scenario goes to the Heart of Mr. Law's thrust that Blacks should not spend their money where either they cannot work or are disrespected. A good example he mentioned is the young lady shopping at Barney's who was arrested, not for shoplifting, but for spending too much when she bought a $2500.00 ladies bag!

Black Nationalism 14. Voting Equals Democracy is a way to empower Blacks who hold the "balance of power" as Malcolm said!

James Clingman in "Exiting the train of consumption" in *Daily Challenge* Holiday Edition, December 24-27, 2013 wrote: "We have been so programmed to believe that having 'things,' especially the best and highest priced things is the key to our personal value. We are mesmerized by luxury and excess and have become obedient consumers who will rush out, sleep out, and even knockout someone else just to have the latest fashion, gadget, or whatever anyone is selling." He reminded, Sharazad Ali once said,

BLACK NATIONALISM
ALIVE AND WELL

"Black folks brag about how much we pay for things, and White folks brag about how little they pay."

Black Nationalism 15. ... And "Children Shall Lead Them!"

As such, the best expression of economic nationalism today is the Montgomery Boycott in "New Wine Skins," which is consistent with the elevated consciousness of the times and Blacks coming of age. All this goes to say, Black Nationalism as a strategy and a reality is absolutely necessary for the salvation of Africans in America. In view of prevailing conditions, social, economic, educational, Blacks must form a "united front" no matter how difficult. It is interesting, however, despite the tremendous struggles for the right to vote and the realized potency of the Black vote, on his radio program Gary Byrd mentioned the percentage of Blacks who voted in the 2008 and 2012 National Election for the President. He mentioned Barack Obama as probably the most potent and dynamic Black candidate in a long time. Yet, only 62 percent of Blacks voted! One has to wonder what it will take to have a higher turnout.

Blacks must equally recognize and return to the potency of economic nationalism as the ancestors have done in their creating wealth through mutual benefit societies, formation and sustaining black banks and insurance companies, purchase and holding property, as well as executing meaningfully "Buy Black" campaigns that support Black enterprise.

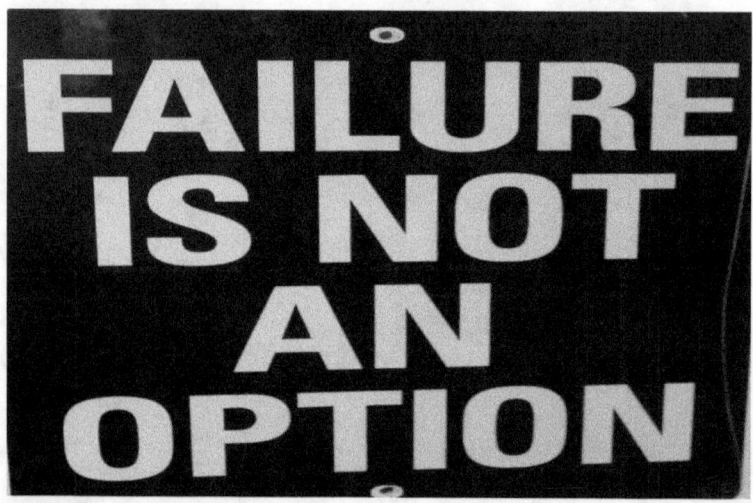

Black Nationalism 16. Yes, "Failure is not an Option" is a message very apropos to any struggle.

Black Nationalism 17. Dr. John Henrik Clarke, long a light and Black Nationalist theorist, no longer with us but whose spirit lives on in Clarke House in Harlem beside his beautiful wife, Sister Sybil Williams-Clarke and their escorts.

BLACK NATIONALISM ALIVE AND WELL

2. Who's Betraying Us Today?
By
Dr. Fred Monderson

Recently I listened to an old tape by Dr. John H. Clarke, entitled "The New World Order" which is really "The Old World Order" in "new wine skins." It was particularly interesting when he came to the part on Booker Taliaferro Washington. First he explained and soft-pedaled that Booker T. did a "little Toming" and then he emphasized his accomplishments so we could stand on the shoulders of this giant, decades later. Importantly, Dr. Clarke asked: "Have you really read Washington's 'Atlanta Compromise' Speech?" at the opening of the Cotton States Exposition on September 18, 1895, and reproduced in his Autobiography *Up From Slavery*. As such I decided to re-read this important document.

What is significant about this document, the speech, Washington and his detractors, is that this was a perilous time for Black people but it was also a time of action and futuristic human creativity. Of course, he was not the only activist! Nevertheless, in those times Washington sought and was able to broker the best deal available to our people in his day. Now, if the "measure of the man" as Dr. M.L. King later put it, "is not where he stands in time of comfort and convenience but in time of challenge and controversy," then the legacy of Washington speaks for itself. He found Tuskegee Institute at a time when the nation was experiencing rapid industrial change amidst an enormous influx of foreign immigrants particularly when one third of the South's population was Black and conservative terror was having a field-day with Blacks.

FREDERICK MONDERSON

Black Nationalism 18. On the mural wall of Amun-Ra, depictions of Bob Marley, Dr. Erik Williams, Malcolm X, Marcus Garvey, Kwame Nkrumah, Toussaint L'Ouverture, and Haile Selaisse as well as Harriet Tubman and Maurice Bishop.

In his Speech, Washington praised the Sponsors of the Exposition for allowing Blacks to participate in the creative process of the forward looking developments then transforming the society. In his view, Washington also recognized, despite the far-reaching implications of the franchise, political power and election to high office, these were probably less meaningful than securing the "40 acres and a mule" because such would have put them at the bedrock of the society. His idea would be better than at the top where they "won" and "lost" power and then were truly powerless with the failure of Reconstruction. His "cast down your bucket where you are" admonition to both Blacks and Whites was indeed the true nature of the "Atlanta Compromise." He realized our people were in a hostile environment and he did the best he could.

This was an age of the Ku Klux Klan and White Citizens Council when whites perpetrated all forms of hideous behaviors against Blacks to re-institute a rigorous caste system in the South. Even in literature Blacks were being grossly depicted and the racist writer Thomas Dixon wrote *The Clansman* and *The Leopard's Spots*. In

BLACK NATIONALISM
ALIVE AND WELL

the latter he established the dictum: "One drop of Negro blood makes a Negro. It kinks the hair, flattens the nose, thickens the lips, puts out the light of intellect and lights the fires of brute passions." On the other hand, he painted southerners as Ladies and Gentlemen of substance in a "world of culture and chivalry."

Black Nationalism 19. Dr. Yosef ben-Jochannan pictured on the same above mural with the famous quote from the *Papyrus of Hunefer* indicating the "Origin of the ancient Egyptians."

Understanding the power of the pen, this is what Washington had to contend with. By the time of Washington's death in 1915, Hodges in *Black History* (1971: 155) would write: "Despite Washington's

FREDERICK MONDERSON

attempts at conciliation with White America, race relations went from bad to worse during his leadership. By the time of his death in 1915, more than 3,000 men and women had been lynched in the United States. Most of the mob murders occurred in the South, and most of the victims were Blacks."

Black Nationalism 20. One of "Our Fathers," Dr. John Henrik Clarke, who himself did "A Long and Mighty Walk."

White racists projected their sexual frustrations and guilt onto the Blacks, and it became an obsession to accuse Black males of "Rape" at the slightest pretext. Ironically, only about 19 percent of "lynched" Blacks had even been accused of sex offenses. "The Southern lynch mobs, often in collusion with racist law enforcement officers, considered hanging too conventional. They often tortured their victims, riddled them with bullets, mutilated them sexually, and burnt them alive. These lynching bees were sometimes 'advertised' in advance and people came from miles around, as if for a gala social gathering. Some even brought their children, and a carnival atmosphere prevailed – with an undercurrent of hatred and violence, especially when the pitiful victim was dragged into view."

BLACK NATIONALISM
ALIVE AND WELL

Thus, since Washington realized we were not going any place and in that precarious position, he needed to cultivate good relations to progress gradually with a view to making inroads in agriculture, mechanics, commerce, domestic service and the professions. Perhaps his analogy is like the rush for intellectual achievements in that age equated with the rush for political power that left Blacks lacking in the crucial fundamental areas of meaningful progress in the society. He says: begin at the bottom, not at the top!

To the whites, his "separate as the fingers, yet one as the hand" seems to foreshadow *Plessey V. Ferguson's* 1896, "Separate but Equal" Supreme Court ruling which was in fact, "separate and unequal." We should not blame Washington because, Whites upturned his advice! He did, but with a different voice, speak of the "highest intelligence and development of all" while believing "that the agitation of questions of social equality is extreme folly."

Black Nationalism 21. "Two Great Ones," Manhattan Borough President Percy Sutton and Mayor David Dinkins. Two Harlem and New York political icons; Sutton did much for Harlem and the Black cause, while Dinkins did a great deal for the Borough of Manhattan and the City of New York.

FREDERICK MONDERSON

Black Nationalism 22. Radio Legend, Gary Byrd, creator of the **GBE** (Gary Byrd Experience) "Global Black Experience."

Washington recognized: "It is important and right that all the privileges of the law be ours, but it is vastly more important that we be prepared for the exercise of those privileges. The opportunity to earn a dollar in a factory is worth infinitely more than the opportunity to spend a dollar in an opera-house."

Then he appealed to Whites to help solve the South's problems by giving Blacks opportunities in the fields, forest, mines, factories, letters and arts and with god's help "administering absolute justice." Material prosperity for all, he predicted, "will bring into our beloved South a new heaven and a new earth."

BLACK NATIONALISM
ALIVE AND WELL

Black Nationalism 23. Dr. John Henrik Clarke on the same Brooklyn mural stating an unmistakable fact: "The role of history is to tell a people what they have been, where they have been, what they are, where they are, where they still must go, and what they still must be!"

In elaborating on the significance of Booker T. Washington, Prof. John Clarke realized the man recognized the realities of his age. Consider that Washington was born a slave in Virginia. Norman Hodges in *Black History* (1971: 153) wrote: "Washington moved to West Virginia along with his family, after emancipation. He entered Hampton Institute at 16, earning his keep as a part-time custodian on the premises. The school - then known as the Hampton Normal and Agricultural Institute - was a center for 'practical' education. Washington trained to become a brick mason, but he later entered teaching. Invited to teach at Hampton, he stayed there until being called to Tuskegee, Alabama, to organize and head a new school for Blacks. He has described how the great Institute started as a ramshackle, one-room building, and how he sat under an umbrella at his desk when it rained, because the roof leaked so badly!"

FREDERICK MONDERSON

Nevertheless, from 1881 to 1915 he made it a school of worth, as he had a more futuristic view of where he wanted his people to be, let's say in a hundred years. Let's face it, a century later Tuskegee is a credible, functional and historic institution that has contributed enormously to Black educational, economic, intellectual, scientific and social advancement and even more.

Sure the negative side has been the "Syphilis Experiment," but we have had enormous scientific and agricultural advances under George Washington Carver. John P. Davis in *The American Negro Reference Book* (1967: 554) writes: "Booker T. Washington attracted to Tuskegee Institute the ablest minds he could; the development there of distinguished bibliographer Monroe N. Work was one of the greatest contribution ever made by a Negro institution to scholarship." In his action program, as early as 1900 Washington sent Tuskegee graduates to Togo in West Africa to teach them agricultural skills, over a six year period. Graduates were also sent to the Anglo-Egyptian Sudan in 1906, as Washington had a tremendous interest in African well-being. In the famous "Tuskegee-Hampton Approach," Washington and his White allies developed a program for missionaries in Africa.

He was interested in the plight of Africans all over. He helped form the Congo Reform Association and National Negro Business League. He lunched at the White House and with boxing champ Jack Johnson. His wife was equally involved in social issues for she was President of the National Federation of Afro-American Women that had affiliates in more than 16 states. Davis (1967: 683) noted Washington planned "a large scale conference on the problems of Africa and people of African descent."

"The International Conference on the Negro met at Tuskegee on April 17, 18, and 19 in 1912. The delegates and the agenda expressed the close interplay between the missionary movement and Negro educational institutions, as well as the extent to which Pan-African thinking was also a force that could not be ignored. It was officially reported that people were present from eighteen foreign countries or colonies, and that they included representatives of

BLACK NATIONALISM
ALIVE AND WELL

twenty-five missionary societies and twelve religious denominations. The Negro mission boards were all represented, but less than a dozen Africans were present among over a hundred delegates.

Black Nationalism 24. Black Power in its classic sense with (from left to right), Charlie Rangel, David Dinkins, Bertrand Aristide, Jesse Jackson and Major Owens.

FREDERICK MONDERSON

Black Nationalism 25. Rev. Charles Norris, Sr., Pastor of Bethesda Missionary Baptist Church of Jamaica Avenue in Queens was tremendously incensed in the statement: "Have you seen what they are doing to my President Barack Obama!"

The African scholar Edward Blyden sent a letter and Rev. Mark Caseley Hayford brought an address prepared by his famous brother, A. Caseley Hayford."

BLACK NATIONALISM
ALIVE AND WELL

Black Nationalism 26. The "Sons of Africa" buried in the historic "African Burial Ground" in Foley Square, Lower Manhattan.

The Tuskegee Choir excelled under the leadership of William Grant Still. The famous "Tuskegee Airmen," of World War II, would equally distinguish themselves in legendary exploits. All these have been guideposts along the path that Washington probably envisioned and set out.

Now contrast those accomplishments with much of what is going on in our community today. Despite all that has been achieved, today our condition is one of plight. It was startling to hear Jesse Jackson rattle it off on the radio recently. We are number one in basketball and football bowl games and last in graduation; last in employment, but first in prison. Many of our people live in sub-standard housing.

FREDERICK MONDERSON

With more than 1 million people incarcerated, Blacks and Latinos make up more than 90 percent of the inmates. We have the highest incidence of Aids, Diabetes, Strokes, and other health and medical conditions disproportionate to our percentage of the general population. We are first among foreclosures and our communities are being overrun by non-Blacks.

In the movie "Liberation of L.B. Jones" it was said jokingly that Blacks traditionally controlled "the numbers," "undertaking" and the "liquor business." Face it, the state has taken over the numbers business; I don't know much about undertaking; but now whites and Asians flood our communities with liquor stores.

Black Nationalism 27. Dr. James McIntosh and Sister Betty Dobson, Co-founders and Co-Chairs of **CEMOTAP** (Committee to Eliminate Media Offensive to African People).

Consider, practically every grocery store, "bodega" sells beer, restaurants and bars sell beer, wines and liquor. Now, add to this how voluminous liquor stores have saturated the black community. For example, in Brooklyn, New York, in North Crown Heights, in a 10-Block stretch along Nostrand Avenue from Atlantic Avenue to Eastern Parkway there are liquor stores between Bergen Street and St. Marks Avenue; at Prospect Place; St. John's Place; and at Eastern Parkway. There is a bar at Bergen Street and another between St.

BLACK NATIONALISM
ALIVE AND WELL

John's and Lincoln Place. These figures are not reflected in other communities. To each his own, but alcohol contributes significantly to diabetes and other illnesses. Yet, the entertainer "Puff Daddy" recently announced a new brand of liquor he was promoting: "I'm building a new brand," he said.

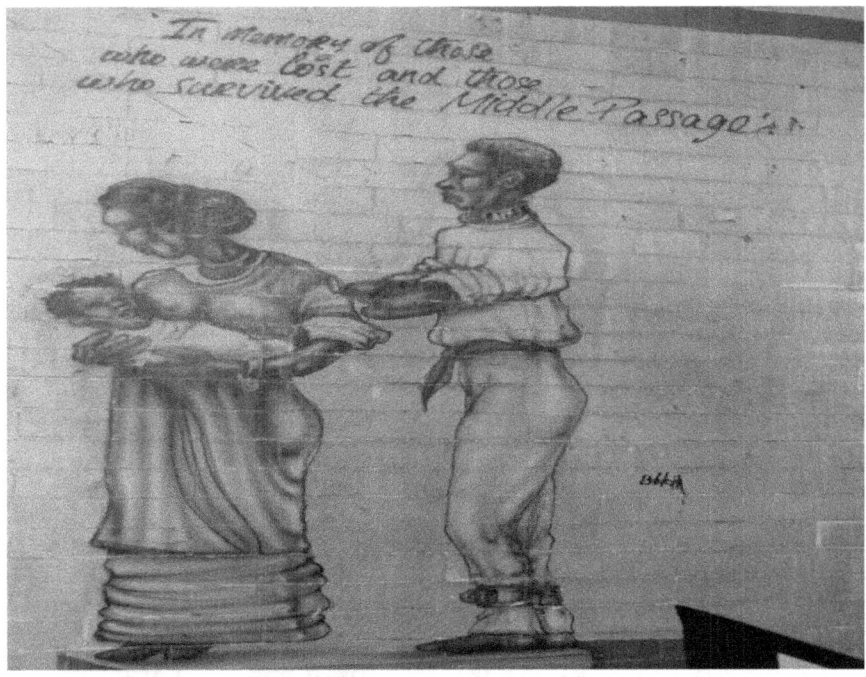

Black Nationalism 28. The African family, shackled and on the auction block, as depicted on the mural!

More than 95 percent of the stores in our community are owned by non-Blacks, viz., vegetables, grocery, fast food, laundry, liquor, clothing, book-stores, nail salons, novelties, pharmacies, furniture, carpets, appliances, and so on. Today Blacks own a few barbershops, fewer beauty-salons and an occasional "mom and pop" store fighting to stay in business.

This is to say, with so much going on in those perilous times after slavery, Blacks were able to work, save and purchase significant

FREDERICK MONDERSON

parcels of property. In many areas they controlled the economic lifeblood of the community. In the many riotous behaviors the first things Whites did was to destroy the community's economic base, but still our people persevered!

There is need to truly evaluate Booker T. Washington who achieved so much and left us a living legacy in Tuskegee Institute, where on his monument are inscribed the words: Booker T. Washington, 1856-1915 – "He lifted the veil of ignorance from his people and pointed the way to progress through education and industry." It's a challenge to understand how so many are learning and earning so much today and still Blacks are high on the poverty scale; they face high unemployment, police misconduct and racial profiling, "Black on Black" crime is out of control, drugs plague our community, substandard housing conditions retard our health, and, despite the traditional ones, no new and significant institutions are being built to serve our people into the future. Equally, there's the ever-present need to know more about our history in Africa and America which is not being met.

This civil rights commentary is the first in a series to look and analyze significant people and documents in our history so the young can have points of reference in their forward and upward march until that day, as Dr. King has said: "when Black men and White men, Jews and Gentiles, Protestant and Catholics," and all others will be able to join hands together, sitting at the table of brotherhood. There they will hopefully proclaim achievement of the fundamental principles of life, liberty and the pursuit of happiness as envisioned in the Declaration of Independence, the Constitution and the litany of statues, tenets and doctrines that aspire to the indivisible nature of America and the lives and happiness of Americans, of which Blacks are unquestionably a part, as they would say, "like old money."

BLACK NATIONALISM ALIVE AND WELL

Black Nationalism 29. Many facets of the mural depicting issues in the Black experience.

3. BEN CARSON, SERIOUSLY?
By
Dr. Fred Monderson

Recently, a Washington lawmaker described the Affordable Care Act maliciously dubbed "Obamacare," as "the most dangerous law in American history." This week, at a social conservative gathering, the famed and now retired neurosurgeon from Johns Hopkins Hospital Center and member of the Heritage Foundation, Dr. Ben Carson, described "Obamacare as worse than slavery." **Tragic**! In a visit to a South American Republic this writer overhead a taxi driver railing at another motorist, "I know you bought your license, but at least learn to drive!"

Dr. Carson is clearly a highly skillful and successful surgeon. However, his comments regarding the Affordable Health Care initiative set forth by President Obama reflects either an abysmal ignorance of African/American history and race relations or a severe psycho/cultural pathology which impels him to seek his "thirty

FREDERICK MONDERSON

pieces of silver" in the form of approbation from powerful white supremacists who fear and hate President Obama.

> ### THE UNDERGROUND RAILROAD AND ABOLITIONISM IN NEW YORK CITY
>
> Nineteenth century New York City was an epicenter of activities for the abolition of chattel slavery. The grand theory of republicanism, a political system that protects liberty through a steadfast rule of law, echoed loudly in all circles of the city and created a hotbed of abolitionism. The ideals of the Declaration of Independence and the Revolutionary War helped fuel the Underground Railroad and the many conductors who, at great personal risk, shuttled scores of brave souls to freedom. In addition to such prominent figures as John Quincy Adams, the Rev. Henry Ward Beecher, the Rev. J.W.C. Pennington, and the Tappan Brothers, there were simple business owners, journalists, inn keepers, and laborers who made an indelible mark on human history.
>
> The Underground Railroad sites in New York City listed above are just some of the stations significant to that passage; however, there are many places throughout the five boroughs that will remain as secret today as they were at that time.
>
> *New-York, May 8, 1758.*
>
> RUN *away on Monday last, from* John Hastier, *of this City, Goldsmith, a lusty well-set Negro Man, named Jasper, about 5 Feet 6 Inches high, speaks good English, and understands the Silversmith's Trade. Had on when he went away, a brown Forest Cloth Coat with flat Pewter Buttons, blue Waistcoat, with same Sort of Buttons; a Leather Breeches, with the like Buttons, old Hat, brown Yarn Stockings, and old Shoes. Whoever takes up the said Negroe, and secures him so that his Master may have him again, shall have* FOUR POUNDS *Reward, and all reasonable Charges paid by*
> n° M8   JOHN HASTIER.
>
> "[In New York] I saw more of the foolishness, wickedness, and at the same time the invincibility, of American Negro-hate, than I ever saw elsewhere." – Samuel Ringgold Ward

Black Nationalism 30. Description of factors related to the **Underground Railroad** in which "Runaways" were assisted in their flight from slavery.

Inasmuch as lawmakers are enormously wealthy, the lawmaker in question may have bought, or inherited, his seat while still being ignorant of American history. Dr. Carson, on the other hand, may have been too busy conducting brain surgery to have truly studied American slavery, as well as its psycho/cultural aftermath, to make such a reckless, perverse comparison. Let us not forget that Malcolm

BLACK NATIONALISM
ALIVE AND WELL

X reminded us, "The slave master used overseers and the method of divide and rule to control the slaves!" In an earlier version of today's developments, the Republicans used Michael Steele to attempt the defeat of President Obama. He was a dismal failure and was subsequently fired. Whether Ben Carson is a "Judas Iscariot" or not only time will tell! Nevertheless, in the record of the oppressor; the lawmakers especially, have historic ties to odious legislation that terrorized and victimized significant segments of the American population. Dr. Carson, one of perhaps very few Blacks afforded a platform at the ultra conservative Family Research Council's meetings and probably at several other such gatherings, raises questions as to his motivation, purpose, audience and intent, as well as his knowledge of history, certainly of Black history! It is thus appropriate that a mini-history lesson be used to enlighten these individuals like Dr. Carson and others on some of the "most dangerous laws passed in American history!"

Perhaps in his narrow-mindedness, what the Congressman meant refers to are times when the law as applied to all Americans it is dangerous but when applied to African Americans it is not! Nevertheless, in Dr. Carson's case, he certainly knows medicine but does not fully realize that a Black Republican, people of his hue, *a la* Michael Steele, J.C. Watts, Allen West, "who all sat by the door," ultimately found it closed. Thank goodness, he has his profession on which to fall back. In the minds of many Black people especially in that rant against Obamacare, Dr. Carson has certainly fallen from grace and many young students who were inspired by his "gifted hands," must now wonder whether psyche and spirit have been impaired!

The intent of this essay is to show, some of the most odious laws, sketched below, which proved to be infinitely more oppressive and dangerous as applied to African Americans in this country, more than the Affordable Health Care law. This meaningful and comprehensive health care law is designed to address the needs of millions of Americans who have no medical coverage and can only

FREDERICK MONDERSON

rely on the immediacy of Emergency Room care. Two things can thus be considered in this case. The article in *The New York Times* of October 6, 2013, referenced the hundreds of millions of dollars this Anti-Obamacare movement is collecting and disbursing.

Black Nationalism 31. Samori Marksman, Radio Personality of Station **WBAI**.

BLACK NATIONALISM ALIVE AND WELL

Black Nationalism 32. Professor James Blake, who is always on point on Black History.

Black Nationalism 33. Locations in the Bronx and Brooklyn where "Stations on the Underground Railroad" were located.

FREDERICK MONDERSON

Given that speakers are paid a fee for their presentation, it is fair to ask whether Dr. Carson is but one recipient of this money-mill. Second, the article mentions the thousands of persons being trained to extend the task of "informing the public about Obamacare." Granted, some policy laws as huge as Obamacare may have some faults in their initial roll-out. These "pseudo-patriots" such as Dr. Carson, however, are not interested in repairability but in destruction. Which great idea has not had setbacks before being perfected? Surely we can name Medicare, Social Security, the conquest of space, even formation of the Union of the United States which is still trying, after nearly two and a half centuries, to perfect itself! Most importantly, it is not inconceivable that there may be much misinformation in the anti-Obamacare strategy, but the Affordable Care Act was a principal issue in the Obama Campaign Platform. It was passed by Congress, upheld by the Supreme Court and is the law of the land. Even more important, it is hardly likely to be repealed despite some 42 attempts by House Republicans to repeal this historic piece of federal legislation!

In school, youngsters are reminded that even the brightest students dropout; and that even the most brilliant people sometimes say dumb things! Dr. Carson certainly knows medicine but his understanding of the forces and realities of history is a failure. Perhaps, in his present mental state, if this was an operation his patient would probably come out seriously impaired. When Vice President Dan Quayle mis-spelled potato as **p-o-t-a-t-o-e** he disappointed a great many. Likewise, when Dr. Carson stood with the Conservative Family Research Council and pronounced that President Obama's Affordable Care Act, maliciously called Obamacare, was the "worse law since slavery," not only did he disappoint untold numbers of adult Blacks, but his status as an icon to many young Blacks took a severe hit! As for this writer, as an American, I feel I must share my thoughts on this misguided statement. Particularly, because similar ones have been expressed among people who have either conspired with or have been funded by surreptitious individuals who plotted to disrupt, subvert and/or obstruct the orderly function of the United States government under the legal administration of President

BLACK NATIONALISM
ALIVE AND WELL

Barack Obama, twice elected by a majority of the American people. These persons are thus guilty of treason!

```
MANHATTAN                                   16. ISAAC T. HOPPER HOME
                                            (The Women's Prison Association)
14. AFRICAN BURIAL GROUND                   East Village
    NATIONAL MONUMENT                       110 Second Avenue
Lower Manhattan                             (between E. Sixth and E. Seventh Streets)
Interim African Burial Ground Visitor Center New York, NY 10003
Ted Weiss Federal Building
290 Broadway                                17. MOTHER A.M.E. ZION CHURCH
(between Duane and Reade Streets)           (former address, identified by a plaque)
New York, NY 10007                          TriBeCa - Plaque erected at:
                                            158 Church Street
African Burial Ground National Monument     (at Leonard Street)
Duane and Elk Streets                       New York, NY 10007
(adjacent to the Ted Weiss Federal Building)
New York, NY 10013                          Current address:
                                            146 W. 137th Street
15. THOMAS DOWNING'S                        (at Malcolm X Boulevard)
    OYSTER HOUSE                            New York, NY 10030
(no longer exists)
West Village                                18. THE QUAKER MEETING HOUSE
Former location:                            (now the Brotherhood Synagogue)
Wall & Broad Streets                        Gramercy Park
New York, NY 10005                          Gramercy Park South
                                            (between Third Avenue and Irving Place)
                                            New York, NY 10003

19. DAVID RUGGLES' BOARDING HOUSE           23. MACEDONIA A.M.E. CHURCH
(no longer exists; identified by a plaque)  Flushing
TriBeCa                                     37-22 Union Street
36 Lispenard Street                         (between 37th and 38th Avenues)
(at the corner of Church Street)            Flushing, NY 11354
New York, NY 10013
                                            STATEN ISLAND
QUEENS
                                            24. DR. SAMUEL MCKENZIE
20. THE 1694 FRIENDS MEETING HOUSE              ELLIOT HOUSE
Flushing                                    (now a private residence)
137-16 Northern Boulevard                   Livingston
(between Main & Union Streets)              69 Delafield Place
Queens, NY 11354                            (between Bard and Davis Avenues)
                                            Staten Island, NY 10310
21. BOWNE HOUSE
Flushing                                    25. SANDY GROUND HISTORICAL
37-01 Bowne Street                              MUSEUM
(at 37th Avenue)                            Sandy Ground
Flushing, NY 11354                          1538 Woodrow Road
                                            (between Dexter and Lynbrook Avenues)
22. KING MANOR MUSEUM                       Staten Island, NY 10309
Jamaica - King Park
53rd Street & Jamaica Avenue
Jamaica, NY 11432
```

Black Nationalism 34. More locations of "Stations of the Underground Railroad" in Manhattan, Queens and Staten Island.

Let me then first point out some milestones in American History, whether legislative or under cover of legal sanction, that have been the hall-marks of the notion of "the Ugly American." In this vein, it

FREDERICK MONDERSON

would be helpful to separate Pre - and Post-1863 *Emancipation Proclamation* issues to establish the context in which Dr. Carson, especially, is not only ignorant, but perverse, malicious and spiteful. This is sadly predictable, considering his alignment with a conservative heritage mindset that reeks of terrorist activities against Blacks in America. It is an established fact that after President Obama's 2008 victory, Senator Mitch McConnell publicly boasted, "I intend to make Barack Obama a one-term President." Morgan Freeman, the Academy Award winner, appearing on CNN's Piers Morgan, asserted that the Senator's statement was "racist!" Freeman's comments also would be apt to Dr. Carson's statement.

Now, history has shown that to secure Southern support for acceptance of the initial United States Constitution, the founding fathers established the 3/5th Clause or the *Compromise of 1787*, in which enslaved Africans were counted as "three fifths" of a White person or to have 5 Blacks counted as 3 Whites. Let us also remind Dr. Carson that many a "founding patriot" sent slaves to fight for America's freedom in the Revolutionary War; that one free Black, Crispus Attucks was the first to fall in the fight for America's freedom. This means that among America's first patriots was a **Black Man**, a bona fide hero!

The *Compromise of 1820* was also called the Missouri Compromise. It stipulated, among other things, that Maine would be admitted to the Union as a free state, and Missouri as a slave state. The remainder of the **Louisiana Purchase** (1803) would not become a slave state.

Following the *Compromise of 1820*, in 1832, the *South Carolina Nullification Act* forced President Andrew Jackson to dispatch federal troops to check the rebellious action. Nearly 250 years later, Jesse Jackson pointed out that, South Carolina; home state of former Senator Jim DeMint, who now heads the Heritage Foundation; on whose website Dr. Carson's photo is prominently displayed; and who wanted to create President Obama's "Waterloo;" that this southern state supported 36 state prisons and 1 state college. It is not

BLACK NATIONALISM
ALIVE AND WELL

surprising in such a former "rebellious slave state," that Blacks are the principal occupants of its state prisons and hardly represented at its state college or colleges!

Black Nationalism 34a. Harriet Tubman, Liberator, Intelligence Agent and Humanitarian.

FREDERICK MONDERSON

Black Nationalism 35. There is a message in the man's attire.

Among its many mandates, the *Compromise of 1850* not only sought to establish north/south, free state/slave state regional balance, but established the *Fugitive Slave Laws* in which, oftentimes both free and enslaved Blacks were returned to southern servitude. Sometimes they were returned from the north to Black slave owners who were often active participants in a system of inhumanity that brutalized and debased the bodies and souls of untold numbers of other African people held in bondage through judicial and administrative fiat.

Black Codes were the legal mechanisms by which enslaved Blacks were dehumanized, controlled and psychologically and often physically emasculated in a system of exploitation that generated great wealth through the plantation culture for principally southerners in the "lynching states." Perhaps, not surprisingly despite this, in the 2012 election, the Republican candidate Mitt Romney won all the southern states with history of lynching. So much for the "New South!"

BLACK NATIONALISM
ALIVE AND WELL

Black Nationalism 35a. Dr. Leonard James and the young men he schooled.

In 1857, Chief Justice Roger Taney issued the *Dred Scott Decision*, a ruling that Dred Scott, an enslaved African American seeking his freedom, was not a citizen and could not bring suit in a United States Court. Even more, this apologist for slavery further ruled, that based on American history, "The Black man has no rights which a White man must respect!" Dr. Carson ought to be aware that even after his outlandish disparagement of President Obama's most important legislative accomplishment by a **Black man** held in the highest esteem by untold millions of African and other people worldwide; there would be at least one conservative heckler in that group who would have shouted "The Nigger has spoken!" Perhaps it would be, "The Nigger Doctor has spoken!" Then again, while his camp has previously thought the President of the United States, Barack Hussein Obama is a "Nigger," perhaps in his misguided mind, Dr. Carson may also think, though he has probably moved from the door, that he is not a "Nigger." But somewhere along the line he will

FREDERICK MONDERSON

be reminded, especially if his strategy as a tool of presidential debasement, does not work!

Black Nationalism 36. Sojourner Truth Social Reformer, Orator and humanitarian.

Abraham Lincoln was very intelligent; a great man and President who realized, "a house divided against itself cannot stand;" and as such, he put his heart, his administration and his life into the *Emancipation Proclamation*. This bold and courageous act paved the way for the *Civil War Amendments* - 13th, legally ended slavery; 14th, gave citizenship to individuals born or naturalized in the United States; and the 15th, which empowered Black men with the legal

BLACK NATIONALISM
ALIVE AND WELL

status to exercise the franchise. However, under cover of law, these legislative milestones were often assaulted and desecrated by southern conservatives who were the "powers that be." They were part of one of the most terrifying period in American history which the historian Professor Rayford Logan called "the Nadir," because of the perennial perpetuation of horrific acts of terror against Blacks.

That conservative movement, to win political control of the "prostrate south" during and after Reconstruction, formed "white redeemers" such as the Ku Klux Klan, White Citizens Council, Knights of the White Camelia, etc., and began to systematically terrorize Blacks using fear, lynchings, tar and featherings, and other intimidating actions, and consigning many Black individuals to an inequitable "share cropper system" of economic peonage. In conjunction, Southern conservative lawmakers enacted the "Grandfather Clause," which ruled that "If one's grandfather had voted previously then one could vote." This strategy was used to instill fear and exclude Blacks from the polls since their enslaved grandfathers could not have voted before the 15th Amendment of February 1870. The "Grandfather Clause" was repealed in 1915 because of its inequity and as a pillar of "Jim Crow." A legal requirement that Blacks pay a "Poll Tax" to vote was instituted and Blacks were required to take a "Literacy Test" which some with doctors degrees could not pass because of the educational machinations involved. All these shenanigans employed contributed to a *de facto* and *de jure* "Jim Crow" state of affairs across the south especially in which ex-slaves were relegated to second class citizenship and were perennially victims of terrorism at will. Meanwhile, the "White Primary" became the order of the day, precluding Blacks from running for elected office and enabling Whites to control the political process! All of this occurred while the federal government pandered to the whims of arch conservatives, irrespective of the party to which they belonged.

FREDERICK MONDERSON

Black Nationalism 37. Frederick Douglass - Publisher, Orator, Author and American Statesman.

Many of those events and circumstances culminated in the 1896 Supreme Court ruling of *Plessey v. Ferguson* that established a "Separate but Equal" rule, which was, in actuality, "Separate and Unequal." This significant ruling particularly affected the education of young children and especially enabled state enforced residential segregation. Thus, more than a year ago in 2011, a CBS 60-Minutes

BLACK NATIONALISM
ALIVE AND WELL

program, investigating a Civil Rights case of murder in which the principal perpetrator was still alive, yet no one was talking but the victim's family, revealed more than 100 unresolved Civil Rights murders. The report also pointed out, in order to run for and hold political office, individuals had to belong to or espouse the policies of the "lynching states" terrorist ideology. Thus, in that environment and under cover of state law and politics, racially motivated mob violence, lynchings and murder were never seriously challenged in territory under conservatives' control.

Under these unjust laws, Black Americans were denied the fundamental rights of the United States Constitution. Among others, these included Exclusion from Jury Duty, Denial of Freedom of Speech, Voting Rights, and the Right to Assemble. They were also excluded from union jobs until, on the eve of World War II in 1941, A. Philip Randolph, a Black activist labor leader threatened to March on Washington! In response, President Roosevelt took some action and the Congress of Industrial Organizations, sister arm of the American Federation of Labor, began enrolling and facilitating the hiring of black workers. At the end of World War II and having succeeded President Roosevelt, President Harry Truman desegregated the armed forces because Blacks had served gloriously to defend this nation as they had in every war in which American has ever been engaged. Even more importantly, the racist behavior of America had begun to be affected by the "winds of change" sweeping the post-war world.

FREDERICK MONDERSON

Black Nationalism 38. Dr. James McCune Smith - Doctor and Author.

In 1954, Thurgood Marshall, long in the vineyards of challenging laws oppressive to Blacks, was able to successfully argue *Brown V. Board of Education of Topeka, Kansas* that, in fact, overturned *Plessey v. Ferguson*. This significant legal victory forever changed America although racism and discrimination changed its *modus operandi* but still essentially remained the same, if not becoming worse. Lest we forget, however, the movement for change was led by a number of individuals who took a stand against the "Bull

BLACK NATIONALISM
ALIVE AND WELL

Connors of the South," the Klan and the ensuing hatred and racial insanity they represented. This profound movement was led by leadership stalwarts as Reverend Shillingsworth, Martin Luther King, Rev. Abernathy, Harry Belafonte, Rosa Parks, Kwame Toure (Stokely Carmichael), Fannie Lou Hamer, Malcolm X, Reverend Lowery, Jesse Jackson, Andrew young, and Viola Liuzzo, Andrew Goodman, Michael Schwerner and so many more who stood up to preserve the American Dream. Today these courageous leaders and martyrs would be tremendously surprised, if not sickened, by Dr. Carson's stunning remarks since, in American politics, it has always been, "Where you stand is where you sit and where you sit is where you stand!" Congressman Charlie Rangel explained that the Anti-Obamacare Movement was predicated and driven by hatred for President Obama, a Black male and, therefore, one would have to wonder how Dr. Carson, also a Black male himself could align himself with persons filled with such conservative and racial venom!

Gerrymandering was essentially a Republican creation though Democrats have also practiced it. Yet, it encouraged and ably assisted voter suppression. Presidents Kennedy and Johnson's "Great Society" which supported the 1964 Civil Rights laws and the 1965 Voting Rights law required a provision which insisted that the voting law must be extended every 25-years in order for them to remain effective. In an interesting development, despite Dr. Ben Carson "sitting at the king's table, eating his meat," and having climbed to the pinnacle of his profession to make that outlandish proclamation; if the Voting Rights law expires, Dr. Carson and his children and grandchildren will not be able to vote! However, and even more important, it is evident that the group with whom Dr. Carson is comfortably aligned, the Republicans were accused of innumerable and unimaginable skullduggery on election day at the last two Presidential elections and all under cover of law. Despite their treasonous planning to subvert the government, no one was arrested. Yet, they lost once and will lose again because their record stands serenely blemished!

FREDERICK MONDERSON

Black Nationalism 39. The Brothers, Arthur and Lewis Tappan, Entrepreneurs and Reformers.

Let us not forget, Sarah Palin who, to make political points in her losing 2008 effort to run for president, accused President Obama of "palling around with terrorists." Today, in 2013 she is like a spent comet lost in the great void of the cosmos; even teaming with or "Palling around with Ted Nugent, profound dis-respecter of President Obama. Notwithstanding, the record forcefully shows that after the 2008 presidential election, a group of rich and powerful individuals got together and planned to subvert Mr. Obama's Presidency. This formed the fundamental strategy of the Republican Party going forward. It earned them the "Party of No" badge of shame! Some people have rightfully called this behavior treason because these persons plotted to subvert the legislatively constituted United States government under the leadership of President Barack Hussein Obama.

BLACK NATIONALISM ALIVE AND WELL

What happens in the dark ultimately comes to light and though only visionaries could see such early treasonous machinations; *The New York Times* of Sunday, October 6, 2013, front page and p. 18, article entitled "A Crisis Months in the Making" exposed the repeated strategy after the 2012 election and named names. It does not take intellectual genius to realize that the same 2008 actors were very much involved and are now exposed in this article. Ed Meese, a named principal conspirator, was United States Attorney General under President Ronald Reagan. In as much as his name surfaced in this article, it established continuity of nefarious, some say racist, treasonous, Republican activity for 2008, possibly decades down to today. Since many of these old and new conservative activists, articulated a "take no prisoners legislative strategy" and who planned and executed behaviors intended to subvert the will of the American people expressed by the second election of the President of the United States, they should, in fact, have been arrested for their treasonous behavior. The elders have often said, "Show me your company and I will tell who you are!" It is clear that Dr. Carson is quite at home with individuals implicated in treasonous words and deeds. Perhaps this deluded individual feels that his Republican pals will hold moderate tones in his presence as they berate other African Americans!

Dr. Carson ought to awake from his misguided slumber and recognize the world has become aware and **several millions of Africans worldwide** are outraged and feel strong revulsion for Dr. Carson, because of his disgusting distortion and omission of the historical record by his shameful, subjective assault upon a public policy set forth by President Obama which is intended to make the human rights of people lacking medical care more affordable and hence more accessible to millions of Americans who had been denied that right.

FREDERICK MONDERSON

Black Nationalism 40. Ministers Reverend Henry Ward Beecher and Henry Highland Garnett.

Black Nationalism 40a. Ms. Pusey, Education activist, "folk heroine" and resident of Brooklyn, New York.

This self-negation of Dr. Carson, a physician and a person of African descent is unfortunately not necessary. It was prevalent during

BLACK NATIONALISM
ALIVE AND WELL

slavery, for the slave owner would instill the illusion among the house slaves that they were more valued than the field hands. This practice induced and created a class within a caste resentment among the enslaved. Predictably, it encouraged betrayal of each other in order to find favor from the slave owners. Are people like Dr. Carson currently in 2013 likewise? Such person openly pander for the "thirty pieces of silver" available to them in the form of approbation by the powerful and callous of heart in the USA?

Black Nationalism 41. Sonny Carson admires the poster-bill for his Biography-movie, **The Education of Sonny Carson**.

FREDERICK MONDERSON

Black Nationalism 42. Marjorie Matthews, education, health care and social activist beside an associate.

4. SONNY CARSON: BORN VISIONARY
By
Dr. Fred Monderson

For the longest, Robert "Sonny" Carson has held the New York City Council in disdain. Perhaps rightly so, for he knew, in all probability, in view of the recent scandal of the Council, who so vehemently and disdainfully rejected the Community's street naming request, on his behalf, he may very well be looking down from that ancestral perch, shaking his head and exclaiming "I told you so!"

Perhaps if he was here these days, Sonny would have marched on and picketed the Council for its flagrant misappropriation of public funds. This is something no group has done so far. However, when it comes to money, Sonny did recognize the value. In fact, he recognized the potency of an economic boycott, and, while taking lots of heat for this, he led several boycotts of the targets' initiation of some inappropriate action towards people of color in Brooklyn.

BLACK NATIONALISM
ALIVE AND WELL

Now in view of the unending police misconduct across the country, police brutality, racial profiling, nooses being hung in public view, the Sean Bell verdict and marches to close down main arteries of the City of New York, and now the recent Congressional interests on holding hearings on police behavior, Sonny would say there is only one answer, the **ECONOMIC BOYCOTT**.

Remember when, according to Dick Gregory, businessmen threatened to kick in Richard Nixon's door and say "What's wrong with you boy?" Then, until Black folks come together, draw a line in the sand, and offer a moratorium for an economic boycott they will not be taken seriously. Let's for argument say, for a period of 90 days Blacks refuse to go in these stores, businesses, car dealers, etc., and object to purchase of all but essential necessities. In Brooklyn and across New York, as if at all possible, as a microscopic example, imagine downtown Fulton Street, Flatbush Avenue, Church Avenue, Atlantic Center, Kings Plaza, Queens Boulevard, Fordham Road in the Bronx, all these vital economic points, beginning to see no customers for weeks. Then imagine the idea spreading across the country, as hundreds of billions of Blacks dollars will be held back for a specified time, there will most certainly have to be "change."

Black Nationalism 43. Wearing the lion skin, Ptah stands with scepter and ankh with the Sphinx and Pyramid at his rear, the beetle, ankh and obelisk represented beside the emblem of Sankofa, "Return to Fetch it!"

FREDERICK MONDERSON

Short of taking the struggle to this next level, the oppressors will concede our right to protest and wait out the cooling off period. When Mayor Bloomberg was asked about the recent Sean Bell verdict protest, the TV clip showed all he said was: "This is America and people have a right to protest. In some countries people do not have this right." Of course, he moved from believing the shooting was "excessive" to the belief that judicial verdicts are inviolate. Now, while the masses did not accept the O.J. Simpson verdict; they did accept the Robert Black verdict; and the innumerable verdicts from Rodney King to Sean Bell. We must remember Zimmerman got away with murder of Trayvon Martin, so too Dunn in killing young Davis. Also of note is the young man K. Johnson of Valdosta, Georgia whose mysterious death is not coming under federal scrutiny since the state botched the investigation. One thing for certain, Sonny Carson did and would have kept his activism focused on all these issues.

Black Nationalism 43a. Mother showing the young the many roads that diverge from the straight and narrow!

Like most urban youth, Sonny first served time in the US Army in Korea and upon returning home ended up in prison for indiscretions of youth of his time. Incarcerated, there he seemed to find himself

BLACK NATIONALISM
ALIVE AND WELL

and upon release set about on a road of social and nationalist activism. First he advocated for jobs in places where Blacks shopped and then he moved to mom and pop ownership of small businesses and with time his name and popularity began to grow.

Black Nationalism 44. Dr. Leonard Jeffries makes a point at an event following the death of Sonny Carson.

Black Nationalism 45. Jitu Weusi speaks at an affair honoring Sonny Carson shortly after his passing.

FREDERICK MONDERSON

Black Nationalism 45a. Very young Erik Monderson poses with Jitu Weusi.

Sonny Carson, very early played a pivotal role in halting construction of the Federal Office Building in downtown Manhattan, when it was discovered, during the Dinkins Administration that this area had been an African Burial Ground. With the **Black Watch Movement** he spearheaded the effort for serious recognition of the historic nature of the site that laid the foundation which resulted in the Chi Wara Memorial in Foley Square before both Federal and State courthouses. This began the recognition of the site as having national historic significance and everything that developed regarding its landmark status flowed from his efforts. He was opposed, however, to treatment of the bones of the African Burial Ground, taken away for anthropological study, though some were returned and reinterred.

BLACK NATIONALISM
ALIVE AND WELL

There is nothing like success to breed success and over the years Sonny expanded his activism into education, fueled by a nationalist outlook, reflective of the maladies that gave birth to the Civil Right Movement. While Langston Hughes, the Harlem poet, could write of seeing "rivers," Sonny rightfully saw death. First Patrice Lumumba, the name of his own son, Malcolm X, and later Martin Luther King, Jr. There were many more in between. He often grieved at not being able to save Tupak Shakur and later Biggie Smalls. These two deaths particularly disturbed him. Black violence spawned by the crack epidemic, the emergence of gangster rap brought more death and according to Sonny, "I'm tired of attending funerals," particularly for young people.

Sonny was certainly known, and by that time a principal of the "School of hard knocks," his reputation attracted attention nationally. During the second Bill Clinton administration, the Commerce Secretary Ron Brown was killed in a plane crash, and while the nation mourned for this hero, Sonny Carson received an official and specific "Do not come to the funeral" dis-invitation from the government. Nevertheless, Sonny continued to attend funerals for the good, the bad and the indifferent.

Black Nationalism 46. Ma'at wearing her emblematic feather headdress with outstretched arms stands for truth, righteousness and justice.

FREDERICK MONDERSON

However, there was more to Sonny than funerals. After his "Success" in the Ocean-Hill-Brownsville school boycott that changed New York City Board of Education hiring practices, created de-centralization and opened the door for Black and Latino administrators, he had come of age. Naturally, many people viewed him negatively and have never forgiven him for opening the door to community control and minority administrators and teachers. More importantly, it sent a message to the powers that Blacks were tired, had matured through activism with a more universal consciousness about local, national and international affairs and would be involved thenceforth.

Black Nationalism 47. Map of the Nile, the Red Sea and flora of the landscape.

From social and civil activism, education activism and economic activism, Sonny "Abubadika" "AB" Carson, moved into organization building. He was a founding member of Malcolm-King

BLACK NATIONALISM
ALIVE AND WELL

College's evolution into Medgar Evers College of the City University of New York. Sonny Carson was a founding member of the Bedford-Stuyvesant **Restoration Corporation** on Fulton Street. Its goal was to revitalize the Bed-Stuy community in North Brooklyn through low-interest loans and economic developing skills through job training.

Sonny Carson founded "The Committee to Honor Black Heroes" and successfully renamed Malcolm X and Marcus Garvey Boulevards in Brooklyn and the Malcolm X and Toussaint L'Ouverture schools. He laid the groundwork for renaming Fulton Street for Harriet Tubman Avenue. At the height of the crack epidemic, he founded **The Black Men's Movement** and **Black Men Against Crack**. He was a founding member of the December 12 Movement.

While he consistently remained an education activist from his days as chairman of the **Education Committee of the Urban League**, Brooklyn Branch, his other involvements included the already mentioned attending funerals. He also took on unscrupulous landlords on behalf of tenants, leading boycotts of Korean stores because of their treatment of Blacks. He fought against the then Bureau of Child Welfare that caused much disruption of families. Many kids were taken from their homes. Sonny took on the Giuliani administration for its callous treatment of Blacks and in wake of the "Million Movement," he launched a "Million Voter Drive" in New York to unseat the Mayor, whose popularity was saved by the tragedy of September 11, 2001.

FREDERICK MONDERSON

Black Nationalism 48. At Akbar's funeral, Sonny Carson in yellow hat (center) is surrounded by several others including George Murden (left) and former Brooklyn Deputy-Borough President Ms. Jeanette Gadsen (facing).

Black Nationalism 49. Robert Matthews, former **Chairman of Community Board 8** in Brooklyn.

For most of his career, Sonny Carson was concerned, challenged and saddened by the music industry's spawning "Gangsta Rap," which portrayed Black women in a disgusting manner. At one point he

BLACK NATIONALISM
ALIVE AND WELL

challenged the music giant Sony in a face off entitled "Sonny Versus Sony." He also challenged the young lyricists to "tone it down," but encouraged them to continue to create constructive lyrics.

As a lifelong vocation and saddened by its debilitating behavior towards Blacks, Sonny challenged the Prison Industrial Complex. For decades he fought the psychological emasculation that prisons in America perennially debased and subjected Black manhood to on a daily basis. As such he received hundreds of calls from across the nation regarding prison conditions and police misconduct. Just as, near the end of his life, he recognized the viability of the vote, he equally fought for the rights of prisoners to be enfranchised after paying their debt to society. Today this is an issue Attorney General Eric Holder and Republican allies are pushing. Equally, Sonny wanted to establish libraries in prisons so that prisoners could undertake literacy enhancement efforts to aid their understanding of prison duties and responsibilities, as well as the workings of the wider world. Sadly, he hoped Mike Tyson, from his past position of visibility would have played a role in this effort as part of his "Give back." Alas, Mike Tyson was a "no show!"

The greatest accomplishment of Sonny Carson, considered his "final triumph," was the repatriation of the "Runaway Slave" to Ghana in West Africa to create a site of African American pilgrimage particularly those seeking and exploring "Roots" on the Continent.

The "Runaway," Samuel Carson, ran away from slavery, served in the US Navy and died during the Mexican War in 1845. He was buried in the Brooklyn Navy Yard. In the mid 1990s, the Navy discovered his ancestor's remains and handed it over to Sonny. Immediately he began advocating for Black Veterans, who were buried there, then a segregated Black Cemetery. He published in the New York *Afro Times* a number of names of Black veterans buried in the Navy Yard hoping their families would trace their names and seek to connect with their ancestors' services. The government owes

FREDERICK MONDERSON

these people accumulated money for their ancestors. That is provided they can prove the relationship.

For "**The Runaway**" Sonny created the **Bones Committee** that met for nearly two years and decided to bury him in Ghana. While the millions of slaves who came to the Americas came through the **Door of No Return**, Sonny created a **Door of Return**, using his ancestor, Samuel Carson. While this happening got good publicity around the globe, it was practically blacked out in the United States. However, amidst all the preparatory events before **the Runaway's** departure, there was a ceremony held in Prospect Park's Drummers' Grove. These events were photographed and published in the *Daily Challenge*, July 31-August 2, 1998, as a centerfold piece. Later it was registered as historical art with the Library of Congress, by the photographer and writer Fred Monderson.

Upon his return to the United States Sonny continued his lifelong work of activism in the many diverse areas that challenged Black and Latino people. Brooklyn was paid one of the most revered "Going Home" ceremonies involving churches, a march from Brooklyn Bridge through the Black Community, and forums to honor the home grown "bad boy," Sonny Carson, who evolved into a local folk hero; having made lasting impressions on his community as he tried to help better its lot. For his unending efforts in aid of community betterment and empowerment, we remember Robert "Sonny" "AB" Carson, born May 18, the day before Malcolm X.

BLACK NATIONALISM
ALIVE AND WELL

Black Nationalism 50. Black American Leaders on wall behind the happy lady, as seen from her smiling face.

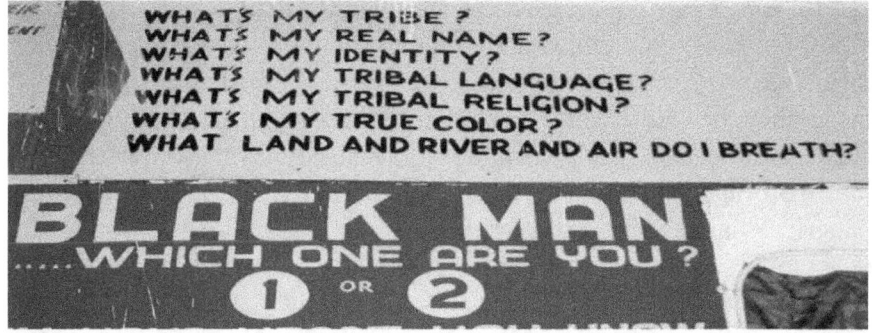

Black Nationalism 51. **Black Lady II**. Judge Phillips asks, "Black Man, which one are you?"

Black Nationalism 51a. Gil Noble at the podium to introduce **CEMOTAP**'s Guest Speaker – Dick Gregory in 2005.

FREDERICK MONDERSON

5. Reflections on Race in America in 2006
By
Dr. Fred Monderson

At the conclusion of the 2008 National Elections and in view of the Republicans' trouncing or 'thumpin' and particularly regarding 'Blacks and Politics' it is appropriate that some reflection be cast on the issue of Race in America with its ramifications on voting, leadership and office holding, responsibility and accountability as it also contrasts with other voters, leaders and office-holders as we begin the long and arduous journey into the 21st Century. As such, a careful eye must be focused on the condition of Blacks and their allies, the poor, challenged and voiceless. Some have argued how in this "Age of Foreign Terrorism," the term "Terrorism" can equally be applied to 'Nineteenth Century African-American History.' As such, the question that can be posed must be: "Is there evidence in the historical record of a biological determinant for race in America?" and "What have been the ramifications of this pattern of behavior?"

Black Nationalism 51b. African people saying hello as is customary in their friendly frame of mind.

BLACK NATIONALISM
ALIVE AND WELL

Black Nationalism 52. Dr. Adelaide Sanford makes a point at affair honoring Sonny Carson after "he passed" to join the ancestors.

Black Nationalism 53. Dr. James C. McIntosh shows off the newest issue of the **Freedom Fighters Journal**.

In answering, we can easily look to Gunnar Myrdal (1900: 90) who mentions how President Thomas Jefferson, at the start of the 19th Century, enumerated the differences between Black and White in his

FREDERICK MONDERSON

time, a belief long and consistently held in this country since. He lists: "'color, hair form, secretion, less physiological need of sleep but sleepiness in work, lack of reasoning power, lack of depth in emotion, poverty of imagination and so on.' In all these respects he is inclined to believe that 'it is not their condition, then, but nature, which has produced the distinction.'" This view was further underscored by John Calhoun in his "Disquisition on Government" speech in the 1840s where he defended the institution of slavery as practiced in the south that essentially terrorized Blacks as if saying they were unfit for liberty. McKitrick (9-11) states, according to Calhoun that liberty "is a reward to be earned, not a blessing to be gratuitously lavished on all alike; a reward reserved for the intelligent, the patriotic, the virtuous and deserving; not a boon to be bestowed on a people too ignorant, degraded and vicious, to be capable either of appreciating or of enjoying it." Even further: "Now, as individuals differ greatly from each other, in intelligence, sagacity, energy, perseverance, skill, habits of industry and economy, physical power, position and opportunity, the necessary effect of leaving all free to exert themselves to better their condition, must be a corresponding inequality between those who may possess these qualities and advantages in a high degree, and those who are deficient in them." This was the racial mindset that permeated 19th Century America. And, according to the old adage, "ideas die hard" particularly pernicious ones that are part of an agenda.

Black Nationalism 54. The artist Sapp in hat to the right and working his paint palette has produced this masterpiece on Sly's Trophy Shop wall that is no longer on display but preserved in this writer's effort.

BLACK NATIONALISM
ALIVE AND WELL

Black Nationalism 55. One of the many mythical scenes of early Africa painted by the artist Sapp.

Simply put, if there is no claimed biological determinant, then there would not have been a need for the 1964 Civil Rights Act! Decades after Jefferson and Calhoun, at the start of the 20th Century, W.E.B. Dubois stated pointedly, "The problem of the Twentieth Century is the problem of the color line (Race)." Importantly yet inappropriately however, many people view the issue of race and racial discrimination and its debilitating effects as one of prejudice but this is altogether wrong. Racial discrimination rightfully is determined by the allocation of rights, responsibilities, privileges, immunities as well as reward and punishment. When these entitlements are not allocated and on the basis of equality, disrespect and inequity step in and this becomes the basis for "second class citizenship" and the seed germ of racism.

The concerned question is particularly cognizant since in his 2005 Inaugural Address Pres. George Bush (43) raised the issue by saying 'We must work to end racism in America.' Nearly three years later we could similarly argue, despite seeming Black gains, particularly in politics, not much has changed in race relations in America. Poverty, prison incarceration, joblessness, suspicion and prejudice are still factors for Blacks in American life. Importantly, we cannot afford to forget Henry Kissinger had said "Let us put the Blacks on

FREDERICK MONDERSON

the back burner." However and significantly, we need remember in the 1950s, 1960s and 1970s untold numbers of White scholars, viz., Kenneth M. Stampp, *The Peculiar Institution* especially Chapter 4, 'To Make Them Stand in Fear' (1956); *The Era of Reconstruction* (1965); Erik L. McKitrick, *Slavery Defended: The Views of the Old South* (1963); John L. Thomas, *Slavery Attacked* (1965); David B. Davis *The Problem of Slavery in Western Culture* (1966); Eugene D. Genovese *The Political Economy of Slavery: Studies in the Economy and Society of the South* (1965), *The World the Slaveholders Made* (1969); Alan Grimshaw (ed) *Racial Violence in the United States* (1969); C. Vann Woodward *The Strange Career of Jim Crow* (1957); Albert P. Blaustein and Robert L. Zangrando (eds) *Civil Rights and the Black American* (1968); Gunnar Myrdal, *An American Dilemma: The Negro Problem and Modern Democracy* (1944)(1962); Thomas F. Gossett *Race: The History of An Idea* (1963); Robert William Fogel and Stanley L. Engelmann *Time on the Cross* (1974); Richard C. Wade *Slavery in the Cities, the South, 1820-1860* (1964); and Winthrop Jordan, Lothrop B. Stoddard, etc., were all awarded PhDs for researching, studying and writing about African and African-American history and the issue of race in America. Today this odious and pernicious practice is still a viable question of historical inquiry and should remain on the "front burner" because it bears upon relationships between Blacks and Whites in this country. All should be reminded, the great American President Abraham Lincoln once said, "Silence in face of wrongdoing is to be culpable for that wrong."

BLACK NATIONALISM
ALIVE AND WELL

Black Nationalism 56. Ossie Davis, actor, activist and beloved husband is flanked by two righteous brothers.

Black Nationalism 57. Hawking the **Amsterdam News** is Brother Abdul Haqq, while the Journalist Playtel Benjamin, "The Sword of Obama," purchases a copy.

FREDERICK MONDERSON

> IN ANCIENT TIMES, MANS IN-
> HUMANITY TO MAN, CAUSED DIFFERENT
> GROUPS AND TRIBES TO BAN TOGETHER
> IN THEIR DEFENSE. THEY WERE WITHOUT
> PHYSICAL WEAPONS. CONSEQUENTLY
> THEY DEVELOPED THEIR GIVEN ANATOMY
> INTO A FIGHTING TOOL, WITH SYMBOLS
> OF DIFFERENT ANIMALS AND FOWLS.
> EVERY RACE ON EARTH DEVELOPED SUCH
> TOOLS. CHINA, WITH SYSTEMS OF KUNG FU,
> 157 STYLES EMERGING THEREFROM;
> JAPAN WITH SYSTEM OF KARATE, NENJU

Black Nationalism 58. An Expression explaining how fighting systems came about by various peoples.

All this is significant because we Blacks in America have not only worked to build this great nation with free labor as kidnapped and enslaved Africans; we have fought in every American war from the French and Indian Wars in 1756-63; the Revolutionary War 1776-1783; the War of 1812 from 1812-1815; the Mexican War 1845; the Civil War from 1860-1865; the Spanish-American War from 1898-1901; World War I during 1917-1918 (1914-1918); World War II from 1941-1945 (1939-1945); the War against Communism 1947-1996; the Korean War from 1950-1952: Vietnam War from 1964-1975; to Grenada, Kosovo and First and Second Gulf Wars, Iraq, Afghanistan. When given the chance to fight we have voted to make democracy a living and practicable experience for many across the globe! We have fought for an education to become better citizens who can contribute something worthwhile to society. Importantly we have even become activists to help America live out the true meaning of its creed as Dr. Martin Luther King enunciated it: "We hold these truths to be self evident that all men are created equal and are endowed by their creator with the god given right to life, liberty and the pursuit of happiness."

BLACK NATIONALISM ALIVE AND WELL

However, and regarding the recent elections, party house-cleaning is not altogether new, for this nation has a tradition of 'throwing the bums out' every 8 to 12 years. If we look at a brief history of the pattern of party elections this is quite apparent.

1860   Lincoln (Rep)
1864   "
1868   Grant   (Rep)
1872   "
1876   Hayes   (Rep) Disputed
1880   Garfield (Rep) close
1884   Cleveland (Dem)
1888   Harrison (Rep) close and the Democrats could have won
1892   Cleveland (Dem)

1896 to 1932 is considered the Age of Republican Supremacy.

1896   Grover Cleveland resigns. He refuses to support William Jennings Bryant.
1896   McKinley won (Rep)
1900   McKinley won. He was assassinated. Teddy Roosevelt succeeded to the Presidency.
1904   Roosevelt   (Rep) elected
1908   Taft wins over McKinley (Rep)
1912   Teddy Roosevelt (Rep) wins to kick Taft out
1912   Wilson (Dem) wins because Republicans split between Roosevelt and Taft.
1916   Wilson re-elected owing to World War I.
1920   Harding (Rep) won on restoring the country to normalcy after the war. He was succeeded by Coolidge.
1924   Coolidge (Rep)
1928   Hoover (Rep) defeats Al smith.

1932 to 1968 is considered the Age of Democratic Supremacy and this is particularly aided by a wholesale change of party by Blacks who had started voting Democratic in defection from the party of Lincoln.

1932   F. D. Roosevelt (Dem)

FREDERICK MONDERSON

1936   F. D. Roosevelt (Dem)
1940   F. D. Roosevelt (Dem)
1944   F. D. Roosevelt (Dem). Roosevelt died in 1945 after being elected four times and was succeeded to the Presidency by Harry Truman.
1948   Truman   (Dem) wins re-election
1952   Eisenhower (Rep) Beats Adlai Stevenson.
1956   Eisenhower   (Rep) Re-elected
1960   John F. Kennedy (Dem) beats Richard Nixon. He was assassinated and succeeded by Lyndon Johnson.
1964.   Johnson   (Dem) defeats Goldwater
1968   Nixon (Rep) defeats Hubert Humphrey. Wallace was a third party.
1972   Nixon (Rep) re-elected. He resigned owing to his involvement in the Watergate break-in scandal, and was replaced by Gerald Ford.

There have been three significant moments of change in political parties in government. These occurred at approximately 36 year intervals.

1972   Nixon   (Rep) defeats McGovern
1976   Carter   (Dem) defeats Gerald Ford
1980   Ronald Reagan (Rep) defeats Jimmy Carter
1984   Reagan   re-elected (Rep)
1988   George Bush (Rep) elected against Michael Dukakis
1992   Bill Clinton   (Dem) defeats George Bush
1996   Clinton (Dem) re-elected
2000   George Bush   (Rep) defeats Al Gore
2004   George Bush (Rep) re-elected by defeating John Kerry
2008   Barack Obama defeats John McCain

BLACK NATIONALISM
ALIVE AND WELL

> SHOTOKAN, JUDO, JIU JITSU, AIKIDO, KOREANS WITH TAE KWAN DO, HAPKIDO, EUROPE: WRESTLING, BOXING AND OTHERS. SLAVE DESCENDANTS OF THE UNITED STATES HAVE SEARCHED FOR A SYSTEM OF PHYSICAL POWER, WITH A TWO LEGGED ANATOMY AS HUMAN, THE MIND OF FATE DEALT THE FIERCE LOOKING GORILLA OF BODY STRENGTH AND THE GNAT, OF NO PHYSICAL EFFORT, BUT TO SURVIVE ON MENTALITY ALONE. TOGETHER AFRICAN SLAVE DESCENDANTS, HAVE DEVELOPED THE GO-RILLA GNAT SYSTEM OF DIVERSE MOVEMENTS IN SCIENTIFIC DEFENSIVE FIGHTING.
> THE CONSUMMATE POWER OF BLACK MANS SELF DEFENSE AND SELF DEFENSE. THIS SYSTEM ALLOWS AN OPPONENT ONE MISTAKEN MOVEMENT (WHAT HE SAYS, WHAT HE DOES). THEN IT IMMOBILIZE HIS FIGHTING INSTRUMENTS BY BREAKING HIS ARMS AND LEGS AND CLAWING HIS EYES OUT. THEN SYSTEMATICALLY DESTROYING HIS ANATOMY A SYSTEM WITH CIRCULAR MOVEMENTS OF DEATH WITH FATALITY-1 THROUGH 24
> "MASTER TECHNIQUES TO KILL"

Black Nationalism 59. Another explanation of how fighting systems came about.

Black Nationalism 60. Image of President Barack Obama serving his first term.

Clearly, the nation clears house every 8 to 12 years. Once in every 30 to 36 years there is a long-term division and shift in party alignment. Despite party change in Congress after the 2006 Mid-term national election, voters must remain vigilant. Such a view is consistent with a recent issue of *Caribbean Life* newspaper, where the legendary civil rights activist and entertainer Harry Belafonte made a startling revelation that there are great similarities between politics, policies and practices of the Democrats and Republicans in terms of not helping the poor, people near and below the poverty

FREDERICK MONDERSON

line, within which a great many Black people fall. We must insist the Democrats address pressing issues of these people.

The seriousness of the issue of second-class citizenship based on race in America is highlighted when, recently at the "Martin Luther King Jr. Memorial Ground Breaking" in Washington, D.C., as Andrew Young spoke, both he and Jesse Jackson broke into tears. They were not crying for Dr. King but for the condition of our people in America, many of whom were miles away from realizing "the Dream." While Dr. King had seen the "Promised Land," his "Dream" was beginning to take on solid form with this Memorial but there were still many obstacles to that reality. This is what drove these two great Black Americans to tears at this momentous moment

I remember someone last year criticizing the commercializing of his birthday as stores hawked the Martin Luther King Day "Sale!" Dr. King was not about "Sales," he was about racial injustice, equality, segregation, jobs, housing, health care, and plight of the poor, dispossessed, and disfranchised. Since his time, the prison industrial complex has come to play a significant role in the life of Blacks. Jesse Jackson got a lot of mileage when he pointed out that the state of South Carolina had 36 state prisons and 1 state college! Naturally, the history of racial discrimination and psychological emasculation has spawned a form of racial hatred so much so that Black men are now killing Black men in unprecedented numbers. Perhaps Willie Lynch has won, somewhat! Though Dr. Leonard James simply sees these "victims" as "wounded!"

> HELLO! - It's nice to see you. Welcome to our home. "Slave One" PLEASE, IN YOUR SPEECHES OR CONVERSATIONS HERE, NEVER INDULGE IN ANY RACE HATING REMARKS AGAINST: Other Groups, Colors, Religions or Races. Remember, the real God made mankind: White, Black, Brown and other colors. If you hate a person because of his color or race, you must hate God!...."THEN, WHO THE HELL ARE YOU!" Our theater, "Slave One", represents UNDERSTANDING of RESPECT and LOVE, for ALL of GOD'S HUMANITY! Please feel at home here in our theater. We know who you are. We love you. All the best to you. COME AGAIN PLEASE. God Bless You.

Black Nationalism 61. Slave Theater I is a veritable storehouse of remarkable wisdom.

BLACK NATIONALISM ALIVE AND WELL

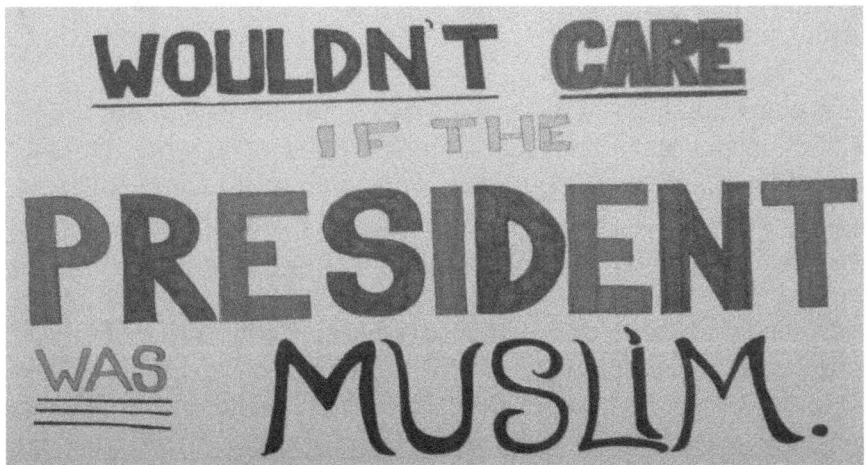

Black Nationalism 62. Sign carried in the 2010 "Rally on the Mall."

Listening to "Barber Shop Talk" in the Deli recently, one discussant said to the other, "Well, America is ready for a Black President, as Rev. Al Sharpton could have won in 2004 if he had more support." The other responded, "America is not ready for a Black President, man we cannot even get in the Fire Department, much more the White House. Yesterday, November 13, 2006, the (NY) *Daily News* showed the NY Fire Department is 91% white, with more than 200 firemen, only 12 are Black." Less than a decade ago, *Newsday* ran a five-part series entitled "It's a White Man's World" and showed the untold numbers of businesses and institutions run by White men. In many respects, little has changed!

Regarding Rev. Al Sharpton's run for the Presidency in 2004, he was a "winner" having completed the race, been a part of the debates, fund raised, enjoyed Secret Service protection, energized Blacks and raised their political consciousness, established chapters of his organization National Action Network nationwide, and encouraged Blacks to run for offices in their locality, all while understanding and being part of the American political and presidential process.

FREDERICK MONDERSON

Despite the fact he was championing grassroots issues that affected broad masses of the population, he lost; perhaps, because of his color, and maybe his activism, since many other candidates ended up advocating his issues.

How many times have you seen the movie "In the Heat of the Night" with Sidney Poitier and Rod Steiger? Remember when the rich southerner Endicott slapped Virgil Tibbs in front of Chief Gillespie, and the Black Butler in Sparta, Mississippi. If I recall, in an original showing, the Butler was shown telling other Blacks that Virgil slapped Mr. Endicott, but this part was cut and not shown in recent showings. However, and particularly in this "2006 Era of Political Correctness," Gillespie was called "Nigger Lover" and told to "Get rid of the Nigger" and when Purdy brought his sister to the Chief to complain of her being pregnant by one of the Chief's men, the brother Purdy would tell the Chief, "Not to Keep a Nigger in the Room." All this says, they would not show a Black man, no matter how respectable slapping a White man on TV, but they would show "White trash" calling a Black man "Nigger" no matter how respectable or professional he was. They do this to President Obama in 2013, even though he has been elected twice by the American people. In 2014 Ted Nugent, a "has been hack" and psychopath vented his racial venom by attacking the humanity and integrity of President Barack Obama. Consider that they would "Bleep" certain curse words on TV but would air the "N" word. A good example is the movie **RFK** where someone referred to a statement of Bobby Kennedy by responding "son of a B." While TV would bleep the "B Word," it won't bleep the "N Word."

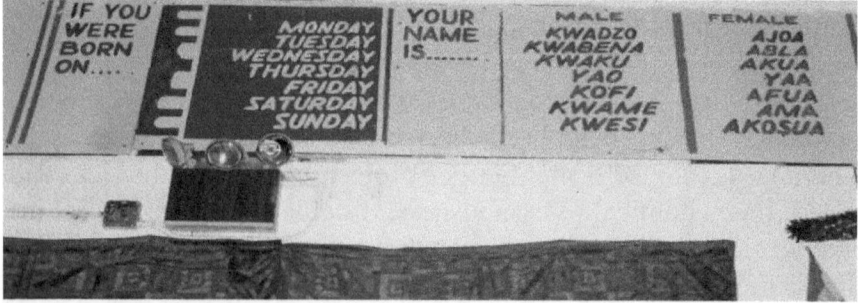

Black Nationalism 63. The names are yours for the taking.

BLACK NATIONALISM
ALIVE AND WELL

Black Nationalism 64. It took "Marbles" for this guy to wear this shirt at the 2010 "Rally on the Mall."

The early morning Steve Harvey radio show on Monday of Thanksgiving 2006, discussed the issue of a White comedian, Michael Richards, who played Kramer on TV, went on a racial diatribe at the "Laugh Factory." His jokes were "flat" and were heckled by a Black member of the audience and he responded, "Nigger shut up!" "Nigger," "You're a Nigger" *ad nausea*. Perhaps if it was a White member of the audience he would simply have said, "Shut up, Sir." Being on stage in the public eye, entertainers should expect to be heckled if their material is "off base." What is troubling is the use of the "N" word in such a demeaning and psychologically emasculating manner, that is complimentary to denial of rights, responsibilities, privileges, immunities, rewards and encourages punishments. A commentator said he was simply "caught." Well, what of the others who are not "caught?"

FREDERICK MONDERSON

Black Nationalism 64a. While Dr. James McIntosh, Co-Chair of **CEMOTAP** and **BEPAA** speaks about Malcolm X at Clarke House; Black Panther and Nationalist Shepherd listens attentively.

Such behavior is commensurate with the mindset directed towards O. J. Simpson. As stupid as Simpson has been in airing his narcissistic and warped mentality as well as love for the limelight, the jury ruled that OJ was not guilty! Yet many people refuse to accept this. When the jury ruled in favor of others similarly charged, case in point, the Robert Blake "Beretta" character, everyone accepted the jury verdict, because they had ruled on the guilt or innocence of a white defendant. Yet they challenged the jury decision because it concerned a Black defendant. This in no way exculpates OJ Simpson for his disgusting mentality and behavior. Equally, everyone accepted the Zimmerman verdict. Well … today his wife has confessed how much of a brute he truly is!

BLACK NATIONALISM
ALIVE AND WELL

> KWAME NKRUMAH AND PATRICE LUMUMBA
>
> THESE MEN ARE WELL RESPECTED IN THE BLACK MAN'S WORLD. A DREAM OF A GREAT CONTINENTAL FAMILY WITHIN A UNION OF AFRICAN STATES. HERE NO BORDERS ARE RECOGNIZED. ONE PEOPLE - ONE BLACK WORLD - ONE REAL GOD. THIS DREAM WAS DEFICIENT AND SHALLOW, IT NEVER CALLED FOR THE RETURN TO AFRICA OF THE CHILDREN OF SLAVES - ALL 250 MILLION. LIKEN TO A SHIP WITH ALL SAILS AND NO ANCHORS.
>
> →

Black Nationalism 65. The Judge oftentimes told the truth.

In a somewhat related story regarding race in America, *Caribbean Life* November 14, 2006, p. 3, entitled "Politics and Economics not favoring Blacks says Malveaux and McKinney" which holds, "Look at what is happening in the labor market right now" Malveaux said. "On the one hand you have a headline which says the unemployment rate (nationally) has dropped to 4.4 percent – for whites – but 8.6

FREDERICK MONDERSON

percent for us (Blacks)." This is twice as much and in some urban areas the claimed percentage of unemployed Black youth especially is between 40 and 50 percent.

Now let's look at some recent developments of issues colored by race which begs the question of whether there is a double standard relating to Black and White relations in this United States of America.

We remember Assemblymen Roger Green and Clarence Norman, because of their legislative prominence were persecuted, prosecuted and convicted for something like $5000.00 or less. When we contrast that with Comptroller Alan Hevesi, who according to his TV political campaign Ad said, "I am a good Comptroller who did a stupid thing" and clearly broke the law by using "a state-paid staffer who chauffeured his ailing wife for three years." He repaid New York State $172,688.00, and one has to wonder where are the "Gung Ho" prosecutors and when will Mr. Hevesi be tried? What will be his penalty? Will he go to jail? Perhaps there is a double standard based on race! Let us not forget the untold numbers given lengthy sentences under DA Joe Hines tenure using questionable and tainted evidence.

Harold Ford Jr., the Tennessee Congressman who ran for Senate in his home state, was by some accounts, a "Clean Negro." Remember this term J. Edgar Hoover used when he wanted to replace Dr. King as a reputable Black leader. Mr. Ford was well liked, he supported all the "Good" issues, viz., Gun Control, Anti-Abortion, he took a position on Stem Cell Research, etc. His campaign literature tells of his position on Reforming the Educational System; Affordable Health Care; Technological Innovation; Energy Self-sufficiency; Balancing the Budget; Making America Competitive Again; Protecting Workers' Pensions; and Anti Pork-Barrel Legislation, etc. Yet, when it came for the south to elect a Black Senator, the Republicans rolled out a "White Woman" from a Playboy Club who in the end said, "Harold, Call me!" This "strategy" is reminiscent of the "Willie Horton ambush" of the Democratic Presidential Candidate Dukakis when he was defeated by the Republicans and

BLACK NATIONALISM
ALIVE AND WELL

President George Bush, the elder in 1988 elections. Willie Horton, a Black convict was either pardoned or released by Dukakis as Governor of Massachusetts. Subsequently, he committed a crime and the Republicans used this "Black syndrome" to defeat the Democrats. Let us not forget the Smith woman who drowned her two children and said "A Black man did it!"

Black Nationalism 66. Dr. Fred Monderson on board a Felucca on the Nile River.

The *Daily News* of Saturday November 4, 2006, p. 4 reported: "An Evangelist who advises President Bush and is an outspoken opponent of gay marriage dropped a bombshell yesterday when he admitted buying methamphetamines from a gay escort he was visiting, supposedly for a massage." He said: "I called him to buy some meth but I threw it away," "I was buying it for me, but I never

FREDERICK MONDERSON

used it. I was tempted. I bought it, but I never used it." No one would ever believe a Black man if he said something like "I bought drugs and threw it away." More important, however, this moralist was probably delving in the nut butter! Moreover, in his confession, he mentions his "dark side" and this is consistent with Webster's Dictionary that lists some 40 entries on Black and all are negative, except the one that describes being in business and making a profit which means being in the "Black." Equally too, American Express did have a Black gold credit card at $10,000.00 minimum. But these are only two examples of "Good Black!"

Several people echoed the view that it was "racism that robbed Attorney Alton Maddox of practicing law in New York State." More than ten years later, he is still disbarred.

The new "icon" Flavor Flave has been accused of debasing black women on TV. Many have commented that this is a come down from his earlier revolutionary stance as a "Public Enemy." While his buffoonery is acceptable, intellectual and professional Blacks are not given their proper respect in terms of equal treatment. This does not mean all White persons practice racism but a great many do!

"Mr. T," the "Super masculine menial" and buffoon has returned to the TV screen, and despite and after the fact when "Lot wife turn a pillar of salt," Senator Trent Lott is being called the "Comeback Kid" in Washington D.C. as he tries to become a leader in the Senate again, despite his praise of Senator Strom Thurman, the Southern segregationist who vilified Blacks while having and keeping a Black daughter under wraps. One thing is certain, neither Al Sharpton nor Jesse Jackson are considered "Good Negroes" and have taken their "hits" but like that famous "Bunny" they keep on "ticking." This is because they keep the interests of the people on the "front burner" and speak for those without a voice.

BLACK NATIONALISM
ALIVE AND WELL

Black Nationalism 67. Activist icon Jitu Weusi on the Protest Circuit fighting for the best in Education.

Black Nationalism 68. The power of reading is the message of this mural.

FREDERICK MONDERSON

Black Nationalism 68a. Delegates to the All-Caribbean People's conference in Barbados, August 1, 2010

As we move forward, think, sympathize and suffer for the betterment of this great nation, we must work, pray, and advocate for the betterment of an America where 'our children will be judged by the content of their character not the color of their skin.' Even more, we must all work for the betterment of humanity under the philosophical construct of the fatherhood of God and the brotherhood of man! Until then we must fight in the schools, boardrooms, work places, hospitals, voting booths, and legislative arenas for until 'equality and justice rolls down like a mighty stream,' the Struggle Continues!

Black Nationalism 69. Again, the "Old Master" is at it again.

BLACK NATIONALISM ALIVE AND WELL

Black Nationalism 70. New York City Councilman Jumane Williams at the Martin Luther King celebration at "Sharpton!"

6. HARRIET TUBMAN: LIVE FREE OR DIE!
By
Dr. Fred Monderson

Boys and Girls High School on Fulton Street in Bedford Stuyvesant hosted a Celebration and Commemoration of "Harriet Tubman Day" sponsored by Councilman Al Vann with Dr. Sheila Evans-Tranumn, Associate Commissioner for the New York State Education Department and a number of high profile political figures invited or in attendance. What was significant was the packed house with school kids who came from all over, from PS 44, PS 81, PS 243, PS

FREDERICK MONDERSON

262, PS 304, PS 305, PS 308, PS 335, MS 336, MS 354, MS 394 and many other schools. The Boys and Girls Jazz Band Ensemble produced one of the most exciting young sounds in Brooklyn, and Taneqa Stephens did a wonderful rendition of **Lift Every Voice and Sing** (The Black National Anthem), while the Vanguard Youth Council Dancers did an excellent performance of **Mary Don't You Weep** and the **Voices from the High** were smashing.

Councilman Al Vann came on stage to explain this year's celebration is on the 9th not the traditional 10th of March and with that he said to the audience: "When I say Celebration, you will say Harriet Tubman. We abolish the 'N-word' and replace it with Harriet Tubman." With that said, he set in motion a rockin' and rollin' that characterized the place for the rest of the performance. Everyone who said the word Celebration got a thunderous Harriet Tubman!

Mr. Vann gave a graphic description of the Underground Railroad and added "Very few abolitionists had the courage of Harriet Tubman." He extolled her determination, persistence, and courageous insightfulness to free her people.

Reverend Jeff Thompson of Concord Baptist Church did the Invocation praising the courage and conviction of Harriet Tubman and thanking god for giving us the spirit and conviction of Harriet Tubman. Then he decried the political, social and economic injustice faced by our people and asked God Almighty to let 'Justice roll down like water, and righteousness like a mighty stream,' so there would be hope for tomorrow.

The new Principal at Boys and Girls High School, Mr. Spencer Holder praised Harriet Tubman's vivacious and spirited courage to bring people from a state of mental and spiritual bondage to one of freedom. The thunderous "call and response" of "Celebration with Harriet Tubman," by the overwhelmingly young audience, over and over again, caused the beautiful lady, Harriet Tubman, to appear,

BLACK NATIONALISM
ALIVE AND WELL

brought back from the ancestral realm. She stood there with her Union Coat and Hat, pistol and musket and the show was on!

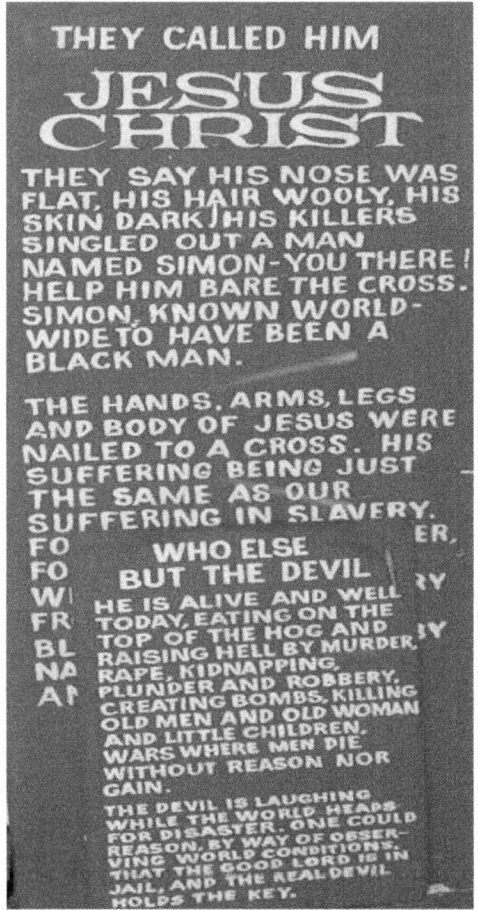

Black Nationalism 71. Here the message takes a religious bent.

Miss Tubman then went into a moving and graphic depiction of the events of her life. She said she had to "work the fields but could not eat the crops." At five years old she had 1 job, at 7 she had 2 jobs. She was a babysitter. "If the baby cry, I get beat" she recounted. By age 10 she was hired out to Mr. Cook. By age 12 she had 4 jobs. She

FREDERICK MONDERSON

never had a pair of shoes until she was grown. She asked do you know what an overseer is then responded that overseers are supervisors! She had a near death experience at age 13 where she was knocked out cold by the brick of a supervisor and in that stupor, she "Heard the lord talking directly to me." In her vision she could see her sisters crying on chain gangs. Mamas crying, "Please don't sell my babies." The Lord told her, "You don't have to be scared for I will be with you always."

She recognized that "God has no favorites; he rains on all, Black and White." She began praying. When I sweep, I pray. When I plow the ground I pray, asking the lord to change the overseer. When the lord did not change the overseer I shot him dead."

Her owner was Doc Thompson. She was able to be hired out and earned and saved $300.00. Doc Thompson said that is not enough. By that time she had married John Thompson who was free. Then she ran away with him, because people thought after her accident she was as dumb as Kojo. "Kojo was so dumb, when you told a joke he would laugh one month later!"

She ran away from Bucktown, Maryland and entered barns, attics, way stations all the way along the Underground Railroad. It was no railway but places where people were kind enough to extend assistance to people fleeing slavery. From Bucktown on the Chesapeake she crossed over into Pennsylvania and "I was free!"

The abolitionist Mr. William Still ran the Underground Railroad and when she volunteered was told, this is man's job. She responded, "Mr. Still, God don't care who done his work as long as it gets done" and with that she became one of his best drivers. With that she brought family, friends and neighbors out of bondage. When challenged by frightened slaves who questioned her knowledge about where they were going she would take out here pistol and tell them, "Dead folks don't talk. Go on or die. I prefer to see you dead than a slave. With that I never lost a passenger. I never ran my train off the track."

BLACK NATIONALISM
ALIVE AND WELL

Black Nationalism 72. Little Black Angels sure are cute.

"They called me the Black Moses. Moses used a stick to part the seas. I used courage and the Underground Railroad to free my people." I built my home in Albany, New York. Mr. Lincoln passed the Emancipation Proclamation freeing us.

"I married my second husband, Mr. Nelson Davis. He was 32 while I was 68. He was a sick man from the Civil War and I nursed him till his death."

"Mr. Vann invited me here. God does give me something to do. God chose Africans above humanity. We gave the world gospel, blues and other music. We still able to love even though we had such hardships. You think because we dead we don't see. We are concerned with reading scores. I was beaten in my time when I tried to read. Go to the library and get a book. African children don't let the N-word ruin you. It's not what they call you; it's what you answer to. Forget names. Adults teach the kids about their history. Love, respect each other." She asked the audience to "Please give a round of applause for Mr. Al Vann." Then she asked them to sing a verse of the song: "My eyes have seen the glory of the coming of the lord."

FREDERICK MONDERSON

Black Nationalism 72a. "Mother Africa" doing her thing painting a wonderful environment.

Members of the Clergy in attendance included Bishop Figeroua, Rev. Craig Gaddy, and Rev Parker of Wayside Baptist Church, Rev. Thompson and Rev. Waterman. Community leaders included Dean R. Jones and Dr. John Flateau and William H. Boone from Medgar Evers College, Dr. Gerald Dees, Carl Roberts, Ruth (Something) President of the 81st Council, B. Jones of Community Board 3 Land Use Committee and his wife, as well as Mrs. Al Vann. Also in the audience were the legendary Jitu Weusi and his brother Job Mashiriki, President of Black Veterans for Social Justice, both community activists. The descendants of Harriet Tubman proudly took their place on stage and savored in the many accolades and tributes paid their courageous ancestor on this her special day.

Assemblywoman Annette Robinson began by saying "We are the survivors of the legacy of Harriet Tubman. To my colleagues in government and to the family of Harriet Tubman, this is a day set in history. It epitomizes the spirits of our ancestors who resides in the shark infested waters. We praise Harriet Tubman for saying 'Live Free or Die.' We must look and see who we can bring along in the

BLACK NATIONALISM
ALIVE AND WELL

journey. Health Care, human rights, living wage, a good education are issues we must fight for. We must continue to struggle. No struggle, no progress." Continued Assemblywoman Robinson, Nina Simone sang "I wish I knew how to be free and not have these hands holding me." Margaret Walker said "Let a new earth rise, let another world begin, let a second generation full of courage issue forth and let a people loving freedom come to growth."

Borough President Marty Markowitz gave a wonderful praise to Harriet Tubman and a passionate and heart-felt charge to the young people. First he praised the accomplishments of the numerous Blacks who benefited from the legacy of Harriet Tubman.

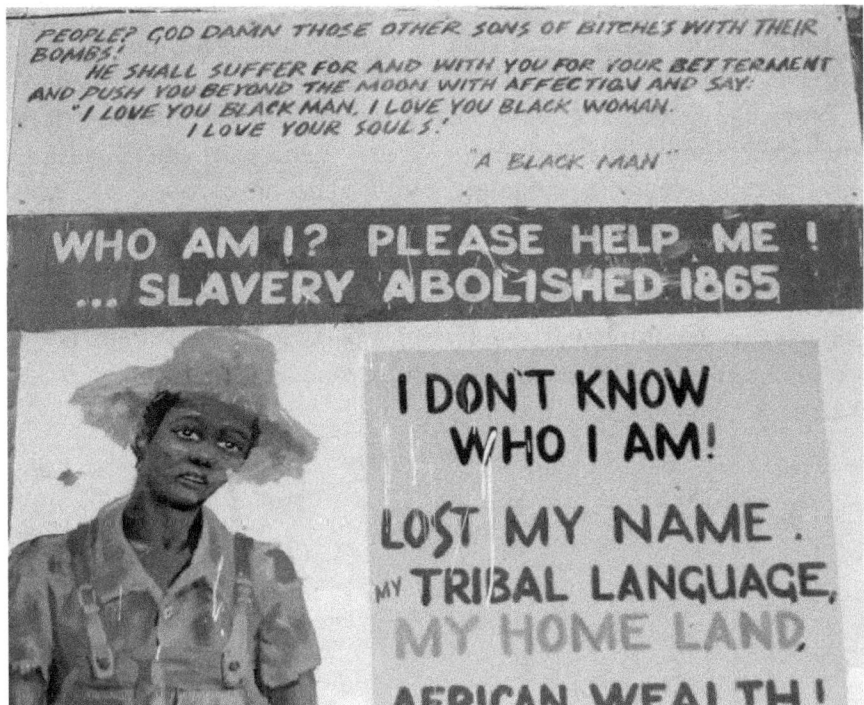

Black Nationalism 73. The belief is this fellow is lost!

"The principal of Boys and Girls High School is an outstanding educator, a crucial heir to the legacy of Harriet Tubman, who was a

FREDERICK MONDERSON

beacon of freedom" said Mr. Markowitz. Marty continued, "2007 is a high time with epic achievements, openings and opportunities for African Americans. Brooklyn has the largest African American population in New York City, and USA. They send a new member of Congress in person of Yvette Clarke to continue the work of Shirley Chisholm. Blacks were appointed to many crucial positions in New York State as David Patterson. The first Black African American Lieutenant Governor (Mr. Patterson later became Governor of New York State); Elliott Theodore Jones, Jr., was appointed to the highest seat in the State Court of Appeals. The new Chief of Brooklyn North is Gerald Nelson. Charlie Rangel in the House of Representatives is in the most powerful position in Congress as Chairman of the House and Ways Committee. Jay-Z was hosting Barak Obama along with Beyonce and Def Jams records as I speak."

BLACK NATIONALISM ALIVE AND WELL

Black Nationalism 74. Congressman Harold Forde and Erik Monderson at "Sharpton's Tribute to Dr. M.L. King."

The Boro President said "The finest career is in business. Rodney O'Neil, Kendall Shenall, Reginald Davis, Carl Horton, Andy Fudge, John Thompson, Max Siegel, yes, an African American is the new President of NASCAR, Oprah Winfrey in South Africa, these are all legacies of Harriet Tubman's contributions. "Every student here must have a future to be Harriet Tubman, an Al Vann or Annette Robinson. You have to be there. It's your responsibility to be free of hate." Al Vann turned around and praised Marty Markowitz for his passionate and sincere message to the young people. Vann said Marty "You're fired up."

FREDERICK MONDERSON

Dr. Sheila Evans-Tranumn, Associate Commissioner for the New York State Education Department was the next speaker and waded right into it by praising the actress: "Ms. Tyrell did an excellent job on Harriet Tubman." She said further, "Focus not on the past but on the future, for every great journey begins with a dream." Looking at the young people she said "Within you is the patience, strength and passion to reach for the stars and to change the world. We need world changes. Change ourselves, change our community." To the adults she continued, "We must groom from an early age the young people whose responsibility it is to change the world."

"We must teach children you have the power to change," and to the young people she insisted, "You must move from being a lawyer to a judge to the head judge. Move from being a doctor to head of a medical institution."

Black Nationalism 75. Jim Butler, union leader and fierce fighter for his constituencies.

"I'm African American, southern and being in America," she said, "has been a challenge. I went to a Black College from NYC schools rather than accept a scholarship to a college I would not fit in."

BLACK NATIONALISM
ALIVE AND WELL

"Teach children they have the power to change the world. But, you can't help anyone if you can't help yourself" she continued.

"Harriet Tubman had a vision or dream to free herself then free others. We say Massa, can we be free in 2007. We ask too many people to give us freedom."

Black Nationalism 76. Reverend Al Sharpton poses with two Black "heavyweights."

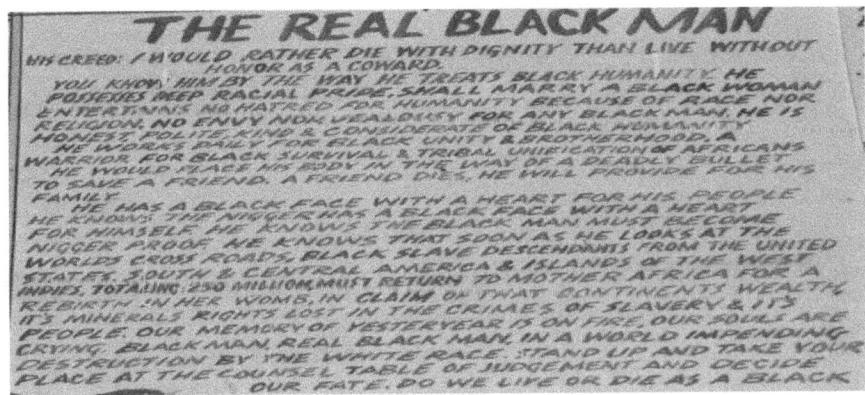

Black Nationalism 77. Question is, "Who is the Real Black man?" He asks and answers his own question!

FREDERICK MONDERSON

By now she was in full swing. "We must fight for freedom. We're too polite. We want to please everybody. We can't do that" she kept exhorting. "I'm not looking to be Ms. Congeniality. In order to free others you must free yourself."

"Your liberty comes with a price Adelaide Sandford told me. She said, understand the burden of liberation." "What happens when the rubber meets the tar" is tantamount to reality.

"Liberation comes with a price" she continued. "If we don't fight for liberation no one will. Changing the world means taking risks. You can take risks when you know there is a higher person looking over you."

"I had reason in my mind. My liberty or my death!"

"'Stay black and die. Liberty or death' is what I was told as a young girl!"

"If you don't change things, our children will suffer."

"Who will challenge the Board of Education to put Black Studies back in our curriculum? If we don't change then our children will be consigned to low performing schools."

"Barak Obama is not the only smart African American in America" she insisted, "I wish I knew the people who know our history."

"Every great dream comes with the responsibility" that you must pay a price for your success.

"Harriet Tubman said, I freed 1000 but could have freed 1000 more, if they only knew that they were slaves. May the spirit of Harriet Tubman be with you" she exhorted. "If you don't do it then our children can't do it. Can I get some African American warriors! We must be free!"

BLACK NATIONALISM
ALIVE AND WELL

Black Nationalism 78. This is a really cute one!

Black Nationalism 79. New York State Governor David Patterson.

FREDERICK MONDERSON

7. A. Philip Randolph's March on Washington, D.C. in 1941
By
Dr. Fred Monderson

Who was A. Philip Randolph? If we read his writings, we would realize he was one of the most brilliant minds of his age, Black or White. Randolph was confronted with the problems facing Black people in the first half of the 20th Century and he ably articulated and effectuated a leadership role that raised the issues and advanced the cause of Black freedoms and quest for equality in the Depression and Post-Depression age. A die-hard advocate of labor, Randolph saw Black salvation in America from a position of labor activism that brought integration in the workplace but more importantly allowed the worker to demand and receive a decent wage to help raise his family. Beyond this milestone, he advocated mass movements and demonstrations to secure equality and social justice, and civil and human rights.

Black Nationalism 79a. Marcus Garvey, Mohammed Ali and Stevie Wonder are featured in this mural on Sly's Wall in Brooklyn.

BLACK NATIONALISM ALIVE AND WELL

To understand the struggles of A. Philip Randolph, one has to understand the condition of Black people by the time of the Great Depression in 1929 and the significance of the election that followed in 1932.

Black Nationalism 80. A. Philip Randolph, activist, labor leader and President of Sleeping Car Porters of America.

From the time of Abraham Lincoln's **Emancipation Proclamation** (1863), and the Radical Republicans in Congress who were instrumental in securing the 13th, 14th, and 15th Amendments to the Constitution (1865-1870) and numerous Civil Rights legislation in the 19th Century as a result of **Reconstruction** (1865-1877), Blacks had voted Republican, the

FREDERICK MONDERSON

"Party of Lincoln." Yet, substantive issues were not addressed in the "age of terror," especially in the South.

John P. Davis in *The American Negro Reference Book* (1967: 63) recounts how after disappointments with the Teddy Roosevelt and Howard Taft Administrations, things got no better and Blacks looked for relief. "In 1912 they were willing to turn to any group that promised some hope. To some Negroes, Woodrow Wilson seemed to provide some hope when he said, during his campaign, that he wished to see 'justice done to the colored people in every matter; and not mere grudging justice, but justice executed with liberality and cordial good feeling." Shortly after Wilson's inauguration, it became clear to most Negroes that they could not rely on Wilson or his party for support in their efforts. Soon, segregation was reintroduced in the nation's capital and in the offices of the Federal government."

Still, this political party commitment continued through World War I (1914-1918), the great economic advances of the 1920s and passed the great Stock Market Crash in 1929, which ushered in the Great Depression. Yet, despite their loyalty to the Republican Party that generally won most elections, Blacks were for the most part, ignored and their condition never improved in the "age of terror" in which they lived.

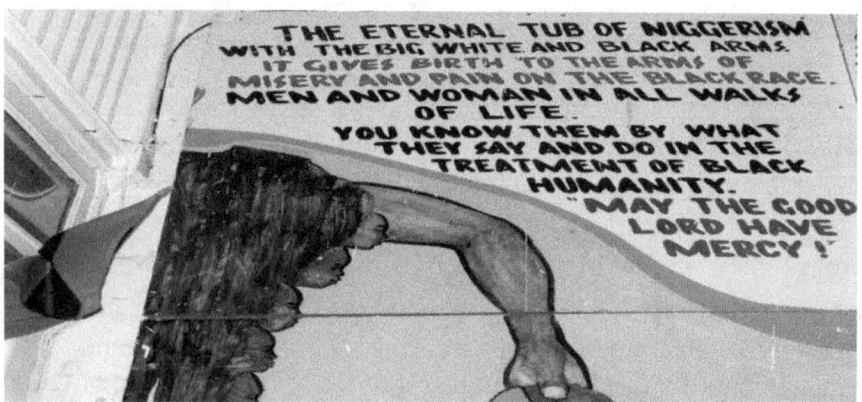

Black Nationalism 81.   The Big contradiction! "May the Good Lord Have Mercy!"

BLACK NATIONALISM
ALIVE AND WELL

In this, the first few years of the Depression hit home hard and Blacks were doubly affected, being the last hired and first fired. Therefore, Blacks decided to switch parties in 1932 and voted overwhelmingly for the Democrat Franklin Delano Roosevelt, who proclaimed and promised the "New Deal." They repeated this support again in 1936 and again in 1940. As such then, while the "New Deal" sought to seriously confront the wrenching conditions of the Depression with its "Alphabet Programs," the issue of the day was jobs. Interestingly enough, as the "drums of war" in Europe began to beat louder and louder in the minds and hearts of the American people, the war industry of the "home front" geared for the inevitable. In this one place where jobs were in great supply as the nation fed the "Lend-Lease Program," the ugly face of racism and discrimination sought to exclude the Black man, confining him to a few jobs in the most degrading and dead-end positions of janitor, sweepers and elevator operators. The record seems to show, for example, of the thirty thousand jobs in New York City, only 142 were held by Blacks in the above mentioned positions and this example was indicative of the broader social condition of Blacks in the nation's workforce.

Accordingly, Executive Order 8802 issued June 25, 1941 stated, "Whereas there is evidence that available and needed workers have been barred from employment in industries engaged in defense production solely because of considerations of race, creed, color, or national origin, to the detriment of workers' morale and of national unity."

Bradford Chambers in *Chronicles of Black Protest* (1968: 174) recounts how: "In the armed forces, segregation was still the official government policy, a carry-over from the Civil War. Black newspapers reported 'race riots at Fort Oswego; discrimination at Fort Devens; Jim Crow Conditions at Camps Blanding and Lee; and the edict – 'Not to shake a Nigger's hand at Camp Upton.' The Baltimore Afro-American called for thousands of Black men to desert rather than serve in army camps in the South."

FREDERICK MONDERSON

Black Nationalism 82. Congressman Charlie Rangel hugs young Erik Monderson at "Sharpton's affair for Dr. King."

Into this mix, A. Philip Randolph had been active for more than two decade, primarily as a labor-unionist but more interested in the well-being of Black people, then generally referred to as Negroes. As early as 1935 he became President of the Brotherhood of Sleeping Car Porters on the railroad, but also active in the National Negro Congress, Co-Chairman of The American Committee on Africa, as well as Co-Chairman of The American Negro Leadership Conference on Africa.

BLACK NATIONALISM ALIVE AND WELL

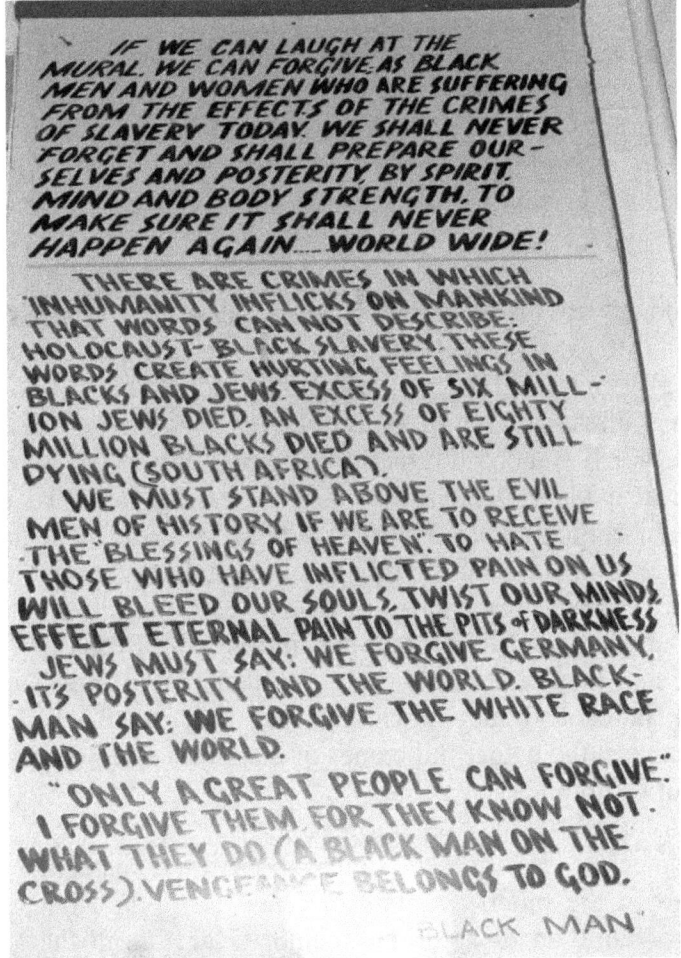

Black Nationalism 83. Laugh, laugh, laugh!

Philip Foner in *The Voice of Black America* (1972: 808) tells about A. Philip Randolph. "Born April 15, 1889, in Crescent City, Florida, Randolph finished high school in Florida, worked his way north and subsisted on odd jobs while attending City College of New York. (He never earned a college degree, and was mostly self-taught). Together with Chandler Own, a young black law student at Columbia University, Randolph became active in the Socialist party, and both edited *The Messenger*, a radical black journal of opinion

FREDERICK MONDERSON

which endorsed Socialism and was a leading voice of the "New Negro" in the post-World War I period. Randolph was asked by the Pullman Porters to help them organize, and in 1935, after twelve years of hard struggle, the Brotherhood of Sleeping Car Porters, with Randolph as president, forced the Pullman Company to recognize it."

In his address to the National Negro Congress held in Chicago February 14, 15, 16 in 1936, of which a pamphlet is in the Schomberg Library in Harlem, New York, and in Foner (1972: 810-811), where after speaking of the problems facing Europe on the eve of World War II Randolph turned to the condition of the Black man in America in that "Depression" and "New Deal" era. To this he stated: "Our contemporary history is a witness to the stark fact that Black America is a victim of both class and race prejudice and oppression. Because Negroes are black, they are hated, maligned and spat upon, lynched, mobbed and murdered. Because Negroes are workers, they are browbeaten, bullied, intimidated, robbed, exploited, jailed and shot down. Because they are black they are caught between the nether millstones of discrimination when seeking a job to join a union."

"Thus, voiceless in thirteen states; politically disregarded and discounted in the others; victims of lynch terror in Dixie, with a Scottsboro frame-up of notorious memory; faced with the label of the white man's job and the white man's union; unequal before the law; Jim-Crowed in schools and colleges throughout the nation; segregated in the slums and ghettos of the urban centers; landless peons of a merciless landlordism; hunted down, harassed and hounded as vagrants in the Southern cities, the Negro people face a hard, deceptive and brutal capitalist order, despite its preachments of Christian love and brotherhood."

BLACK NATIONALISM
ALIVE AND WELL

Black Nationalism 84. People praying for President Obama outside the White House.

Further he indicated, Black progress must come through admission into the industrial and craft unions, to which he opined: "The craft union invariably has a color bar against the Negro worker, but the industrial union in structure renders race discrimination less possible, since it embraces all the workers included in the industry, regardless of race, creed, color, or craft, skilled or unskilled. Thus, this congress should seek to broaden and intensify the movement to draw Negro workers into labor organizations and break down the color bar in the trade-unions that now have it. The next instrumentality which the workers must build and employ for their protection against economic exploitation, war and fascism is an independent working-class political party. It should take the form of a farmer-labor political organization. This is indispensable in view of the bankruptcy in principles, courage and vision of the old-line parties, Republican and Democratic."

FREDERICK MONDERSON

Randolph says further, as Foner (1972: 813-814) pointed out: "The fight for civil and political rights of the Negro peoples can effectively be carried on if only those organizations that are pushing the struggles are broadened and built with a wider mass base. Those organizations that are serving on the civil-rights front effectively for the Negro are the National Association for the Advancement of Colored People and the International Labor Defense. It needs to be definitely understood, however, that the fight in the courts for civil and political rights cannot be effective except when backed by a broad nationwide, if not international, mass protest through demonstrations in the form of parades, mass meetings and publicity."

Black Nationalism 84a. Two beautiful ladies on a visit to **Clarke House** in Harlem to hear Dr. Leonard Jeffries speak on Malcolm X.

He cautioned, Foner (1972: 814) continued: "The task of overcoming the enemies of democratic institutions and constitutional liberties is too big for any single organization. It requires the united and formal integrating and coordinating of the various Negro

BLACK NATIONALISM
ALIVE AND WELL

organizations – church, fraternal, civil, trade-union, farmer, professional, college and what not – into the framework of a united front, together with the white groups of workers, lovers of liberty and those whose liberties are similarly menaced for a common attack upon the forces of reaction, backed by the embattled masses of black and white workers. The united front strategy and tactics should be executed through methods of mass demonstration, such as parades, picketing, boycotting, mass protests, the mass distribution of propaganda literature, as well as legal action."

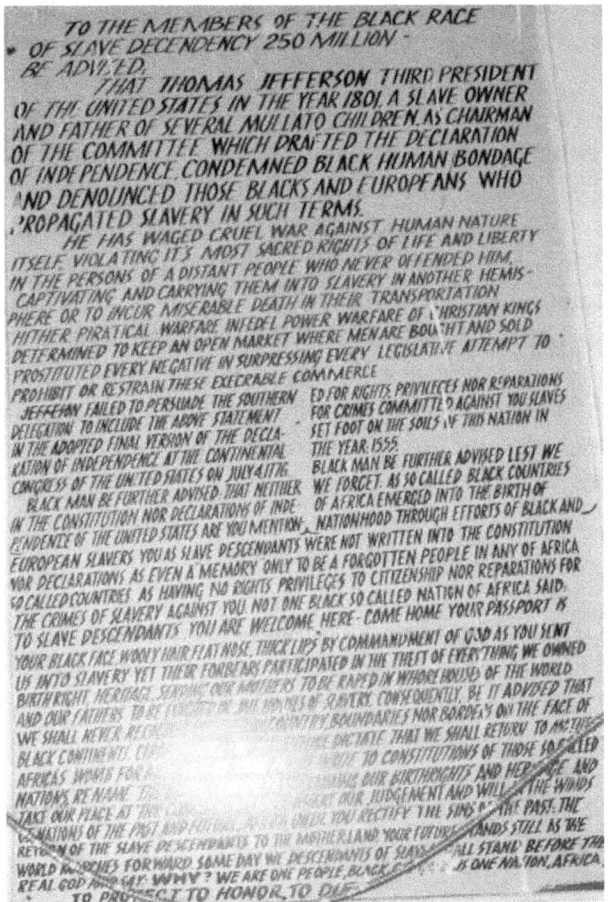

Black Nationalism 85. Well, read the message.

FREDERICK MONDERSON

"The salvation of the Negro like the workers must come from within," he believed. Then he chronicled challenges facing Blacks, particularly during the 1930s. He indicated: "These issues should be obvious, clear and simple, such as prevention of stoppage of relief, cuts in relief allotments, layoffs of relief workers or workers in any industry, discrimination in the giving of relief, exorbitant rents, evictions, rent increases, police brutality, denial of free assembly, freedom of the press, freedom of speech to unpopular groups, denial of civil rights to Negroes, access to public utilities and forms of transportation, such as the Pullman car."

He called Blacks to be involved and advocated: "Wage struggles around war upon Ethiopia by the fascist dictator Mussolini, strikes and lockouts of black and white workers, the amendment to the federal constitution or the adoption of social legislation such as the Retirement Pension Act for railroad workers, fight for the freedom of Angelo Herndon, the Scottsboro boys, the Wagner-Costigan anti-lynching bill, the violations of the Wagner Labor Disputes bill, the forcing of teachers to take the oath, the goose-stepping of the students in the school system thru the R.O.T.C., the abolition of the color bar in trade-unions, the murder of Shoemaker in Tampa, Florida, exposing the menace of the American Liberty League, William Randolph Hearst and the Ku Klux Klan, and supporting the movement of John L. Lewis for industrial unionism."

Such is the task of the Negro people as Randolph outlined them. Nevertheless, continued Randolph: "To meet the task, the Negro peoples, pressed with their backs against the wall, must face the future with heads erect, hearts undaunted and undismayed, ready and willing and determined to pay the price in struggle, sacrifices and suffering that freedom, justice and peace shall share and enjoy a more abundant life."

BLACK NATIONALISM
ALIVE AND WELL

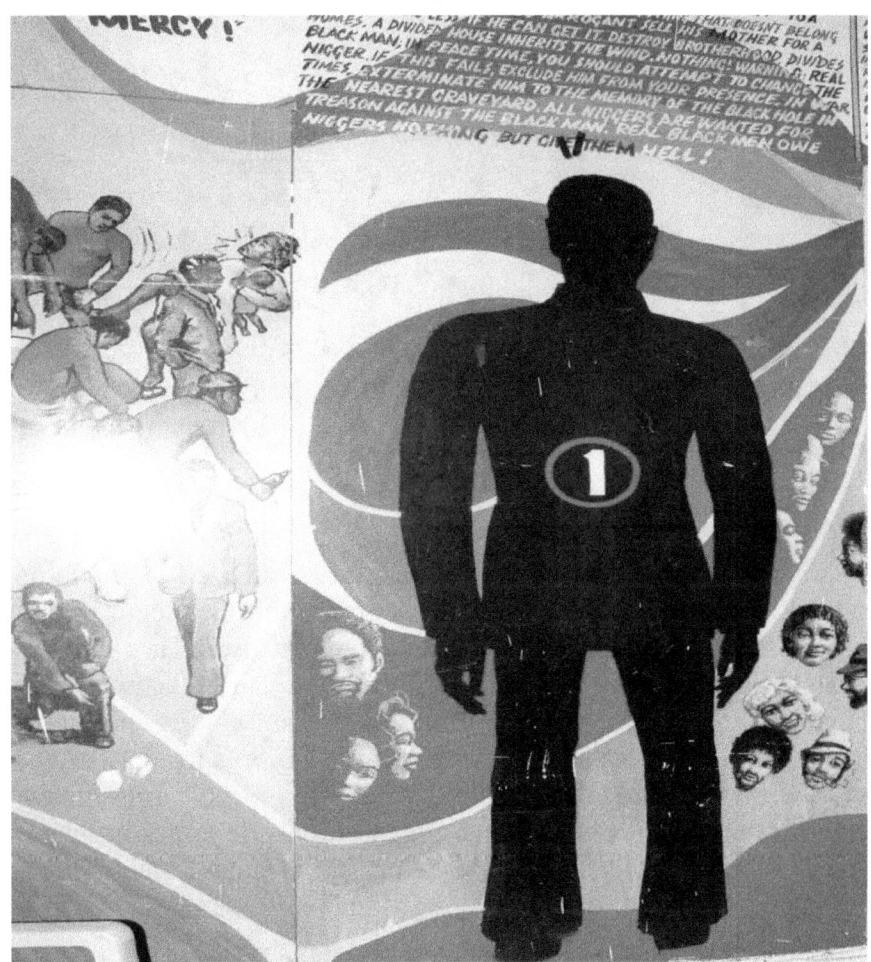

Black Nationalism 86. This image is subject to interpretation.

FREDERICK MONDERSON

Black Nationalism 86a. Delegate at the Podium at the "All Caribbean People's Conference" in Barbados in 2010.

In a further speech, upon its 150th anniversary entitled *The Crisis of the Negro and the Constitution* in Foner (1972: 816-817) Randolph stated: "Freedom is never given; it is won. And the Negro people must win their freedom. They must achieve justice. This involves struggle, continuous struggle. True liberation can be acquired and maintained only when the Negro masses possess power; and power is the product and flower of organization – organization of the masses, the masses in the mills and mines, on the farms, in the factories, in churches, in fraternal organizations, in homes, colleges, women's clubs, student groups, trade-unions, tenants' leagues, in co-operative guilds, political organizations and civil-rights associations."

Still, despite the organizing and speech-making, Blacks continued to face major obstacles and difficulties in the society. All this, and despite the sympathetic attitude of the President's wife, Eleanor Roosevelt and even the efforts of the "Black Cabinet" who consulted with President Roosevelt himself. As the war unfolded in Europe,

BLACK NATIONALISM
ALIVE AND WELL

Blacks sought meaningful jobs in the war industries from which they were generally excluded. It was time for action!

Black Nationalism 86b. The Honorable Minister Louis Farrakhan, Leader, The Nation of Islam!

In January, 1941, A. Philip Randolph, as head of **The Brotherhood of Sleeping Car Porters Union** issued a call for a "March on Washington, DC.," insisting "Ten, twenty, fifty thousand Negroes" would gather on the White House Lawn on July 1, 1941, to demand the federal government end discrimination in civilian and military job contracts. Importantly, however, if we look to Randolph's activism we get a broader view of the overall condition of Black in the depression years leading to the war, despite their voting record as Democrats.

FREDERICK MONDERSON

Randolph was joined by other Black leaders Walter White, Adam Clayton Powell, Jr., and Frank Crosswaith to demand, according to Chambers (1968: 175) that the "federal government take action to stop discrimination in the defense industries and the armed forces." Imagine, 9 years later and three significant Democratic victories and Blacks were still waiting for significant changes in the American social and civic order. Chambers (1968: 175) continued: "The idea of a black revolt in a time of crisis threw Washington into a panic. President Roosevelt called the March leaders to Washington and tried to persuade them to call it off." They refused! Interesting, for people don't generally refuse the President!

The Program of the March on Washington on July 1, 1941 was as follows:

1. We demand, in the interest of national unity, the abrogation of every law which makes a distinction in treatment between citizens based on religion, color, or national origin. This means an end to Jim Crow in education, in housing, in transportation and in every other social, economic, and political privilege; and especially, we demand, in the capital of the nation, an end to all segregation in public places and in public institutions.
2. We demand legislation to enforce the Fifth and Fourteenth Amendments guaranteeing that no person shall be deprived of life, liberty or property without due process of law, so that the full weight of the national government may be used for the protection of life and thereby may end the disgrace of lynching.
3. We demand the enforcement of the Fourteenth and Fifteenth Amendments and the enactment of the Pepper Poll Tax bill so that all barriers in the exercise of the suffrage are eliminated.
4. We demand the abolition of segregation and discrimination in the army, navy, Marine Corps, air corps, and all other branches of national defense.
5. We demand an end to discrimination in jobs and job training. Further, we demand that the FEPC be made a permanent administrative agency of the U.S. Government and that it be given power to enforce its decisions based on its findings.

BLACK NATIONALISM ALIVE AND WELL

6. We demand that federal funds be withheld from any agency which practices discrimination in the use of such funds.

7. We demand colored and minority group representation on all administrative agencies so that these groups may have recognition of their democratic rights to participate in formulating policies.

8. We demand representation for the colored and minority racial groups on all missions, political and technical, which will be sent to the peace conference so that the interests of all people everywhere may be truly recognized and justly provided for in the postwar settlement.

Black Nationalism 87. Barack Obama and the winning galvanizing "Yes We Can" logo.

The March never happened, because of necessity President Roosevelt signed Executive Order 8802 on June 25, 1941, days before the March date. This Executive Order banned discrimination in the war industries and government training programs, and established a President's Commission on Fair Employment Practices.

FREDERICK MONDERSON

Black Nationalism 88. Amiri Baraka, Poet Laureate of New Jersey and nationalist extraordinaire.

Nevertheless, while **FEPA** (Fair Employment Practices Act) banned selective job discrimination, desegregation of the Armed Forces had to wait until the death of **FDR**, end of World War II and the new Harry Truman Administration, when the Armed Forces Act officially ended discrimination in the military.

BLACK NATIONALISM
ALIVE AND WELL

Black Nationalism 89. "Washing an Ethiopian White?"

Notwithstanding, most of the other issues mentioned in the program had to be hard won in the late 1940s, the 1950s and well into the Civil Rights struggles of the 1960s and beyond. We can never forget Frederick Douglass' statement: "Power concedes nothing without a struggle."

FREDERICK MONDERSON

Black Nationalism 90. Amiri Baraka (Leroy Jones), extraordinary revolutionary poet and one-time Poet Laureate of New Jersey, his home state.

Fortunately, in sweet irony, it was Randolph who actually originated the 1963 March on Washington. Davis (1967: 476) wrote: "The march on Washington originated with A. Philip Randolph, militant head of the Brotherhood of Sleeping Car Porters. It was organized and programmed by Bayard Rustin, former field secretary of **CORE**, who also organized the New York City school boycott. Every Negro protest organization working for integration was represented, as were a number of white or mixed supporting organizations representing labor, churches and civic and various liberal groups. Martin Luther King, Jr., James farmer, Roy Wilkins, A. Philip Randolph and John Lewis were the principal speakers."

Randolph was unquestionably a brilliant mind, consummate activist, jailed for 2 years while editor of the *Messenger* during World War I and whose ideas laid the foundation strategies for the later Civil Rights Movement. He initially called for a United Front Movement. Unfortunately Randolph has not gotten the credit he deserves for the pivotal and avante garde role he played as a Civil Rights activist who made a difference in the 20th Century.

BLACK NATIONALISM ALIVE AND WELL

Black Nationalism 91. Rev. Jesse Jackson with Judge Bruce ("Cut 'em Loose Bruce") Wright.

8. Marcus Garvey and Black Nationalism
By
Dr. Fred Monderson

Marcus Moziah Garvey, born August 17, 1887 and died in 1940, is numbered among the greatest Africans of the 19th and 20th Centuries for his daring, visionary character, organizational ability, charismatic personality, outspokenness and forward thinking as well as mobilization abilities that has shown the way to so many engaged in struggle to uplift African people worldwide. I'm reminded during the First Emancipation Day festivities in Ghana, West Africa, during August 1998, when President Jerry Rawlings celebrated the return of activist Sonny Carson's great-great grand-uncle, Samuel Carson, he equally honored Marcus Garvey for his early insistence that Blacks in the Diaspora identify with and celebrate their African heritage and

FREDERICK MONDERSON

culture. One of Garvey's famous lines is that he looked at the Black man, degraded, dehumanized and debased as Africa lay prostrate resulting from the slave trade and slavery, rampant European imperialism and colonialism, at the turn of the 20th Century. In response, he said: "Black man, where are your men of big affairs?" Looking around, he could not find any. So he created organizations as the Universal Negro Improvement Association, the African Communities League, the Black Cross Nurses, Black Madonna and Child, and founded the Black Star Line, and gave Blacks the Red, Black and Green flag as a nationalist heritage. Red is for the Blood, Black is for the color of the people and Green is for the land and this trilogy unites Black people worldwide.

For combat he formed The African Legions, whose outfit, Thompson described as: "arrayed in black uniform with red seams, red shoulder-straps, and a red band around the collar of the tunic, [who] will go forth to conquer Africa, even if it means as their leader says, walking knee-deep in blood and grime." Garvey even made influential titles as the Duke of the Nile, Earl of the Congo, formed the African Orthodox Church, and so much more. He made himself Provisional President-General of Africa. Symbols, ethos, cultural motifs, institutions, organizations, military organs, propaganda literature, are all needed by a people seeking to prolong their existence, dignity and gain respect from others in a oftentimes hostile world. Much of this Marcus Garvey insisted on as he laid the foundation for Black men and women to stride towards advancement, upliftment and progress. Garvey coined the phrase "Black is Beautiful." He said Black people were "a gifted race with a proud past and a great future." He founded his own media to get his message to the people. *The Negro World* publisher published his message on a weekly basis. He also had a daily newspaper called *The Negro Times*. He targeted the Black masses worldwide but his philosophic, economic, and cultural and motif messages were challenged and curtailed by the colonial apparatus that controlled Africans worldwide. In this regard, again Thompson wrote: "Garvey's newspaper *The Negro World* was banned and heavy penalties were imposed on people found reading or even possessing copies of it. The punishment in certain colonial territories for

BLACK NATIONALISM
ALIVE AND WELL

possessing *The Negro World* was five years imprisonment with hard labor. In Dahomey, formerly French West Africa, it was life imprisonment. The paper was also suppressed in Trinidad, British Guiana, Barbados in the West Indies, and all French, Italian, Portuguese, Belgian and some British colonies in Africa."

Nevertheless, when we consider the state of the Black World in 1915 when Garvey came to America and where we are today, clearly he was a significant pillar and a driving dynamo that propelled our people along to achieve and face the many challenges still awaiting us in the 21st Century. No wonder, almost a century after his arrival in America people still practice his philosophy and identify with his goals and aspirations.

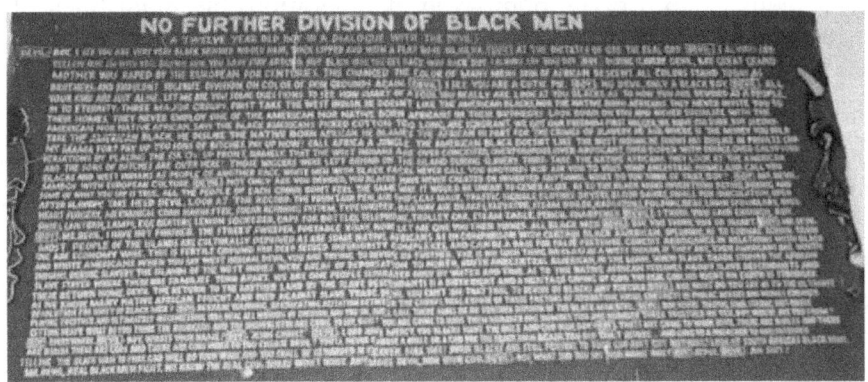

Black Nationalism 92. Judge Philips calls this, "No further Division of Black Men."

Interestingly enough, men of great ideas have disagreements but some of these leaders even though they have a people's well being in mind, can sometimes go over the edge and spew vile vituperation or even conspire against and sometimes murder their competitors, who seem to challenge them for leadership. In an age of Booker T. Washington, W.E.B. DuBois and others, Marcus Garvey was looked upon as a foreigner, even though he is now considered a pillar in the foundation of Pan-Africanism and in the struggle for economic emancipation and social justice in this country. Just as DuBois

FREDERICK MONDERSON

challenged Washington he challenged Garvey. In that era of Jim Crowism, lynchings and fear and intimidation of Black people, one leader accused the other. DuBois accused Washington of serving the White man's interests, saying only his own "Talented tenth" idea was most practicable. Garvey accused DuBois of being a "Traitor to the race" and a "White Man's Nigger." DuBois on the other hand, said Garvey was "insane" and "without a doubt, the most dangerous enemy of the Negro race in America, and the world. He is either a traitor or a lunatic." How harsh could they be! Nevertheless, and strange enough they ended up, with the passage of time, seeing the wisdom, foresight and honest concern for African people, of those they once vilified. Thompson says Dubois would later confess: "Garvey was an extraordinary leader of men and regarded his movement as 'one of the most interesting spiritual movements of the modern world.' In another place, he had said of the Garvey movement: 'Shorn of its bombastic exaggeration, the main lines of the Garvey plan are perfectly feasible. What he is trying to say and do is this: American Negroes can, by accumulating and ministering their own capital, organize industry, join the Black Centers of the South Atlantic by commercial enterprise and in this way ultimately redeem Africa as a fit and free home for Black men.'"

Naturally and sometimes, institutions, ideas, speeches and even memorabilia can be forgotten or perish but the written word, can last forever for it freezes the individual's thoughts in time and can be resurrected later to be used for the initial purposes intended. In this case, *The Philosophy and Opinions of Marcus Garvey* has captured the essence, ideas, philosophies and aspirations as well as insights of the man who brought great hope and enlightenment to so many people of African descent throughout in Africa, America, the Caribbean, Latin America, Europe and even Asia.

Here in these United States, Marcus Garvey and his teachings in more ways than one influenced many a movement dating back to the first decades of the 20th Century. In his organizational building approach he held conventions in the late teens and early nineteen twenties. There were spectacular parades with pomp and great reverence. Harlem was lit-up by the reverence and revelry

BLACK NATIONALISM
ALIVE AND WELL

associated with his movement. Some of the local separatist and nationalist groups and individuals Marcus Garvey influenced from that time included Roy Innis and the *Congress of Racial Equality*; Elijah Mohammed and the *Nation of Islam*; Noble Drew Ali, Queen Mother Moore who had such tremendous influence on many modern leaders as Martin Luther King, Malcolm X, Sonny Carson, Jitu Weusi, Conrad Worrill, Herbert Daughtry, and many more. All drew inspiration and ideas from his economic, political, separatist, nationalist, cultural and historical beliefs and practices as well as Pan-Africanism, in which Garvey, his movement and his "cubs" played a role. In Africa as well as the Caribbean and Middle and South America, Marcus Garvey equally influenced Nkrumah and a whole host of African nationalists and independence seekers. In Ghana under Nkrumah the Ghana Shipping Line was formed to replace the Black Star Line and there was a Black Star Square in the capital. Even the Ghanaian flag with its colors of red, gold (yellow) and green, with a black star copied the similar colors of the Garvey Flag adopted by the UNIA.

> AWARDING CERTIFICATES WITH THE WHITE CHAINS, GREENS, BLACK CHAINS AND THE MASTER LINK CHAIN, REPRESENTING A STANDARD OF IN SELF DEFENSE AND SELF OFFENSE. STUDENTS MUST VISIT THE HOMELAND OF THE AFRICAN SLAVES WITH KNOWLEDGE OF THE RED BLOOD SPILLED DURING SLAVERY AND WITH A COMMITMENT TO THE DEAD BLACK SLAVES OF HISTORY: TO ACT AND FEEL BLACK WORLDIZED TO A BLACK MAN'S IMAGE WITH MASTERFUL KNOWLEDGE OF THE GO-RILLA COMMANDMENTS AND THEIR PURPOSE.

Black Nationalism 93. "Go-Rilla Commandments" and their Purpose.

FREDERICK MONDERSON

In Tony Martin's Preface to the Majority Press Centennial Edition of *The Philosophy and Opinions of Marcus Garvey* he writes: "The history and contents of the book are a metaphor of the Black experience of the last five hundred years. Careful perusal of these pages reveals much more than the dreams and achievements and the trials and tribulations of the most successful Pan-African movement of all time. They reveal much also of the strengths and hopes, of the failures and frustrations besetting scattered Africa in its tedious meanderings out of the quagmire of slavery and subjugation."

According to Martin, "The Black struggle in the western world, like all struggles of oppressed peoples everywhere, has produced leaders of exceptional ability and unswerving dedication to a cause. In these pages we see the singleness of purpose, the breath of vision, the belief in the righteousness of his work, the boldness born of conviction, that made Marcus Garvey both the most loved and the most feared and hated Black man of his time. Qualities like these in leaders from Toussaint L'Ouverture to Nat Turner to Martin Luther King, Jr. and Malcolm X have always helped sustain this struggle when the need was greatest." Even further, Martin continued, "The price of such leadership has always been too high. All of the names enumerated above suffered martyrdom. Marcus Garvey escaped the assassin's bullet only to be jailed, deported, hounded and harassed." He did affirm Leadership means everything – **PAIN**, **BLOOD**, **DEATH**!

Today the world knows Marcus Garvey, while the people who conspired against him for the most part have gone down in oblivion and the influence he wielded helped fan the whirlwind of African independence following World War II. The timelessness of his ideas still inspire young people, Pan-Africanists and conscious thinking individuals who can gain from his experiences, trials, tribulations, triumphs, failures, betrayals and vision. Except for those who lived before his time, all great Black man who have imprinted on their time, unquestionably benefited from the ideas of Marcus Garvey.

BLACK NATIONALISM
ALIVE AND WELL

A perusal of the Table of Contents of the book *The Philosophy and Opinions of Marcus Garvey* shows how wide was the breadth of the man's thinking, a man essentially self-taught at a time when education for Africans anywhere in the world was a hard won sacrifice. He wrote about "Propaganda, slavery, force, education, miscegenation, prejudice, radicalism, government, evolution and the result, poverty, power, universal suspicion, dissertation on man, race assimilation, Christianity, the function of man and traitors."

Black Nationalism 94. A Compatriot from struggles at and with **National Action Network**.

Then there is "Present Day Civilization, Divine apportionment of earth, universal unrest in 1922, world disarmament, causes of wars, the fall of governments, great ideals know no nationality, purpose of creation, purity of race, man know thyself, a solution for the world peace in 1922, god as a war lord, and the image of god." Even further, "the slave trade, Negroes' status under alien governments, the Negro as an industrial makeshift, lack of co-operation in the

FREDERICK MONDERSON

Negro race, White man's solution for the Negro problem in America, the true solution of the Negro problem, white propaganda about Africa, the three stages of the Negro in contact with the White man, Booker T. Washington's program, belief that race problem will adjust itself a fallacy, examples of White Christian control of Africa, the thought behind their deeds, similarity of persecution, shall the Negro be exterminated? Africa for the Africans, the future as I see it." Finally, "Emancipation Speech, Christmas Message, Easter sermon, Convention speech and statement on arrest." These words have been so piercing and influential they were instrumental in galvanizing Kwame Nkrumah as he chaired the 5th Pan African Conference in Manchester, England after World War II in 1945 and in his struggles to free Ghana and assist in African decolonization.

In this country, Raymond Hall in *Black Separatism in the United States* (1978: 66) wrote offering a synopsis of Garvey and his movement. "Marcus Garvey was the UNIA's sole architect. The movement's values, in essence, reflected only slight differences from those of mainstream America. Lewis makes the point, however, that Garvey's ideological creation is paradoxical. Garvey's militant call for Black Nationalism might be too quickly called extremely radical, but its content and emphasis, all reflected 'the conventional American world view.' That is, in exhorting Blacks to be proud of their Blackness and Black historical achievements, 'Garvey was merely turning the white American's racial chauvinism on its head.' His ideas of justice and world order were based on the nation-state concept, which most Americans would embrace. His economic philosophy, like Washington's and most Americans,' was bourgeoisie. Finally, "except for its emphasis on the return to Africa, the only 'radicalism' in Garvey's thought (was) his basic assumption that Black men could and would manage their affairs in the same manner as did White men."

BLACK NATIONALISM
ALIVE AND WELL

Black Nationalism 95. "The Messenger, Elijah Mohammed, founder of the Black Muslims of America.

Assessing some aspects of Garvey's economic philosophy, Hall believed while Garvey influenced many, others also in turn influenced him. He wrote: "Clearly, Garvey proposed to bring to fruition Washington's goal of 'economic separatism' in urban America. Washington had been concerned about economic separatism - or Black independence - in the rural South, and Garvey applied his philosophy to urban America, with the Back-to-Africa

FREDERICK MONDERSON

label as an added incentive. He knew that black people had already had large doses of economic self-determination from Washington and of Back-to-Africa from Bishop Turner, Blyden, and others; he therefore had to combine the two with dynamic variables. Perhaps he saw that it was necessary to augment economic independence and Back-to-Africa with race chauvinism, pride in one's racial heritage, glorification of the African past, confidence in oneself, and other ego-bolstering tactics."

Vincent Bakpetu Thompson in *Africa and Unity*: *The Evolution of Pan-Africanism* praises Garvey for the many slogans he coined in seeking African unity and progress. These included: "Africans for the Africans," "Renaissance of the Black RACE," "Ethiopia Awake," "Look for me in the eye of the storm," "Man love your brother," "Up, you mighty race, you can accomplish what you will." His "One God, One Aim, One Destiny" sought to unite Africans and determine the road ahead. As a compliment to his "One destiny" belief Garvey declared: "Therefore, let justice be done to all mankind, realizing that if the strong oppress the weak, confusion and discontent will ever mark the path of man, but love, faith and charity toward all, the reign of peace and plenty will be heralded into the world and the generation of men shall be blessed." Yet still, he did believe passionately: "No one knows when the hour of Africa's redemption cometh. It is in the wind. It is coming. One day, like the storm it will be here. When that day comes all Africa will stand together. Any sane man, race or nation that desires freedom must first of all think in terms of blood. Why, even the Heavenly Father tells us that 'without the shedding of blood there can be no remission of sins?' Then how in the name of God, with history before us, do we expect to redeem Africa without preparing ourselves – some of us to die."

He continued: "Wake up Ethiopia! Let us work towards the one glorious end of a free, redeemed, and mighty nation. Let Africa be a bright star among the constellation of nations." Even further, the declared objectives of Garvey's Organization were stated thus: "To establish a universal confraternity among the race; to promote the spirit of pride and love; to reclaim the fallen; to administer to and

BLACK NATIONALISM
ALIVE AND WELL

assist the needy; to assist in the development of independent Negro nations and communities; to establish a central nation for the race, to establish commissaries or agencies in principal countries and cities of the world for the representation of all Negroes; to promote a conscientious spiritual worship among the native tribes of Africa; to establish universities, colleges, academies and schools for the racial education and culture of the people; to work for better conditions among Negroes everywhere." Finally, Thompson summed up Garvey's program with its four principles that are hallmarks of the Pan-African movement today: "first, the common destiny of all Africans and the need for continental unity as a prerequisite for dealing with the numerous problems; second, the 'Negro or African Personality;' third, the repudiation of all foreign rule and control and the eradication of all its vestiges which are retarding the grown of African man; and, fourth, social change including cultural regeneration and reactivation of the world's cultures."

Black Nationalist 95a. Long-time Black Nationalist Brother Tarik James Haskins in the audience at Clarke House to hear about Malcolm X.

FREDERICK MONDERSON

Clearly a visionary, Garvey hoped to create an African world state that mirrored the universalism of the Catholic Church. He argued that: "Our union must know no clime, boundary or nationality. Like the great Church of Rome, Negroes the world over must practice one faith, that of confidence in themselves, with One God, One Aim, One Destiny ... the founding of a racial Empire whose only natural, spiritual and political limits shall be God and Africa at home and abroad."

Black Nationalism 96. The "Lion in Brooklyn!"

BLACK NATIONALISM
ALIVE AND WELL

Black Nationalism 96a. New York City Councilman Jumane Williams with Erik Monderson at the 2013 "March on Washington."

FREDERICK MONDERSON

Black Nationalism 97. Erik Monderson shakes hands with two New York State Senators, John Sampson and Erik Adams.

Certainly his influence has been immeasurable and his name became enshrined in motifs as schools, parks, and even streets today bear the name of this Pan-African and nationalist icon who helped get us here today. However, while we can give Garvey great grades for his efforts in mobilizing "400,000,000 Negroes" around the world we ought to pay some attention to the mistakes he made, trusting in others who betrayed him, meeting with the Ku Klux Klan, underestimating the power of Europeans who controlled those 400,000,000 Negroes through colonialism and the role of Ethiopia and Liberia as pawns in Global white supremacy, imperialism and power politics. His Black Star Line, with traitors aboard, coupled with mis-management, was an alligator that bled the UNIA, his return to Africa through the Liberia experiment was un-researched and betrayed, the "Negroes in America" who conspired and had him arrested, are all causes of his failures. Nevertheless, no matter what happens, when the people believe in you, your ideas, vision or name never die and this is why we celebrate and give Marcus Garvey such

BLACK NATIONALISM
ALIVE AND WELL

high marks today, August 17. On his arrest he remarked, "You have caged the lion but his cubs are running free out there!" Those cubs have indeed made their mark! God Bless Marcus Garvey and his timeliness as his ideas, efforts and charisma helped Black people to see the light at the end of the tunnel! Happy Birthday Marcus Moziah Garvey!

Black Nationalism 97a. "Mother" in her numerous varieties.

Black Nationalism 97b. Enduring mother's love for a child!

FREDERICK MONDERSON

9. Marcus Garvey and the UNIA
By
Dr. Fred Monderson

Marcus Garvey brought a new impetus to the needs and aspirations of Black people in America from his Harlem, New York, based Universal Negro Improvement Association. Founded in 1914 in Jamaica, West Indies, under a philosophy of Black "redemption" and "self-improvement," the UNIA soon became a force to be reckoned with in the United States, where the masses flocked to join, precisely because of its message of hope and pride. Foremost, Garvey felt, only the Black man can save the Black man! Naturally and for many reasons, he had his detractors or critics! Yet, calling the devil white, Garvey denounced White America for the tribulations of slavery and the aftermath it had visited upon the Black man. Still, white liberals were impressed by his self-help philosophy and even the KKK was "happy" that he wanted to take Blacks "Back to Africa."

Black leaders were especially critical, accusing him, says W.E.B. DuBois, of being a "visionary" and A. Philip Randolph, according to Bradford Chambers in *Chronicles of Black Protest* (1968: 165) accused him of "outright exploitation of the Black man." Nevertheless, it's interesting how time and history has put Garvey in proper perspective. DuBois later praised Garvey, while A. Philip Randolph despite his enormous Civil Rights efforts, had been retired to the "old folks home" of history to pass out his days. He does have a statue in Union Station, Washington, DC. Garvey, on the other hand, has remained to this day, a vibrant and motivating symbolic icon as the people, in time, got to know more about the man and his ideas. His red, black and green flag remains a living symbol of Black Nationalist aspirations.

BLACK NATIONALISM
ALIVE AND WELL

Black Nationalism 98. Education Icon Jitu Weusi and State Assemblywoman Inez Baron on the Firing Line protesting Mayor Bloomberg's choice of Chancellor for the City of New York's Board of Education.

Marcus Moziah Garvey, born in Jamaica on August 1, 1887, was impressed with the work of Booker T. Washington after reading *Up from Slavery*. He wrote Washington with the intent of setting up a Tuskegee-like school in Jamaica. Booker T. invited him to come to America in 1915 and by the time he arrived in 1916, the Tuskegee icon had died. Nevertheless, Garvey settled in Harlem, New York, and began to plant the seeds of UNIA there in 1917. By the time of the Versailles Peace Conference of 1919 ending World War I (1914-1918) Garvey boasted he had set up 19 branches of the UNIA throughout the United States. Within those few years, the movement had lit a fire under the downtrodden and Garvey's star began to rise.

John Hope Franklin in *From Slavery to Freedom* (Sixth Edition) (1987: 320) explained: "The basis for Garvey's wide popularity was his appeal to race pride at a time when Negroes generally had so little of which to be proud. The strain and stress of living in hostile urban communities created a state of mind upon which Garvey capitalized. He called upon Negroes, especially the ones of the darker hue, to follow him. Garvey exalted everything black: he insisted that black stood for strength and beauty, not inferiority. He

FREDERICK MONDERSON

asserted that Africans had a noble past, and he declared that Negroes should be proud of their ancestry. In his newspaper, *The Negro World*, he told Negroes that racial prejudice was so much a part of the civilization of the whites that it was futile to appeal to their sense of justice and their high-sounding democratic principles. With an eye to the growing sentiment favoring self-determination of dependent peoples, Garvey said that the only hope for Negro Americans was to flee America and return to Africa and build up a country of their own. On one occasion Garvey cried out: "Wake up Ethiopia! Wake up Africa! Let us work toward the one glorious end of a free, redeemed and mighty nation. Let Africa be a bright star among the constellation of nations." However, while he sent missions to Africa to explore land options, no one was ever repatriated back to Africa. Equally importantly, many of the people who surrounded Garvey, it can be pointed out, worked against him and his people's best interest.

Black Nationalism 98a. Barry Campbell and members of his organization, Veterans Quality of Life (The Forgotten Ones) that helps veterans get various forms of benefits.

BLACK NATIONALISM
ALIVE AND WELL

Black Nationalist 98b. Celebrated author, columnist and Harlemite Herb Boyd offers wisdom on the "Life and Times of Malcolm X" at Clarke House in Harlem.

Notwithstanding, Garvey was a master analyst, tactician, orator and man of action! Apprenticed in his youth as a printer, Garvey began printing his newspaper, *The Negro World* to get his message out and this certainly helped in expanding membership in the UNIA. After his travels in Latin America and Europe and then coming to America, he became acutely aware of the plight of Africans worldwide. Perhaps he looked in the mirror as Malcolm X would later say. According to Franklin (1987: 323), Garvey asked: "Where is the Black man's Government?" "Where is his King and

FREDERICK MONDERSON

Kingdom?" "Where is his President, his Country, and his Ambassador, his Army, his Navy, his Men of Big Affairs?" He said, "I could not find them and then declared, I will help to make them." That was the cataclysmic moment, when looking in the mirror, one sees the messiah!

Garvey then created titles to fit the positions of "men of big affairs." The nobility he created included: "Knights of the Nile, Knights of the Distinguished Service Order of Ethiopia, and Dukes of the Niger and Uganda." He also created the Duke of the Congo. His auxiliary organs included the Universal Black Cross Nurses, the Universal African Motor Corps, and the Black Eagle Flying Corps and to promote commerce between Africa and America, the Black Star Line.

Black Nationalism 99. Gentleman holds photograph of Judge John Phillips, founder and proprietor of the Slave Theater I and II in Brooklyn, whose powerful "Images decorated Mon's living room!"

Nonetheless, and again, many of the people who worked for him made the Black Star Line his "Achilles Heel." The captains, for the

BLACK NATIONALISM
ALIVE AND WELL

most part, sabotaged the ships so that they required more and more resources to operate and this became a drain, siphoning off resources for other projects. However, within four years after its founding in Harlem in 1917, the UNIA held its 1921 convention and Garvey put on a spectacular show of pomp, pride and performance.

Black Nationalism 100. Beauty - Physical and Botanical, "Kiss the Rose!"

Bradford Chambers' in *Chronicles of Black Protest* (1968: 165) offers commentary on Garvey's "Back to Africa Movement" in which he wrote: "The 1921 convention of the UNIA in New York was a prime example of Garvey's use of pageantry. Led by Garvey, in a uniform of purple, green and black – with gold-braid trimmings and a helmet crowned with flowing white feathers – 50,000 Garveyites and partisans from Harlem marched down Lenox Avenue. With flag and bands they paraded to Madison Square Garden for a mass rally. There they proclaimed Garvey the Provisional President-General of Africa. Splendid was the pomp and ceremony of the occasion. There was an invocation by the black archbishop of the African Orthodox Church, which Garvey created (complete with a Black Holy Trinity, a Black Christ of Sorrow, and a

FREDERICK MONDERSON

Black Madonna)." Also on display were contingents from the African Legion, the Black Cross Nurses, the African Motor Corps, and the Black Eagle Flying Corps. Garvey also had assistants in his role as President-General of Africa.

Even further, Bradford (1968: 166) continued: "He told his followers that Black men's only hope was to build an independent nation in Africa where they could choose their own leaders. He criticized interracial organizations such as the NAACP for their lack of concern for the ordinary black, and urged Black people to do something for themselves."

Naturally, Garvey like all great revolutionary visionaries who challenged behemoth systems of oppression, was betrayed, jailed, deported and died alone in London in 1940, far from his beloved UNIA in Harlem.

John Hope Franklin and Isidore Starr in *The Negro in 20th Century America* (1967: 110) quoted Garvey in which he states: "To fight for the African redemption does not mean that we must give up our domestic fight for political justice and industrial rights. It does not mean that we must become disloyal to any government or to any country wherein we were born. Each and every race outside of its domestic national loyalty had a loyalty to itself; therefore, it is foolish for the Negro to talk about not being interested in his own racial, political, social and industrial destiny. We can be as loyal American citizens as British subjects as the Irishman or the Jew, and yet fight for the redemption of Africa, a complete emancipation of the race."

Franklin (1967: 112) outlined the main points of the Preamble of the UNIA as stated by Garvey. "The Universal Negro Improvement Association and African Communities League is a social, friendly, humanitarian, charitable, educational, institutional, constructive, and egalitarian society, and is founded by persons, desiring to the utmost to work for the general uplift of the Negro peoples of the world. And the members pledge themselves to do all in their power to

BLACK NATIONALISM ALIVE AND WELL

conserve the rights of their noble race and to respect the rights of all mankind, believing always in the Brotherhood of man and the fatherhood of God. The motto of the organization is: One God! One Aim! One Destiny! Therefore, let justice be done to all mankind, realizing that if the strong oppress the weak confusion and discontent will ever mark the path of men, but with love, faith and charity towards all the reign of peace and plenty will be heralded into the world and the generation of men shall be called blessed."

Black Nationalism 101. Oh, that sweet angel called **MOTHER**!

Franklin (1967: 112) further added that the declared objectives of the association are: "To establish a universal Confraternity among the race; to promote the spirit of pride and love; to reclaim the fallen; to administer to and assist the needy; to assist in civilizing the

FREDERICK MONDERSON

backward tribes of Africa; to assist in the development of Independent Negro Nations and Communities; to establish a central nation for the race; to establish Commissaries or agencies in the principal countries and cities of the world for the representation of all Negroes; to promote a conscientious Spiritual worship among the native tribes of Africa; to establish Universities, Colleges, Academies and Schools for the racial education and culture of the people to work for better conditions among Negroes everywhere."

In a speech delivered at Liberty Hall, New York City, on November 25, 1922, Garvey outlined "The Principles of the Universal Negro Improvement Association" as presented in *The Philosophy and Opinions of Marcus Garvey* (New York: Athenaeum, 1971: 93-100):

"Over five years ago the Universal Negro Improvement Association placed itself before the world as the movement through which the new and rising Negro would give expression of his feelings. This Association adopts an attitude not of hostility to other races and peoples of the world, but an attitude of self-respect, of manhood rights on behalf of 400,000,000 Negroes of the world...

"We represent a new line of thought among Negroes. Whether you call it advanced thought or reactionary thought, I do not care. If it is reactionary for people to seek independence in government, then we are reactionary. If it is advanced thought for people to seek liberty and freedom, then we represent the advanced school of thought among the Negroes of this country. We of the UNIA believe that what is good for the other fellow is good for us. If government is something that is worthwhile; if government is something that is appreciable and helpful and protective to others, then we also want to experiment in government. We do not mean a government that will make us citizens without rights or subjections without consideration. We mean the kind of government that will place our race in control, even as other races are in control of their own governments...."

"I desire to remove the misunderstanding that has been created in the minds of millions of people throughout the world in their

BLACK NATIONALISM
ALIVE AND WELL

relationship to the organization. The Universal Negro Improvement Association stands for the Bigger Brotherhood; the Universal Negro Improvement Association stands for human rights; not only for Negroes, but for all races. The Universal Negro Improvement Association believes in the rights of not only the black race, but the white race, the yellow race and the brown race. The Universal Negro Improvement Association believes that the white man has as much right to be considered, the yellow man has as much right to be considered as the black man of Africa. In view of the fact that the Black man of Africa has contributed as much to the world as the white man of Europe, and brown man and yellow man of Asia, we of the Universal Negro Improvement Association demand that the white, yellow and brown races give to the black man his place in the civilization of the world. We ask for nothing more than the rights of 400,000,000 Negroes...."

Black Nationalism 102. Michele and Barack Obama dolls surround that of Abraham Lincoln.

FREDERICK MONDERSON

"We of the Universal Negro Improvement Association ... desire to bring together the 15,000,000 of the United States, the 180,000,000 in Asia, the West Indies and Central and South America, and the 200,000,000 in Africa. We are looking toward political freedom on the continent of Africa, the land of our fathers."

"The difference between the Universal Negro Improvement Association and the movements of this country, and possibly the world, is that the Universal Negro Improvement Association seeks independence of government, while the other organizations seek to make the Negro a secondary part of existing governments. We differ from the organizations in America because they seek to subordinate the Negro as a secondary consideration in a great civilization, knowing that the Negro in America will never reach his highest ambition, knowing that the Negro in America will never get his constitutional rights....You and I can live in the United States of America for 100 years, and our generations may live for 200 years or for 5,000 more years, and so long as there is black and white population, when the majority is on the side of the white race, you and I will never get political justice or get political equality in this country...."

"We are not preaching propaganda of hate against anybody. We love the white man; we love all humanity because we feel that we cannot live without the other. The white man is as necessary to the existence of the Negro as the Negro is necessary to his existence. There is a common relationship that we cannot escape. Africa has certain things that Europe wants, and Europe has certain things that Africa wants and if a fair and square deal must bring white and black with each other, it is impossible for us to escape it. Africa has oil, diamonds, copper, gold and rubber and all the minerals that Europe wants, and there must be some kind of relationship between Africa and Europe for a fair exchange, so we cannot afford to hate anybody."

BLACK NATIONALISM ALIVE AND WELL

Black Nationalism 103. This message is about freedom of worship!

Black Nationalism 103a. Barry Campbell leads his contingent down Fifth Avenue at the 2013 Veterans Day parade in Manhattan.

FREDERICK MONDERSON

"Wheresoever the cause of humanity stands in need of assistance, there you will find the Negro ever ready to serve."

"He has done it from the time of Christ up to now. When the whole world turned its back upon the Christ, the man who was said to be the Son of God; when the world spurned him and spat upon Him; it was a Black man, Simon, the Cyrenian, who took up the cross. Why? It was because the course of humanity appealed to him. When the Black man saw the suffering Jew, struggling under the heavy cross, he was willing to go to His assistance, and he bore the cross up to the heights of Cavalry. In the spirit of Simon, the Cyrenian, 1900 years ago, we answered the call of Woodrow Wilson, the call to a larger humanity, and it was for that we willingly rushed into the war ...."

"We have not forgotten the prowess of war. If we have been liberal minded enough to give our life's blood in France, in Mesopotamia and elsewhere, fighting for the White man, whom we have always assisted, surely we have not forgotten to fight for ourselves, and when the time comes that the world will again give Africa an opportunity for freedom, surely…black men will march out on the battle plains of Africa, under the colors of the red, the black and the green."

"We shall march out, yes, as Black American citizens, as Black British subjects, as Black French citizens, as Black Italians or as Black Spaniards, but we shall march out in answer to the cry of our fathers, who cries out to us for the redemption of our own country, our motherland, Africa."

"We shall march out, not forgetting the blessings of America. We shall march out, not forgetting the blessings of civilization. We shall march out with a history of peace before and behind us, and surely that history shall be our breastplate, for how can man fight better than knowing that the cause for which he fights is righteous? How can man fight more gloriously than by knowing that behind him is a history of slavery, a history of bloody carnage and massacre inflicted upon a race because of its inability to protect itself and fight? Shall we not fight for the glorious opportunity of protecting and forever

BLACK NATIONALISM
ALIVE AND WELL

more establishing ourselves as a mighty race and nation, never more to be disrespected by men? Glorious shall be the battle when the time comes to fight for our people and our race."

"We shall say to the millions who are in Africa to hold the fort, for we are coming 400,000,000 strong."

Black Nationalism 104. Reversing the process of enslavement!

Thus, Garvey was indeed an immortal African thinker whose timely appearance on the world stage became a wind beneath the Black

FREDERICK MONDERSON

man's sails and helped propel him, with not simply the wherewithal to improve himself in the significant parameters of social development. He instilled a new and forward reaching type of thinking that has helped him reach higher and higher heights. As a publisher, Garvey wrote and inspired his people on every conceivable subject from Propaganda, slavery, force, education, miscegenation, prejudice, radicalism, government, evolution and its results, poverty, power, universal suspicion, dissertation on man, race assimilation, Christianity, the functions of man, and traitors.

Then he wrote on Present day civilization, Divine apportionment of the earth, universal unrest in 1922, world disarmament, causes of wars, world readjustment, the fall of governments, great ideas know no nationality, purpose of creation, purity of race, man know thyself, a solution for world peace in 1922, god as a war lord and the image of god. Then he wrote some more on the slave trade, Negroes' status under alien governments, the Negro as an industrial makeshift, lack of co-operation in the Negro race, White man's solution for the Negro problem in America, the true solution of the Negro problem, white propaganda about Africa, the three stages of the Negro in contact with the White man, Booker T. Washington's Program, belief that race problems will adjust itself a fallacy, examples of White Christian control of Africa, the thought behind their deeds, similarity of persecution, shall the Negro be exterminated, Africa for the Africans, and the future as I see it.

Truly the man was a visionary well ahead for his time, a great thinker and man of action, whose success still propels Blacks and perhaps it was inevitable that he be betrayed and brought down. Convicted and handcuffed on his way to Atlanta federal Prison, he uttered, "You have caged the lion, but the cubs are still running around out there." And as equally inevitable, "Truth crushed to earth shall rise" and Garvey's aspirations and visions for the Black man is alive and well today under the Red, Black and Green.

BLACK NATIONALISM ALIVE AND WELL

Black Nationalism 104a. Following Sonny Carson's death, singers and dancers from Ghana came to pay tribute and so the Brothers did the **PUSH Ceremony** with the youngest Brother there!

10. Have We Forgotten Sonny Carson? By Dr. Fred Monderson

"A people who have forgotten their past, are like a tree without roots."

Have we forgotten Sonny Carson? If so, we have also forgotten Queen Mother Moore, Fannie Lou Hamer, Barbara Jordan, Sojourner Truth, Mary McLeod Bethune, Rosa Parks and Coretta Scott-King, Mother Jordan, great Black heroines who now rest with the Ancestors comprising the Black Pantheon!

FREDERICK MONDERSON

Naturally, we have not forgotten Martin Luther King, Jr., or Malcolm X. Equally, others have not forgotten for they too promote Martin Luther King Sale and Malcolm X Sale. What a pity!

Why has not a sale day set aside for Sonny Carson on May 18; Paul Robeson; Kwame Nkrumah; Marcus Garvey, August 17; WEB DuBois; Jackie Robinson; Countee Cullen; Claude McKay; Langston Hughes; Booker T. Washington; Frederick Douglass; Martin Delaney; Henry Highland Garnett; David Walker; Nat Turner; Crispus Attucks; and so on. So, if we're promoting sales let's remember everyone.

Black Nationalism 105. Sonny Carson accompanied by two Brothers, Rodney Adams (left) as the poster bill for the movie **The Education of Sonny Carson** stands over their shoulders.

Imagine, since Black people shop so much on the two aforementioned sale days; imagine how much more they would spend if sale days were promoted on the birth and death days of the above. After all, isn't it about money? Nevertheless, and naturally, since some may think this is an exercise in futility, I beg to differ. It is, however, to prove a point that some of our leaders' names are not

BLACK NATIONALISM
ALIVE AND WELL

commercially lucrative. Hence, we must struggle to retain control of their image, persona and philosophic outlook and revolutionary perspective. Hopefully this book is a first step!

Sonny Carson remained obdurate in his revolutionary outlook and demands for Black liberation through economic emancipation, educational advancement and social upliftment. He adamantly opposed the prison industrial complex for its evisceration of the psychological aspirations of Black manhood, trampled upon constantly on a day-to-day basis. Sonny was, however, acutely aware, our people contribute much to their travail by boldly walking into traps set by their captors and oppressors.

Sonny "AB," Abubadika Carson, was equally and unalterably opposed to the scourge of drugs in our community; police brutality; racism; inferior education; joblessness; the lack of encouragement for respectable and admirable leaders and leadership. He despaired that young people do not have sufficient credible contemporary heroes to emulate. That is, despite sports figures, actors and musicians, who are constantly fed to the young on a false and deceptive premise.

In fact, one of the major fights Sonny had with the musical giants, Sony, ET. Al. is their fostering the portrayal of Blacks as gangsters through the lyrics of their promoted music. Unfortunately, as our demands for Black ownership in the music industry proved successful, the lyrics never got better. It's like Rev. Al Sharpton said in his eulogy for James Brown, "'How did we get from 'Say it loud, I'm Black and proud' to 'Bitches and hos?'"

FREDERICK MONDERSON

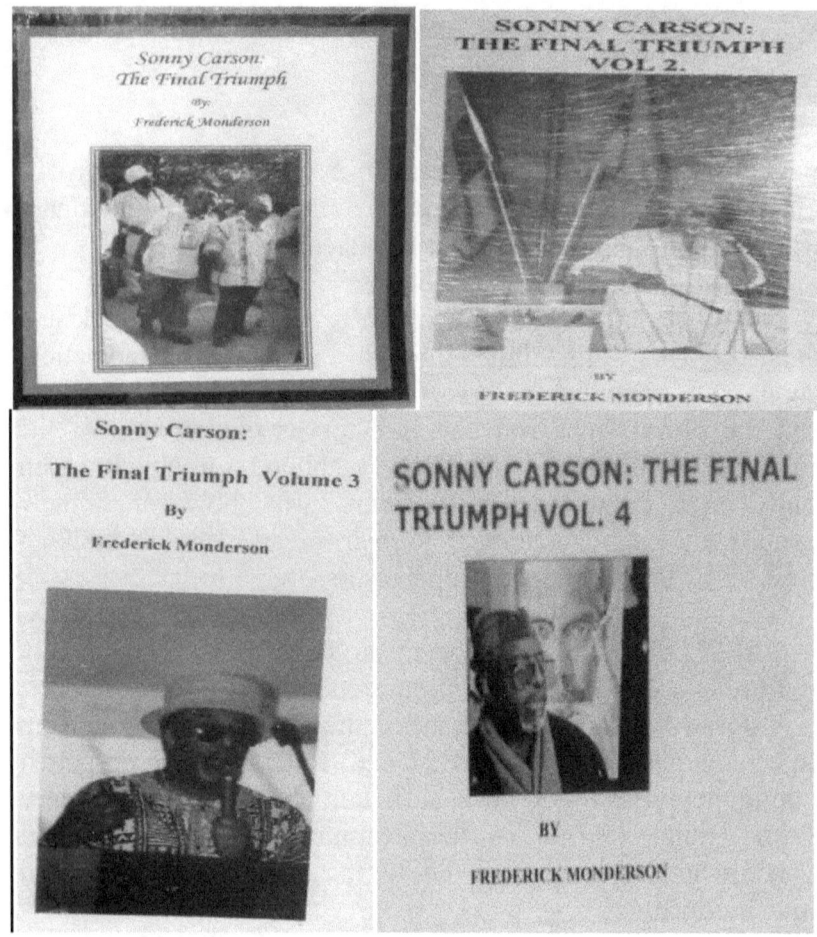

Black Nationalism 106. Sonny Carson's *The Final Triumph* in 4 volumes.

Championing creative and clean musical lyrics in his "Tone it down" admonition, Sonny Carson proved a multi-issue activist. Granted, he got bad-publicity for the Ocean-Hill-Brownsville struggle to decentralize the New York City school system owing to its improper representation of Blacks and Hispanics in teaching and administrative positions, he remained steadfastly an education advocate. He was concerned with the plight of derelict landlords, poor housing, and lack of ownership of the economic infrastructure of the Black community. As such, particularly when merchants dealt

BLACK NATIONALISM
ALIVE AND WELL

egregiously with Black patrons, he led economic boycotts that were not universally praised. Sonny Carson founded; was a founding member; or advocated the founding of several organizations. The Restoration Corporation in Bedford-Stuyvesant that spawned economic revitalization of this hub of the Black community is one such entity. He was active in the evolution of Malcolm-King College into Medgar Evers College. Despite this at one of its graduation ceremonies he complained; saying, "I thought I was in Greece. Where are the drums, the preponderance of African cultural motifs that connect with the African heritage?"

Black Nationalism 107. The "Man" and "Master" Judge John L. Phillips, responsible for the murals of the two movie houses, "The Slave Theater I and II."

FREDERICK MONDERSON

In 1968, after the assassination of Martin Luther King, the then Mayor John Lindsey personally appealed to Sonny Carson as a leader of substance to quell any acts of looting and violence. And, Sonny accepted the challenge.

Sonny Carson founded the Committee to Honor Black Heroes and set about changing the names of streets, Viz., Malcolm X Boulevard, Martin Luther King Boulevard and instrumental in naming Harriet Ross Tubman Avenue. He also changed schools such as Malcolm X and Toussaint L'Ouverture and had a host of others in the pipeline before his demise. He also founded Black Men Against Crack and the Black Men's Movement. Despite his advocacy against police brutality and misconduct, many top brass in the Police Department respected Sonny for his principled activism.

Sonny Carson's **Final Triumph** came when the U.S. navy discovered the remains of Sonny's ancestor Samuel Carson, "The Runaway," who served and died in the Mexican-American War in 1845. He was buried in the Brooklyn Navy yard. Utilizing one of his strengths, Sonny set up the "Bones Committee" that met for nearly 2 years and finally resolved to repatriate "The runaway" through "The Door of Return" into Ghana. In this he created a memorial site of pilgrimage for African-Americans seeking their cultural and ancestral roots in Africa.

That farcical display of New York City Council denying the naming of a street in Bed-Stuy for Sonny Carson is more of a shame on their part. As one commentator wrote: "The Revolution was in the hearts and minds of the people;" and so it was whether in the street or the park, the name Sonny Carson still resonates in the minds and hearts of the people. That is why today Bed-Stuy is called **Abubadikaville**!

BLACK NATIONALISM ALIVE AND WELL

Black Nationalism 108. Mr. Caldwell, President of the 77th Precinct Council shakes hands with Erik Monderson.

Now, with all the challenges facing Blacks today; not discounting many who act foolishly; if we think about it, only Al Sharpton is out there as a true activist. Hence, we cannot afford to forget Robert Sonny Carson, "AB" Abubadika, and what he stood for in terms of Black elevation and advancement, educational upliftment, creative but respective musical lyrics, decent housing, and full-employment for Blacks, while saying no to police brutality, racism and racial profiling. May the spirit of Sonny Carson prevail!

FREDERICK MONDERSON

Black Nationalism 108a. The Brothers doing **PUSH**!

11. MARJORIE MATTHEWS: HEALTH CARE ADVOCATE EXTRAORDINAIRE!
By
Dr. Fred Monderson

For years, in fact decades, Marjorie Matthews had been an activist, advocate, leader and humanitarian in the Bedford Stuyvesant and Central Brooklyn communities. In fact, she had been a conscience of these communities and as a parent had been a gadfly holding educators to the highest standards, not simply for her children, but children in general. With a child in Brownsville school district, she would surprise teachers, appearing in their classrooms, enquiring about her child while casting a penetrating and critical eye on how others were doing.

BLACK NATIONALISM
ALIVE AND WELL

Mrs. Matthews was a member of Community Board 3 in Bedford Stuyvesant and worked out of their Restoration office, soon rising to be Chairman of Transportation with membership on health care and other committees. Because of her dedicated efforts towards community upliftment, Ms. Matthews was appointed to the Kings County Community Advisory Board during the tenure of Enid Forde who was chairman. She served under Dr. Waldaba Stewart, became chairman herself and was succeeded by Ben Whitehorn and Dr. Frederick Monderson who was followed by Mr. Kenneth Campbell.

Black Nationalism 109. Marjorie Matthews, extraordinary education, health care and community activist.

Years later upon her passing, the Community Board decided on naming one of its conference rooms in honor of Ms. Matthews. The ceremony was held in the main conference room with Dr. Monderson as the event's Master of Ceremonies. He in turn invited Mr. Jitu Weusi, that veritable community activist, educator and social icon. When it was his turn to speak, as he rose he said, "You

FREDERICK MONDERSON

may know me as Les Campbell, I was a teacher in Brownsville and Ms. Matthews would often come to my classroom because one of her daughters was my student." Then he went into how as apparent advocate, especially during the Brownsville-Ocean-Hill struggle to decontrol the educational system resulting in the creation of School Planning Boards, Ms. Matthews was an active member. She often worked with and kept Sonny Carson, who spearheaded that movement when he was Chair of Brooklyn Congress of Racial Equality, on his toes, challenging him and also advising him and the movement.

Mrs. Matthews greatest accomplishment seems to have been after she succeeded to the Chairmanship of the Kings County Community Advisory Board and began the process of not using the term advisory but insisting on, what Agnes Abraham, a later Chairman, often likes to say, "Keeping the fire under the feet" of politicians and Ms. Jean Leon, the then Executive Director of the hospital. Though many have chosen to down-play Ms. Leon's leadership, working in consort with Marje, Ms. Leon initiated the structural transformation of health-care in Central Brooklyn by forcing the powers that be to begin the many phase re-construction of Kings County.

In her leadership role, Ms. Matthews earned the appellate -"When Marje Matthews speaks, people listen!"

The hospital entered a phase where the institution's reputation was suffering because of the outdated facility that led to an antiquated system of treatment or patient care. At that time, some did argue, Mayor Giuliani did not favor building the hospital. Yet, some even believed, the city was paying to hoard the building materials somewhere in Pennsylvania. Taxing her skillful organizational abilities to steer the hospital through these challenging years, Ms. Leon found an ally in Marje Matthews even though as Chairman she insisted on top quality administration. The old master tactician also teamed up with Jim Butler, head of the local union and orchestrated a massive health care demonstration in front of Kings County, blocking all traffic on Clarkson Avenue where the people jeered the Mayor calling him names. The impact was so profound, the city

BLACK NATIONALISM
ALIVE AND WELL

relented and agreed to fund Phase I of the reconstruction program. It was their finest hour!

Black Nationalism 110. His Imperial Majesty Haile Selassie.

In this strategic organizational success was actually born the aphorism? "When Marje Matthews speaks, people listen!" However, not content to sit on her laurels, Ms. Matthews began training young members in the dynamics of health care advocacy at a time when Health and Hospitals Corporation's young yet senior administrators were coming into their own, demonstrating their meticulous knowledge and organizational abilities as the hospital system began to remake itself.

FREDERICK MONDERSON

Then Marje took Frederick Monderson under her wings and taught him the inns and outs of health care advocacy and who the principal players were. As such, whether it was HHC's headquarters, the Bronx, Kings County or any hospital where health care matters came under review, if Marje was there, people came to expect she would say something and it would be meaningful.

Working in consort with Jean Leon and Jim Hansen, the master architect and planner, always with a smile and pleasant disposition, Marje launched Phase I in building the Bed Tower and oversaw the G-Building makeover setting in motion the overall greater makeover of the hospital landscape; while seeing to better training of the staff to complete the full cycle of health care transformation in Central Brooklyn. As fate would have it, the Bed Tower, D-Building, would welcome Ms. Matthews at the end of her life's journey. "You are what you are" is the true reality as a person's life work comes to an end. Contributions made to the betterment of the society in general and mankind in particular are testimony to a life of service. As such, thankful colleagues rushed to show gratitude to Marje Matthews by extolling her name in the Conference Room, having her image made a permanent fixture and establishing the Marje Matthews Award to reward the countless people involved in ongoing advocacy for the betterment of health care recipients in the City of New York under the unrelenting efforts of New York city's Health and hospital Corporation.

BLACK NATIONALISM ALIVE AND WELL

Black Nationalism 110a. Dr. Leonard Jeffries speaks at Clarke House on Malcolm X but delves into how things are getting better in Africa and does so by the use of illustrations.

12.   "A BLACK AGENDA?"
By
Dr. Fred Monderson

On Thursday January 29, 2009, radio personality Bob Law, of *Night Talk* fame, sponsored a Forum and posed the provocative question, "In wake of the Obama victory, should there be a Black Agenda or Black Strategy?" He asked further, "Is it necessary?" This was held at Bethany Baptist Church on Marcus Garvey Boulevard in Brooklyn. The Panelists consisted of Council Member Charles Baron and his wife, newly elected Assemblywoman Inez Baron, as well as columnist Herb Boyd, Assemblyman Karim Camara, Divine Pryor, Ph. D of Medgar Evers' New Leadership Council and Eddie Ellis,

FREDERICK MONDERSON

Executive Director of the New Leadership Policy Group, a branch of the New Leadership Policy Group at Medgar Evers, College of City

Black Nationalism 111. Collage of "The Prophet Marcus Moziah Garvey." May he live forever!

University of New York (CUNY). Apparently they were responding to a position taken by Illinois Congressman Jessie Jackson Jr. among others that, "This is a post-race generation," particularly since the 2008 election of Barack Obama as President of the United States.

After Bob Law had set out the parameters of the discussion, Assemblywoman Inez Baron began by saying: "Peace and power. Now is an exciting time to be alive. Make it real in our community,

BLACK NATIONALISM ALIVE AND WELL

block by block organizing to create solutions before taking it to a national level."

Council Member Charles Barron, commenting on the recent popular election of now President Barack Obama explained there was a 62 percent Black turnout and this was the largest ever; 95 percent of Black voters and 43 percent of White voters voted for Barack Obama. He did emphasize these numbers. However, what is interesting about the percent of Black turnout is, though this was 62 percent and the highest, it also raised questions about Black voter participation. Now, everyone has agreed the Obama candidacy, given all the phenomena attached to it, particularly the post election memorabilia grab, one has to wonder what it would take to get even higher Black turnout rates. After all, this was one of the best "Black candidates" ever and we were so far from 100 percent which means there must be more registration and voter participation.

Again, Charles Baron, commenting on a statement by Newark Mayor Cory Booker, perhaps echoing something Colin Powell said about Barack Obama, is that he is "an American who happens to be Black," was an issue of contention. Baron used the analogy of "a doctor who happens to be Chinese." No, he is a Chinese doctor, the Councilman emphasized! Personally, I think there is a big difference between what Powell and Booker said, even though it seems they said the same thing. Powell seemed to be viewing the issue from the top down or a national or international perspective and Booker from a local or bottom up approach.

Baron went on to point out, if Jesse Jackson, Sr. had not run in 1984 and again in 1988, there would be no Barack Obama! He also pointed out some of the pitfalls of Jesse's campaign is that they included calls for reparations and insistence on a Black Agenda. He also pointed to the forgiving nature of Obama who could forgive John McCain, Hillary Clinton and Joe Lieberman. Jokingly he said, perhaps "Farrakhan should have done the Invocation; Jesse Jackson the Introduction; and Rev. Wright the Benediction."

FREDERICK MONDERSON

Assemblyman Karim Camara pointed to the historic conflicts between the leaders DuBois and Washington; Dr. King and Malcolm X; and Louis Farrakhan and Jesse Jackson. Then he asked whether this is the "end of Black politics?" Commenting on statistics for poor educational performance, high rates of prison incarceration, poor health and economics in the Black community, these things requires there be an urban agenda. Emphasizing spirituality and economic development he insisted "government is one resource; but we must return to our spiritual tradition. We must have business and religious leaders at the table to discuss the issues and problems."

Always the story teller, Bob Law began telling stories of how the community can act in unison to correct a problem. He mentions one night on his *Night Talk* show, a young woman was in need of a liver transplant worth $100,000 and he asked the audience to donate and voila, they did, and so she got the funds. Again, he mentions a similar such action to buy the *Lorraine Motel* where Dr. King was shot and this the audience also did, then handed it over to the King Center to complete the process of turning it into a museum. Further he told of how a church group appealed to a supermarket for assistance and was rebuffed by the owner. That Monday every member from the church who shopped at the supermarket told the cashier, "I'm from church X." On Tuesday the pastor called the supermarket and enquired if anyone from his church shopped there. The excited owner responded, "Oh yes. We had so many people from your church, I'm really pleased." The pastor replied, "Just as I told them to shop there, I can tell them not to shop there." The owner fell in line. It does, however, underscore the power of the pulpit as it can affect spending. Finally, he told of how word went out from 500 churches one Sunday, "Don't buy a certain product" and by Tuesday the pastor got numerous calls.

BLACK NATIONALISM
ALIVE AND WELL

Black Nationalism 112. Senator Erik Adams shakes hands with Erik Monderson at Sharpton's Affair.

FREDERICK MONDERSON

Black Nationalism 113. Malcolm X will live forever!

Therefore, Bob Law urged we must "use our tangible and intangible wealth." Tangible wealth is money and intangible wealth is whatever else. Then he began arguing how the ground has shifted under blacks by giving statistics showing: 10 percent of Black Americans are 2 weeks from poverty; 70 percent of Black Americans live in 10 major cities, but they are nearly 100 percent consumers. Blacks own one half of one percent of the nation's wealth. While White unemployment rate is 6%, that of Black is 35% and among Hispanics its 80%; 96% of Blacks are dependent on income outside of their neighborhoods.

Elsewhere and equally relevant, Martin Luther King III commenting on whether his father's dream has been fulfilled offered: "As long as there are 37 plus million people living in poverty, the dream will not be fulfilled; as long as we live in a nation where more than 47 million have no health insurance, the dream has not been fulfilled, as long as we live in a nation where the criminal justice system has

BLACK NATIONALISM ALIVE AND WELL

millions of people and just about 50 percent of those are people of color, the dream will not be fulfilled." Clearly these disparities require some form of response and that must be part of a broader Black agenda.

I'm reminded of the movie, *The Education of L.B. Jones* where the statement was made that traditional Black businesses were "Numbers," "Liquor Stores" and "Funeral Parlors." Well, the states have seized the numbers business, Blacks have lost liquor stores, and often many are now owned by Koreans. Who knows which way the funeral business will go in future? He also gives as an example of dwindling Black local businesses. In the Black community, Koreans now own more than 90% of vegetable stands, nail salons, cleaners and now liquor stores. I was once in Maryland visiting friends who took me to buy some seafood. As you probably know, Maryland is famous for crabs. Would you know, the one seafood place we visited was owned by Koreans and they hired no Black help? Yet, would you also believe, as we waited untold numbers of Blacks were lined up to purchase seafood from this store. This is a perfectly good example of outsiders coming and controlling a resource in the Black community, then selling it back to us. Talk about 1200 percent consumers! Then Bob Law talked of how Disney, Viacom and Clear Channel have control of the airwaves and the FCC no longer pays much attention to Black ownership of this media that now comes under the heading of minority ownership. As such, Black ownership is in the decline and remaining Black radio is kept poor by design.

FREDERICK MONDERSON

Black Nationalism 113a. Members of **"The Brotherhood**," Ofori Payton (left); Diallo, Bishop Shivers (second from right); Atiim Ferguson and the Bishop's son who presents Sonny Carson "Holding Forth the Light."

Next it was Eddie Ellis, an ex-felon and now Executive Director of the New Leadership Policy Group at Medgar Evers College assisted by Dr. Divine Pryor that is spearheading a new project of return to integrate felons coming home. Mr. Ellis' definition of success is "When opportunity meets preparation." He pointed out, "We always had a Black Agenda. What has happened is the ability to move that agenda forward." He mentioned, 25,000,000 people have a prison

BLACK NATIONALISM
ALIVE AND WELL

record in this country; 700,000 coming back to urban centers; each year 25,000 ex-cons are returning to New York City; 7 neighborhoods in New York provide 75% of all prisoners in New York; and that 75% of all prisoners are Black!

Black Nationalism 114. In Haiti, Connie Lesold of Crown Heights, Brooklyn, and Madame Marie Rene, Founder and Chancellor of the University of the Haitian Academy (First in New York and then in Haiti,) sandwich **Sister** who was the sole survivor of a convent demolished during the Earthquake.

Journalist Herb Boyd introduced two acronyms. TEP and TOP. When he realized he would be on the panel he taught of it being staffed by talent, eloquence and perspicacity and The Obama Paradox. He reminded many on the left voted for McCain. "We have to develop an economic stimulus initiative, which should emphasize,

FREDERICK MONDERSON

'Unless you advertise in my media, I will not buy your product." But we must also Buy Black.

Bob Law asked to be reminded of Adam Clayton Powell's mantra: "What's in your hand?" The answer is $1,000,000,000,000 (one thousand billion) earning power of American Blacks! Spend it wisely. Create an economic development fund; save independent schools; spend your dollars among Black businesses. He went on to say many young Blacks are beginning to believe the "Biggie Smalls" reality is their own, rather than the Barack Obama's. Strange that recently, Dr. Leonard Jeffries said Black youth are leading with their pants down rather than with their brains. We see even Japanese youth are emulating Barack Obama as they learn English. So, where does that leave our kids?

Stay tuned, another meeting on the Black Agenda will follow.

Black Nationalism 115. Much loved by all Americans, President John Fitzgerald Kennedy!

BLACK NATIONALISM ALIVE AND WELL

13. CEMOTAP, RON DANIELS AND HAITI
By
Dr. Fred Monderson

To celebrate Dr. James McIntosh's 62nd Birthday, April 24, 2010, his Co-Chair of **CEMOTAP** Betty Dobson invited Distinguished Scholar Dr. Ron Daniels to speak on "The Rise of Haiti." In keeping with a previous pronouncement by Dr. McIntosh that "Betty determines who speaks" while he "focuses on World Peace," the Keynote Speaker was right on target, with his "A Game" as he reflected on past, present and future scenarios on Haiti, in light of recent developments. Upcoming, on May 22, **CEMOTAP** will celebrate 23 years and have Haki Madhabuti as Keynote speaker.

To begin, 83 year-old Rev. Norris, Pastor Emeritus of Bethesda Missionary Church opened the proceedings with a prayer. With a blessing he began, "What a privilege it is to carry everything to God in Prayer. Oh what trials and tribulations we face, Oh what pain we often bear, because we do not carry everything to God in prayer." Then he sketched out his relationships to the principals and gave his blessings before he had to depart.

In introducing the Guest Speaker, Dr. McIntosh informed Dr. Ron Daniels, founder and President of the Institute of the Black World, was helping Haiti before it was popular, long before the earthquake. For long, he took medicine, school supplies and people to Haiti. This spotlight is so appropriate for a man seeming to possess boundless energy, remarkable vision and an articulateness that compares with the best of modern orators. He indicated Dr. Daniels had written the "Black Pledge."

FREDERICK MONDERSON

Black Nationalism 116. The Presidential Palace in Haiti after the Earthquake that wrecked havoc on that poor island.

In a tour de force oration, some call an "A-GAME," Dr. Daniels waylaid the issue of Haiti, focusing on a multitude of contexts, viz., history, culture, religion, medicine, liberation, Pan-Africanism, ethnicity, tourism, the Clintons, and the roles of indigenous and Diasporian Haitians as well as Black Americans in the Renaissance of the New Haiti. The master, in articulated artistry, sketched side by side murals of the significance and symbolism of the old and new Haiti. To achieve such, he pointed to Haiti as being contextualized within the Haitian Revolution; but even this phenomenon needs be assessed within a broader framework of greater and more deadly implications of the slave experience, the MAAFA or Great Enslavement. To explicate such, he referenced two phenomenal classics, Eric Williams' *Capitalism and Slavery* and Walter Rodney's *How Europe Under-Developed Africa*. A third equally important volume in the tragedy and triumph of Haiti is C.L.R. James' masterful *The Black Jacobins*, about the Haitian Revolution.

First, Ron Daniels referred to a *New York Times* article of Friday, April 23, 2010, wherein the "Professor at the Beer Summit" Skip Gates decried calls for reparations because "Africans were involved in the Slave trade." Pointing out that slavery existed from the earliest times, Daniels insisted British and American chattel slavery

BLACK NATIONALISM
ALIVE AND WELL

was different and much more brutal! He did admit some Africans were involved in selling other Blacks, but as stooges of the White man. He likened this behavior to the drug dealer plague in the Black community; but these too are also stooges of the drug barons who poison our communities. Nevertheless, and whereas from ancient times people were considered slaves from military, cultural or ethnic perspectives; New World slavery was racial! Previously persons were enslaved from circumstances, but they had families, owned property and could even attain high levels in a society, but this was not so in the Americas.

He argued that while any slavery should not be condoned, Africans did not initiate Trans-Atlantic Slave Trade nor were they its primary beneficiaries. They did not get ships and begin trading with the New World; but Africans were brutally victimized in the institutions of slave trade and slavery. This is why, because of his fact, Africans should not have overlooked, but have had a passion for, Haiti because of the incredible phenomenon of its experience. He argued, the Haitian Revolution was the most phenomenal compared to the other two, American and French; that is, within the context of human rights in that age. As such, the American Revolution, whose watchword was "life, liberty and the pursuit of happiness" was about political representation within the British Empire. However, the French Revolution was class representation within the French cultural context. The Haitian Revolution was about physical freedom and liberation of the human spirit. All this developed within the rise of Europe, its expansion overseas and subsequent conquest, extermination, domination and exploitation of non-white people, giving rise to the notion of "white supremacy."

FREDERICK MONDERSON

Black Nationalism 117. President Lynden Johnson, successor who established continuity of President Kennedy's "Great Society Program" which brought to fruition the **1964 Civil Rights Act** and the **1965 Voting Rights Act**.

Europeans intruded into Africa, Daniels explained, and diffused Africans all over the New World; to be enslaved in European plantation culture, manned by Europeans, benefitting Europeans and Europe. In that horrifying experience, European overseas expansion was fueled by economic theories of "bullionism," "specie accumulation" through "mercantilism" that regulated "balance of trade" and other capitalist and imperialist strategies and practices as propounded by the Adam Smiths of the age. In this unusual experience Europeans continued a practice of conquering, brutalizing and killing while instilling a superior/inferior people oriented mentality. As Dr. Daniels pointed out, "No where until now, was race used as a basis for subjugation of a people."

BLACK NATIONALISM
ALIVE AND WELL

Black Nationalism 118. President Bertrand Aristide of Haiti who erected this memorial to the **Haitian Constitution of 1801** in homage to Toussaint L'Ouverture (1743-1803).

Then he showed even ancient chauvinism was based on culture, nationality, but never on race. Even the Greeks, the ancient Greeks, saw non-Greeks as inferior because of their nationality, not their

FREDERICK MONDERSON

race! Cletus, Commander of Alexander's regiment was African. So too, the Romans who viewed others not on race but culture. Sappho and Aesop were Africans. They were African Emperors and many of the theorists of the early Christian church, the "church fathers" were Africans. Herodotus, the "father of history" praised the ancient Ethiopians as "the most just of men." The most beautiful people! Certainly he did not consider them inferior. Only until the Atlantic Slave Trade with its horrendous "Middle Passage" and dehumanizing "Triangular Trade" was race made a factor. Here was the "crafting of race" and white over Black with "Black at the back and base" of the "White supremacy myth."

Therefore, the nature of "white supremacy" is such that white is superior and black is inferior and all shades lie between. This was instrumental in the old adage: "If you are white, you're right; if you're brown you could stick around; if you're yellow, you're mellow; but if you're black, get back!" So they crafted the theory of race, and created Caucasoid, Mongoloid and Negroid races of peoples, with Negroid or black farthest from white. To divide and further subjugate the black race they bastardized them; then they created octoroons, quadroons, maroons, etc.

Dr. Daniels explained; the American Revolution (1776-1783) was essentially a fight between the British and their colonial kin. Africans were enslaved as less than humans. The French Revolution (1789-1791) was a class struggle among French men. Both the British and Americans and the French were involved in subjugating, exploiting and dehumanizing Africans in institutions of slavery while still proclaiming "All men are born free and are created equal, endowed by their creator with life, liberty and the pursuit of happiness" and equally calls of "liberty, equality, fraternity." This exclusion meant Africans were not men!

BLACK NATIONALISM
ALIVE AND WELL

Black Nationalism 119. The National Cathedral after the earthquake that was so devastating.

The Haitians stood up! They said No! "We are men! No to slavery! Haiti will be free!" They launched the Haitian Revolution to uphold the contention, rid their island of slavery and in process, unintentionally sent a message to nations that subjugated fellow men. These Black men and women of Haiti gave us dignity when we were down on our knees. This stance was to ultimately prove very costly for Haiti.

Black Nationalism 120. President Bertrand Aristide and friends in New York.

FREDERICK MONDERSON

The Haitian Revolution was led by Toussaint L'Ouverture, who, though he won the battle lost the war. After defeating the French he believed he could develop a cordial relationship with France. He was a statesman! However, while some French wanted to accommodate his aspirations, creating Haiti as an Overseas Department with Toussaint L'Ouverture as its governor; then along came Napoleon Bonaparte who viewed such actions as "uppity" and insisted Haiti must be re-conquered. In order for him to confront the British and Americans in North America, he had to hold on to Haiti. In order to exploit the enormous potential riches of the Mississippi River valley, he had to subjugate Haiti! So Napoleon invited Toussaint to France and kidnapped him. Toussaint died in a French dungeon. The Haitians got serious and declared their independence from France under Dessalines on January 1, 1804.

Buckman came to Haiti from Jamaica in 1791 and proved a tremendous force to the revolution. The leaders, men and women, "prayed and provided the spiritual power that undergirded the revolution." Haiti had sent Black men to fight at the "Battle of Savannah" during the American Revolution. These soldiers "had learned the ways of the white man." They learned military techniques in the American Revolution and put them to good use against the French, British and Spanish. Equally they had seen "The white man's god!" They had seen the behaviors of those who preached and practiced the white man's religion. This they rejected, prayed and affirmed, "Our God is a just God! Our God will not fail us." What they were recognizing was one god no matter what he was called.

BLACK NATIONALISM
ALIVE AND WELL

Black Nationalism 121. Heroes of the Haitian Revolution are enshrined in statue.

Black Nationalism 122. The People and their Liberators in Haiti.

FREDERICK MONDERSON

Black Nationalism 123. Marcus Garvey among other art expressions.

Black Nationalism 124. Washington Avenue, a street, dedicated to Mary Pinkett.

14. WASHINGTON AVENUE NAMED FOR MARY GLOVER PINKETT BY Dr. Fred Monderson

The venerated Mary Glover-Pinkett was immortalized in a street naming on her birthday, September 8, 2005 in her beloved Crown Heights, Brooklyn. Washington Avenue from Atlantic Ave to Eastern Parkway will now be named Mary Pinkett Avenue. The City Council has also approved a measure to extend it down to Park

BLACK NATIONALISM
ALIVE AND WELL

Avenue. Now, a move is afoot to also extend the new street name from Atlantic Avenue to Empire Blvd.

Black Nationalism 125. Image of Marcus Garvey as portrayed by Ron Bob Semple.

Mary Pinkett was an extraordinary citizen, a wonderful person, and full of charisma, intellect, very articulate and tremendously religious. A fighter, she had the gift of charm and so many she befriended, clashed with, debated and even challenged people of all persuasions. In turn, they sang praises of her ability to persuade, cajole and bring them around to see it her way. A lover of children, she knew and supported the benefits of education; she had a deep sense of loyalty and cared deeply for elder citizens. She was a good and staunch

FREDERICK MONDERSON

friend; her arms were always reaching out. "Thank god for Mary Glover-Pinkett."

The first African American woman to serve in the New York City Council, church member and labor leader, Mary Glover-Pinkett left Brooklyn and New York City a better place than she found it. As such, then, the individuals who came out to honor her at the memorial sang praises of her personality, abilities, daring, articulateness and an overall caring, loving spouse and good friend and colleague.

Councilwoman Leticia James sponsored the Ceremonial Co-Naming of Washington Avenue in Honor of the late Council Member Mary Glover-Pinkett where special thanks was given to the Parks Department; Community Boards 2, 8, and 9; Medgar Evers College; Police Officer Jamal Moore; Ms. N'Kenge Simpson-Hoffman; Lafayette Presbyterian Church; "Cake Man Raven" and NYPD Color Guards.

Rev. Clinton Miller of Brown Memorial Baptist Church offered the Opening Prayer and the National Anthem, the **Star Spangled Banner** was sung by Police Officer Jamel Moore and Ms. N'Kenge Simpson Hoffman sang the Negro National Anthem, **Lift Every Voice and Sing**. After remarks by Mrs. Sahidha Murell, Mary's former Chief of Staff and Ms. Mary King the former Legislative Aide; Dr. Edison O. Jackson, President of Medgar Evers College spoke of his acquaintance with Mary. He praised Mary Pinkett for her untiring and valuable support for Medgar Evers College. Initially intending to name a Lecture Hall in Mary's name, he now proposes to name the new building on Bedford Avenue for Mary Glover-Pinkett. He wants, besides students and faculty, "even the people driving down Bedford Avenue will see the building and know Mary Glover-Pinkett."

Police Commissioner Raymond W. Kelly praised Mary for two decades ago he commanded the 84th Precinct and this is where she lived and he heard and learned from her. Marty Markowitz, Borough

BLACK NATIONALISM
ALIVE AND WELL

President of Brooklyn, praised Mary. He tells of how years ago the Rabbis told him, "You want to please us, do like Mary does!" Ms. Lillian Roberts, President of District Council 37, Ernest Logan, Executive Vice-President, CSA and Mrs. Ophelia Perry, President, Church Women United, all lavished praises on Mary Pinkett for her sincerity, honesty, care and concern for the young and old, love of education and for being a staunch labor leader and church person.

Mr. Robert Matthews, Chairman of Community Board 8 spoke in praise of Mary Pinkett, so too did Dr. Fred Monderson, Chairman of Board 8's Transportation Committee who was appointed to the Community Board by Mary Pinkett some 20 years ago. He also worked with Mary on the "Save the Franklin Avenue Shuttle" campaign, one of her victorious accomplishments. Pearl Miles, District Manager of Community Board 9 spoke in praise of the hardworking, serious and charming Mary Pinkett. The Manager of Community Board 2 also praised Mary.

Black Nationalism 126. Logo of Al Sharpton's "Keepers of the Dream 2011."

Later at the Luncheon, Mike Gerstin, Candidate for Judge in Brooklyn praised Mary for her desire to "Serve her community and to serve nobly." Sahidha Murrell her Chief of Staff again praised

FREDERICK MONDERSON

Mary Pinkett saying "So many people continue her legacy. So many people owe so much to her. She demanded a lot from everyone. She made women stronger. She's our angel but Mr. Pinkett is our Saint." Chanina Sperlin said, "If she felt for something she was there. Mary worked for the entire community, African Americans, Caribbean Americans, Jewish and Haitians. Anne Bowen told of how Mary kept the BMT from being eliminated and how she forced the MTA to keep the B-51 to City Hall, Pace University and Chinatown from being eliminated also. Jackie Mitchell said she learned very early from Mary, 'the squeaky wheel gets the grease. Once you identify the problem, what you do about it is what matters!' "You feel a sense of empowerment from her. People were devoted to her because she gave personal attention to their problems."

Black Nationalism 127. Dr. Roscoe Lee Brown (right) and an associate, both members of "Tuskegee Airmen," famous fighters during World War II.

Connie Lesold praised Mary for the work she did with her husband Helmut on the "Franklin Avenue Shuttle" and "Eastern Parkway Reconstruction." However, more forcefully she affirmed: "Mary Pinkett's work would have died on the vine had it not been for the hard work of Dr. Fred Monderson who fought for the Franklin Avenue Shuttle, wrote more than half a dozen articles on the Shuttle

BLACK NATIONALISM
ALIVE AND WELL

for the *Daily Challenge* and proposed the street naming as Chairman of Traffic and Transportation for Community Board 8."

Black Nationalism 128. Toussaint L'Ouverture, Haitian Liberator.

Mr. William Pinkett also came in for some praise because he shared his wife with the community for the 28 years she served in the council. He thanked the people who shared their reflection of Mary and special thanks for the "309 Lafayette Crew." He reminded all of Mary's working philosophy: "Look out for one another. Don't dwell on differences. Keep an eye on the prize. Keep looking forward." In the video tribute to Mary she tells the Human Rights Commission "We want equal rights, equal access" and to "The Monarch of City Hall" she said: "Be the Mayor of the entire city!"

FREDERICK MONDERSON

15. Rev. Al Sharpton: The Next Level and Earned Ascent

By

Dr. Fred Monderson

In recent months a number of friends have approached me with a single question: "What do you think of this Sharpton thing?" As a free and critical thinker I could only respond: "I think it was the best thing that has happened to Sharpton." Then they would assume a puzzling countenance with a follow up: "Well, explain." In as much as I have not done so, I now venture to offer my considered opinion.

I thought then and now the government made a mistake with Sharpton! They should have thought it out first and then said, pardon the pun: "Rev. Sharpton, we know you are concerned about this matter and are moving to resolve this issue, so you should go home." They did not and this set in motion a consciousness raising and mobilization of people and sentiment, unimagined. "The Pope called for the First Crusade; Jitu Weusi called for the First African Arts Street Festival; and when Sharpton does and calls for people to get arrested, they come running. Talk about Love Offering!"

Importantly, after his lengthy imprisonment, Sharpton emerged thinner, fitter, and more conscious and with a vision of salvation for the nation's downtrodden, silent victims and the dispossessed, disenfranchised and discriminated against. All this, with a view to polishing and brightening America's image at home and abroad. Yet still, as such, it leaves me to wonder who are making those decisions in Washington.

BLACK NATIONALISM
ALIVE AND WELL

Black Nationalism 129. Charles Finch III, in Washington, DC, commenting on the significance of the election of Barack Obama as President.

FREDERICK MONDERSON

Black Nationalism 130. Reverend Al Sharpton, "Abubadika" Sonny Carson and Reverend Wyatt Tee Walker at **National Action Network** headquarters.

As a young and aspiring student-nationalist in 1974, some friends were expecting me to run for Congress. That notwithstanding, so much has happened since then, with family, college, community, job, etc., that such a dream was not realized. Still, along the way, and trained as a historian, I see a litany of parallels in governments making similar mistakes that left them in the dust. Even more important, the individuals who "spoke truth to power" ended up having significant impact on the issues of their time and the challenged governments ended up with cake on their face, to say the least.

If we look back far enough we can see, first, as "the good book" says, imprisoned Moses challenged Pharaoh and the end result was catastrophic for that nation and antiquity. The Bible tells of Daniel in the Lion's Den and the brothers Shadrack, Meshak and Abednego, whom Nebuchadnezzar imprisoned in the fire, were protected and this did not do much for his image. The establishment and its interests had

BLACK NATIONALISM
ALIVE AND WELL

Black Nationalism 131. Ladies and Gents of all hues.

Delilah cut Samson's hair and both columns and the walls came tumbling down. Herod had Salome dance, and then cut off John the Baptist's head. However, he served his function in validating the coming messiah. Then, the Romans and their corroborators killed Jesus and two millennia later his movement, Christianity, boasts a following of more than a billion believers.

FREDERICK MONDERSON

The Church censured Copernicus and look where we are today, in the heavens. Then Napoleon imprisoned Toussaint L'Ouverture and this emboldened Dessalines and Christophe to create in Haiti a Black beacon of hope in a raging sea of turbulence, racial and economic. This in the aftermath of the British iron fist against the American colonists that forced the founding fathers to challenge that juggernaut and the result was an American nation, the tenacity of whose founders created a system that has survived for centuries and is a great hope for mankind. In this, Nathan Hale, challenged the British, and was sorry he only had one life to give for his country. As testimony to such martyrdom, and in the tradition of its purpose, this country is being challenged today to enact reforms to live out its creed. Lest we forget, Thomas Jefferson said: "When I think there is a just God, I tremble for this nation."

In Harlem, Marcus Garvey was betrayed and imprisoned after he had galvanized Black people worldwide, resuscitated their cultural history, created their "men of big affairs," and began economic and political organization that was to have world-wide repercussions. All the while he emphasized "Africa for the Africans, those at home and abroad." That Africans should have a voice in their own destiny he argued; and upheld their right to own the land they lived-on and worked. In this effort, he was able to found the Universal Negro Improvement Association, the Black Cross Nurses, the historic and mystical Red, Black and Green flag, and created the notion of Garveyism and its Garveyite followers. He was betrayed, this "Black Moses," accused, tried and imprisoned. On way to the Atlanta Federal Prison, a handcuffed, Garvey prophesized: "Look for me in the whirlwind!" Then he scoffed at the powers: "You have caged the tiger but the cubs are running free out there!" Today Marcus Garvey is regarded as an authentic Black hero, an ancestor of merit and substance.

We will not be turned back! "I feel no way tired," Rev. Cleveland believed, "We've come too far to turn back now. I don't think he brought me this far to leave me now." Without a doubt, Sharpton is a significant leader in this forward thrust.

BLACK NATIONALISM ALIVE AND WELL

Moving right along, the British imprisoned Mahatma Gandhi and the result was non-violent creative protest that ended in creation of a nation state called India, where Britain simply walked away, out of frustration, defeated, again.

In Africa, Kwame Nkrumah, Jomo Kenyatta, Albert Luthuli, Sekou Toure, Namdzi Azikwi, Ahmed Ben Bella, and a whole host of others were all imprisoned in the struggle to decolonize Africa and end the cultural, educational, political and economic dehumanization and exploitation of African people. Lumumba was imprisoned then killed in the Congo. The end result was a victory for the people, defeat for colonialism and a realignment of "North-South" relationships.

In that thunderstorm that Harold Macmillan called the "winds of change;" that odious system of apartheid imprisoned Nelson Mandela and that gentleman, possessing the wherewithal, weathered that racist storm! Truly, "one man can become a majority if his truth is sound and he persists in the ideals of his conviction," so much so that when the world finally catches up with him, then it will see the light and the prize he struggled for. The end result was not simply the end of apartheid, the creation of a non-racial South Africa, but in the process a Truth Commission exposed the horrors of that deadly apparatus, called the racist apartheid regime. Revealed, were the methods of oppression where the government killed Steven Biko and so many others, seeking to right the wrongs of a society warped by the notion of racial superiority.

FREDERICK MONDERSON

Black Nationalism 132. The "Young Al Sharpton" listens attentively to concerns of "The People."

At home, Rosa Parks was arrested and she set in motion a firestorm that did wonders for the image of America as it sought to examine itself and expose the insidious lacerations created in actions against itself, against its citizens. In that turbulence, Martin Luther King emerged and in forcing the American system to examine itself, he was imprisoned, where he penned his famous "Letter from a Birmingham Jail." This action of imprisonment did more for the cause of social justice in America than most would understand. For, it undergirded the struggle and laid the foundation for the notion of Dr. King's "Dream." So much so, decades later, after the "King Holiday" many people now see the wisdom of King's creative protests, recognizing his was a battle cry for the poor and downtrodden. Certainly Jesse Jackson, Andrew Young, John Lewis, Julian Bond, Fannie Lou Hamer, and so many others got their heads busted and were imprisoned and the collective successes of their efforts has helped in the transformation of America, where so many people, ethnicities, persuasions and physicalities benefited.

BLACK NATIONALISM
ALIVE AND WELL

Black Nationalism 133. "The Savior!" In his true self! Look at both but closely at the picture to the left!

Sonny Carson was arrested and ended up fighting the system by keeping tabs on the Prison Industrial Complex and its attitudes towards Blacks, Hispanics and other peoples of color. In addition,

FREDERICK MONDERSON

Carson extended his activism to honoring Black Heroes, effectively naming streets, schools, etc., in their honor, viz., Martin Luther King Boulevard, Malcolm X Boulevard, Malcolm X School, Akbar Place, etc. With far reaching implications, he was instrumental in returning a runaway slave, his ancestor; Samuel Carson, who in 1845, served in the Unites States Navy; to Ghana, for internment, opening "The Door of Return!" This was a highlight of the 1998 First Emancipation Day Festival held in that nation, August 1, 1998. This significant gesture remains the guiding light as he continues to struggle to reclaim the bones of so many other enslaved Africans in America.

Today we recognize, so many of our progressive ministers were jailed. The institutional builder Rev. Daughtry and the venerated Malcolm X have certainly made their contributions, emerging from prison, new men, more enlightened and ready to work for the people's salvation.

Rev. Al Sharpton came of age in the backdrop of all these happenings. He carved his own path of activism in his climb from humble beginnings. His is the true story of living the "American Dream." Yet, some say the legal system was unfair to Sharpton in giving him 90 days of imprisonment for his Vieques protest. Perhaps not so, for the instrument of that action, the presiding judge was simply following the law for repeat offenders, which Sharpton certainly was. Consider that he had been arrested before as he forced New York City to confront its racial attitudes when four New York City policemen shot Amadou Diallo 41 times. Officer Weatherspoon, of "100 Police Officers Who Care" found a 42nd bullet! Look at the litany of high and low who followed this African American genius, Al Sharpton, to be arrested. Can I just mention David Dinkins, Ed Koch, Charles Rangel, Major Owens, even Floyd Flake, and the rest you know. This Diallo protest effort was the work of a visionary who, in the tradition of the American system shed light beyond the Blue Wall of silence. All this coming after Howard Beach, Bensonhurst, Tawana Brawley, Abner Louima, Anthony Baez, James Byrd, Sean Bell, racial profiling, etc.,

BLACK NATIONALISM
ALIVE AND WELL

statesmanship following the wrongful verdict in the "Rodney King" trial and so many other "trials."

Black Nationalism 134. New York State Governor David Patterson embraces Erik Monderson at Al Sharpton's "Keepers of the Dream 2011" affair.

FREDERICK MONDERSON

In 1994, when I endorsed Al Sharpton for Senator against Daniel Moynihan, I believed then and still do, that he is the quintessential American nationalist steeped in the tradition of the founding fathers Crispus Attucks, Thomas Paine and Patrick Henry. Then as now, I measured his idealism, as it became refined, tempered in struggle to give voice to those victimized by society's institutions and its mindless minions who perpetuate racial, religious, political, and sexual violence and discrimination. This is the record the judge saw "when he threw the book at Sharpton." He saw Sharpton as championing causes that were not popular. His well-documented acts of civil disobedience gave voice of concern of the powerless and many not so powerless. After all, Sharpton helped to raise national attention to urban blight, and youth, education and other social problems that affect Blacks, women, Native Americans, immigrants, disabled, and particularly people from the Caribbean. Strange enough, many victimized by racial violence especially in New York, were from the Caribbean and Africa. And, as a true Pan-Africanist, Garveyite in outlook, he was there, not questioning their national origin. He has been outspoken on Somalia, Haiti, Uganda, shown interest in Jamaica, West Indies, slavery in Sudan and is known around the world, from Algeria to Zimbabwe.

The *Vieques* incident, therefore, was a culmination of a strategy and tactics of civil disobedience in form of demonstrations, sit-ins, boycotts, that was sanctioned by the American Constitution and used so effectively in the civil rights struggle. Now, as he moves to the next level, progressives around the nation can help mold Sharpton's vision as he charts a course for betterment of the American system. But, why not, for Sharpton has great merit! When we consider, what Blacks got out of the 2000 presidential election? They turned out en masse and voted primarily Democratic. In Florida there was significant disfranchisement effort and perhaps in other locations too. Following the questionable results, nothing has been said regarding this constituency. It's like Prof. John Clarke used to say: "When I look for our picture in All of US, we are not there." Paul Robeson's picture is not in that famous one at Rutgers, though he was their star running back. Consider how he was treated.

BLACK NATIONALISM
ALIVE AND WELL

Black Nationalism 135. Commerce Secretary in the Clinton Administration, Ron Brown, killed in an aircraft crash.

As a result therefore, I again support the efforts of the Reverend Al Sharpton for the Presidency of the United States, as I did when he ran for the Senate. His record is as a fighter for justice and equal access to opportunity for all people; the personal sacrifices he has made and the dignity and integrity which he brings to public life are all fundamental assets which eminently qualify him to lead this nation.

FREDERICK MONDERSON

Black Nationalism 136. Great Americans, George Washington, Abraham Lincoln and another great but unknown Black Man.

16. THE BOOK of ESSAYS ON ANCIENT KEMET, THE COLONNADE AND ARCHITECTURAL FRAGMENTS FROM HERE AND THERE

Frederick M. Monderson

BLACK NATIONALISM ALIVE AND WELL

Brooklyn, New York 11216
January 20, 1997

The Copyright Office
Library of Congress
Washington, DC 20559

Dear Sirs,

Heaven moves in mysterious ways! As indicated in my second correspondence, the haste of a deadline of Thursday January 16, 1997, forced me to forget the entry for *The Afro Times* June 8, 1996, where in the sequence on Karnak June 1, 8, 15, 22 and 29, 1996, June 8, 1996, is missing and in the May 25, 1996 *Afro Times* with its part cover front page photograph bearing representatives from Atwell Middle School 61 in Brooklyn, where much of the ideas were forged. I'm now reminded that the cover photograph of the *Colonnade* needs to be affixed. Here I am supplying a new cover with attached photograph of "Columns at Karnak Temple, Thebes, emblematic of Upper and Lower Kemet/Egypt" for the Cover Page, which I neglected to insert. In *Reflections*, in the sequence of the *New American*, December 26-January 1, 1997, "Africa's Early Art Gallery;" January 2-January 8, 1997, "Africa's Early Art Gallery;" January 9-January 15, "Ancient Kemetic Art and Technology;" January 16-January 22, 1997 "Ancient Kemet: Art and Technology;" in the *Afro Times*, January 11, 1997, "Hatshepsut: African Queen Extraordinaire;" and, January 18, 1997, "Hatshepsut: African Queen Extraordinaire" should be inserted. For the third volume, *Architectural Fragments* a Cover Page is provided.

In addition, a page is included of an insert from **USA TODAY** January 10, 1997, entitled "EGYPT HAS DESIGNS ON A NEW VALLEY NURTURED BY NILE," where on page 6A, the Egyptian President Hosni Mubarak "envisions a 500-mile canal that would create a million-acre green strip."

FREDERICK MONDERSON

Black Nationalism 137. Harry Belafonte, the "Quintessential Black Activist" with a youngster.

Embarking on such a massive project to create a new valley by diverting the Nile River and reclaiming millions of new acres of land to fund development wants of his nation's fast developing population, now occupying only 6 % of the land, is proving Mr. Hosni Mubarak a futuristic visionary. Even further, a number of additions are submitted including Smith's *Comprehensive Dictionary of the Bible* (1915: 253) Map of Egypt; Mr. R.S. Poole's Table of the First Seventeen Dynasties; (1905: 364); Temple of Deir el-Bahari. Middle Colonnade. South Wall. Queen Hatshepsut's Expedition to Punt, B.C. 1500. Loading Egyptian Ships at Punt and Middle Colonnade. South Wall. Laden Egyptian ships leaving Punt; Making Papyrus Boat from Wilkinson and Boat on the Nile, showing how the sail was fastened to the yards, and the nature of the rigging also from Wilkinson; the Narmer Palette from *Scientific American* December 20, 1902; from *Scientific American* March 14, 1903 "The Restoration of the Foundations of the Philae Temple" and Underpinning of the Submerged Building of the Island of Philae in *Scientific American*; "The Giant Arsinotherium, the Newly

BLACK NATIONALISM
ALIVE AND WELL

Discovered Horned Monster of Prehistoric Egypt" in *Scientific American* October 17, 1908; and a special added volume to contain additional illustrations included with this mailing. Here I would like to thank Carl Hinds of Remsen Copy Center.

On this national Holiday honoring Dr. King and with President Bill Clinton's historic inauguration festivities underway, and as a 1997 Tribute to Black History Month, I choose to consider the issue of dedication of this important work of serious African American scholarship.

I would like to dedicate **THE BOOK** to the well-deserved recipients. The Title should read: "**THE BOOK of ESSAYS ON ANCIENT KEMET, THE COLONNADE, and ARCHITECTURAL FRAGMENTS: FROM HERE AND THERE.**" "**THE BOOK of ESSAYS ON ANCIENT KEMET,**" "**THE COLONNADE**" and "**ARCHITECTURAL FRAGMENTS: FROM HERE AND THERE**" is dedicated to four people. Three have loved, supported and taught me. These are my mother Mitta Monderson, who sits in heaven, at the right hand of God in Heaven, and I ask that they guide and protect us all; my sister Cherise Monderson-Maloney, who supported me and whose photographs are included as model before those important religious, cultural and architectural masterpieces testifying to a wonderful history of a people, that's a most powerful legacy; and thirdly, Dr. Leonard James, the noted scholar and educator, who for many years recognized the role of architecture in religious history. He taught African History at New York City Technical College, for many years before moving to Stone Mountain, Georgia. He helped so many students, including the present author, to understand the dynamics of the **Process of Historical Evolution** and its impact on civilization. He made us understand the need for paradigms in problem solving skills. He emphasized the importance of a Criteria for Critical Reading; understanding of the Eight Major Social

FREDERICK MONDERSON

Sciences, viz., Geography, Archaeology, Anthropology, History, Sociology, Economics, Political Science, and Psychology, and the utility of applying these principles to read and study, research, write and teach, so central to his educational philosophy. He encouraged study of such topics as Early Christianity; the Western Sudanic States of Ghana, Mali and Songhai; the Slave Trade and Slavery; Abolition; Reconstruction; the Great Awakening. He stressed the significance of the roles of African and African American thinkers and civic and social activists in the person of Edward Wilmot Blyden; Toussaint L'Ouverture, Dessalines and Christophe; Crispus Attucks; Henry Highland Garnett; Peter Salem; Benjamin Banneker; Pointe De Sable; Prince Hall; Denmark Vesey; Nat Turner; Frederick Douglass; John Henry and John Brown. Duse Mohammed particularly interested him as a teacher of Marcus Garvey.

Black Nationalism 138. "Our Father" Marcus Moziah Garvey (1887-1940).

BLACK NATIONALISM ALIVE AND WELL

He showed how the work of the Jubilee Singers helped produce the Harlem Renaissance, with its photographic, literary and musical masterpieces. More importantly, however, Dr. James made his students appreciate how wonderfully exciting it could be to explore Nile Valley cultural history when experienced through the process of inductive rather than deductive methodology. This is a most effective tool, to study history, whether American or otherwise, he taught, and how intellectually rewarding research and writing about the Ancient Africans could be. Dr. James also taught that the Nilotic Civilization extended throughout the Nile Valley and that pre-dynastic Egypt/Kemet, viz., Badarian, Amratian and Gerzean, now Naqada I and Naqada II, created the foundations of the Dynastic period beginning with Narmer/Menes, 3200 B.C. *Nile Year* 1040. He taught the cultural origins were to be found in the south of Egypt. Today we know of Nabta Playa and the significance of the Eastern and Western Deserts to the south of Egypt where evidence for the foundations of Egypt and pharaonic predecessors is to be found. For 30 Dynasties, a strong central government was able to exert effective control over the River Nile using a system of canals, dams, dykes and to provide water in times of scarcity until the next Inundation.

Understanding and challenging the dynamics of the Inundation produced scholars of mathematics, geometry and measurement, and great architectural geniuses. He taught how the social institutions of the Nile Valley culture lent itself to study from political, economic, cultural, artistic and scientific perspectives. How mummification and preservation of the dead lead to advances in anatomy and medicine. He showed how religion and theology guided by astronomy produced wonderful and timeless edifices of temple architecture employing the colonnade as a principal feature. In the construction of such magnificent temples as Karnak and Luxor, Deir el Bahari, the Ramesseum, Abu Simbel, Medinet Habu, ancient Africans set in motion the engines of civilization – Old Kingdom, Middle Kingdom, New Kingdom - Empire; Late Period, particularly Kush, then Greece, Rome and Islam, received inquiry and fueled his and his student's interests for further study. He helped students see inter-

FREDERICK MONDERSON

connections in the social and psychic fabric of the Nile Valley Culture. He taught us sources for study of African history included the Bible, and classical scholars Herodotus, Plutarch, Diodorus, and Strabo. Arabic scholars, Shakespeare and modern writers, some objective and others, pseudo-scientific racists, whose works were studied; are today being challenged by redemptive African scholarship.

Dr. James encouraged his students to see how distortions in history serve social, economic, cultural and political oppression, through discriminatory practices. He asked "What is a distortion?" After discussion he would settle on: "Distortions are the willful twisting of the historical record to suppress the evidence of history for ulterior motives." In this, he cites examples of historical distortion of Samuel Cartwright's *Slavery and Ethnology* (1859), while simultaneously teaching students the critical and proper way to study past phenomena. He taught students to meticulously examine and critique Samuel Cartwright's work which postulated, the view, "Nilotic monuments show only evidence of Negroes as slaves in Egypt from time immemorial." In 1864, Dr. Hunt described the Negro as a "beast." Flinders Petrie taught the "Asiatic Origin of Egypt" and Arthur Weigall's "Flights into Antiquity" were disdainful repletes of the now infamous N-word. Dr. James continued to enlighten his students through cultivation of their critical analytic skills. He was first to point to modern examples of historical distortion, citing the Metropolitan Museum of Art itself having distortions in its museum displays, because this Museum caters to a particular clientele. He queried whether Blacks had the political muscle to challenge the New York's Museum of Natural History to change some of its displays. He pointed out most educational institutions teach two sides to history and culture of the ancient Egyptians/people from Kemet. They were always Brown, Red, and Black but never White, he insisted!

Prof. James spent much time challenging the accuracy of the presentation of the historical record, knowing that in regards to Egyptian/Kemetic civilization, we know no more than 15-20 percent of what we need to know. He cited Herodotus, Diodorus, Count

BLACK NATIONALISM
ALIVE AND WELL

Denon, Volney, Godfrey Higgins, Kersey Greaves, Gerald Massey, Albert Churchward, Carter G. Woodson, John H. Clark and Yosef ben-Jochannan, as well as the Senegalese Cheikh Anta Diop. As to answering the question "What is the purpose of omissions and distortions in history?" Dr. James answered: "It is to deny African identification with the great architectural builders of history and the Egyptian/Kemetic culture." Therefore, he structured his classes to develop a methodology and philosophy where his course emphasized the cultivation of a critical perspective for examining the records and making objective analyses in correcting distortions and including omissions that make Africans proud of their history and culture.

Black Nationalism 139. All the powerful Black "movers and shakers" are shown in this mural.

FREDERICK MONDERSON

From the Egyptian sources came written records and artifactual evidence unearthed in the systematic archaeological excavation and anthropological inquiries these discoveries fueled, arising from the "age of imperialism" which culminated in the Scramble for Africa. The Berlin Congress of 1884 legitimized the Partition of Africa and here began the road to the war in 1914. Prof. James specifically encouraged challenges to analyses of the systematic unearthing of Africa's hidden glories in what Professor John H. Clarke often summed up as: "The people who preached racism colonized history." The end result of this "Rape of the Nile" saw London, Manchester, Glasgow, Oxford, private collections, and such nations as France, Germany, Switzerland, Italy, USA, and cities as Brooklyn, New York, Detroit, Boston, Chicago, Philadelphia, and Toronto, Moscow and Sydney, all boast wonderful collections of the artifactual and cultural history of Africa, now comprising major holdings in museum displays. Papyri, artifacts, mummies, chemicals, rocks, etc., were all significant adjuncts of instruction in institutions of higher learning. Through it all, the master teacher saw religion and architecture along with the army and trade. More importantly, however, he saw the educational possibilities, the motivation, and benefits of the systematic conceptual scheme of analysis, that is, the soundest methodology or cognitive structure needed to aid African Historical Reconstruction. Paradigms of this tool comprised, A Criteria for Critical Reading, A Methodological Plan, A Systematic Conceptual Scheme or Framework of Analysis, as well as An Historical Perspective that is Iconoclastic. Such a methodology thus becomes bedrock in sustaining the inquiry necessary to support African historiographic reconstruction.

The use of the Syllogism, a logical tool of analysis, with its congruence in the major and minor premises with their conclusions, he showed, is also an important under-pine of the methodological framework. The 8 major social sciences can thus be utilized in an interdisciplinary approach that examines the Records (Primary and Secondary Sources), to create Critical Historical Comparative Analyses into the Cognitive or Effective Areas of Learning. This approach forces Critical Relearning of any given phenomenon to Generate a New Hypothesis. The second Critical Comparative

BLACK NATIONALISM ALIVE AND WELL

Historical Analysis forces a Reinterpretation and New Generalizations about any social or civic issue. The Methodological Plan of Historical Evolution lets the student see, contrary to racist western scholarship, viz., Hegel, Cartwright, Dr. Hunt, Toynbee, and such persons; Africa has been in the forefront of human progress in art, architecture, astronomy, mathematics, military science, agriculture, gold mining and smelting. Prof. James made his students aware of such Racist Pseudo-Scientific writers and historians as Henry Fairfield Osborne, Edward Ross, Sociologist; G. Stanley Hall, Psychologist; John R. Commons, Economist; James Ford Rhodes, Historian; John W. Burgess, Historian; Josiah Nott, Historian, U. B. Philips, Historian; Arthur De Gobineau, Lothrop D. Stoddard, and the "Banana skin physician" Dr. Samuel Cartwright. Christian Ministers in this category included Charles B. Calloway, Theodore Debose Stratton, William Montgomery Brown; A. Newby, who wrote *In Defense of Jim Crow*; Thomas Dixon, *The Klansman*; and Thomas Nelson Paige all shared the spotlight of negatively characterizing Blacks. Some contemporary racist scientific writers active in the last quarter of the 20th Century were William Shockley, Arthur Jensen and Christopher Jenks. To counter their influence Dr. James introduced his students to "Personalities in Black History." These included Alexander Cromwell; Dr. J. E. Moreland; Dr. Arthur Schomberg; Dr. Carter G. Woodson; Dr. Edward Wilmot Blyden; William Pickens; Booker T. Washington; Marcus Garvey; W. E. B. Du Boise; Blaise Diagne, Dantes Bellgrade; Duse Mohammed; J.E.K. Aggrey; Caseley Hayford; Paul Panda; Malcolm X; Paul Robeson, Harry Belafonte, Dr. John H. Clarke, and Dr. Yosef Ben-Jochannan. To these we may add George G.M. James, Walter Rodney, C.L.R. James, Ivan Van Sertima, Prof. Scoby, Asa Hillard and Dr. Benjamin Carruthers, among others.

FREDERICK MONDERSON

Black Nationalism 140. Replica sample of a Slave Castle on the Coast of West Africa that held the "Door of No Return" through which millions of Africans passed on way to New World enslavement.

He thus showed how Africa has been an active participant in the undulative process of human experience, having both nadir and zenith, high and low points, in cultural evolution as opposed to being confined to the "Darkness" of Conrad. We can see the *causes stimuli* with its internal and external features, and antecedent and precipitate ingredients, acting positively and negatively on the landscape of history in Africa, creating the engines of human progress in the continuity of historical evolution.

Sciences teaches us, early man emerged in Africa with a large brain, hand-axes as technology, developed bi-pedalism and the use of fire. The expansion of cultural units, viz., art, music, government, religion, language, etc., if we use Kemet as an example-Nile boats, fish, agriculture, religious expression, quarrying and building in stone, culminating in the refinement of the cultural units and their extension, consolidation, perpetuation, and expansion now equated with imperialism. These concepts he pointed out were the foundational basis for civilization. This historical process of state development, he showed, is thus also traceable in the Ethiopians, people of Kemet (Egyptians) and Nubians along the Nile. We later

BLACK NATIONALISM
ALIVE AND WELL

see civilization dynamics operating among the Sumerian, Assyrians, Hittites, Persian, Greeks, Phoenicians, Carthage, Rome, Islam, Portugal, Spain, England, France, America, and Russia, mostly outside of Africa. The particularly indigenous African states with civilization pageantry beyond Egypt/Kemet included Meroe, Axum, and Ghana with Sumanguru Kante, its ruler; Sundiata Keita and Mansa Musa from Mali; and Sunni Ali, Askia Mohammed and Sunni Ali Ber, from Songhai. Then Kanem-Bornu, Ashanti, Yoruba, Ibo, Monomatapa, Zimbabwe, Congo, Zulu, and up on the Veldt in South Africa where Moshesh created the Basuto nation, ultimately and diplomatically placed under the Protectorate of the British, thwarting the South Africa's system of Apartheid. The nearby Portuguese colonial holdings in Mozambique and Angola, and the roles of Samori Toure and Mohammed Ali, were lively topics of discussion and research in his class. So too were the roles of Yohanes IV, Menelik II and Haile Selassie I, astute 19th Century and 20th Century Ethiopian leaders.

Therefore this exploration for objective truth in history allowed the student to develop the tools of critical analysis and research techniques as well as the construction of theoretical problem-solving skills to apply in their social situations. This is why this sociologist also taught "Black Community Problems" These insights were then to help his students create a philosophy of history aimed at challenging and correcting distortions and including omissions in African History, systematically implanted by racist Western, European and American historiography. Equally important, Dr. James was himself a graduate of Columbia University's Teachers College, where the young educator, remembered here, attended. What is significant is that though suffering from Dyslexia, yet a young student became committed to reading and developing his mind to combat the external and internal obstacles, so many African American youths face. He demonstrably achieved, and as he did, gained admission to the Masters Program at Teachers College, Columbia University.

FREDERICK MONDERSON

Black Nationalism 141. Celebrants gather for a January 1st Religious Ceremony at a Batey in San Juan de la Maguanas in Dominican Republic.

BLACK NATIONALISM
ALIVE AND WELL

Black Nationalism 142. The Monster and the "Dragon," Bruce Lee.

As such, I would like to also dedicate this book to Mr. Enos Cosby, an African American from a notable American family, a young man

FREDERICK MONDERSON

whose life was tragically and senselessly cut short. I'm reminded of one of the articles in *The Daily Challenge*, Monday June 6, 1994, where I mentioned in "An Open Letter to Senator Daniel Moynihan," Democrat from New York, how firearms were senselessly killing young Americans, especially young Black men. We see this evidence mushrooming in urban communities as memorials, often on walls of abandoned buildings. To recall the incident where, a young mother with her baby at the third floor window, at a time when the New York Knicks won a Championship, an exuberant and misguided fan, fired his pistol in the air and took her life tragically. However you look at it, firearms are killing Americans needlessly.

This dedication of **THE BOOK** to the memory of someone, whose heart was in the right place, academically speaking, is an honor and bodes well for education. This young educator sought to help students and other people with learning disabilities through pursuing a "Special Education" program. **THE BOOK** is a tool the young student would have used, had he known about it. The *New York Times* December 1, 1996 editorial points to significant proportions of young Americans with learning disabilities across this great nation, who spend inordinate numbers of their most productive years confined in correctional institutions because of lack of education and skills. Mr. Cosby's and efforts of others in "special education" can be enhanced if the curriculum exposes young people to **THE BOOK** that would educate them in social, cultural, political, and civic critique of issues affecting their lives. This is especially so when it's known that newspapers reflect the living history of a people, in their experiences on this physical, mental and spiritual plane of existence, we all share.

The art and architecture can offer incentives for young learners, in more detail study of the timeless culture. The illustrations can encourage reading and use of visual images to educate and in process help build perspective gleaned from its use in creative exercise and purposes. When America speaks of the bridge to the next century,

BLACK NATIONALISM ALIVE AND WELL

African-Americans must also seek to conceive of the bridge at the end of that century. We must be conscious of centenary and have knowledge and a consciousness of the archaeological excavation of the land of ancient Kemet/Egypt, a century ago. We must possess the knowledge of history to span that hundred years. The wonderful architectural and religious experiences explored, in **THE BOOK**, should be part of any young brother or sister, for that matter, young people, reading repertoire.

So, it is my gift to the Cosby Family that has given so much to this nation and to say with so many others worldwide, how much sympathy and prayers go out to them. This is special, particularly when on the loss of their beloved; they are mindful and choose to emphasize how other families of victims in similar circumstances have endured in their experiences. Here we need remember; young Black men are being killed across America, oftentimes by other young Black men!

Hopefully, the combination of this piece into a single volume, in three parts, can be used to create modules that would further engage young people, in reading and studying, where they can be encouraged to research the facts and write as part of educating themselves and other youngsters, in the rich cultural history of the Nile Valley experience. It is a powerful course of study that African Americans students and all people, can take pride in, as we prepare for "Black History Month" in February; "Women's History Month" in March; "Stand for Children" in April; "Equality in Education" and "Inclusion of all Americans" and in the free and fair exercise of those cornerstone principles of equality, unity and opportunity that make our nation strong, are goals we must aspire towards.

FREDERICK MONDERSON

Black Nationalism 143. Councilman Charles Barron and his wife, Inez Barron, a "Power Couple," who go all out for the people!

Given the opportunity to examine the fundamental principles of human progress that the Nile Valley helped to promote in furtherance of civilization, we see ancient African cultural symbols migrate and wonderfully represented in the foundations of American Civilization. Just as Egyptian President Mubarak hopes to create a new valley from diverting the Nile to reclaims millions of acres of arable land from the desert; in remembrance of Mr. Enos Cosby and the thousands that are dying and their families, that they be remembered; we must let **THE BOOK** cultivate a new valley of green pastures where millions of young Americans will graze to be educated and enriched by this cultural legacy of ancient Africa. Then a new generation of young people can understand and arm themselves in the century ahead, with hope, faith and the principles and procedures of critical analysis to study science, architecture, art, religion, spirituality, government and enlightenment, realizing that so much can be gained from these ancient Africans. To apply the methodology of a critical perspective to the dynamics of social and civic community action and in efforts that help children, whether in Parent-Teacher meetings, working and reading with the child, etc., a great deal can be learnt from **THE BOOK**. In so doing, the Twenty-First Century will find so many Americans across the bridge with **THE BOOK**, I believe, all the recipients would proudly display on their mantle. Symbolically I wish the brothers and

BLACK NATIONALISM
ALIVE AND WELL

"sisters" could "carry with them," **THE BOOK** for pleasurable and knowledgeable reading while on route to heaven, that great reward beyond. From Here to There, I ask my mother and so many of the great mothers, as Nut, Isis, Ahotep, Hetepheres, Mentuhotep's mother Queen Aam, Teti-Sheri, Aahmes-Nefertari, Hatshepsut, Queen Tiy, Nefertari, Nzinga, Yaa Asantewaa, Phyllis Wheatley, Harriet Tubman, Sojourner Truth, Mary McLeod Bethune, Fannie Lou Hamer, Barbara Jordan, Moms Mabley, "me moms," all as ancestors. Equally, let us not forget the great fathers, Narmer, Scorpion, Den, Der, Imhotep, Khufu, Khafre, Menkaure, Mentuhotep, Senmut, Amenhotep, Thutmose, Akhenaton, Seti, Rameses, Khasta, Piankhi, Shabaka, Shabataka, Taharka, Mansa Musa, Askia Mohammed, Menelik II, Samori Toure, Shaka, Behanzin, Ebenezer D. Bassett, Marcus Garvey, Booker T. Washington, Benjamin E. Mays, Alain Locke, Arthur Schomberg, Paul Lawrence Dunbar, Frederick Douglass, Medgar Evers, Countee Cullen, James Weldon Johnson, Richard Wright, Langston Hughes, James Baldwin, A. Philip Randolph, Whitney Young, Thurgood Marshall, Oscar De Priest, Benjamin O. Davis, Sr., William Monroe Trotter, W. E. B. Du Bois, Carter G. Woodson, John O. Higgins, John Jackson, Paul Robeson, Prof. Scobie, C. L. R. James, Kwame Nkrumah, Sekou Toure, George Padmore, Ralph Bunche, Charles Drew, George Washington Carver, Secretary Ron Brown, Malcolm X and Martin Luther King, Jr., to all "receive them" and extend their warmest hospitality in that just reward, where Maat is the supreme goddess and lady of the heavens.

Black Nationalism 144. If you recall, Putney Swope reminded us, "The Drums carry a message all need to hear!"

FREDERICK MONDERSON

Black Nationalism 145. Quintessential Black Nationalist!

17. Dick Gregory's *Callus on My Soul*
By
Dr. Fred Monderson, a Review.

What a book! We all know of the Civil Rights Movement but this book is the story of one man's involvement. Man of vision, principle, foresight, courage, "distance runner," survivor, loyal, challenger to the system, some call him a "Bear hunter" and epitome of one man becoming a majority. No wonder Ossie Davis and Ruby Dee said: "Dick Gregory is a product of the struggle. He is an activist. We just look like activists."

Dick Gregory's book *Callus on My Soul*, with Sheila P. Moses is an extraordinary book, a unique history of the Civil Rights Movement, a history of Civil Rights Protest by an equally exceptional individual who is a legend in this country and worldwide. A 2000 Copyright by Dick Gregory and Sheila P. Moses and originally published in Hardcover by Longstreet Press, this first Kensington Trade Paperback Printing under Dafina Books is dated 2003.

This work begins with a Dedication to the "unsung heroes and sheroes all over the world, whose names most people don't ever stop to ask: the porters, the taxi-drivers, the dishwashers, and the bell captains at the hotel; the valet at the airport, the waiters and waitresses, the cooks, the teachers, the garbage collectors and the maids." He asks that all people "pray or meditate" with him "every day at noon." Then he asks for "a special prayer for the struggling single parents, the handicapped, and those who are disabled." He

BLACK NATIONALISM
ALIVE AND WELL

also mentions "struggling farmers and the forgotten human rights workers."

Black Nationalism 146. Dick Gregory, "distance runner" some have labeled "The Bear Hunter," who sure knows his facts!

FREDERICK MONDERSON

Then follows Acknowledgements from Dick Gregory, where he mentions "soldiers we lost while writing this book" to which he lists Albert Turner, Dr. Avenia Fulton, Stokely Carmichael and James Farmer "as well as those we lost so long ago: Dr. Martin Luther King, Jr., Medgar Evers, Viola Liuzzo, Chaney, Goodman, and Schwerner, Roy Wilkins, Dr. Benjamin Mays, Robert and John Kennedy, Malcolm X, Tom Skinner, Bob Johnson, Ralph Abernathy, Betty Shabaaz, Jim Sanders, Reverend John Nettles, and those four beautiful girls from Birmingham." He also said "thanks to the good, honest, decent White folks who walked in the shadow of death with us during the movement and today."

Let me say this before I move on, when we consider all the arguments for belief in god, viz., "first cause," "first mover," "beauty of creation," we could also add Dick Gregory's profound faith and religious conviction. Fueled by the power of prayer and an unshakeable belief in god, is what I believe brought him through the many trials and tribulations he faced in fighting for the human, civil, economic and physical and emotional rights of all people!

Acknowledgements follow from Sheila P. Moses thanking several people in assisting the completion and publication of this book.

According to the **Table of Contents**, Callus on My Soul's 301 pages is divided into 31 Chapters and a section on "Fasting" and "Dick Gregory's Weight Loss Program." Spanning his entire life, the Chapters include: Momma, Relief, Her Last Mile, On My Way, Lily of the Valley, To Cast a Stone, Blinded by the Light, Move on Niggers, Turn Me Loose, "Bombingham," Sad November, With His Armor On, In the Snake's Mouth, A Bullet of My Own, Black Power, Code name "Zorro," Nothing But Grace, Redskins, Going Home, The Greatest, Give Peace a Chance, Good or Evil, Happy Birthday Martin, Going the Distance, Let There Be Food, Fire With No Flame, Nothing From History, Blood On My Shoes, On Broadway, Sitting on the Couch, and Callus on My Soul!

BLACK NATIONALISM
ALIVE AND WELL

Black Nationalism 147. Perennial and Quintessential Nationalist, Sister Viola Plummer of the **December 12th Movement**.

FREDERICK MONDERSON

Revisiting the old adage, "Behind Every Great man, There is a Woman," Dick Gregory has confessed he could not swim his "River of Sorrows" without his beloved and god given wife, Lillian Gregory. Again, bless her soul for she was "The wings under his feet," "The Wind in his Sails," "The Gasoline in his Tank," and "The Fire in His Soul." This woman Dick Gregory married who bore him 10 children and her undying love was exceptional, gentle, yet stronger than steel!

Though the book has no Index, a list of some of the names he mentions, with whom he interacted, gone to jail with, entertained alongside, confronted, prayed and fasted with, influenced, assisted, been influenced by and watched die over the years, equally gives a paltry measure of the breadth of the experience he recounts. From Mohammed Ali, Byron de La Beckwith, Harry Belafonte, Marlon Brando, George Bush, Les Brown, Tony Brown, H. Rap Brown, Lenny Bruce, Ralph Bunche, John Carlos, Jimmy Carter, Robert Chambliss, Johnny Cochran, Bull Connor, Daddy-O-Dailey, Angela Davis, Miles Davis, Ossie Davis, Ruby Dee, David Dinkins, Queen Elizabeth, Jim Ellis, Medgar and Merlie Evers, Min. Louis Farrakhan, Walter Fauntroy, Hugh Hefner, Dorothy Height, Aaron Henry, Cathy Hughes, Jessie Jackson, Eunice and John Johnson, Tom Joyner, Clyde Kennard, Coretta Scott-King, Ayatollah Khomeni and the Hostages in Iran, Irv Kupeinet, John Lewis, Coach Leyland Lingle, Abner Louima, Nelson Mandela, Bob Marley, James Meredith, Kwesi Mfume, Jackie Kennedy, Jack Parr, Adam Clayton Powell Jr., Richard Pryor, A. Philip Randolph, Randall Robinson, Haile Selassie, Jim Sanders, Al Sharpton, Tavis Smiley, B. Tommy Smith, Leon Sullivan, Bill Tatum, Emmitt Till, C. Delores Tucker, Maxine Walters, Oprah Winfrey, Stevie Wonder, and Andy Young and Whitney Young,

Finally, in closing a few things in the book needs to be pointed out. "Racism is a form of insanity in this country that we cannot afford to ignore …. We have to talk about it until it goes away. You have to acknowledge the presence of the tumor then cut it out. It may be painful but it will save your life." (P278) "Name one movement in

BLACK NATIONALISM ALIVE AND WELL

the history of this planet in which every single leader has been murdered." "The continent of Africa is the key to the salvation of Black folks in the United States." "Gangster rap is an insult to the Black family. Take a minute to look up the definition of 'gangster' and 'rap.' Gangster means a member of a group of people banded together for some purpose, usually bad or negative. Rap means to deliver short, light blows. For our children, gangster rap means a succession of criminal messages."

"Two of the strongest forces in the history of America are and will remain the Black woman and the Black church. Gangster rap was not created by Black folks; it was created by White folks, to destroy the Black woman and the Black family. Imagine you are a Swedish woman on vacation in the United States. You get in a taxi and the Black driver is listening to a gangster rapper calling Black women bitches and whores. This is your first time in this country, and you don't know anything about Black women. Stay with me now. The next week, you go home to Sweden and two Black American women executives from Xerox with PhD's are there on vacation. Well, you don't see them as two Black women from corporate America – you see them as bitches and whores because that is the image that has been planted in your mind the week before by a Black gangster rapper.

So there you have it. Dick Gregory, an extraordinary individual. Man of courage, tenacity, endurance, integrity and exceptional faith and belief in god. **Callus on My Soul** is a book that must be read, savored and reread again to understand the long road Blacks have come in the United States as well as some of the obstacles still facing them.

FREDERICK MONDERSON

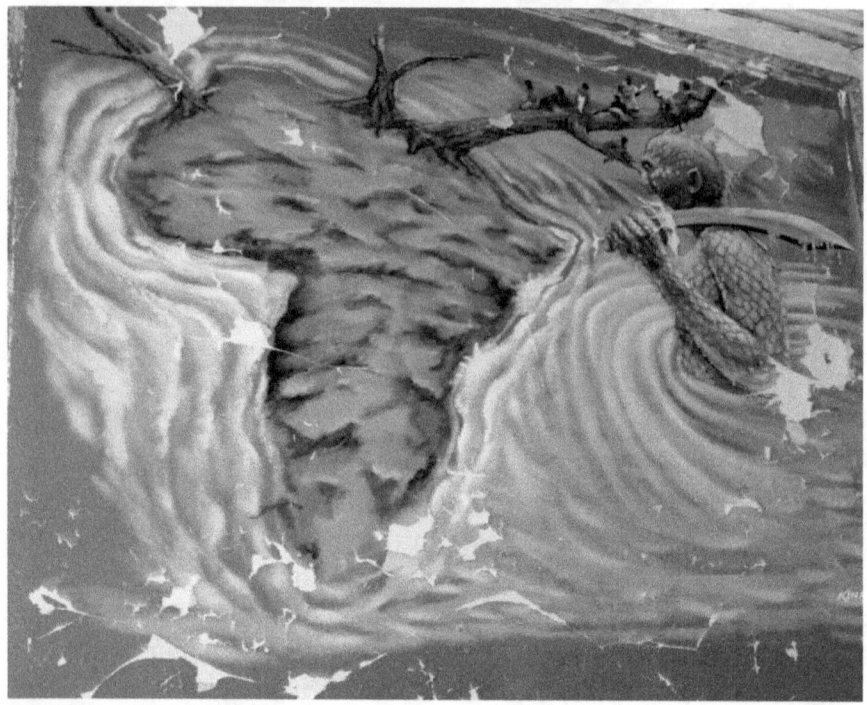

Black Nationalism 148. The continent of Africa under assault!

18. Dick Gregory at CEMOTAP
By
Dr. Fred Monderson

The **Committee to Eliminate Media Offensive to African People** (**CEMOTAP**) with Dr. McIntosh and Ms. Betty Dobson as well as a very active Board of Directors, celebrated their 18th Anniversary with Dick Gregory as its keynote speaker. This writer first met Dick Gregory in 1970 and was pleased to see how well he looked and how hectic a pace he still was able to maintain. Stating that "God and poverty don't dwell in the same place," the master activist, comedian and "Bear Hunter" presented a tour de force lecture on subjects A to Z. That is from Aids in Africa

BLACK NATIONALISM
ALIVE AND WELL

to his 46 years of marriage. When the audience began to applaud him for his martial longevity he reminded them: "This had nothing to do with love, when I got married my wife told me, if you leave me I will hurt you." As he became more successful, one word helped keep him in place: "Half!"

Mr. Gregory talked about how the media misrepresents the news. He was however thankful for the Black media who were responsible for much of the progress Blacks made in this country. He said: "It was Jet Magazine that put Emmett Till on the cover and had it go around the world and this embarrassed America." It forced this country to give a little slack. He talked about Michael Jackson getting a jury of his peers, all White because he was White! "Only thing Blacks did was hold his umbrella." The *London Times* printed an article about the spread of Aids in Africa due to smallpox vaccination. They are in court with the individual who filed for a patent in the US Copyright Office for **AIDS**!

And on and on he went. He said "Eat raw food, fruits and vegetables for seven days to clean out the inside." "Try a little fasting." "Drink 10 to 12 glasses of water per day." "Walking is the best exercise." One thing for sure, the brother is up on his information. Still, his presentation was punctuated with anecdotes of humor. Some cannot be repeated here but I do remember one he told at another occasion when his Brother drove his family to Disney World in Florida. On the highway leading up to Disney he saw a sign that read: **DISNEY LEFT**!

The poor fellow pulled over, was agitated and began to curse. He said: "You mean Disney waited until I got down here and LEFT!" Well, you know the rest.

FREDERICK MONDERSON

Black Nationalism 150. The entrance of a school named for the Haitian Liberator Toussaint L'Ouverture; and, entrance to Medgar Evers College for the Civil Rights advocate killed for registering people to vote.

Black Nationalism 149. Image of Dr. Martin Luther King, Jr. in that memorable pose associated with his "I Have a Dream" speech at the 1963 March on Washington.

BLACK NATIONALISM
ALIVE AND WELL

Black Nationalism 150a. Sonny Carson in a relaxed and pensive mood.

The poor fellow pulled over, was agitated and began to curse. He said: "You mean Disney waited until I got down here and LEFT!" Well, you know the rest.

FREDERICK MONDERSON

Black Nationalism 152. "If you don't stand for something you will fall for anything." This Brother certainly stands for many things and he should be celebrated and commemorated.

BLACK NATIONALISM ALIVE AND WELL

19. JAMES BROWN: A PERSONAL VIEW
By
Dr. Fred Monderson

The passing of James Brown has certainly resonated on distant shores because his musical genius and showmanship as well as his principled positions were known worldwide. Watching **CNN Headline News** many times were repeated something Rev. Al Sharpton said about the legendary 'God Father of Soul,' the 'Hardest working man in show business.' It was that "James Brown made us proud!" The famous song title: "Say it Loud, I'm Black and I'm Proud" had far reaching implications beyond the shores of America. Significantly, as art lyrics, it galvanized a people and inspired them along the arduous path of social change in the dynamics unfolding in the American political and cultural landscape.

Being a foreign born national in a colonial heritage, we knew we were Black, we lived Black, but Black was a closet secret! We were never taught about Black History, about Black America, about Black accomplishments. It was all about the history of the colonizer, in my case the British. For example, books such as J.A. Rogers' "World's Great Men of Color" and "Sex and Race" were published in the 1950s and certainly available in the 1960s, but were unknown in the Black world. There was that language, cultural, historical disconnect between American Blacks, British Blacks, Dutch Blacks, French Blacks, Spanish Blacks, African Blacks! This is what the principal adherents to Pan-Africanism as well as Marcus Garvey struggled to combat. They created that notion of the Black Diaspora and James Brown's lyrics and affirmations filtered throughout as a rallying cry making Black men and women proud of their skin color and by extension reinforcing ties with Africa.

FREDERICK MONDERSON

Black Nationalism 153. Queen Mother Moore on the road and in company of wonderful people.

Black Nationalism 153a. Jitu Weusi (left); Sonny Carson, Atiim Ferguson and Joshua (right); on way to attend the Malcolm X Parade in Bushwick, Brooklyn.

BLACK NATIONALISM
ALIVE AND WELL

In the British West Indies, Guyana to be exact, we equally never realized the potency of the cinema and its carefully regulated inculcation of a foreign cultural manifesto for control of a colonized people. We were constantly fed the Tarzan movies in which Hollywood reduced the Africans to mere buffoons. We enjoyed the John Wayne movies and the westerns particularly those featuring Native Americans. Then there was that movie, I don't remember its name when "James Brown and the Famous Flames" came out of the cold and did a "song and dance" with the spin around the mike, those quick shuffles, the slide, a drop to his knees and had the cape thrown over him. Finally he did the split. He was, like, the first Black Action Hero to me and many others of my age group. After that, all my young companions were doing the drop down and the split. This is how we were turned on to James Brown in the early sixties. In fact, in High School, I remember a fellow student Scantlebury whose pants were split doing the split as he saw James Brown doing it, and we all had a good laugh. After that we were moved and sang along and danced as the James Brown hits kept coming.

Black Nationalism 154. The High School on Fulton Street in Bedford-Stuyvesant in Brooklyn, where Nelson Mandela visited and which will be renamed for the South African icon.

FREDERICK MONDERSON

Black Nationalism 154a. Jitu Weusi, another Brother, Angela Weusi, Sonny Carson and George Murden at the African Street Festival on Boys and Girls High School grounds.

While "Sex Machine" and "Papa's Got a New Bag" were entertainment boasts, "Say it Loud, I'm Black and I'm Proud" was an unequivocal philosophical and principled statement right in the kisser to the powers that be, the establishment, racist institutions, the media, everyone with an agenda of Black suppression. This crystal clear statement was very important for many reasons but for historical affirmation it was significant. In another somewhat similar situation, from Biblical times, the Queen of Sheba had said "I'm Black and Comely" and a great deal of ink was spilled by publication media to reinforce the notion of Black inferiority. The distorters mis-quoted the Queen saying she instead said, "I'm Black, but comely" implying a sort of self-hatred, an aversion to being

BLACK NATIONALISM
ALIVE AND WELL

Black, yet affirming she was still pretty or beautiful. However, there was no mistaken what James Brown said and meant!

Black Nationalism 154b. Cherise Maloney speaks to an attentive Sonny Carson on Boys and girls grounds.

FREDERICK MONDERSON

Black Nationalism 154c. Cherise Maloney, George Murden and Sonny Carson who greets an admirer.

The significance of James Brown's song is that as a creative songster, an artist, a leader, he had the people singing and dancing to

BLACK NATIONALISM
ALIVE AND WELL

this new shibboleth, north and south, east and west, and these beyond the shores of the United States were in-tuned with this genius. All of a sudden "Black was Beautiful" and we could be proud of it. Remember when he said he wanted to be a teacher but he felt like a preacher, or something like that!

Black Nationalism 154d. Michael Hooper of "Roots Revisited" and "Legendary Basketball Coach" Mr. George Murden.

Even more meaningful his creative genius was like fuel to the Civil Rights Movement as it affirmed its stance in those troubled times. Naturally, like all leaders, when he said "Hit Me!" the anti-Black forces did just that, but Maceo and the band played on! Meanwhile the "God-father of Soul" had etched his place in the minds, hearts and feet of the people. More importantly, he influenced generations of song and dance men and women, Black, Brown and White. "Mr.

FREDERICK MONDERSON

Dynamite," "The Minister of Superfunk," "Soul Brother No. 1," in his *Autobiography*, once referred to those who did follow his lead in funk, soul, jazz, rhythm and blues, pop, and even the later original creation hip hop, "I taught them everything they knew" he said, "but not everything I know."

Black Nationalism 155. Here's a historic intersection in Brooklyn where Harriet Ross Tubman Avenue meets Malcolm Boulevard. It is interesting that Sonny Carson played an important part in naming these two streets.

Strange, it is how coincidences seem to pile one on top of the other. More than a year ago, Al Sharpton held an affair at the Apollo and James Brown was there. The Rev. carried on about how his dad had brought him to the Apollo to "See James Brown" and now he confessed, "Dad, today I'm honoring James Brown." His dad never believed his son would aspire to the U.S. Presidency. I also took my son Erik to see the Rev. and James Brown on that occasion at the Apollo. James Brown was a standard bearer of Blackness who made us all proud. Through it all, I don't think he ever used the "N" word in any of his lyrical creativity and that was significant!

BLACK NATIONALISM
ALIVE AND WELL

Black Nationalism 156. Sonny Carson examines and discusses the bones of his ancestor Samuel Carson, **The Runaway**, with Atiim Ferguson and others in attendance.

Black Nationalism 156a. Flying the Colors!

FREDERICK MONDERSON

Black Nationalism 156b. Prof. James Smalls (left), an unnamed "Brother," Sonny Carson and Mzee Mora (right).

20. Perspectives on Sonny (AB) Carson By Dr. Fred Monderson

The roles of historical figures who impact on their community, nation and in an extra-national manner are sometimes not readily discernible to the general public but with time things have a tendency to come to the fore. One such character, who has had a similar impact on American history, with aforementioned repercussions, is Robert "Sonny" Carson. Paradoxically, while the general public has not recognized this important historical person, his immediate community with whom he interacted and impacted upon wanted to make sure that he was not forgotten.

BLACK NATIONALISM
ALIVE AND WELL

Upon his death the Black community, from diverse parts of the states came to pay last respects to Sonny "Abubadika" "He who leads his people" ("Abubadika" "AB") Carson. This is a title given him by a Ghana Chieftain who visited America in the early 1970s. While not as extravagant a send-off as that given to U.S. President Ronald Reagan, this President of the Committee to Honor Black Heroes, the community in a manner reminiscent of the Biblical story of the individual who would not let the angel depart until he had blest him, insisted that Sonny get all the trimmings accorded his due respect. Like Prof. John H. Clarke has often said regarding African-American funerals, "We put him away nicely." In that, with ceremonies at The House of the Lord Church, Friendship Baptist Church, Brown Memorial Baptist Church, gatherings in the Restoration Plaza and a *tour de force* march with funeral cortege from the Brooklyn Bridge, down Flatbush Avenue, up Fulton Street and across Troop Avenue to Gates Avenue then down Gates to Brown Memorial Baptist Church on Washington and Gates Avenue, Sonny got his "well-deserved due." A week later, dancers from Ghana gathered with the community at the Malcolm X School in Bed-Stuy to give more due to Sonny.

Jitu Weusi, center, of the Black Solidarity Day Committee and founding member of The East Cultural Organization, is flanked by supporters Basir Mchawi, Michael Hooper, Abubadika Sonny Carson; Weusi; Frederick Moderson and others. (Photo: Lem Peterkin)

Black Nationalism 156c. The Caption contains the message.

FREDERICK MONDERSON

Black Nationalism 156d. Sonny Carson in an analytic mood.

Anyone not familiar with the man could easily ask, "Why all this?" The answer is simple.

Black Nationalism 157. Close-up of the street name of the Super-Nationalist, Malcolm X.

BLACK NATIONALISM
ALIVE AND WELL

MALCOLM X

Black Nationalism 157a. The Legendary Malcolm Little turned Malik El-Hajj Shabazz, Malcolm X.

Sonny Carson was an extraordinary individual. He was also a man of vision, courage, fortitude, daring and with a big heart and a big smile. He emerged from a poor upbringing, was involved with drugs and crime, a gang-leader, he went to jail and saw first-hand the debilitating experiences of that institution. The Book and Movie, **The Education of Sonny Carson** chronicles his early years, the dynamic challenges facing urban Black youth in the post-World War II decades, his time in jail and it recounts and sets the stage for the ultimate transformation he would experience upon his release from prison.

FREDERICK MONDERSON

Almost instantly Sonny Carson became concerned about people, their problems and the aspirations to meet those challenges. As he rendered assistance "he used guile, all the while with a big and beautiful smile." However, it was never misunderstood that beneath that broad smile was a serious, determined and courageous leader who was well respected for his commitment and consistency when facing challenges.

Black Nationalism 158. Sonny Carson (left), Atiim Ferguson (center) and James (Chief) Parker (right), "The Brotherhood."

BLACK NATIONALISM
ALIVE AND WELL

Black Nationalist 158a. Senator Montgomery, Sonny Carson and Omowale Clay, testify at the Medgar Evers Congressional Hearing on Police Brutality convened by Congressman John Conyers and a Congressional delegation.

Black Nationalism 158b. Congressmen John Conyers (left), Major Owens (right) and Coleman (center) comprising the male members of the Congressional Delegation holding "Hearings on Police Brutality" in New York City especially.

FREDERICK MONDERSON

Black Nationalism 158c. John Conyers and other members of the Congressional Delegation conducting "Hearings on NYC Police Brutality," which is a national trend.

Upon his return from prison Sonny became aware of social and psychological inequities facing Blacks within that industrial complex framework, not only in New York, but across the nation as a whole. This is why he dedicated his life to offering assistance to persons caught within the perilous web of that emasculating experience. But he did not stop there. He saw social disparities in economic opportunities and employment practices, education, housing as well as in locations where Blacks spent their hard earned dollars.

In this latter respect, Sonny realized many stores operating in the Black community were White owned and so staffed. He often organized economic resistance. He said if we could shop here we could work here. He faced opposition at first but gradually doors were opened, Blacks were hired leading eventually to recognition of Black ownership. Hence was born the notion of the economic boycott. But Sonny did not stop there. His activist "mojo" was working. He became involved in education, was a member of **CORE (Congress of Racial Equality)** and all this was happening within the context of the national Civil Rights Movement, the Black Muslims and emergence of Malcolm X, the "5

BLACK NATIONALISM
ALIVE AND WELL

Percenters," the Black Panther Party, the Anti-Viet Nam War resistance on college campuses as well as all forms of movements for change across the American political, human and civil rights landscape. By the 1970s Sonny Carson had come of age as a fully fledged activist of national standing tremendously aggrieved at loss of Malcolm X and Martin Luther King. Similarly in the 1990s that compassionate side of him would be further aggrieved in loss of Biggie Smalls and Tupak Shakur.

Black Nationalism 158d. At his funeral parade banner extols Sonny Abubadika Carson as the Founder of the Committee to Honor Black Heroes.

FREDERICK MONDERSON

Black Nationalism 158e. Mother Jordan and son walk behind Dr. Delores Blakeley in the funeral parade for Sonny Carson.

Black Nationalism 158f. At the start of the funeral parade beside New York Technical College near the Brooklyn Bridge, Councilman Charles Barron, Abdul Haqq, Rev. Herbert Daughtry and Reverend Mother Jordan and her son.

BLACK NATIONALISM
ALIVE AND WELL

Black Nationalism 158g. The funeral parade works its way down Fulton Street towards the Bedford Stuyvesant community.

Black Nationalism 158h. View of the parade from the rear as the two highest individuals sits on the horse-drawn cortege.

FREDERICK MONDERSON

Black Nationalism 159. The school Sonny Carson was instrumental in naming for Malcolm X, El Hajj Malik el Shabazz.

BLACK NATIONALISM ALIVE AND WELL

Black Nationalism 159a. Lumumba Carson, son of famed activist Sonny Carson.

FREDERICK MONDERSON

Black Nationalism 160. Professor Kelson Maynard steadfastedly at what he does best, preparing for the next lecture, as a "classroom teacher."

Black Nationalism 160a. At the funeral and flanked by Ali Lamont and Rasheed Allah, "Pops" holds high the impending street name of Harriet Tubman Avenue.

BLACK NATIONALISM
ALIVE AND WELL

Sonny became a member of **The Republic of New Africa** and was elevated to status of a Judge before his untimely passing. This group wanted southern states set aside for Black independence contending that they would never have equal status in America. However, realistically considering the social, political and military history of this nation that has been and is a difficult proposition. Perhaps he ultimately realized this and thus he maintained his anti-White beliefs because of how that group had treated his people in America. The walls of his office were plastered with pictures of lynched Black men to serve as a reminder of the history of this heinous experience. Still, he was a principled man and was never satisfied with the explanation of the implications of Black Muslim murder of Malcolm X. However, while respecting the principles and program of Kwanza, which he incidentally made a special effort to participate in annually, he was later incensed that the leader would allow the flag to be changed or rearranged so the government could issue a postage stamp for Kwanza.

Black Nationalism 160b. The funeral parade finally arrives at Restoration Plaza where Sonny Carson "Held Court!"

FREDERICK MONDERSON

Black Nationalism 160c. Dr. Segun Shabaka (left); and John Branch, founder of the African Poetry Theater in New York (right).

His constantly working incisive and analytic mind, possessing a profound understanding of the change agents acting across the national landscape, political assassinations, murders, jailings, the infusion of drugs into the Black community, his travels abroad in Africa and elsewhere, by the mid-1990s Sonny Carson had come of age again. He had grown from a mere hill to a mountain of a man.

Sonny Carson's enlarged status was manifest when in 1995 his activism took him to the Brooklyn Navy Yard where coincidentally the US Navy discovered they had buried Samuel Carson "The Runaway" and turned his remains over to this grand-nephew Sonny Carson. There were several hundred names of Black Veterans also handed over to Mr. Carson. These were published in the New York **Afro Times** and are included in the book, **Sonny Carson: The Final Triumph** by Dr. Fred Monderson.

BLACK NATIONALISM ALIVE AND WELL

Black Nationalism 161. The famed Malcolm X, El Hajj Malik Shabazz, "More than just a man," an extraordinary leader and visionary.

21. PROFESSOR GEORGE SIMMONDS: UNSUNG HERO
BY
FRED MONDERSON

On Monday October 6, 1997, scholars, students, colleagues and community residents with their children came out to the Victoria 5 Theater in Harlem, to honor Professor George Simmons, an unsung hero of the African American community. A parade of speakers

FREDERICK MONDERSON

recounted how Professor Simmonds has educated, trained and assisted so many in the most unselfish manner. This is why, so many were proud that we were able to honor this giant of a man, while he was still alive.

William X, host and student, colleague and confidant of Dr. Simmonds spoke of how he was encouraged to be a scholar, speaker and organizer in the interest of the welfare of Africa and African Americans, thanks to the work and attitude of the scholar, Dr. George Simmonds.

Black Nationalism 162. Prof. George Simmonds embraces "young Fred Monderson" on a visit to Middle School 61, Gladstone Atwell in Brooklyn.

BLACK NATIONALISM ALIVE AND WELL

Black Nationalism 162a. Rev. Charles Norris, Sr., "Spiritual Father" of the **CEMOTAP** Movement and Pastor Emeritus of Bethesda Missionary Baptist Church.

22. Dr. YOSEF A. A. BEN-JOCHANNAN: A Tribute. By Dr. Fred Monderson

Sitting and listening recently to one of Dr. Ben's lectures given back in 1997, I realize he is near 95 years old, at least! Equally and considering he has had more than half a dozen strokes, and as a student of his, I thought he certainly deserves a tribute from me, before it's too late! I came to realize, Dr. Ben is an extraordinary man of many talents, but principally a man who held the African woman in the highest esteem. He taught us in the beginning was the African woman! Creation came out of the African woman! As the obelisk is a small pyramid on a tall base, this is the pedestal upon which Dr. ben-Jochannan placed the African woman. He honored

FREDERICK MONDERSON

the Black Woman who is the source of the Black Family! He taught us the Black Woman is a Goddess! He also led the light to the Nile Valley. He said, "I took Egypt to destroy White supremacy!" It's like Marcus Garvey said, "the cubs are running free out there," and thanks to Dr. Ben, intellectual cubs are challenging the historical records' distortions, omissions and are vigorously engaged in putting Africa in its proper place in world civilization history through its accomplishments in Nubia and Egypt, Nile Valley, cultures that gave so much to the world.

Black Nationalism 163. Dr. Josef ben-Jochannan, elder, nationalist, author, lecturer and early self-publishing promoter.

The Twentieth Century has been blessed with great African and African-American writers and historians. These include Dr. W. E.

BLACK NATIONALISM
ALIVE AND WELL

B. Du Bois, Dr. Carter G. Woodson, Dr. Kwame Nkrumah, Dr. Ivan Van Sertima, J. A. Rogers, Dr. Cheikh Anta Diop and Dr. Leonard James of New York City Technical College of the City University of New York, among others. This outstanding collection of brainpower equally extends into the Twenty-First Century. However, none of these giants surpass the literary production, commitment, tirelessness, and sincere dedication of Dr. Yusuf Alfredo Antonio ben-Jochannan. Outspoken visionary, ahead of his time; controversial historian and scholar, who is "not afraid to take an iconoclastic and individual if a somewhat idiosyncratic point of view;" Dr. Ben was always prepared to defend his position, irrespective. His friends and students, affectionately call this father, teacher, historian, friend and Egyptologist, "Doc Ben." In fact, back there in the early 1970s when even "Black folks" did not readily accept "Dr. Ben," Has anyone ever wondered how he got his name? It was a young man named "Barney" and myself Fred Monderson who first started calling him not "Dr. Ben" but "Ben Jo" and the name stuck and finally when another student Curtis Dunmoodie picked it up we began calling him "Dr. Ben" in defiance of those "feather bedders" who said "Dr. Ben has no Ph.D."

Black Nationalism 164. At the "Tribute to Prof. George Simmonds" at the Victoria 5 Theater in Harlem, "Young" Fred Monderson sat at the feet of his heroes, with Dr. Ben in light suit.

FREDERICK MONDERSON

Ever cried for Dr. Ben? This statement once made me cry at New York City Technical College. I hurriedly took the train to 125th Street in Harlem, before Prof. George Simmonds calmed me down, showing me Dr. Ben's Doctorate in Anthropology on the wall. That is what some of the "false prophets" still do today in academia to him and others! And so you ask them to match their literary production with their in-clandestine vituperativeness and they cannot! Period!

Black Nationalism 165. Dr. Yosef ben-Jochannan delivers a Lecture with a number of his Self-published works in background.

Here is a serious scholar, Dr. ben-Jochannan, who spent a lifetime researching, writing, and defending the integrity and intellectual capabilities of African people worldwide. Dr. Ben pioneered in indigenous ancient African terminology. Imagine a European-American scholar discovered an African woman in Ethiopia and named her "Lucy" after an Englishman's song "Lucy with Diamonds." Dr. Ben said no! Her name is *Denk Nesh* not Lucy!

BLACK NATIONALISM
ALIVE AND WELL

Black Nationalism 166. Sister Dr. Betty Shabazz, wife of Malcolm X, who always said, "Find the Good and Praise it!"

FREDERICK MONDERSON

In 1989, Doc Ben celebrated fifty years of visiting ancient Kemet, Ta-merry (Egypt) and the Nile Valley cultures. This prolonged involvement has under-girded the basis of his researches, speeches, writings and educational efforts and tours. Equally, he began and for some time maintained archaeological digs on the Island of Elephantine and elsewhere. Alas, these have been discontinued.

This writer was happy to be a part of that epoch making tour that marked Doc Ben's Fiftieth Anniversary visiting the ancient African "holy-land" and the next year for the First Nubian Festival. More importantly, I met "Doc Ben" in early 1972. This was right after the publication of his seminal works, *African Origins of the Major Western Religions (1970)*, *Africa: Mother of Western Civilization (1971)*, and *Black Man of the Nile* (1972), later *Black Man of the Nile and His Family*. The style of his writings, copious nature of referents employed to defend things African, and his Afrocentric pioneering approach makes Doc. Ben, a very well-respected elder, and a much sought after speaking attraction, a man who "tells it like it is!"

Black Nationalism 166a. Celebrating **KWANZAA** in New York.

BLACK NATIONALISM
ALIVE AND WELL

Dr. ben-Jochannan has compiled an impressive thirty odd publications! He helped set the stage for a whole new approach in interpreting Africa's contributions to civilization and its legacy. He lit the fire of intellectual and cultural consciousness in Africans worldwide. The style of dress with an Afrocentric flavor in America is also credited to him. Establishing connections between Africans in America, Africa, the Caribbean and South America, Asia and Europe are all attributed to Dr. ben-Jochannan, a man of vision, seer, and intellectual giant. Many of his books challenged the distortions of Europeans in writing, publishing and dissemination of knowledge about the arts, sciences, religion, etc., of the ancient people today called Egyptians. Dr. Ben has rightly included omissions and corrected distortions systematically implanted and perpetrated by racist Western, European and American historiography that have falsified the historical past with a prejudiced interpretation. Dr. Ben dared to expose the hypocrisy of western scholarship. He attacked the foundational pillars upon which a false legacy rests.

Black Nationalism 167. Dr. Fred Monderson sits beside his mentor and friend, Dr. Yosef ben-Jochannan, at a Harlem lecture.

FREDERICK MONDERSON

Black Nationalism 168. Honorable Robert "Sonny" Carson, venerated activist, always insisted young people "Stay in School."

Very early he also expressed the view some scholars are confused because they were taught with a wrong premise. In his own right, and as a result of his teachings, he had no choice but to produce, publish and distribute his works without the aid of major publishing

BLACK NATIONALISM
ALIVE AND WELL

firms. He was thus a pioneer in self-publishing, launching Alkebu-Lan Publishing Company and appealing and winning the support of many upcoming nationalists as they purchased his books in first edition form!

Black Nationalism 168a. Sonny Carson and his son, Lumumba Carson, at the funeral for **Allah U Akbar**.

FREDERICK MONDERSON

Initiating a new approach to history and the end result was an exposition and critical analysis of dynamic forces of Europe and Africa in struggle to claim heritage of the ancient and modern historical record. Dr. Ben addressed professionals, laymen, clergy, students and educators. He stressed vitality, resilience and creative expressions that shaped the modern African personality and worldview. Such an approach found ready ears among a people yearning for factual information about their illustrious African past in effort to free their minds. They were enthused by the positive nature and potency of their cultural African heritage as "Ben" outlined it. He also took great pains to explain that there were lusterless pages in Africa's past. Nevertheless, his concern fueled their emerging aspirations. This outlook brought Dr. Ben the adulation and respect so deserved of a grateful people. They understood and welcomed his contributions among the litany of great African-American literary artists.

As such, Dr. Ben's writings, lectures and educational tours over the years have stressed two essential themes. The first is that the emergence of civilization, viz., science, religion, government, architecture, agriculture, philosophy, and the arts, began in Africa. The mouth of these utterances became the conduit of today's Egypt and the Nile Valley. In his approach, Dr. Ben has shown how the structural foundations of western civilization developed from discoveries and scientific applications in this ancient African land. Lastly, he took great pains to show the writing and teaching of modern history have been distorted to elevate Europe and degrade Africa, which is clearly wrong and must be rectified. This fundamental view helped establish the need for African historical reconstruction and interpretation particularly as we navigate this new century and millennium.

BLACK NATIONALISM
ALIVE AND WELL

Black Nationalism 169. Another view of Dr. Ben-Jochannan delivering a lecture at the Dempsey Center in Harlem.

FREDERICK MONDERSON

Black Nationalism 169a. Allah U Akbar, whose funeral drew some important persons, is shown on horseback.

The second of Dr. Ben's themes has been that Africans worldwide should be proud of their ancestors' accomplishments. The arts and sciences that today govern the world are Africa's legacy. African-Americans should take and show great pride and dignity in their history and heritage. They must respect themselves and carry themselves with that dignity and pride. They can and must teach the young how to identify with Africa. In so doing, they must study and visit Africa. Yet, they must also be aware of the machinations of cultural imperialism and cultural genocide at work challenging their

BLACK NATIONALISM
ALIVE AND WELL

every forward movement. Further, the young must immerse themselves in an African-centric intellectual perspective and research, write and teach others in turn. They must study languages, French, especially for this is where a tremendous body of recovered knowledge is located. In so doing, German, Swahili, Greek, Latin, Coptic and *Medu Netcher* or Hieroglyphics, must also be learnt for there is much that must be learnt also. Importantly, they must struggle to correct the recent distorted history of Africa's past. In this way, future leaders would help to better the lot of humanity and save the world from its impending moral, psychological, spiritual and scientific destruction. To accomplish these objectives the good doctor has supplied a reservoir of information from his life's researches.

Black Nationalism 169b. Sonny Carson, Atiim Ferguson and Mr. Wright, in tearful moment, came to pay respects to Akbar.

FREDERICK MONDERSON

Black Nationalism 169c. Richard Green of the Youth **Collective** came to pay his respects to Akbar.

The author's major thesis of his *African Origins of the Major "Western Religions"* is that African religious practices were denigrated and called "Fetishism" and "Paganism" despite such religious practices laying the foundation for all subsequent religion. In fact, these ancient thought processes, he showed are the fundamental bases of Judaism, Christianity and Islam. He showed and argued that these ideas were first developed and nurtured in Central Africa among indigenous peoples and then extended throughout the Nile Valley. They found greatest fruition in Kemet (Egypt) and were preserved by its civilization advances and the nature of its geography. After centuries, millennia, of oral formulation, the early knowledge was first written down in the "Pyramid Texts," then "Coffin Texts," and the later *Book of the Dead* or *Book of Going Forth By Day*, "Book of Gates," "Book of Knowing Ra," and the "Mysteries of Sais" (Egypt), etc In this intellectual awakening giving impetus to advances in science and social principles benefiting humanity, Africa's second cultural daughter, Kemet, rose to greater prominence than did the eldest, Ethiopia, he explained. He stressed and still maintains today, despite

BLACK NATIONALISM
ALIVE AND WELL

all the "new evidence" that civilization began to the south of Egypt! Again, now we know of religious, artistic and other advances discovered in the Eastern and Western Deserts of Upper Egypt, primarily at **Nabta Playa**, west of Abu Simbel in Upper Egypt.

Black Nationalism 170. The revered Reverend Dr. Martin Luther King, Jr. (1929-1968).

FREDERICK MONDERSON

Another of Dr. Ben's works is *Africa: Mother of Western Civilization*. Its major thesis holds that the fundamental laws, principles, philosophies, ideas, arts and crafts that educated the west, are indigenous to Africa through the Nile Valley cultural experience. For critical teachers who face this dilemma he has some advice. As such, he wrote: "The only credentials necessary in the experience of African history, otherwise mis-nomered 'the Black Experience' and 'Black Studies' are the documented proofs and the sources from whence they are taken."

Black Nationalism 170a. Attorney Carl Thomas is interviewed for a local program.

BLACK NATIONALISM
ALIVE AND WELL

Black Nationalism 170b. "In the Name of Allah U Akbar."

For this reason, *Africa: Mother of Western Civilization* is an enormous compendium of referents, facts, sources, illustrations, and analyses that challenge laymen and scholars alike. It suggests all educators and lay persons alike become involved. It opens new vistas and a wide array of historical sources relating to the significance of Africa in world civilization.

Black Man of the Nile and his Family marks the third of the trilogy of Dr. Ben's seminal works. This particular source represents the maturity of his thoughts and presentations. It also contains a number of objectives the author seeks to accomplish.

FREDERICK MONDERSON

The first of these objectives is, "an attempt to create in young African, African-American (Black person), and all other African people, a sense of belonging in the great African heritage." It is, writes Dr. Ben, "specifically directed to those who have criminally demasculinized, denuded, and otherwise denigrated the Africans of their **CULTURAL**, **ECONOMIC**, **POLITICAL**, **SCIENTIFIC**, **SPIRITUAL**, and all other forms of their heritage and human decency." To this we should add the intellectual heritage as preserved and represented in Egypt.

It also presents, **"AFRICAN ORIGINS OF EUROPEAN CIVILIZATION"** in a manner whereby, "scholars can find interesting use for it in their research; as much as the layman can for processing information."

Dr. Ben views his role as gadfly presenting, "pertinent information needed in the African peoples' **RE-IDENTIFICATION** with their great ancestral heritage." Lastly, he continued, the: "major desired accomplishment this volume seeks to achieve, is to provide anthropological evidence in the ancient heritage of the Africans" and their contributions all over the world.

Another work of his, *From Abu Simbel to Ghizeh*: *A Guide Book and Manual* is in itself a useful piece of writing. But, there are other books including:

BLACK NATIONALISM ALIVE AND WELL

Black Nationalism 171. Dr. Yosef ben-Jochannan sits beside a friend with young Senator David Patterson, who will later become Lieutenant and then Governor of New York State, in light coat, standing in rear.

Sir Francis Bacon (1561-1626) admonished, "Some books are to be tasted, others to be swallowed, and some few to be chewed and digested." This much can be said of the trilogy of Dr. ben-Jochannan's works, *Black Man of the Nile and His Family*, *Africa: Mother of Western Civilization*, and *The African Origins of the Major Western Religions*. The others are equally interesting! Everyone must buy and read these books and pass them on to others particularly your sons and daughters.

FREDERICK MONDERSON

Black Nationalism 172. The highly respected and admired South African icon and freedom fighter who spent 27-years in prison to finally dismantle apartheid and whose autobiography was entitled "A Long Walk to Freedom."

Finally, as a student of his, and based on observations and analytic critique, this writer would like to add a 12-point summation of how we can view Dr. Yosef Alfredo Antonio ben-Jochannan's contributions as an unselfish and fearless historian, researcher, author and orator elucidating correction to the historical record systematically distorted to elevate Europe and denigrate Africa,

BLACK NATIONALISM ALIVE AND WELL

while wrecking psycho-social debasement of the African psyche, spirit and persona.

1. We must praise and show thankfulness for the man who, for more than a century, challenged the behemoth of western intellectual oppression of Africa and her offspring while enlightening many to the wonders of a creative African cultural heritage.

2. We must commend Dr. ben-Jochannan for the humanitarian work he did among the Nubians in Egypt and Sudan, viz., Aswan, Daboud, Wadi Halfa, Dongola Province and Fashoda.

3. We must recognize his call to action in the cultural genocide in the African American studies curriculum predating the Afrocentric insistence on multi-culturalism.

4. We should continue to emulate his style of critical analysis of contemporary developments, whether it was historical omissions in Alex Haley's **Roots**; misrepresentation in **King Tut's Exhibition** that is again taking place in America today; taking to task T. Eric Peet's "The Problem with Akhenaton;" Criticism of Father Temple's **Bantu Philosophy**; challenge to another writer's description that Rameses II had "badly abscessed teeth," and so forth.

5. We can appreciate his identifying "**They all look Alike, All**," thus linking Black people across the globe who were victims of racial hatred and cultural aggression.

6. His clarification of the differences between the Black Nationalist and the Black Marxist was very timely and inspiring and still is.

FREDERICK MONDERSON

7. First to outline the **History of the Bible**, he challenged the **Black Clergy Without a Black Theology** and offered a **Black Bible** for Black spiritual and religious consciousness.

Black Nationalism 173. Dr. Leonard Jeffries, Prof. James Smalls and Dr. Lewis, the Ophthalmologist from Harlem who address a gathering at PS 258 in Brooklyn.

BLACK NATIONALISM ALIVE AND WELL

Black Nationalism 173a. Rev. Al Sharpton and Carl Thomas sit and listen attentively to testimony at the Congressional Hearings on Police Brutality.

Black Nationalism 173b. Attorney Carl Thomas gives testimony to the Congressional Delegation on Police Brutality.

FREDERICK MONDERSON

Black Nationalism 173c. Its Ron Daniels' turn to give testimony.

8. We must acknowledge as a human he may have made some mistakes, miniscule as they were outweighed by the foundation of ethical and cultural Ma'at he implanted in the consciousness of African people worldwide.

9. His insistence that all African Americans visit the Nile Valley to imbibe in the cultural heritage and grow from the intellectual exposure, but more particularly their dress code and mannerism among the people must not be construed as the "arrogance of Ugly Americans," was and is still timely and insightful.

10. His outspoken nature, love for Marcus Garvey and his "Philosophy and Opinions," praise of Black Goddesses, critique of Academics who are "fifth columns" made him anathema to people with ill-intentions for African people.

BLACK NATIONALISM
ALIVE AND WELL

Black Nationalism 173d. Members of the audience expressing their cases at the Congressional Hearing on Police Brutality (top); while others sit silently, with Connie Lesold (center) and Marlene Sanders beside her, as events unfold.

FREDERICK MONDERSON

Black Nationalism 173e. Families expressing their grief to the Congressional Delegation about their loss due to violence.

11. Dr. ben-Jochannan had little respect for people in high positions who never promoted the aspirations of their Black subordinates.

12. A staunch Pan-Africanist, he aspired to see accomplished sustained and measurable economic, political and educational empowerment for people of African heritage worldwide.

Therefore, we must recognize that Dr. ben-Jochannan has made a major contribution to African intellectual growth. He created a cosmological vision over time that allowed us to see the light. In fact, he was our light! He taught us how to persevere to persevere! He asked us to standardize our learning, have a standard for our behavior, and don't fear, don't fear defeat, don't fear death!

BLACK NATIONALISM ALIVE AND WELL

Black Nationalism 174. Musical legend Bob Marley featured in this mural in the Bed-Stuy area of Brooklyn.

FREDERICK MONDERSON

23. PRAISE OF DR. BEN BY DR. FRED Mc ONDERSON

1. Historical Overview –

Dr. Yosef Alfredo Antonio ben-Jochannan is a well-respected elder, historian, Egyptologist, author, publisher and speaker who was never afraid to take an individual, a somewhat idiosyncratic point of view and defend it irrespective. Dr. Ben told us, "I took Egypt to challenge White supremacy!" He shined the light for many of us to see and encouraged the acquisition of knowledge. Throughout his career, Dr. Ben emphasized Egypt/Kemet is a Black civilization and whatever Whites found there were latecomers to Egypt after the Middle Kingdom following the Hyksos invasion. He challenged distortion, omission and misrepresentation of the culture. He also paid a price from both Black and White interests. We know the status quo would like to eliminate people like Dr. Ben from the consciousness of young people, but we will not have it! For this all people should look at the history through which he focused and guided our understanding.

Prehistory

The Palaeolithic Period lasted from about 300,000 to 25,000 years ago. It comprised Lower, Middle and Upper Periods. This is called the Old Stone Age.

BLACK NATIONALISM
ALIVE AND WELL

Black Nationalism 175. "Young" Fred Monderson, student of Dr. ben-Jochannan and more importantly, Dr. Leonard James.

The Mesolithic is called the Middle Stone Age. Where we see Homo Erectus, early man, begin the use of more sophisticated stone tools.

FREDERICK MONDERSON

Let us not forget, Zinjanthropus Boise, "near man" had been a tool using Being dated at 1.75 million years old.

In Egypt, Palaeolithic Sites included Merimdeh, the Fayum, Kharga Oasis, and Thebes where Hand axes were found dating to more than 300,000 years. Kom Ombo was also a Palaeolithic site.

In the Palaeolithic Period man used bifacial flint tools, hand-axes and choppers. He began learning to use bone tools. The Mousterian Period is contemporary with the Middle to Upper period and more sophisticated hand tools, hand axes emerged. We also see early burial of man and beginnings of family living. Palaeolithic tools of the Mousterian Period were made of flint, antler, ivory, lance-heads, knives and microliths, or very tiny tools were also made of stone particularly. By the Mesolithic Period the bow and arrow emerged with arrow-heads of flint and later stone. We see carvings of various animals appearing in early art.

A big change occurred in the history of man between the Mesolithic and Neolithic Periods. The Neolithic Period began about 10,000 B.C. The Neolithic Age is characterized by sedentary beginnings as man began to settle down. This is marked by the birth of food production. Women are credited with developing agriculture because of their "stay of home" nurturing responsibility.

In the Palaeolithic Period man's food supply was characterized as 90 percent meats from the hunt and 10 percent agri-vegetation from gathering. The big change occurred with him settling down in communities, beginning to grow crops, domesticating animals and practice a more systematic burial of his dead. We early see containers for grain, use of sickles and evidence of winnowing grain. Equally too, we see the emergence of "division of labor" with men as hunters and women as gatherers of plants; as well as specialization of function. There is evidence of ivory combs, needles, and manufacture of points and knives used in domestic endeavors.

BLACK NATIONALISM ALIVE AND WELL

Three major cultures emerged in Neolithic, Upper Egypt. These are the Badarian, Amratian and Gerzean or Naqada I and II, lasting anywhere from 4500-3100 B.C. The period from 3300-3100 B.C. is considered Proto-dynastic or sometimes Naqada III period.

The Badarian is named after El-Badari in Upper Egypt. This is the site where Flinders Petrie did his Sequence dating techniques. At El-Badari were found ivory figurines having religious significance. There were cosmetic palettes. Jewelry was made of shells, turquoise, and much burnished pottery. Trade seems to have developed in this period.

Black Nationalism 176. Sign indicating the African Burial Ground National Monument served by the National Parks Service of the U.S. Department of the Interior.

The Amratian Period is named after El-Amrah also in Upper Egypt and Merimdeh where we first see bee-hive huts. There was a shrine for the local god. People are seen hunting. A woman sits at a loom. There is a figurine of a dancing lady. The "Bird Lady" figurine in the Brooklyn Museum comes from El-Amrah. The earliest mother goddess figurine comes from this site that is transitional to the Gerzean culture.

Gerzean from El Gerza was characterized with white incised pottery with a ripple pattern. This culture produced the first incised pottery with people and animals. We see also a double-shaped type of pottery, as well as black-topped pottery, with red burnishing of various designs.

The Nagada site, which together with el Gerza characterized the period, is also located in Upper Egypt.

Black Nationalism 177. Sankofa International Academy is one of those institutions Bob Law insisted we support financially and otherwise for the good work they do in educating our youth.

A tomb from Gebelein shows the earliest representation of boats and the first clear figures on pattern. Linen from Gebelein is one of the oldest found. The Gerzean pottery represents variety in pottery form, design and use of material. Some were in regular mud, stone and even alabaster. Whether red, black topped or designed, we see great sophistication in the pottery.

Some pottery changed to votive offerings. Rock carvings show use of bow and arrows with kilts as garments. The Dog Palette in the Louvre depicts mythical animals. The earliest forms of the gods are shown on the high cliffs of the Eastern Desert. Min is the earliest

BLACK NATIONALISM ALIVE AND WELL

example of a god discovered in the Eastern Desert, c. 4000 B.C.; while the "Cow goddess" or Hathor was found at Nabta Playa earlier.

By the emergence of the Dynastic Period nomes were beginning to be delimited with 22 in the south and some 20 in the north. Those in the South were clearly delineated while the exact boundaries of the north were still being worked out. There is much fighting for domination that ends in formation of dynastic period. There are many battle scenes with much pictographic representation. The Scorpion King is shown as Horus. Other predynastic kings and animal guises are shown. The most distinguishing thing to emerge here is the Register, a method of representation in art that separates the chaos of predynastic from the order of the dynastic period which was ushered in by Narmer the conqueror from the south. Much evidence from this period comes from Hierakonpolis, the earliest capital of Egypt and Abydos. Many battle scenes depict the process of unification.

King Scorpion is depicted on a macehead from Hierakonpolis. He is shown opening a new canal with scenes of defeated enemies. He wears the White Crown, symbol of the south. There is much controversy regarding the kings Narmer, Menes and Hor-Aha. We were told earlier Narmer married a queen from north, Lower Egypt, to solidify the unification. This is incorrect for now she is said to be from Gebelein in Upper Egypt! This brings us to the end of the Prehistoric Period.

Discoveries at Qustol in Nubia or Ethiopia.

The discoveries at Qustol in Nubia show the paraphernalia we associate with Kingship, such as White Crown, palace façade, Horus bird, incense burner that we see in Egypt at around 3100 BC, evident

FREDERICK MONDERSON

in Nubia some 200 years earlier. Equally too, the Eastern Desert is Upper Egypt has revealed Petroglyphs or markings on stone on the walls of the high shelters of the Wadis. They clearly show the earliest god-figure, Min; leaders, boats, cattle, earliest form of the writing, etc.

Black Nationalis178. Entrance to **The Ancestral Chamber** or **The Well** a sort of **Door of No Return**! Interesting, but Sonny Carson created **The Door of Return** by repatriating his ancestor, **The Runaway**, Samuel Carson, to Ghana to create a site of pilgrimage for African Americans seeking their ancestral roots in Africa.

By the time of the First Dynasty, writing was fully established having laid the grounds for later perfection. Much research, particularly since Post-World War II, has shown Upper Egyptian origins of the writing developed from local flora, fauna, geographic and human motifs. Diop, Arnett and others have presented evidence of rudimentary development of writing in cliffs along the upper areas of the Nile. While Winkler argued they were Mesopotamian in origin; Wilkinson dates them to 1000 years before possibly Mesopotamian contacts.

BLACK NATIONALISM ALIVE AND WELL

Dynasties

The Archaic Period, Dynasties I and II, is important for the formative beginnings of government, religious expression, establishment of the military, trade patterns, burial of the dead, etc. The most reliable record of the kings of Egypt is the **Tablets** listing the order of these rulers. The **Palermo Stone** begins with the predynastic kings and has been commented on by Josephus, Eusebius and Manetho. The **Turin Papyrus** is now a fragmented relic in that museum. The **Tablet of Karnak**, created by Thutmose III of the 18th Dynasty, was stolen in 1864 by Prisse de Avenges and taken to the Louvre. At that time it listed 64 kings though only 48 names were legible. The **Table of Abydos** is one of two such sources still in its original place. It lists 76 kings from Menes or Narmer to Seti I. Five of its cartouche names of kings are blank. We will get to this later. Its companion, the **Second Abydos List**, found in the Temple of Rameses II at Abydos, now resides in the British Museum. The **Sakkara List** was found in a tomb of an Old Kingdom **Noble Roy** listing a small number of kings and still resides in its place or deposit. While the nation's capital was at Hierakonpolis, at Unification, it was changed and administered from Memphis. The kings of the first two dynasties were buried at Abydos. However, while Memphis remained the Capital city, new kings chose to be buried at Sakkara, within the Memphis vicinity.

FREDERICK MONDERSON

> For all those who were lost
> For all those who were stolen
> For all those who were left behind
> For all those who were not forgotten

Black Nationalism 179. The engraved message on the wall of the "Ancestral Chamber" says it all!

We know the **Old Kingdom** was a Period of creativity, building upon and solidifying the form of government, religious worship, building enterprise, emergence of Pyramid Texts and much more. Trade flourished, river navigation and transportation of large stone became perfected. The art of medicine made great strides, particularly to treat injuries from principally building in stone and in whatever military ventures the pharaohs engaged in. The Priesthood emerged as a powerful body that perpetuated the religious philosophy of the God King, conducted religious worship and oversaw the cult of the dead. In time they became very powerful, "a state within the state."

The "Pyramid Texts" represented on the walls of tombs of fifth and sixth dynasty pharaohs represent the earliest recorded writings that spelt out the fundamentals of Egyptian religious beliefs. This is one of the highlights of Dr. Ben's work. As some of his followers may know, Dr. Ben is an anthropologist; historian, engineer and he also taught religion. His problem with the "Major Religions" is that not only did they come after this great flowering of African religious thought, while the "Pyramid Texts" remain unchanged for some 5000 years; the 2500 years of the Bible has seen many, many revisions that to this day still has not changed the negative representation of the African in its content.

BLACK NATIONALISM ALIVE AND WELL

Let me now review some of the firsts Dr. Ben has enlightened his students about Egypt.

1. The first tunnel was dug during the Old Kingdom to create a passageway between the two great pyramids.

2. The first representation of a moving image shows a hound running after a gazelle from the Old Kingdom.

3. The first evidence of people being depicted in motion was made by a Middle Kingdom artist named Mertisen.

4. There were 70 pyramids built in Egypt. He taught us about the silt pyramid, the natural pyramid, the step pyramid, and the true pyramid. There was also a bent pyramid.

Black Nationalism 180. Entrance into **The Well** showing continents, symbolisms and names and dates of African buried therein.

5. He showed the prominence of women in ancient Egypt/Kemet. Dr. Ben put the black woman on a pedestal. He informed that Narmer's queen was given prominence; so too were other queens throughout the nation's history. Narmer's son Aha built a large tomb at Abydos for his mother. The society believed women transmitted divine genes. Peseshet was a "Lady Director of Lady Doctors." That is why I named my granddaughter Jayde "Peseshet" after her.

6. Imhotep was the first physician to step out from the mist of history. He came from an architectural family; his father was an architect and presumably his grandfather. He built the Step-Pyramid at Sakkara.

7. Quarrying and transportation of large stone was greatly developed as early as the Old Kingdom.

8. The practice of medicine had reached unprecedented levels by Old Kingdom times.

Middle Kingdom – The Middle Kingdom was a period of Unification, Consolidation, Reorganization, Expansion and Cultural Flowering, following the collapse of the Old Kingdom that had ushered in the First Intermediate Period. The Kings Intef and Mentuhotep united the country and provided the wherewithal to transition the form of government, nature of the military, schools of art and thought, religious practice, and much more. The temple of Mentuhotep at Deir el Bahari is a masterpiece of Egyptian architecture that transitions from the Old Kingdom to New Kingdom architectural and artistic building techniques.

Egyptian town life leaves practically no records because of perishable materials used in domestic construction. Only tombs have evidence of the people's existence. Tombs were profusely illustrated with scenes of the dead, evidence of the "Coffin Text," a continuation of the "Pyramid Texts" of the Old Kingdom which was later replaced by the "Book of the Dead" or "Book of Coming Forth by Day."

BLACK NATIONALISM
ALIVE AND WELL

Language was highly developed during this time. In fact, the language for most of the later period was based on Middle Egyptian.

The **New Kingdom** saw the expulsion of the Hyksos invaders and development of Imperial adventures with a rise in prominence of Thebes; Amon Worship principally characterized the period; Temple and Tomb construction expanded; and arts and crafts developed. Reorganization of the military aided warrior pharaohs to go abroad, conquer peoples and places, bring back wealth and enslaved peoples, many of whom were given as booty to enrich the Priesthood who built great temple to praise Amon-Ra, god of great beneficence to his adherents. Science, art, medicine, transportation, trade, medicine, quarrying, astronomy and astrology was enhanced through the efforts of this priestly body.

The New Kingdom essentially ended with the 20th Dynasty when even the Ramessides were proving to be weak pharaohs. The 18th Dynasty was dominated by the Amenhoteps and Thutmoses, including Hatshepsut; while the 19th Dynasty comprised Rameses I, Seti and Rameses II who essentially dominated the duration. The 20th Dynasty, following in the name of illustrious predecessors fielded 2 strong pharaohs, Rameses II and IX, while the others were all weak. The 21st through the 24th dynasties were all embroiled in squabbles, none being stable. This invited the Ethiopians or Kushites to descend the Nile, conquering Thebes and ultimately all of Egypt. They became the only rulers who dominated and controlled the Nile River Valley from the Headwaters to the Mediterranean.

FREDERICK MONDERSON

Black Nationalism 181. View from within **Circle of the Diaspora** or **The well** where the following engraved symbolism recounts the religious and philosophical belief systems, not simply of Africans, but of other people also.

The **LATE PERIOD** represents the beginning of the end of native Egyptian rule of the ancient land that ends with the 26th Dynasty.

Following Khasta, Piankhy, Shabaka and Taharka were the outstanding pharaohs of the 25th Dynasty. The Late Period Revival began in the 25th Dynasty was continued into the 26th Dynasty. This signaled the end of African rulership of Egypt and Persians, Assyrians, Persians again conquered the ancient land. Finally "Alexander the Great" essentially began Greek rule which was continued by Ptolemy Soter upon his death and this rule was ended by Roman conquest.

Greeks and Romans – Temples at Edfu, Esneh, Kom Ombo, Isis and Kalabsha were built using Egyptian and Nubian architectural practices with Greek and Roman innovations.

II. What is the proper attire/behavior in the Temple?

BLACK NATIONALISM ALIVE AND WELL

Dr. Ben has always insisted on a particular dress code and mode of behavior when visiting any temple in Egypt. That is to say, no short shorts and any such attire! He frowned on European visitors who enter the holy places practically naked as if sunning themselves. He advised against entering the Sanctuary, "Holy of Holies," the most sacred place in the temple. In ancient times, only the Pharaoh or High Priest could enter this place where the god rested. The Guides, because of their work, enter the Sanctuary often carrying those they are guiding! Still, many have no idea of what is being said in this instance and so permit anything, behavior or otherwise.

The "Shabaka Proscription" was made against some people who plotted a murder in the temple. As such, Dr. Ben advised, be on your best behavior, think only positive thoughts and look, learn and enjoy your visit.

Before you go, it's advisable that you read as much as possible so what you see on the monuments will be more easily understandable. Get yourself a good camera and lots of film, 20-25 rolls. Today we're into the digital photography age. Enjoy your pictures and boast about what you saw!

One of the Axioms of Dr. Ben has been, "Only the documented sources are what determine the interpretation of the subject." Writing always played a significant role in the development of religion and as far as is certain, Egyptian religion is older than the dynasties.

When it comes to the writing there is clear evidence, contrary to 19th Century European scholarship followed over into the 20th Century with claims of Asiatic and Indo-European and Semitic origins of the Egyptian language; Diop, Arnett, even Winkler have shown there is clear evidence of the emergence of writing in Upper Egypt and Nubia in the shelters on the high ridges of the Nile and in the Wadis of the Eastern and Western Deserts. Again, the flora, fauna, geography and people provided the basis for the language stock.

FREDERICK MONDERSON

Now, since we know mathematics was already developed by the First Dynasty and a coherent body of religious doctrines was available by the Old Kingdom, it's safe to say centuries of preparation went into these developments. For example, we know the earliest evidence of Greek writing is found at Abu Simbel and dated to the fifth century. Homer "wrote" his **Iliad** and **Odyssey** and this has been dated, with some stretch to the eighth century. Some have tried to argue these events go back centuries before they were written down. Are we to believe such early and profound ideas as the pyramid texts did not take centuries to become coherent in their evolution, thus stretching the origins of writing back into the fourth millennium?

Bases of Knowledge – Thoth, scribe of the gods is also recognized as the inventor of writing as well as astronomy, measurement, music and other forms of knowledge. His female counterpart was Seshat, goddess of building, often shown with the pharaoh "Stretching the Cord" in building a temple.

Black Nationalism 182. Circle of the Diaspora – Close-up evidence of the map of Africa and the West carved in the floor of the Memorial.

BLACK NATIONALISM ALIVE AND WELL

24. THE GOLDEN AGE OF WEST AFRICA
By
Dr. Fred Monderson

Introduction:

The middle age of African history comprised the Medieval Sudanic empires of Ghana, Mali and Songhay that accomplished all the characteristics of African civilization. In those areas considered the bedrock of African high-cultural experience and development, viz., economics, politics, and culture, the accomplishments were tremendous. However, while cultural developments are important, geography has also been significant in shaping the emerging culture of this expansive sub-continent. For example, the Western Sudan and the Sahara are curious environments. Evidence indicates in earlier times the Sahara was very fertile, teeming with game and had many rivers, supporting a significant population. Importantly, however, in *African Glory*, J.C. DeGraaf-Johnson, informs the Roman occupation of North Africa decimated the wildlife of this region. In late ancient history leopards, lions and elephants once roamed this area and have now vanished. J.C. De-Graaf-Johnson mentions 3,500 animals killed in 26 games given by Emperor Augustus Caesar, to amuse the people of Rome. Pompey, Roman general and emperor slew 600 lions, 315 being males. Julius Caesar killed 400 lions in the shows he gave. Warfare also bears some fault. Nevertheless, more animal and plant-life were destroyed by man than by other geographic or climatic factors; aiding desertification of the region since.

FREDERICK MONDERSON

Black Nationalism 183. ANKH - "Egyptian Symbol of Life!"

We know culture is the most viable and vital dynamic of any civilization. Bernard Fage mentions fragments of coal found at Jos, Nigeria in West Africa that was radio-carbon dated at "greater than 39,000 years." These dates range from the Middle Stone Age to the

BLACK NATIONALISM ALIVE AND WELL

New Stone Age, showing man in West Africa using fire some forty thousand years ago. Whether Jos, Nigeria, or sites in the Sahara were continuously occupied is difficult to tell. However, Nok culture does show occupational stratification at 3500 B.C., 2000 B.C., 900 B.C. and 200 A.D. This West African site is therefore considered a "transitional" culture, from stone to metal workings.

Basil Davidson's *Lost Cities of Africa*, mentions the Frenchman Lhote's discoveries in the Sahara at places occupied by "Negroes" from the earliest times. Producing "beautiful and sensitive realism in art," these Africans originated naturalistic human portraiture very early, laying the cultural foundations for West African Sudanic Art with its religious and spiritual dynamics.

The history of the Western Sudan is generally recounted by Islamic scholars charting the rise and expansion of Medieval states, where the success of these empires were due to trade, good government and strong armies. Islam played a pivotal role, helping to destroy Ghana, aiding Mali and was a factor in Songhay's rise and final destruction. In these cultures and nation states, accomplishments were made in higher education, where literacy flourished and scholars produced academic manuscripts; where philosophy, law, astronomy, mathematics and medicine were taught at the Universities of Sankore, Djenne and Timbuktu. The *Tarik as-Sudan* and *Tarik al-Fattah*, as primary sources recount, the history of *Bilal es-Sudan* "land of the Blacks," during this period. Art was primarily supported by the state and royalty. And so, they blended African conventions and social needs with Islamic ideas. Still, despite the importance of the large states, the Western Sudan has no uniform art style; each culture in their region producing their own characteristics, whether sculpture or other forms of gold or precious metals artifacts.

FREDERICK MONDERSON

Economic factors played a pivotal role in this agricultural region influenced by the desert, the Sudanic belt, the forest region, the Niger River Valley and the Atlantic Ocean to the westwards. The area supported sedentary hoe farming, with millet, maize and rice as staples. To support industrial activity two sets of craftsmen, blacksmiths and professionals jewelers, dominated the work of base and precious metals. Gold of Western Sudan became legendary. E.W. Bovill's *The Golden Trade of the Moors* mentions large gold production as late as start of the sixteenth century. By this time, however, much of the gold trade was diverted to the Atlantic coast after the destruction of Songhay. Still, estimates show "gold from the Gold Coast was accounting for an amount that has been estimated at about one-tenth of the total world supply at that time." This was an immense total from one state.

International, regional and local markets developed from the trans-Saharan trade. In these markets one could find cloths, thread, straw hats, mats and calabash bowls. Much of this was decorated with geometric and other patterns. Craftsmen worked in glass beads, did leather work and made iron hoes. The book trade was lucrative. Gold, however, characterized the "Golden Age of West Africa."

From the time of Ancient Ghana, scholars estimate the Trans-Saharan trade exported some 9 tons of gold annually. Much of this was in the form of well worked jewelry and coins of gold. Goldsmiths worked with twisted thread and ingots, using a variety of art forms. Weapons of swords and daggers were of iron and copper. However, royal weapons were made of gold. Goldsmiths made bracelets, rings and necklaces. The state awarded "toe rings" of gold, for bravery. The sword scabbard of the royal interpreter and instruments of the king's musicians were made of gold. Ceremonial sabers, lances and arrow quivers were made of gold. Also, trappings of horses and royal dinner plates were made of gold. Royal dogs were leashed in gold.

The forest region provided an abundance of wood for smelting metals and sculpturing. Jean Laude's *The Arts of Black Africa*

BLACK NATIONALISM
ALIVE AND WELL

describes tools of sculptors as, "various types of adzes, broad-axes, chip axes, hollow chisels, and double-edged knives." They used "leaves for polishing the finished sculpture and special palm-oil preparations for obtaining an artificial patina." Natural ingredients were used for colors as kaolin for white, charcoal for black, and sometimes ochre for red and yellow.

Black Nationalism 184. LATIN CROSS - "Christian Faith."

Ghana

Medieval Ghana filled a transitional gap in the civilizations of Africa. In fact, many West African peoples as the Akan of Ghana have legends of migrations from the Nile Valley. They believe in the divine death and birth of the founder of the royal lineage. There are similarities in the ram's religious symbolism in Egypt, Kush and much of West Africa. The figure 8, as a religious symbol "suggests life, death, and rebirth forever repeating itself." Lastly, the West African concept of time is viewed cyclically and not lineal as in Europe.

The migration towards West Africa was fueled by invading Assyrian and Persian forces attacking peoples of the Nile Valley. Equally, the eclipse and fall of Kush, miseries of dynastic strife and the search for wealth are other factors in the early population shift. Importantly, advances in iron smelting at refineries of Meroe, transformed cultural standards and ways of life. Ghana therefore benefitted from resulting demographic and cultural migration, fueled by technological advances of this early period.

Scholars differ on Ghana's beginnings, though consensus believes Soninkes were the founders of the state, while the Sisse clan supplied its rulers. They provided kings, governors of provinces and the principal political officials. The Kante clan, on the other hand, provided the artisans who worked in metals as blacksmiths, goldsmiths and silversmiths. Other clans also worked in agriculture, animal husbandry, boat building and the manufacture of clothing.

In 722 Al Fazari called Ghana the "land of Gold," while Al Masudi the "land of gold beyond Sijilmasa." In the 9th Century, Al Hamadhani described Ghana as a "country where gold grows like plants in the sand in the same way as carrots do, and is plucked at sunset;" and Ibn Hawkal thought the ruler of Ghana "the wealthiest of all kings on the face of the earth on account of the riches he owns and the hoards of gold acquired by him and inherited from his predecessors since ancient times." In the 11th Century, Al Idrisi and Al Bekri wrote descriptions of Ghana, while Al Bekri commented on the gold of Ghana and the lucrative system of taxation utilized by the government, noting "all gold nuggets found in the kingdom were reserved for the king, only gold dust being left for the people." Also, the "king owns a nugget as big as a stone," weighing about thirty pounds. Gold came from the mines of Fulme and Bambuk in the

BLACK NATIONALISM
ALIVE AND WELL

forest regions. While the king of Ghana did not seek to ascertain this source of gold, much later, the kings of Mali and Songhay annexed the lands of the forest and claimed ownership of the mines.

Ghana was famous for sustaining a trans-Saharan trade in gold for salt and utilizing an elaborate system of taxation. According to Al Bekri, "for every donkey load of salt that enters the country, the king takes a duty of one gold dinar and two gold dinars from everyone that leaves. From a load of copper the king's due is five mitquals and from a load of other goods ten mitquals."

Black Nationalism 185. TANIT - "Islamic Faith."

FREDERICK MONDERSON

Sijilmasa to the north and Awdaghost to the south were the rendezvous and market center destination for the caravan trade across the Sahara. Exploiting the "silent trade," made Ghana rich and powerful. Gold miners of the forest exchanged gold for salt in the "silent trade." Ghana was destroyed by fanatical Muslims in search of gold.

Mali

Sundiata Keita was born a cripple who overcame his handicap and became the 12th King of Mali, ascending the throne in 1234. Within twenty-one years, he turned the tiny vassal state into the powerful and flourishing Empire of Mali. Three factors are credited with his rise and the growth of Mali. The first is the favorable or central location of his state. Second, the unsettled political conditions of the time of transition in the Western Sudan enabled this warrior to become a statesman. Third, his courage, wisdom and ability to overcome adversity and rally his people to greatness, was a plus.

Sundiata Keita was also an able administrator who understood the significance of gold of the Sudan and importance of the trans-Saharan trade. He quickly conquered the gold producing regions of Bure and Bambuk to the south. Thus, while Ghana never actually controlled the gold producing regions, Mali had control over them before Sundiata's death. The empire's boundaries were extended to the north. He also exploited the agricultural base of the Niger River Valley, introducing cultivation and weaving of cotton. In 1255, he died after laying the foundation for the Empire of Mali and providing it with a flourishing capital.

BLACK NATIONALISM
ALIVE AND WELL

Black Nationalism 186. **GYE NYAME** - "Supremacy of God."

Within a century, the Mali Empire's four main towns of Jenne, the capital Niani, Timbuktu, and Gao had become thriving commercial centers of the Western Sudan. In 1353, Ibn Khaldoun, an Arabic scholar and traveler, reported seeing a caravan of merchants from the

FREDERICK MONDERSON

east with 12,000 loaded camels heading for Mali. At an estimated 300 pounds per camel, the volume of trade staggers the imagination. This volume of merchandise certainly needed security guaranteed by a large and effective army. This force in turn provided the political stability that attracted the merchants who paid the taxes to conduct business during "The Golden Age of West Africa."

Songhay

Songhay next rose to prominence with a monarchy and continued the system of government. The empire became divided into four regions and each headed by a Viceroy. The Army had a Commander-in-Chief. There was a Council of Ministers who advised the Government headed by the king. Officers of the government included a Chief Tax-Collector, Finance Minister, Minister of Foreigners, Minister of Property, and Minister in Charge of Rivers, Lakes and Fisheries. Judges administered the courts impartially. One of Songhay's greatest rulers was Askia Mohammed.

In *Black History*, Norman E.W. Hodges credits Askia Mohammed with some remarkable innovations. He came to the throne in 1491 by a coup d'état. He presided over "establishment of schools, a uniform system of weights and measures, the improvement of taxes and credit procedures, reorganization of the armed forces, the promotion of more foreign trade, and the creation of an effective governmental administrative network throughout the land." Lastly, Muslim law based on the Koran, became the basis for administering justice in the state.

BLACK NATIONALISM ALIVE AND WELL

Black Nationalism 187. LEGBA - "Guardian of the Crossroads."

In essence, towards the end of the Sixteenth Century, Songhay grew powerful from the stability of a mixed economy. This consisted of

FREDERICK MONDERSON

farming, fishing, and cattle-raising. The trans-Saharan trade was important. They were also successful in uniting against rivals. Throughout the land security was enforced and political stability reigned. Intellectual activities flourished at Sankore University. Islam became the state religion. In 1591, Songhay was attacked by an Islamic force from Morocco, who introduced guns into the Western Sudan. Still, Songhay's demise is actually blamed on internal and external factors. Importantly, however, firearms changed the nature of African warfare and weak leadership of Africans also hurt Songhay.

Results of the Moroccan conquest saw Muslim marauders refusing to replace the governmental structure they destroyed; demise of the army and disruption caused by the war affected the important trans-Saharan trade; the Moroccans disregarded the level of cultural sophistication attained in literacy. Destruction of Songhay began in 1591 ending two millennia of West African cultural and civilization growth in culture, government and economics. Literacy and learning had progressed to a high level until discontinued. This began a downward spiral leading to the slave trade that further decimated Africa and Africans.

Black Nationalism 188. Fred Monderson pets the brown bear.

BLACK NATIONALISM ALIVE AND WELL

25. CENTRAL BROOKLYN FAMNILY HEALTH NETWORK 2009 LEGISLATIVE BREAKFAST BY DR. FRED MONDERSON

Kings County Hospital Center hosted its Annual Legislative Breakfast on Friday, January 30, 2009, 10:30 AM, amidst the most serious challenge to its health care services in years. Owing to the economic conundrum facing the nation and state, this time it's for all the marbles in this most turbulent state of affairs. To top it all, Jean C. Leon, Senior Executive Director of the Central Brooklyn Family Health Network, who for years has provided outstanding leadership to this important institution is now retiring and being replaced by Mr. Antonio Martin, equally and eminently qualified. Just as the Community Advisory Board and the Auxiliary has supported Ms. Leon, so too will they support her successor, making Kings County advocacy a priority at Federal, State and Local levels of government, in order to keep serving the Central Brooklyn community.

Even more important, when we examine the Zip Codes serviced by Kings County Hospital Center, coming from all across the boroughs, this hospital is not simply a Central Brooklyn, but really a New York City institution of health care, a "medical battleship" of remarkable potential. Nevertheless, to understand the significance of this legislative breakfast and the importance of this hospital and Family Health Network, one has to examine the numbers and variety of medical care rendered in this community.

To combat this problem and vigorously advocate the respective government agencies, the hospital attracted a most impressive array of legislative leaders who fired up the crowd, and once issued their

FREDERICK MONDERSON

marching orders, agreed to help turn things around. The elected officials in attendance included Ms. Yvonne Graham, Deputy Borough President of Brooklyn; State Senator Eric Adams; Assemblymen Nick Perry and Hakeem Jeffries; Councilmen Kendall Stewart and Matthew Eugene; and those who could not attend sent their representatives. In attendance were: Carolyn Sanders-James from the Mayor's Office; Cathleen McCadden representing Councilwoman Darlene Mealy; Carl Luciano for Al Vann; G.G. Elliot for Letitia James; Alan Joseph for Ed Towns and Anita Taylor for Yvette Clarke; and Wendy Powell for Assemblywoman Rhoda Jacobs.

Also in attendance were James Connolly and Reverend Jamieson who did the Invocation, Mr. Alvin Young for HHC at 125 Worth Street. From the Administration, Mr. George Proctor, Mr. Warren Hanson, and Ms. Agnes Abraham, Chair of Kings County Advisory Board, as well as Ms. Cleopatra Jones, Chairwoman of East New York Diagnostic and Treatment center; and Mr. Leon Crooks of the Bedford Stuyvesant Alcoholic and Treatment Center. Ms. Josephine Bolus of the HHC Board of Directors was in attendance and Ms. Guerrero accompanied Ms. Graham.

While Cynthia Moseley, Assistant Secretary, Community Advisory Board at Dr. Susan Smith McKinney Nursing and Rehabilitation Center did the Introduction, Ms. Gloria Thomas, member of the DSSM and KCHC Boards, did the Welcoming Address and pointed out "While there are cuts across the board in every category, we cannot afford to have cuts in health care," and "we will fight tooth and nail for our hospitals." She did add further, there were 5 hospitals closed within Central Brooklyn. From this writer's knowledge, these are Brooklyn Women's Hospital, St. Mary's, Brooklyn Jewish, Caledonian and Kings Highway Hospital. This means the patients from these areas will naturally flood Kings County, whose mandate is to care for any and all who walk through its doors, whether they have the ability to pay or not.

BLACK NATIONALISM
ALIVE AND WELL

Black Nationalism 189. **BARON** - "Male Cemetery Guardian."

FREDERICK MONDERSON

Ms. Leon pointed out the Health and Hospitals Corporation health care system is the safety net for New York City, and this is threatened. She added, "We pay a mortgage for the hospitals, and the new building (R-Bldg. replacing the old G-Bldg.) runs $75 million a year."

In an **Overview** of the financial situation one gets to understand the gravity of the calamity facing the nation's health care in general and that of New York State and locally, Kings County Hospital in particular. Therefore, let's look at the numbers.

The **Deficit Reduction and Executive Budget** proposals include Medicaid funding reductions to hospital, nursing homes and home care providers as well as reforms that could increase funding for ambulatory care and care to uninsured patients. The estimates of the amounts of cuts and provider taxes to Kings County Hospital Center are $12.6 million and that to the New York City Health and Hospitals Corporation (HHC) hospitals and nursing homes is nearly $300 million on an annual basis.

* The HHC estimate is comprised of $115 million in across-the-board rate reductions and provider taxes, $138 million in cuts as a result of a new hospital inpatient reimbursement methodology and other reductions, and a loss of $44 million from the implementation of new nursing home rates.

* The Kings County estimate is comprised of $13.6 million in across-the-board rate reductions and provides taxes, and an increase of $1 million as a result of the new inpatient methodology and other changes. Kings County could also gain up to $25.4 million from proposed reforms.

Positive Changes to Expand Coverage: HHC supports the proposals to streamline the process for those enrolling or re-certifying for Medicaid, Child Health Plus (CHP) and Family Health Plus (FHP). Limitations on FHP enrollment for public employees

BLACK NATIONALISM
ALIVE AND WELL

and 19-20 year olds who do not reside with parents are also eliminated. HHC supports the proposal to expand FHP eligibility from 150% of the federal poverty level to 200% FPL if new sources of Federal funding can be secured and not through the use of supplemental Medicaid payments that public hospitals currently receive. These changes will benefit the increasing number of New Yorkers without health coverage and the safety net providers who serve them.

Investments: A portion of the nearly $300 million cut to HHC (and all of Kings County's $13.6 million cut) could be offset by investments in ambulatory care and through a new indigent care pool that will increase reimbursement to teaching hospitals providing care to uninsured patients. HHC could receive up to $171 million from this new initiative. Kings County could receive up to $25.4 million. However, these increases are not guaranteed and are a result of funding redistributions among other hospitals in New York State that will be contested during budget negotiations.

Hospital Inpatient Funding: While HHC is supportive of the goals for reforming hospital inpatient reimbursement rates, and have publicly participated in a state workgroup to devise a new system, HHC has serious concerns with the newly proposed methodology that does not adequately reflect the public hospitals' actual costs of providing care. HHC's hospitals rely primarily on Medicaid funding because they serve higher numbers of Medicaid patients when compared to almost all other hospitals. Because HHC hospitals have little opportunity to cross-subsidize their expenses through other payers, the negative impact of changes in Medicaid reimbursement are more keenly felt by the public hospitals.

FREDERICK MONDERSON

Black Nationalism 190. Cherise Maloney and Clive Monderson sandwich Dr. Fred Monderson of Brooklyn, New York.

*   The proposed formula does not capture the true value of Kings' labor costs including physician salaries and the value of pensions and other fringe benefits.

*   The proposed formula also does not include approximately $60 million in New York City's EMS which has historically been included in HHC's Medicaid rates. This is, in effect, a $60 million cut to the City of New York.

*   In addition, HHC was exempted without explanation from receiving funding for hospitals proposed to ease the transition to the new methodology.

BLACK NATIONALISM ALIVE AND WELL

Black Nationalism 191. MANMAN BRIGITTE - "Female Cemetery Guardian."

Skilled Nursing Facilities: HHC's four, large skilled nursing facilities currently provide high levels of care on a daily basis to more than 3,300 patients. Many of these patients have no other options for care in New York City. The proposal to move to a

FREDERICK MONDERSON

new reimbursement system would decrease funding by more than $44 million.

For example, in Brooklyn, the Dr. Susan Smith McKinney Nursing and Rehabilitation Center will lose $10.9 million. On Staten Island, the Sea View Hospital Rehabilitation Center and Home will lose $9.2 million. In Manhattan, Coler Goldwater Specialty Hospital and Nursing Facility will lose $37.3 million and Gouverneur Healthcare Services loses $3.7 million in State funding.

The Bottom Line: While Kings County would see a net increase in funding, even with the proposed investments, HHC still faces more than $127 million in reductions and the Dr. Susan Smith McKinney Nursing and Rehabilitation Center will lose $10.9 million. A loss of the amounts of funds of this magnitude cannot simply be absolved and New York City's entire public hospital system will be unable to sustain services at their current levels.

In her address, **Deputy Boro President Graham** pointed to the "incredible transformation of Kings County and a large part of that credit goes to Ms. Leon." She continued, Brooklyn is facing a near catastrophic crisis, especially since it has alarming rates of Diabetes, Asthma, AIDS, and Infant Mortality. This will create a hemorrhaging of jobs impacting on families. There must be alternatives to the draconian cuts. Health Care is a right!"

State Senator Eric Adams, in referring to Ms. Leon, believed the "Firmness of a person's spirit tells much of the character. She has done so much for us all." He added further, "When the affluent catch a cold we get the flu. Well, right now the affluent have pneumonia, so guess what that has done to us." He pointed out there needs to be a grassroots mutiny and we must stop the hemorrhaging of health care. Even further, "Conditions do not make a person; conditions determine what a person is made of. There is need for real conversation with leaders. The community must be mobilized. These numbers are real. Education and health care should not be part of the surgeon's knife."

BLACK NATIONALISM
ALIVE AND WELL

Councilmember Kendall Stewart presented Ms. Leon with a City Council Proclamation pointing out she was an Assistant Director at Woodhull Hospital, Director of Quality Management at Metropolitan Hospital, Deputy Executive Director and Chief Operating Officer at Harlem Hospital before being appointed Senior Executive Director at Kings County Hospital Center in 1995, and then head of the Central Brooklyn Family Healthcare Network.

Assemblyman Nick Perry praised Ms. Leon in saying she "raised Kings County from the lows to a high standard," and that "good nurses don't die, they don't fade away either." Even further, we must make sure the people of Brooklyn do not carry a disproportionate health care burden. We must reduce emergency room costs which is triple clinic costs. We must target real problems in health care."

Assemblyman Hakeem Jeffries commended Jean Leon for hard work and dedication. He said these are difficult times with the state having a $15-billion budget deficit, "But we can't balance the budget on the backs of Brooklyn. A more progressive Income Tax structure is needed in New York State. The wealthy are not paying their fair share." He gave an example of the imbalance in the tax structure: "Whether you make $5000.00, $500,000.00, $5,000,000.00, or $5,000,000,000,00, you pay the same tax. These are challenging times and so we must restructure the tax system."

Councilmember Matthew Eugene described Kings County as the best hospital in Brooklyn. "It is an asset for our community. It serves immigrants in this community who have nowhere else to go. Therefore, we must do everything in our power to save the hospital to continue its good work."

FREDERICK MONDERSON

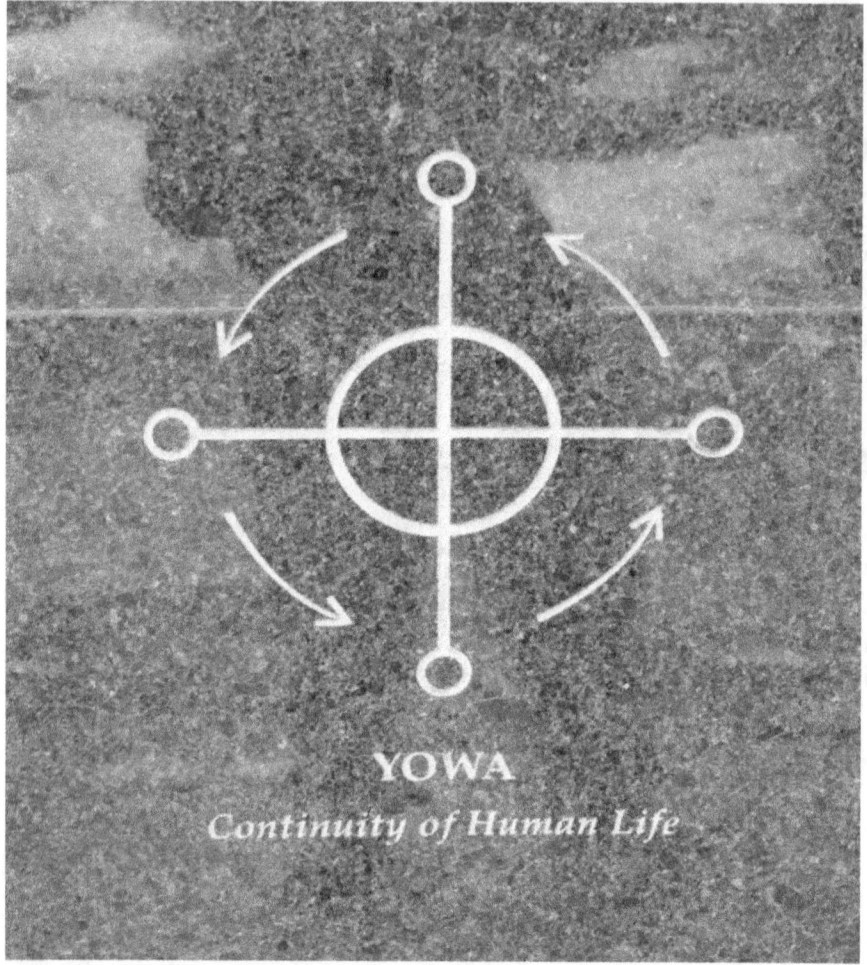

Black Nationalism 192. **YOWA** – "Continuity of Human Life."

All the elected officials promised to return to their respective levels of government. Everyone also hoped their constituency would call the Governor, and their city, state and federal legislators and demand health care and education not suffer in this budget crisis.

BLACK NATIONALISM ALIVE AND WELL

26. SONNY CARSON: "Torch Still Burning" By Dr. Fred Monderson

When Sonny Carson passed away, I called a friend to inform him of this. His response was: "Sonny Carson dead, God help us!" Now, two years later, while Black Americans have won with the election of Barak Obama to the US Senate, Al Sharpton's Candidacy for the US Presidency, in addition to Bill Thompson being re-elected as New York City Comptroller, as well as a few other pedestrian successes, we have still lost ground on many fronts.

Fresh from his 2004 presidential win, in his 2005 inaugural address, President George Bush called for an end to racism in America! Now, such a recent pronouncement reflects the living nature of an odious and institutional practice very much alive in 21st Century America. Coupled with police brutality, the rising rate of Black incarceration in the Prison Industrial Complex, as well as the media's negative depiction, the problematic existence of Blacks underscores how much ground we have lost since Sonny's demise.

The New York Times, in full color, recently featured and depicted the condition of a particular jail and its overcrowding in Africa. Equally, another front page article and depiction featured a young woman with a baby who was married from puberty to a man nearly three times her age. In still another front page article, *The New York Times* again critiqued how Blacks were "improving" in their academic grade point averages as if by sleight of hand that cheapens the process.

FREDERICK MONDERSON

Black Nationalism 193. MEDICINE WHEEL - "Native American Circle of Life."

On this year's **Black Solidarity Day**, November 7, 2005, the *New York Daily News*, featured on top of the comics section a cartoon about "Cannibal toys" belonging to "shaded persons," implying Blacks! Imagine, **Black Solidarity Day** in America 2005, and a major daily with a significant Black readership, the editorial board would print anything that equates Blacks with cannibals! or even print anything with reference to cannibals! No ethnic group in New York or anyplace would be disrespected in this

BLACK NATIONALISM
ALIVE AND WELL

manner on their special day or on any day. They would let that paper know it and so would have Sonny Carson had he been around. Rising Black unemployment, high incidents of health concerns victimizing Blacks, and then the shameful and incompetent unpreparedness and inadequate response to Hurricane Katrina are issues that need particular attention and are not addressed. Add to this the threat to ideologically move the US Supreme Court further to the right, all helps to underscore the many challenges facing Blacks in America and worldwide.

Sonny would certainly be involved in activities to address some of these issues. Now away from the scene, this voice, a champion of Black rights is no longer being heard. Nevertheless, let it not be said with his passing Sonny Carson is forgotten! His symbolism is alive! His legacy is assured! His "Torch Is Still Burning! His *nom de guerre* "Abubadika" is still an inspiration!

Sonny Carson's **Final Triumph** was the recovery of the bones of the "Runaway Samuel Carson," the planning and organizing for his re-location and actual return to Ghana, creating a site of pilgrimage for African Americans in that West African country. The symbolism of this significant return, first time anyone came back through the "Door of no Return," creating the "Door of Return" was the final masterpiece in the gallery of masterpieces the master has created. I hear tell; travelers from Philadelphia and other parts of American have traveled to view the runaway's final resting place, beside the female slave Crystal from Jamaica, as they were interred on August 1, 1998.

FREDERICK MONDERSON

Black Nationalism 194. NKISI SARABANDA – "Signature of the Spirit."

What all of this means regarding Sony Carson, his struggles and legacy? A man who has spent a lifetime struggling in causes of Black political and economic empowerment, educational advancement, and dealing with the demeaning and disgusting portrayal and inculcation of the musical cultural phenomenon, police brutality, racial profiling, Prison Industrial Complex, Sonny Carson's legacy must not die! We must tell the young Sonny Carson was a product of his environment; a young Black man coming of age in New York in the Post-World War II era; serving in Korea; going to prison and coming out to begin a movement that sought justice and equality for Blacks; an uncompromising education activist who fought the Ocean-Hill-Brownsville battle to bring about community control of schools and their economic destiny; as well as seeking to solve the problems and challenges of intra-African dynamics in their "day to day survival" aspirations, are fundamentals of what Sonny Carson was all about and what he should be remembered for.

BLACK NATIONALISM ALIVE AND WELL

Black Nationalism 195. NSOROMMA - "Guardianship."

27. Senmut
By
Dr. Fred Monderson

Senmut was an Egyptian nobleman who lived during the reign of Queen Hatshepsut in the XVIII Dynasty, about 1490-1470 BC. He came from a poor family but luck, intelligence, fortune and hard work helped him reach the top in Egyptian society. His lowly background is surmised from the poor tomb he built for his family. Some scholars believed that Senmut was a scribe. Others think he was a general in the army of the Queen's father, Thutmose I. Hatshepsut loved her father. He made her co-regent with Thutmose II her half-brother. Still, the old king was aware that she would have political and social difficulties in the male dominated world of the

FREDERICK MONDERSON

pharaohs. Possibly Thutmose I may have advised her alliance with "strong males" in the kingdom. Thus, her fortune became intertwined with Senmut's and theirs rose and fell together.

The Queen married Thutmose II. They had a girl child named Nefer-re. When Thutmose I died, Hatshepsut pushed aside young Thutmose III, her co-regent, and made herself ruler of all Egypt. Shortly after, she claimed to be the son of Amon (Amun, Amen) and this declaration helped solidify her claim to be king of all Egypt. Senmut was well liked by Hatshepsut. Many people believed Senmut was behind all this, since he headed a political party with powerful individuals in the country. William C. Hayes in *The Scepter of Egypt II* (Cambridge, Mass: Harvard University Press, 1959, p. 106) says, "He received some 80 titles from the Queen and became the most powerful man in the kingdom." In *Ancient Records of the Egypt*, J.H. Breasted informs: "He was the Minister of Finance, Minister of Works, Hereditary Prince and Count, Wearer of the Royal Seal, and Sole Companion." Other titles were Great Father, Tutor of the Princess Nefru-re, Conductor of Festivals, Overseer of the Gardens of Amon, Chief Steward of the King, Overseer of the Prophet of Montu, Overseer of Administrative Officers, and Imy-Weret Priest, and so on.

Black Nationalism 196. View of Deir el Bahari temple from the north showing the two ramps and three colonnades.

BLACK NATIONALISM ALIVE AND WELL

Senmut was a famous architect, among others, of the Eighteenth Dynasty. He built two tombs for himself. The first was dug out of the hillside above the village of Abd el Qurna. Breasted's *History of Egypt* explained, "This elaborate tomb (No. 71) was built before he became powerful. It was decorated with a wonderful ceiling pattern and contained scenes of the Egyptian afterlife." Barbara Mertz in *Black Land, Red Land* notes Senmut, "Employed several bright colors such as yellow, blue, red, and green in its decoration. His family members and household helpers as well as his horse and a pet-ape were buried in and around the tomb. The horse, a mare, was twelve and a half hands high. Both animals were mummified."

From this site we know the names of Senmut's father Ramose, "the Worthy," and his mother, Hatnufer, "Lady of the House." His beloved sister was Ahotep "the Justified." Amenhotep, a younger brother and Harmose, a musician, with his lute lying beside his coffin, were all buried here. Also buried here were a young servant and an old woman Priestess of the God Amun. Senmut had another brother, Senmen, who was probably older. He too seems to have had royal children as protégées. His charge was Senenyah and probably Nefru-re. Senmen was also buried on a very steep slope of the hills at Sheikh Abu el-Qurna where Senmut was probably interred. H. de Garis Davies in "The Tomb of Senmen, Brother of Senmut" in *Society of Biblical Archaeology* (1913: 382) informs: "Higher upon, on the same hillside, is a feature unique in the necropolis, a group of man, woman and child, carved out of a great boulder, the back of which is still left in the rough." Interestingly enough, this is the prototype of the Mount Rushmore phenomenon in American political history, but it is not generally known.

Senmut had several close friends who helped the Queen rule the country. Their names were Nehsi, Chancellor, who led an expedition to Punt. Thutiy and Thutnofre were Treasurers. Puyemre was the Second Prophet of Amon. Hapuseneb was the Vizier or Prime Minister. Ineby was the Viceroy of Nubia. Dewaemhen was the First Herald, and Tetenre, a Scribe.

FREDERICK MONDERSON

Black Nationalism 197. ASASE YE DURU - "Divinity of Mother Earth."

Senmut built the great Deir el-Bahari Funerary Temple of Queen Hatshepsut, at Thebes. Built five hundred years later, it is located on the West Bank of the Nile, near the XI Dynasty Temple of Mentuhotep II, which served as its model. Here he had his second tomb, with a long sloping corridor, secretly dug under the Queen's temple. Throughout the temple, Herman Kees in *Egypt: A Cultural History* says Senmut, "dared to have figures of himself carved

BLACK NATIONALISM ALIVE AND WELL

behind the doors of the chapel shrines such as the rock-shrine of Hathor, and to have a new rock-tomb cut for himself under the forecourt of the temple so that he could rest within the sacred precinct." Hayes adds: "Senmut inscribed his name some 70 times in out-of-the-way places in the Queen's mortuary temple." This secret, unfinished, tomb was abandoned after his demise. When discovered, Thutmose III's forces defaced and destroyed it.

Hatshepsut's funerary temple is an architectural masterpiece with three platforms boasting lower, middle and upper colonnades. There are two ramps and three courts. The Upper Court comprises a Hypostyle Hall with side entrances to a Sanctuary of Ra (right) and a Sanctuary to Thutmose I and III and the Queen (left). The Central Sanctuary was dedicated to "her father Amon." In the Middle Colonnade the Anubis Shrine is located off to the right while the Hathor Shrine is to the left.

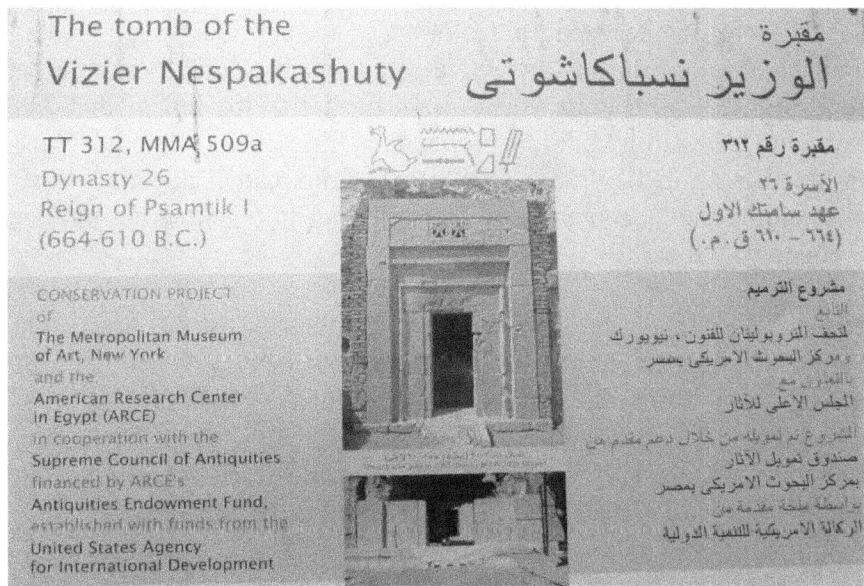

Black Nationalism 198. Image of the Tomb of Vizier Nespakashuty, 26th Dynasty.

FREDERICK MONDERSON

The First Ramp ascends to the Middle Colonnade while the Second Ramp ascends to the Upper Platform with its colonnade that entrances the Upper Court. Important, as the ramps are centrally located they split the Lower and Middle Colonnades. As such, each segment is named for some feature. To the left of the Lower Colonnade is the "Fishes and Marshes Colonnade." To the right is the "Obelisk Colonnade." The Obelisk Colonnade is so named showing two obelisks being transported from Aswan where they were quarried by Senmut and erected in a 7-month period. They were erected at Karnak in the Court with a Hypostyle Hall her father Thutmose I had built. Today one obelisk still stands while the apex of its twin now rests southward near the Sacred Lake. There is an image on the back wall of the Middle Colonnade of her temple showing four obelisks. Some scholars believe, instead of the two known obelisks, four were actually erected at Karnak. Then, the other two have not only disappeared but the whereabouts of their location still remains a mystery.

To the left of the Middle Colonnade is the "Punt Colonnade" showing the expedition to Punt, the boats and rejoicing people on their return. The Hathor Shrine rests further to the left of this. On the right side of this Middle Colonnade is the "Birth Colonnade" just beside the Anubis Shrine. The "Birth Colonnade" depicts events surrounding the Queen's divine birth when Amon visited her mother to conceive the child!

Beyond the Upper Platform with its colonnades is the Hypostyle Hall in the Upper Court that entrances the Sanctuary or "Holy of Holies." Thus, Deir el Bahari had sanctuaries, columns, shrines, courts, ramps, sandstone sphinxes, and Osiride states of the Queen. Some statues are still visible today, as can be seen following the restoration by a Polish team that has worked there for decades.

W. Stephenson Smith in the *Art and Archaeology of Ancient Egypt* (1959: 233) states the temple "combines a broad feeling of openness of space with a nicety of architectural detail which only gradually becomes apparent as one penetrates into the individual parts."

BLACK NATIONALISM ALIVE AND WELL

The architect of the Deir el-Bahari structure's most wonderful innovation was his employing square pillars and polygonal columns. Smith writes, "This variation between pillar and column is one of the reasons for Senmut's success in employing the polygonal channeled column, which had long been one of the happiest of Egyptian inventions."

Black Nationalism 199. FUNTUNFUNEEU DENKYEMFUNEFU - "Unity in Diversity."

28. HANIBAL OF CARTHAGE
By
Dr. Fred Monderson

Egypt began to decline in the centuries before Christ. Greece and later Rome rose to be the military powers in the Mediterranean Sea in this age. The control of economic activity in this region thus led to wars between the maritime and trading nations

FREDERICK MONDERSON

Carthage was an African nation believed to be founded by sea-farers called Phoenicians. They came from the eastern Mediterranean and were considered "Negroid" or by today's standards, Black people. The Phoenicians introduced our alphabet which had 22 letters at first. They were great merchants who carried goods throughout the region in their ships. The role they played was important. This economic beehive became the envy of Rome who wanted to control all trade in the Mediterranean. Therefore, Rome found itself on the road to war with Carthage. It must also be pointed out, while the Phoenicians may have gotten credit for founding Carthage, the occupants were African people.

There were three Punic Wars between Rome and Carthage from 264-241 BC, 218- 201 BC, and 149-146 BC. The conflict was called "Punic" because the Romans could not pronounce Phoenicia. In the "First Punic War" Carthage lost the Islands of Sicily, Corsica and Sardinia to Rome. Up to and including the "Second Punic War," the Barca family was involved. They were all Carthaginian Generals under the names of Hamilcar Barca, the father, Hannibal Barca the son, and Hasdrubal Barca, Hannibal's brother.

Hannibal of Carthage was the one who had the most impact on all the wars. His father was killed in battle and he vowed revenge on Rome. He thought it would be difficult to win from afar against a large confederacy like Rome. She had a large and powerful navy in addition to a large army. A new strategy was needed. Hannibal decided to carry the battle to Rome.

BLACK NATIONALISM ALIVE AND WELL

Black Nationalism 200. HYE WON HYE - "Imperishability and Endurance."

Hannibal outfitted an expedition of 12,000 cavalry, 80,000 infantry and 40 attack elephants. He landed in Spain, fought his way north and crossed the Alps. Crossing this mountain range was quite a feat. Rome had expected a frontal attack. However, this strategy placed him on the back-side of Rome, where an attack was unlikely. How

FREDERICK MONDERSON

do we know Hannibal was an African and Black? A surviving coin depicts a man with African features riding an elephant.

This crossing was difficult at first since the native defenders knew the terrain. It was slow at first but his strategy won out against the odds. Those he defeated were made to join his army in the fight against Rome. Rome had a standing army of 250,000 infantry, 25,000 cavalry and auxiliaries of 750,000 infantry and cavalry.

Cold, weary and battle scarred, Hannibal's army faced a force of 80,000 Romans under the command of Scipio. They met Hannibal at Ticino. Scipio was confident of victory. He threw his entire force at Hannibal. The African General did his homework. His strategy forced the Romans into a group. Then he attacked with his elephants. The Romans broke ranks and then his cavalry charged. Panic-stricken the Romans fled. In another battle at Trebia, he defeated the Romans and killed their general Sempronius.

The Next thing of great importance he did was to cross the Appenines, another mountain range. Here he lost all but one elephant. He also lost an eye. When setting up his forces for the winter, the Romans attacked. He took 1,000 head of cattle, tied cloth to their horns and set it afire. Next he drove them into the advancing Roman formation. As they broke ranks in face of the stampeding fires, he then attacked with his cavalry. Again, at a place called Lake Trasimeno he ambushed another Roman force under the command of Flaminius. The Romans lost 25,000 men. Hannibal lost 1,500 men.

Next Hannibal defeated the Roman Generals Varro and Emilius and their force of 90,000 men. They fought at a place called Cannae. Emilius, 80 Roman Senators who came to watch the battle and 70,000 Romans were slaughtered by Hannibal. For 15 years, the great African General controlled the plains of Rome. He stopped just short of entering the City of Rome.

BLACK NATIONALISM
ALIVE AND WELL

Black Nationalism 201. MATE MASIE - "Wisdom and Prudence."

After many battles with Hannibal in Italy, Rome appointed Scipio commander and gave him a large army. Scipio used Hannibal's strategy. He crossed the Mediterranean Sea and attacked Carthage in North Africa. This forced Hannibal to retreat from Rome to defend his homeland. That's how the threat to Rome was removed.

FREDERICK MONDERSON

On returning to Carthage, Hannibal gathered a force of 55,000 men and 80 attack elephants. He met the Roman army but was betrayed and defeated. The city was walled in a horseshoe-shaped manner to accommodate 200 battle elephants. It had stables for thousands of horses, magazines for war materials and barracks for soldiers. It had libraries, baths, restaurants or public messes and theaters. This was indeed a glorious age in North Africa.

So, Hannibal was considered one of the greatest generals in the history of warfare. He certainly used new and daring strategies to win out against larger forces. He did this for nearly twenty years. Many of his battlefield strategies are still taught in military academies. He was a great African of whom all Africans could be proud. Yet, in opposition, *Delenda est Carthago* – "Carthage must be destroyed" is the way "Cato the Elder" greeted his fellow Roman Senators. This was because Carthage remained a threat to Rome.

In the Third Punic War 149-146 Rome defeated Carthage. She sacked and burned the city. Later it became a Roman Province. Under Roman administration, it was systematically exploited for agricultural purposes. This region of North Africa became the bread basket of the Roman Empire. Wheat, corn, fruits, wine and olive oil were produced. Wood was furnished for heating. They rebuilt the city with Roman architecture. This led many modern scholars to hold that Carthage was Roman. This is not so. It was African first.

There were positives and negatives associated with Roman rule in North Africa. They administered firmly and effectively. They exploited the agricultural base of the province. They also built roads connecting much of the territory. The most important development, however, was how climatic conditions affected the lives of Romans.

BLACK NATIONALISM
ALIVE AND WELL

Black Nationalism 202. AKOMA NTOSO – "Understanding."

In an Article "On the Longevity of the Romans in North Africa," Lord Talbot de Malahide has shown inscriptions at Constantine and Carthage. He held many lived to be over one hundred years old. The inscriptions do not give cause for this just the fact that Roman officers called Censors went to great lengths to record these ages.

FREDERICK MONDERSON

On the other hand, the Romans destroyed much of the wildlife of North Africa. The Romans exterminated elephants, leopards, lions and bears. There was a great demand for hyenas, ostriches, boars, antelopes. The lions particularly were killed in gladiatorial games held to entertain the Roman people.

The Emperor Augustus Caesar said he gave 26 games to amuse the people of Rome. In them 3,500 African animals were slain. Pompey was another Roman Emperor. At the height of his power 600 African lions were slain in one game to amuse the Roman people. Three hundred and fifteen were male lions. Julius Caesar gave a similar show in which were exhibited 400 lions and the list goes on. All this is documented in J.C. DeGraaf-Johnson's *African Glory*.

Roman rule in North Africa destroyed the wildlife, the vegetation suffered and this aided the desert's expansion. This callousness was a disaster for North Africa because there were no more Hannibals to defend the motherland.

Black Nationalism 203. DWENNIMMEN - 'Humility and Strength."

BLACK NATIONALISM ALIVE AND WELL

29. Mohammed Ali
By
Dr. Fred Monderson

Two important developments took place in Egypt at the start of the Nineteenth Century. The first was the discovery of the Rosetta Stone by Napoleon's military forces in 1799. This discovery was to have far reaching and lasting economic, cultural and social consequences for that North African nation. Egyptology was later born with the decipherment of the Rosetta Stone by Jean Jacques Champollion in 1822. The development created an enormous interest in ancient Egypt. In turn it gave birth to massive tourism in Egypt that transformed the country. On one hand, it has been a buoy to the economy. On the other it has fostered the cultural rape of that ancient African land.

The second most important development in Egypt at the turn of the century was the ascension of Mohammed Ali to rulership of Egypt. He was a general in service to the Turkish Sultan, the Overlord of the Turkish Empire, which included Egypt. Moving very quickly one day, Mohammed Ali initiated a number of changes that placed Egypt on the road to modernization and independence.

Taking advantage of the Nile River's perennial fertility, he made land reforms to the peasants. Their farming methods were organized more methodically. The end result was more efficient production of agricultural bounty. Because of the growing demands of the textile industries in Europe due to the industrial revolution, he made cotton a major crop. The long Egyptian staples were superior to even that produced in America.

FREDERICK MONDERSON

Black Nationalism 204. Tomb of Vizier Nespakashuty, 26th Dynasty, on the slopes of the North Assasif beside the Deir el Bahari amphitheater.

In the end he established Egypt as a major producer and exporter of cotton to the European nations. To strengthen his economic reforms he created a national army. In this military force he placed native Egyptians who had either been excluded from this body or kept at the most menial levels. He created new military forces and elevated Egyptians into the officers' ranks.

The next step was to undermine the Mamelukes who had been Egypt's traditional rulers, in the name of the Sultan of Turkey. In a triumphant year he sponsored an enormous national banquet. He invited the **Who's Who in Mameluke Hierarchy**. He wined and dined them. With all gathered in one large arena, he moved his trusted soldiers in on them and killed them all. He broke the power of the Mameluke control over Egypt.

Mohammed Ali next gave Egyptians some place in the government of their country. Many were sent to European Universities to learn western ideas, technology, statecraft and art of war. He laid the foundations for the growth of a Western educated class. By this time

BLACK NATIONALISM
ALIVE AND WELL

he was lauded as a national hero and though not Egyptian by birth, he became well liked by all.

Finally, he was able to secure from the Turkish Sultan the right to create a hereditary succession for his dynasty in Egypt. Providing, however, this relationship would not become a threat to the Turkish Empire. Mohammed Ali did all these things without taking any loans from the European Powers. In so doing he was not committed to them in any way.

Unfortunately, his successors were not as astute in statecraft and soon became dependent on foreign investment in Egypt. By 1859 the Suez Canal was opened. This was a major achievement for commercial sea-traffic between Europe and Asia. The revenue gained from its operation was important, but, the European nations owned the canal because Egypt had become indebted to them.

Black Nationalism 205. DENKYEM - "Adaptability."

FREDERICK MONDERSON

30. Samori Toure: "Black Napoleon of the Sudan"
By
Dr. Fred Monderson

Samori Toure was born at Bissandugu, in the Niger River Valley in 1830. He died in 1900 and was dubbed "Black Napoleon of the Sudan" for his exploits against the French in West Africa. In the era of African partition and implementation, he held the French at bay for eighteen years. Such action was unthinkable against the disciplined, seasoned and heavily armed European soldiers.

While a young man, the neighboring King Lori Bourama captured Samori's mother and others. Samori offered his services for his mother's freedom. He later escaped and was elected King among his people. As a new King, Samori began to expand his kingdom. This conflicted with the intentions of the French who were extending across West Africa. The French had an eye on the Nile Basin at the other end of the Sudan.

In his expansion Samori seized all lands east of Sierra Leone to the Niger. This territory was estimated at 100,000 square miles. For the daring and initiative of this move, European writers compared him to Genghis Khan and Napoleon.

Samori Toure rejected the titles of king or sultan. He simply preferred to be "Samori, Son of Lafla, African of the Negro Race, Prince of Believers."

He was a Muslim and firm believer in Islam. He offered conquered people the Koran or death. The Madhi, a religious reformer in such places as Khartoum, in the Sudan, also did this.

BLACK NATIONALISM ALIVE AND WELL

So, while extending the political boundaries of his kingdom, Samori also spread the religion of Islam. Throughout it all, he felt that Islam and the Koran strengthened and guided his every action.

The significance of Samori Toure's rise to power, lay in the turmoil facing Africa of that time. This was a time when Africa was being discovered, explored and invaded from all directions by Europeans. The precursors to colonialism, which included explorers, traders, merchants and missionaries all, set the stage for the Berlin Conference to partition Africa. Therefore, Samori's intentions conflicted with many of Europe's interests. In 1881, an impertinent black sergeant in French uniform commanded Samori to discontinue a siege of a place called Kenira. Samori's response was war with France. This conflict lasted for 15 years.

Black Nationalism 206. AKOMA - "Endurance."

Samori used guerilla tactics against the French. He attacked their caravans in the Congo. He even resorted to scorched earth tactics when the French placed him in difficult situations. This besieged African nationalist signed a treaty with France in 1886. He sent his favorite son, Karamook to Paris as a hostage. In another treaty in 1887 he gave up all lands on the left bank of the Niger River.

In 1891, with France on the right bank, along with native chiefs they declared war on Samori. He met them at Kekouner. He had a force of 40,000 men. Over 10,000 were armed with rifles. Some 2,000 were cavalry. The remainders were armed with spears.

The European incursions in Africa were very much understood by other great African nationalists as Moshesh, Menelik, Ja Ja of Opobo and Samori. Similarly, Cetewayo, Behanzin, Samuel Crowther and other prominent nationalists across the continent faced the same problem resulting from implementation of "Partition on Land" as dictated by "Partition on Paper."

The African response to colonial control was sincere, resolute but ineffective. Nevertheless, many Africans gave their lives in defense of Africa as all self-respecting people would in such situations.

In his case, many times heavily armed and superior forces overcame Samori. However, this African general fought courageously and defiantly. Illiteracy does not measure one's capacity for wisdom. Nor can it retard one's expression of what western philosophy calls the virtues. Scholars have claimed Samori acted barbarously and such actions may have solid basis, but the times demanded what it produced. After all, can barbarity be the exclusive behaviors of "naked savages" or "clothed gentlemen?"

His shrewdness has sometimes been called diplomacy by western rulers of the time. Many of them were schooled in the Machiavellian tradition, which held *the ends justified the means*.

BLACK NATIONALISM ALIVE AND WELL

Black Nationalism 207. NSIBIDI SYMBOL - "Love and Unity."

31. RACE: FROM DUBOIS TO OBAMA
By
Dr. Fred Monderson

The question of race in America has for centuries been pervasive, yet, people seem to not want to discuss it for fear it would "upset the applecart" of their comfort zones. Certainly, privileged and not so privileged whites and "accomplished Blacks" seem to want to keep the issue "under the mat," so to speak. Yet, in every walk of life, the questions of "black and white" pervade the American social order and process.

From the beginning when Africans were brought to the Americas as enslaved persons, one of the rationales was that they would be like fly in milk and easily recognized. In those desperate days of that horrendous and inhuman system of slavery, Blacks were confined to plantations as chattel property having been made so by legislative

FREDERICK MONDERSON

fiat. They seldom ventured outside of their masters' domains. Whenever they "traveled" they were easily recognized and so this was in keeping with one of the premises on which they were brought to the Americas. Blacks could not blend in with the general population. This characteristic has dogged Africa's sons and daughters not simply in America but also in Europe. Today the reality is "driving," "walking," or "shopping" while Black! That is not to say, a small percentage of Whites who are learned and rational have not been devoid of the prejudices that characterize the greater percent of their fellows.

Practically every thinker of significance in American history has expressed some sentiment that reeks of racial bias against Blacks because of the color of their skin. This is traceable throughout the eighteenth and nineteenth centuries. The birth, expansion and continuance of the Ku Klux Klan way of life and thought have proved race is an issue that will not go away. The age of lynching, approximately 1870-1930 seems to indicate racists in America were seeking a "final solution" to the African race. Having thrown everything including the kitchen sink, was only the resilience of Blacks and by the grace of god that enabled their survival and continuance.

BLACK NATIONALISM
ALIVE AND WELL

Black Nationalism 208. "The African Burial Ground Way" at Elk Street in Lower Manhattan.

At the start of the Twentieth Century the great African American scholar W.E.B. DuBois, after his extensive researches came to the conclusion that race would be the most significant issue in American relations among its peoples. He wrote, "The twentieth century would be the century of the color bar." How true he was! This realization continued throughout the ages of the depression, the two world wars, the Civil Rights Movement and brought us to the end of the 20th Century. In this new 21st Century, after the chaotic and devastating first decade, a new leader emerged with vision for change to help repair the image of "ugly America." As he seemed to make strides in creating a new climate for national and international relations, the

FREDERICK MONDERSON

issue of race reared its ugly head seeking to derail his candidacy. Nevertheless, this effort was eventually spearheaded by powerful Republicans and their rich conservative allies. However, Barack Obama, in a masterful speech which some have praised as one of the most significant for its leadership content and intent; called on America to come to grips with its history of race and race relations. As a candidate who did not begin his campaign on a race platform but one who sought to help and bring change to his beloved America, he was thrust into the spotlight of this important issue.

We know in the process of historical evolution, internal and external factors impact and have sometimes positive and sometimes negative influences on the development of growth. This is a perfectly good example that this issue, swept under the rug and not being addressed would surface and sort of catch all persons flatfooted.

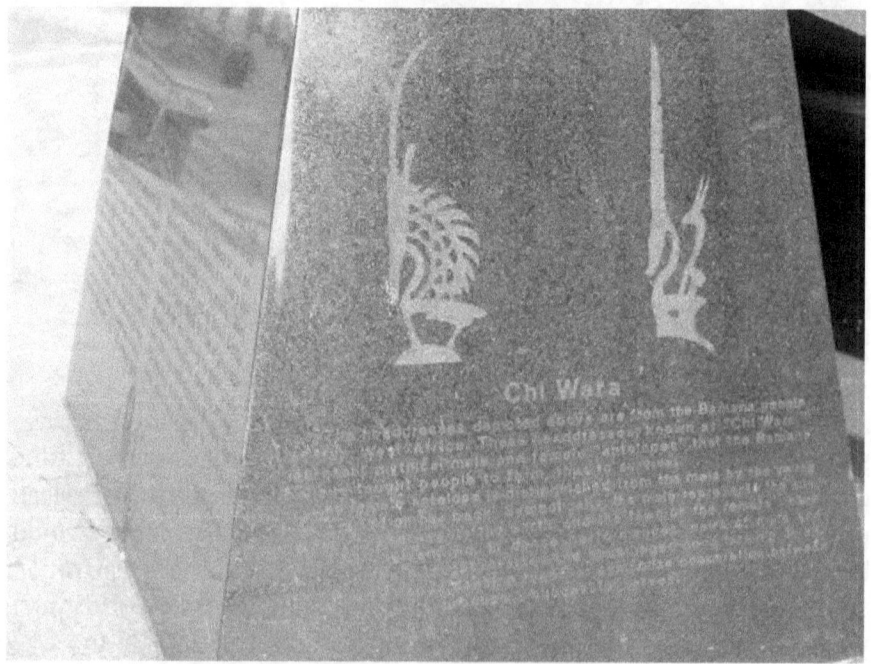

Black Nationalism 209. **CHI WARA** – "Symbol of the Spirit of the African Burial Ground" in Foley Square.

BLACK NATIONALISM ALIVE AND WELL

32. Black Men in Chains, Revisited
By
Dr. Fred Monderson

The Michael Jackson trial again forces us, as Black Americans, to assess our societal situation in terms of our accomplishments and whether we are unduly scrutinized by law enforcement authorities. Even for the casual observer, this latter seem to border on entrapment for a variety of reasons. These ideas are one individual's views but they nevertheless merit some consideration as they are enumerated.

1. In *American History and Government*, President George W. Bush will be remembered among the twice-elected great Presidents. As such, he will be judged on a number of issues that have plagued his Presidency. Not necessarily of first priority but the issue of race relations in America is certainly one, albeit important. In a memorable speech, at the Second Inaugural Address in January 2005, the President called for an end to racism in America! Mention is simply a reminder of the problem or should I say cancer of racism, with its equally odorous tentacles of discrimination, racial profiling, police brutality, high rates of black unemployment, incarceration, sub-standard housing, etc. The captain of the ship of state must throw these problems overboard, especially through presidential activism or they will remain on board as the state progresses. Just as the *Washington Post*, Saturday June 11, 2005 Lead read "Repairing Senate's Record on Lynching" reports "'Long Overdue' Apology Would Be Congress's First for Treatment of Blacks," then Presidential leadership can also make a difference in other areas of Black mistreatment in American society. After all, between 1882 and 1968 there were 4,743 lynchings in the US, 3,446 Blacks and 1,297 Non-Blacks. A great many of these latter were immigrants. Maryland lynched 27 Blacks and 2 Non-Blacks; Virginia 83 Blacks and 17 Non-Blacks; West Virginia 28 Blacks and 20 Non-Blacks, while Mississippi with 581, Georgia 531, Texas 493, Louisiana 391, and Alabama 347 present disturbing numbers. Better late than never, but still an apology does begin to address the problem. So too, presidential leadership can move the nation forward on so many Black related issues.

Another issue of importance is the Voting Rights Act that will expire in 2007. Imagine a Russian whose country has autonomic weapons pointed at us, not necessarily ready to fire, but nevertheless. Still, a Russian national can come to this country, fulfill the necessary requirement to become a citizen, earn the right to vote and never have to worry about the Voting Rights Act. Where is Presidential or Congressional leadership on this important issue? Then again, the crafters of the 1965 Voting Rights Act probably envisioned weakening of the legislation and required the 25-years renewal.

2. Whether of their own doing or whether unduly law enforcement scrutiny, Black men of prominence are targets. The prisons are full of Black men who are not of prominence. A question which attends this situation is 'Why are these Black men targets?' The answer could very well be, these Black men are targets because, as exceptional personalities, athletes, entertainers, politicians, administrators, they are leaders of their race, though not particularly DuBois' "talented tenth." The actions of nefarious individuals who are "grinding the race axe," by targeting and "bringing down these leaders" especially those who embarrass Blacks, may be pursuing their individual agendas. As such, those who "live in fish bowls" must constantly remain alert to the "baited fish hooks." Therefore, as Black men and women we must remain constantly alert to the "misguided perception that all Black men are criminals."

3. Blacks make up nearly 12 percent of the national population, and while there may not be a combined statistic, if you add up Black men, Black woman and Black youth in prison, the total numbers may

BLACK NATIONALISM
ALIVE AND WELL

range between 80-90 percent of the total prison population. This is a staggering realization but it has even greater reverberations.

First, nearly three quarters of a century ago, Gunnar Myrdal did his *American Dilemma* study. He mentions a 1926 statistic showing that in the South, cops would target, arrest and incarcerate Black males. Upon their conviction, time served and release, the police would follow and threaten them with re-arrest if they would not "snitch" against others engaged in crime. This is like how scientist tracks polar bears that roam the icy tundra.

Black Nationalism 210 The Thurgood Marshall U.S. Courthouse in honor of the Honorable Supreme Court Justice.

Second, many states disfranchise people convicted of crimes. Some states have high percentages of Black men, who, once convicted, lose the right to vote. One statistic showed the District of Columbia boasted nearly 56 percent of Black men who lost the vote for conviction of criminal activity. If you calculate this for states, particularly in the South who practice this political decapitation, one has to wonder if there is a plot or conspiracy to deny the vote, especially since it is such a potent weapon in a democracy. Recently, Republican control of state houses and their efforts to

FREDERICK MONDERSON

manipulate the voting process certainly is a corollary to voter suppression. In fact, many, even the Federal Government has argued, it is designed for voter suppression.

Third, the now former New York State Assemblyman Roger Green, in a Report to Community Board 8 in Brooklyn, a few years ago, told of the Budget fight with then Governor George Pataki. He said the Governor wanted to build jails rather than schools. One jail cell, he said, cost $110,000.00, at that time. The interest on each financed cell was $110,000.00 for a total of $220,000.00. Further, he continued, it cost $90,000.00 a year to incarcerate a teenager and $35,000.00 to jail an adult. Meanwhile, it just costs $12,000.00 or so to attend college for one year. No profits were and are accrued to business interests for Black kids going to college. You do the math!

Fourth, Jesse Jackson was recently quoted as saying South Carolina has 36 state prisons and 1 state college. Is there a connection? It's reasonable to assume across the 50 states there are varying statistical ratios relative to this phenomenon. On a visit to the Criminal Court in Brooklyn, one morning some years ago, coming off the elevator, I observed a number of "Calendars" on the facing wall indicating names of individuals and the Courtrooms their cases were being tried in. Raising this with a friend, he reminded: "That is only the morning calendar." Consider that there is an afternoon session and Night Court in Brooklyn; then multiply this by examining similar developments in the five boroughs and across the state of New York. Then multiply this phenomenon across 50 states and the "collection process" for the Prison Industrial Complex and disfranchisement becomes real and meaningfully stacked against Blacks in this nation. Irrespective, the prison industrial complex is a behemoth business enterprise that emasculates, dehumanizes, and destroys Black psychological, societal, political and intellectual potential. In many cases this is particularly true in "up-state" locals, where many of the jails are situated. Thus, the economies of whole districts are built around the prisons in their vicinity and Blacks are the "cannon fodder."

BLACK NATIONALISM
ALIVE AND WELL

The late activist Sonny Carson, who grappled with and fought the "monster" was a visionary realist. He wanted to establish libraries where Black men in prison would be encouraged to read as a rehabilitative approach to reclaiming their self-respect, combating recidivism, and then play meaningful roles in society having repaid their debt. He had hoped the 2000 incarceration of the pugilist Mike Tyson would have been such a catalyst in building jail libraries, but to no avail. "Tyson never answered the bell!"

Black Nationalism 211. The African Burial Ground, "A Place of Remembrance."

Today it's Michael Jackson, before Kobe Bryant, Williams the basketball player, Mike Tyson, O.J. Simpson, Geronimo Pratt, Dhuruba bin-Waheed, Wayne Williams, you name it. Black men are

FREDERICK MONDERSON

in chains! In the Movie, **The Education of Sonny Carson**, the arresting cop said to Young Sonny, "You people should be locked up!" Sonny responded, "We are!"

On June 11-12, 2005, the Potomac Valley District Championships were held as part of the AAU 2005 season, and hosted by the Marlboro Track Club. It was amazing to see 1000 cars in the parking lot that Saturday morning. Multiply that by parents "who pay the price" in support of their kids who give their all in athletic competition. From four years old to high school students, these young stars are phenomenal.

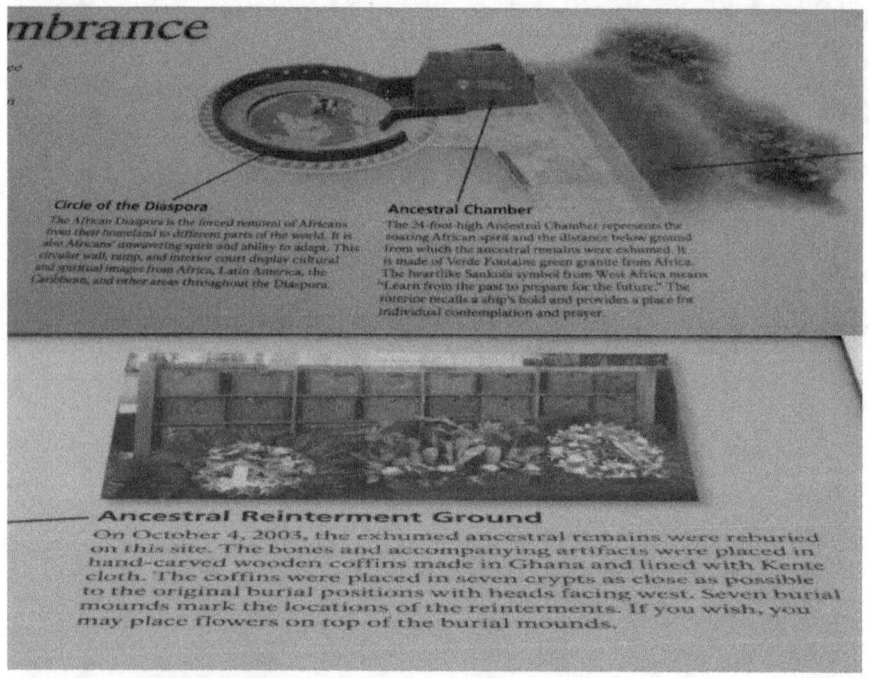

Black Nationalism 212. Mural showing the "Circle of Diaspora," "Ancestral Chamber" and "Ancestral Reinterment Ground."

Ms. Gertie Starks, Registrar of the Marlboro Track Club hosting that week's event was elated at how these young athletes were "well disciplined. There is no fighting, no profanity, no theft and these

BLACK NATIONALISM
ALIVE AND WELL

young people exhibit tremendous teamsmanship." Kudos goes out to the parents who support those kids in the enormous effort needed to sustain the high level of commitment and competition. Congratulations also went out to Coach Greg Crawley of Oxon Hill Boys and Girls Track Club of Roadrunners as he had been doing this for a dozen years. Equally too, the other coaches assisting Greg Crawley include Doug Burrell, Waddell Jones, McCaskill, Lesa Moore, and Greg Smithson. All have been tremendously supportive and were quintessential lynchpins of this venture's success. Imagine if they were cloned, duplicated and cultivated across the nation we would defeat the debilitating morass of Black incarceration and social uncertainty. One thing is certain, these young people are not going to jail! This is the hope for our future!

Activists hold vigil in 1992 to honor those laid to rest in the African Burial Ground.

Black Nationalism 213. Part of the activist demonstrations held in 1992 when the site of the African Burial Ground was first discovered.

FREDERICK MONDERSON

33. Narmer/Menes
By
Dr. Fred Monderson

Some 5,000 years before our age, there was a great Pharaoh of Egypt named Narmer or Menes. In the Hieroglyphic language, *Medu Netcher*, a fish and chisel signified this name. He was the first historical king of Egypt who united the kingdoms of Upper Egypt and Lower Egypt. Before his reign Egypt had cultural growth and unending warfare. As King of Upper Egypt to the south, he conquered Lower Egypt, to the north, and established a united kingdom. Some scholars believe rather than a single event, this was a protracted process.

Nevertheless, Narmer was a warrior king whose home was the Nome of Thinis or This near Abydos, in Upper Egypt. It was the world's first Holy City of Pilgrimage, where God Osiris' heart was buried. However, Dr. Cheikh Anta Diop identified Narmer as Theban! Nonetheless, as king of the Upper Egyptian Kingdom, he wore the White Crown called the *Hed Jet*. He conquered the Lower Egyptian Kingdom whose symbol was the Red crown, called the *Deshret*. To show the two kingdoms united, he chose a Double Crown, called the *Sekhemti*, which was actually a fusion of the Red and White Crowns. According to M.A. Murray in *The Splendor that Was Egypt* (New York: Philosophical Library 1949, 1957: 179), "The vulture goddess *Nekhebt*, of the south protected the king. The cobra goddess *Wazt* of the north attacked the king's enemies. The White Crown of the south and the Red Crown of the north appear to have been another form of the protective goddesses, being in themselves divine. The crown of the south symbolized the 'Lady of Dread,' the crown of the north, 'Lady of spells.' When the two were united into one headdress, the Double Crown, it was known as the 'Lady of Power' or 'Lady of Flame.' As such, for the next 3,000 years the Double Crown was the symbol of a unified Egypt."

BLACK NATIONALISM
ALIVE AND WELL

Black Nationalism 214. The Last and most Terrible Ordeal of the Soul of the Scribe Ani.

Regarding the Red Crown especially, and it being regarded as the emblem of the Lower Kingdom of the north, the earliest identified example has been found among the Petroglyphs of the Eastern Desert of Upper Egypt, in the South. We must remember what the great teachers have said and taught, in terms of the critical study of the Nile Valley experience. Even more important, a few years ago, Zahi Hawass Chairman of the Supreme Antiquities Council in Egypt stated, "The only king whose identity we know for sure is that of King Tut, because we found him in an enclosed tomb as originally buried." Not that others are not who we think they are but a systematic study must be made to verify what we know! However, subsequently to his statement Queen Hatshepsut's mummy was identified by a missing tooth and one discovered in the queen's toilet box. What is significant, nevertheless, while much of what has been written, theorized and accepted particularly of the early part of the history, new revelations require we re-evaluate generalizations that may be wrong!

FREDERICK MONDERSON

We know of Narmer form the "Narmer Palette," a commemorative "document" made of slate. On one side he is shown wearing the White Crown and on the other side he is shown wearing the Red Crown. We have another document called the ceremonial "Narmer Macehead." E.A. Wallis Budge in *The Dwellers on the Nile* (New York: Benjamin Bloom, 1902: 5-6) tells: "This is an extremely important document on which the king records his capture of 120,000 men, 400,000 oxen and 1,200,000 goats." Further, in the mythology, the gods give "millions of years of life" to the king. In addition to the numbers on the Narmer Macehead, the king is shown under a canopy with his wife Neithhotep seated beside him. Many have theorized this was a political marriage in that he chose a wife from the north to signify unity. Now we know his wife was actually a southerner!

The use of crowns of the first document helps us understand the conquest and unification event. The figures of the second document shows mathematical signs denoting each decimal place completely fixed exactly as they were used during thousands of years afterwards. W.M. Flinders Petrie in *The Wisdom of the Ancient Egyptians* (London: B. Quaritch 1940) states: "This tells us that the ancient Egyptians had account-keeping up to millions already developed by Narmer's time." We must believe this was a process developed over a period of time.

BLACK NATIONALISM
ALIVE AND WELL

Black Nationalism 215. Ani, Vindicated in the Day of his Judgment, Comes Before Osiris.

Thinis, near Abydos in the south, was far removed from the center to politically control the united land and effectively relate to nations further north. Narmer changed the flow of the Nile River by building a "white wall." At this spot he built the City of Memphis. It was more centrally located in Egypt and became his administrative capital. This move had political, economic, military and religious significance. Some scholars say he needed the new center to check the rebellious Northern Kingdom. He could also control the copper mines of Sinai and encourage and safeguard trade with the Mediterranean area. He also sent expeditions to the eastern desert. At Memphis he built a temple to the God Ptah, introduced temple services and the cult of the Apis Bull. Thus, Narmer or Menes is credited with introducing or operationalizing central government, kingship and religious practices in Egypt. His conquest of the north represents probably the first organized descent of the Nile with a formidable military force.

FREDERICK MONDERSON

> ## Sacred Tradition, Sacre[d]
>
> The rediscovery of the burial ground revealed that Africans and their descendants buried loved ones with dignity and respect in the 17th and 18th centuries. More than 90 percent of the 419 human skeletal remains were wrapped in shrouds (cloths), and most of the bodies were buried in full-sized coffins. Africans continued other traditional practices such as placing pennies over the eyes to keep them closed. Small artifacts like beads, cowry shells, and cuff links sometimes accompanied the burials.
>
> Community activists, politicians, and many others fought vehemently to preserve the burial ground and to honor this history and culture. Their efforts led to the designation of 0.34 acre of the African Burial Ground as a national monument.
>
> National Park Service | U.S. Department of the Interior

> Despite a 1731 law limiting the number of enslaved Africans who could assemble for a funeral to no more than 12, Africans and their descendants continued to venerate loved ones. Their burial ground was outside the city wall, or palisade, (Chambers Street today) built by enslaved Africans in 1746.

Black Nationalism 216. Evidence of "Sacred Traditions" in the "Sacred Space" and efforts surrounding the fight to preserve the site.

Narmer was married to Queen Neithhotep. They had a son named Hor-Aha who followed his father as king or Pharaoh of Egypt. Narmer was buried at Abydos in Tomb B-10, a small brick lined pit measuring 11 by 9.4 meters. On the other hand, Walter Emery in *Archaic Egypt* (Baltimore, MD: Penguin Books) says, "his Queen Neithhotep was buried at Neggadeh, also in the south of Egypt." V. Gordon Childe in *New Light on the Ancient East* (New York: W.W.

BLACK NATIONALISM
ALIVE AND WELL

Norton and Company) informed: "Her son, Hor-Aha built the Queen's tomb, a magnificent structure measuring 53.4 by 26.7 meters."

Clearly Narmer represents the bridge between prehistoric and dynastic Egypt. His imprint remains in the choice of Abydos as a burial site for the early kings. He shaped the system of government, religious practices and had some influence on religious beliefs.

Black Nationalism 217. Burial scene showing no more than 12 persons the legal amount permitted to attend a funeral.

FREDERICK MONDERSON

Black Nationalism 218. Step-Pyramid of Zoser at Sakkara, forerunner of all its kind.

34. Rosa Parks
By
Dr. Fred Monderson

Sitting on the bus from Washington to New York, the traffic was stopped to allow a motorcade carrying the hearse of Rosa Parks about 11:00 am, Monday October 31, 2005. How fortunate I was to observe this fleeting moment of history back of such tremendous Civil Rights significance! Just then I thought, no one knows or can predict the final events of their departure from this world. The ripple effect of one's actions can set in motion intractable events that can have long lasting local, national and even international implications. As such then, the events Rosa Parks set in motion were so cataclysmic, the forces she unleashed forced the President and the

BLACK NATIONALISM
ALIVE AND WELL

United States government to honor her in the most unimagined manner, lying in state in the nation's Capitol Rotunda. Rosa Parks was the first woman to have this distinctive honor bestowed and the second Black person to have this distinction. The first was a DC policeman killed in the line of duty. It is unthinkable that a Black girl could grow up and have such a profound impact on the American psyche, consciousness and social and political processes. One wonders then, who is a leader and can a quiet and soft spoken person fit that bill?

Black Nationalism 219. The most famous of all the Pyramids of Egypt, the Crowning Triad of the Gizeh Plateau.

But who was Rosa Parks?

Now, to understand the progress of Blacks in America that Rosa Parks helped to significantly further, we could look at the last 200 years at the start of each century or even the first decade of the century. We could also look at the first decade after mid-century. Thus, we could examine 1800-1810; 1850-1860; 1900-1910; 1950-1960; and 2000-2010.

FREDERICK MONDERSON

1800-1810 – Thomas Jefferson's tenure as President; Louisiana Purchase; Haitian Revolution; Britain outlaws the Slave Trade; America outlaws the Slave Trade.

1850-1860 – The Compromise of 1850; Lincoln Douglas Debates; Dred Scott Decision 1857; the Civil War.

1900-1910 – Jim Crowism; Separate and unequal educational opportunities; founding of Civil Rights organizations; emergence of Booker T. Washington and W.E.B. DuBois; Marcus Garvey and the UNIA.

1950-1960 – Nascent Civil Rights Movement; Brown v. Board of Education; Rosa Parks Montgomery Bus Boycott; Civil Rights Revolution.

2000-2010 – Development of Black Political Muscle; Economic powerhouse in Black earning and spending power; election of Barack Obama; the 'realization of Dr. King's Dream.'

These developments teach us, persons such as Rosa Parks have been pivotal lynch-pins in advancement of Black aspirations despite the enormous effort expended to stymie such accomplishments.

Black Nationalism 220. "Sacred Tradition," "Sacred Ground."

BLACK NATIONALISM ALIVE AND WELL

35. BLACK SOLIDARITY DAY: HISTORY AND VISION

By
Dr. Fred Monderson

(This article was first published in the *Daily Challenge* Tuesday, October 28, 1997, p. 2.)

Black Solidarity Day was first organized in 1969, at the height of those years when Blacks were being killed and jailed all across this society. The U.S. government was in an especially reactionary mood towards Black and poor people, while it tried to wage its war in Viet Nam. As a result, Black men and women across this nation chose to make a statement. They believed it was possible that the poor, Whites, Blacks, Latinos, and Anti-Viet Nam war groups could make a political statement that, "We are the huddled victims of a system of racism that was institutionalized."

Yet, there were others who were prepared to seek reform through organizational and electoral politics. Among this group were some persons from New York who thought that it was necessary to impact on society in order to stop the killing of our Black men! At that time, also, Douglas Turner Ward's play, "Day of Absence," was being featured. It concerned a setting in a southern town where Blacks did all the menial work such as garbage collection, shoe shine and all other miserable forms of labor. When all the Blacks were forced to disappear from the town, everything stopped. The town suffered a serious hemorrhage before Whites appealed for Blacks to return.

The reappearance of the Black townsfolk was a clear signal of the interdependence of citizens in the nation. Even more far reaching, however, was the significance that if one group wanted to make a statement in protest of some social injustice, then their absence would seriously affect the functioning of the system.

FREDERICK MONDERSON

In addition, this was also the decade in which Dr. King had struggled with non-violent protest in the Civil Rights movement. As a result, some nationalists began to see reason and logic in Mahatma Gandhi's dictum: "To make change, you must deal with the economic system, in a non-violent manner." The word that symbolized that ideal was *Hartal* (Come together).

The Black minds who spoke on behalf of our people believed that we should come together on one day for spiritual and cultural reawakening. The significance of this was tantamount to a strike. This meant that if Blacks in hotels, schools, banks and other institutions and industries were to stay home on **Black Solidarity Day** – the first Monday in November and the day before the General Elections – then a powerful statement could be made to the powers that be!

The Black family, through its physical and spiritual absence, would surely make such felt. As a result, **Black Solidarity Day** was considered a "Holy Day," not a holiday! Therefore, we needed to recognize that the system was arrayed against us, particularly because we are Black. As that thinking went, the Black church, NAACP, Ultra Liberals, Muslims and Catholics, all needed to join us in this day of solidarity.

Why did they choose the first Monday in November? In the United States, Election Day is important to show that Democracy works and there is equal justice. The organizers of Black Solidarity Day choose to let people understand the inherent contradiction in the system. If we shut down the city, the problem would be highlighted. And following this, our people would vote their conscience and interests the next day, Election Day.

The elders who thought of this strategy included Dr. Carlos Russell, Philip White, Reggie Watts, Dr. Megan McClassen, Eugene Callender and Hosea Williams.

BLACK NATIONALISM
ALIVE AND WELL

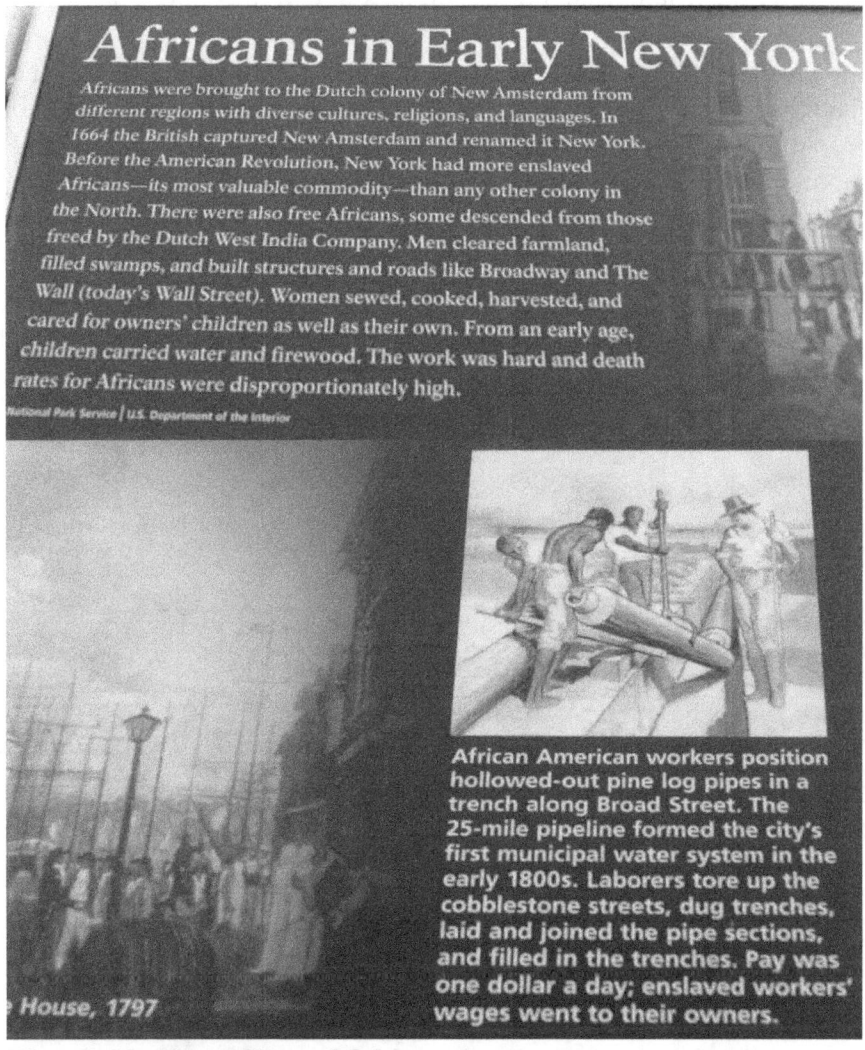

Black Nationalism 221. Africans in Early New York!

The first gathering at the Manhattan Center attracted 15,000 people with speakers including Congressman Charles Rangel and Minister Louis Farrakhan. They all decried the nation's racism, militarism, capitalism and treatment of a significant sector of the population.

FREDERICK MONDERSON

There were too many of us and if we all decided not to spend or buy anything, we would send a powerful message to the oppressor.

Our elders wanted to examine the question of what is the state of the quality of life for the majority of Black people, poor people, Latino people and a host of others who are victimized by inequality and oppression in this country. Therefore, the message should be: "Let there be solidarity in the home, city, nation and internationally among Black people and their allies. Not one of us should die at the hands of another. We should have positive outlooks. We should stop venting necessary energy and support our communities."

Black Nationalism 222. Notice the white guy wears a shoe but the Black does not!

BLACK NATIONALISM ALIVE AND WELL

Black Nationalism 223. Poster for the naming of Linden Park for Sonny Carson.

FREDERICK MONDERSON

Black Nationalism 223a. At the Elombe Brath sponsored Harlem event celebrating 30-years of **"Like It Is,"** Atiim Ferguson, *Daily Challenge* Publisher Tom Watkins, Sonny Carson and Gil Noble.

Black Nationalism 223b. Sonny Carson relaxes with his Chief of Staff Atiim Ferguson (right) and Security Detail of Rasheed Allah (right) and James (Chief) Parker at rear.

BLACK NATIONALISM ALIVE AND WELL

Black Nationalism 223c. Sonny Carson meets Congressman Charlie Rangel.

Over the years, particularly in the 1970s, this method of atonement was very effective. Schools were closed, Blacks did not shop on this day and positive activities were scheduled. Parents demanded that on our "Holy Day," schools be closed. This is what the Citywide Black Solidarity Committee is asking this Black Solidarity Day, Monday

FREDERICK MONDERSON

November 4. They are calling for a citywide march at 12 noon. The marchers will gather at Fulton Street and Malcolm X Boulevard and march to the Brooklyn Bridge. They are insisting that voices be heard on such issues as police brutality, schools mis-educating our youth, economic racism, jobs, gang violence, drugs in the community, and the denial of immigrant rights.

We must stand together or be struck down individually.

The cry is "Show Your Courage. Show your outrage. Don't go to work. Don't go to school. Don't shop." When the goals of this Black Solidarity Day have been accomplished, then the next day, Election Day, November 5, we must turn out in record numbers and vote.

This year, there will be a **Pre-Black Solidarity Day Celebration**, Sunday, November 3, 2013, 2:00 PM at Fort Green Senior Citizens Center, 966 Fulton Street, Brooklyn, NY 11238. Featured will be Bro. Michael Hooper, the Honorable Inez and Charles Barron and Bro. Bob Law. There will be cultural Presentations, martial Arts, and performances by Capoeira Angola, the Afrikan Community Drummers and Children of the International Sankofa Academy. This free even is supported by **Roots Revisited**, **NAAKO, CEMOTAP, BEPAA, DECEMBER 12th MOVEMENT, NBUF, UNIA-ACL, SANKOFA INTERNATIONAL SCHOOL**, and **African Nationalist Pioneer Movement**.

BLACK NATIONALISM ALIVE AND WELL

Black Nationalism 224. Changing Landscape in New York City.

There will also be a 44th Commemoration of **BLACK SOLIDARITY DAY** Monday, November 4th, 2013 at the **Adam Clayton Powell, Jr. Harlem State Office Building**, 2nd Floor Gallery, 125th Street and Adam Clayton Powell Jr. Blvd, under a theme of "Fighting for Political Unity, Cultural Identity and the Movement for Reparations. Here a partial listing of participants includes Amadi Ajamu, Gary Byrd, Bob Law, Honorable Charles and Inez Barron, George Edward Tait, Roger Wareham, John "Watusi" Branch, Jah Man, and many more.

FREDERICK MONDERSON

36. Black Solidarity Day Activities

Black Nationalism 225. Dr. Fred Monderson was on hand for the naming of Linden Park, **Sonny Abubadika Carson Park**.

BLACK SOLIDARITY DAY: Pre-election Rally *Daily Challenge* Thursday, October 30, 1997, p. 4.

An initiation of unity between "Gangs" and activist elders to maintain peace in the community will be presented tomorrow night at the Patrice Lumumba Coalition's African Internationalist Forum at 6:30 p.m. at the Harriet Tubman Learning Center in Harlem.

BLACK NATIONALISM ALIVE AND WELL

Inspired by last week's forum, which allowed young alleged "gang members" to discuss the issue of the nuclear family structure and its variants in crime and youth gang organizations, the event is supported by various activist groups in conjunction with "Afrikaleidoscope," a public affairs radio program produced and hosted by PLC Chairman Elombe Brath. The continuation of the timely topic, Halloween Night will seek to confront the gang-related negative activities associated with the old Celtic holiday of All Saints' Day.

"In keeping with our annual denunciation of Halloween as a 'Devil's night' holiday where White youth participating in illegal acts are considered pranksters and Black and Latinos in similar circumstances are seen as gangsters, the PLC will explain the Halloween ceremony as a "horrifying, haunting history of a blood-sucking tale featuring global goblins, imperialist tricks and threats, wretched witches, capitalist ghouls, vicious vampires and civil rites ghosts plus spooks who sit by the door," said Brath.

Black Nationalism 225a. Councilwoman Una Clarke (seated), as Rev. Calvin Butts and Gil Noble introduces Dr. Benjamin Chavis to Mrs. Gil Noble.

FREDERICK MONDERSON

In addition to an historical analysis of Halloween, the program is slated as a Pre-Black Solidarity Day/Pre-Election Rally. It will also address the current hysteria surrounding gangs.

"One issue we will discuss is how Black and Latino youth are being criminalized by political authorities, the media and the police departments of the capitalist state," said Brath. "We will present an expose of the criminalization of our youth by political sellouts to the Giuliani re-election campaign."

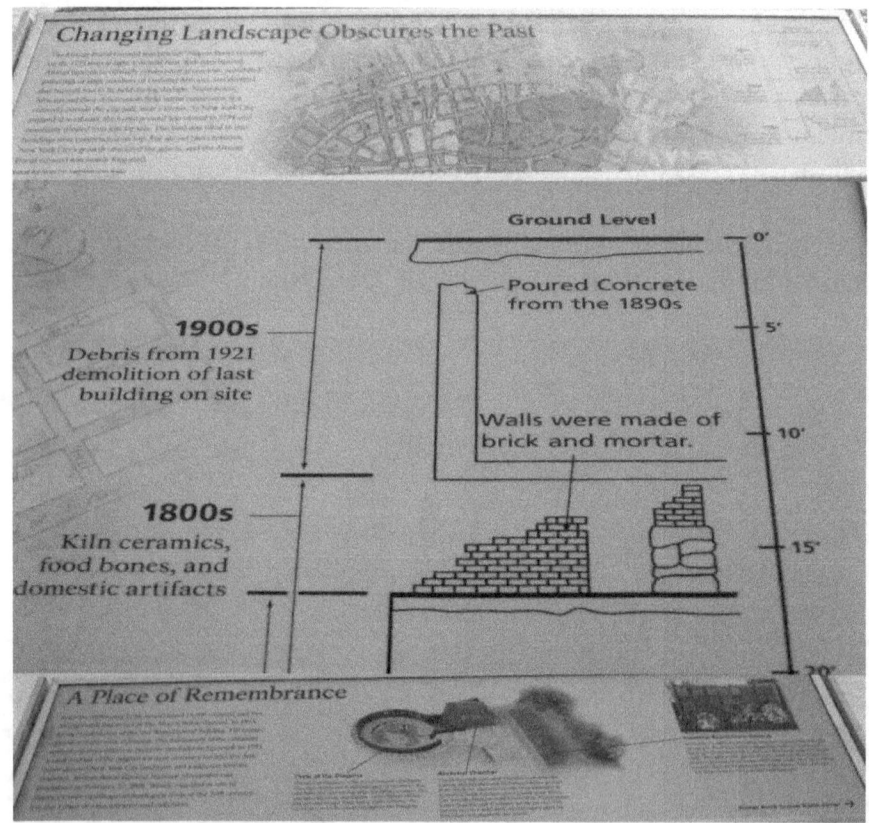

Black Nationalism 226. Changing landscape obscures the past!

BLACK NATIONALISM ALIVE AND WELL

Black Nationalism 227. Sonny Carson as "The Bringer of the Light!"

This theme will be discussed by Black Liberation Movement elders, including "Abubadika" Sonny Carson, a former gang leader (war counselor of the Bishops). Chairman of the Committee to Honor Black Heroes, he is a founder and chair of the December 12th Movement and one of the country's most astute activists on gang culture. Other elders scheduled to speak include Herman Ferguson, a former public school assistant principal, political exile and prisoner. A longtime activist, he is coordinator of the New Afrikan Liberation Front. Other speakers include one of the Catholic

FREDERICK MONDERSON

Church's most radical clergyman, Father Lawrence Lucas, Chaplain at Rikers Island and author of *Black Priest, White Church*; Vincent "Panama" Alba, formerly a member of the Young Lords and Hector Torres, a leading activist working with former gang formations such as the "Almighty Latin Kings" and "Queens Nation" and the "Nietas."

Black Nationalism 227a. Jitu Weusi greets Gil Noble thanking him for 30-years of Television journalist service to the Black Community.

Others scheduled to participate include Wu Tang Clan's Papa Wu, representative of the United Kingdom and a national spokesman for the "Five Percent Nation;" Afrika Bambata of the Universal Zulu Nation; King Tony of the Latin Kings; and a representative of the Nietas. Members of the Bloods and the Crips youth groups are also expected to participate.

BLACK NATIONALISM
ALIVE AND WELL

Black Nationalism 228. Message of the **Chi Wara**!

"The guest elders and activists will attempt to reason with the recently sensationalized attacks in New York's communities of color," said Brath. "This concern is especially important to the loved ones of those who have been victimized by random attacks by such young self-professed gang members who alleges to be the New York counterparts of Los Angeles' original notorious Bloods and Crips."

FREDERICK MONDERSON

Black Nationalism 228a. Rev. Calvin Butts, Pastor of Abyssinian Baptist Church in Harlem, sits between Councilwoman Una Clarke and Mrs. Gil Noble.

Also participating in the forum are Sisters Safiya Bukhari, co-chair of the Free Mumia Abu Jamal Committee, who endured more than eight years of political imprisonment for her activities with both the Black Panther Party and the Black Liberation Army and Sharonne Salaam, founder and chair of People United for Children, an organization that grew out of the infamous Central Park Jogger Case (in which her son Yusef Salaam, along with three other Black and two Puerto Rican teenagers were convicted and imprisoned.)

"This program will deal with the reality of the current hysteria about gangs in New York City and detail how the media is actually using sensationalism to enhance Giuliani's image as a crime fighter who will save the city from alleged barbarism coming from the wretched of the earth ensconced in the ghettoes and other urban centers," said Brath.

BLACK NATIONALISM ALIVE AND WELL

Black Nationalism 229. Lorenzo Pace's Message of the **Chi Wara** Dedication!

"We will show young men and women how they are being 'played out of pocket' by following the script that the ruling class has drawn up and that its political hirelings, along with corrupt labor aristocrats, have bought into," he said.

FREDERICK MONDERSON

Black Nationalism 229a. Red, Black and Green on the Great Lawn, listening to the Minister Farrakhan at the "Million Family March."

BLACK NATIONALISM ALIVE AND WELL

Black Nationalism 230. Self Portrait of the artist Sapp who left public evidence of his work in Bed-Stuy and Crown Heights that has subsequently deteriorated by force of the weather and graffiti. Fortunately this writer has preserved some aspects of his creativity.

37. UNITED AFRICAN MOVEMENT
By
Dr. Fred Monderson

The *Education Committee* of the United African Movement has perfected their unique *Summer Camp* for boys and girls, for which information can be obtained at their new location, Friendship Baptist Church, Herkimer Street, between Bedford and Nostrand Avenues. This is the third year of this program begun in 1994 and continued in 1995.

The UAM's *Freedom Retreat* is a comprehensive African-centered learning experience that is designed to target youngsters ages 8 to 16 years, recognizing they're the leaders of tomorrow and the future of the struggles of the African Liberation Movement. Held at Mountain Valley, formerly Peg Leg Bates Country Club and Resort in

FREDERICK MONDERSON

Kerhonkson, Upstate New York, the two-week Retreat for Boys will be June 30 to July 13, and for Girls, July 14-July 27.

Black Nationalism 231. Mural created by the Artist Sapp.

In addition, a *Rites of Passage* program for Male Boys between the age of 9 and 16 years old is offered by the group from September to June at Harlem Library and July to August at 125th Street Library. There is a similar *Rites of Passage* for Girls, though information is not available at this time of writing. For a fee of $10.00, young brothers are engaged in such activities as: "lectures from volunteers, guest speakers, cultural trips, career exploration and planning,

BLACK NATIONALISM
ALIVE AND WELL

readings, newsletter development, open discussion and a cultural play performed and organized by the young brothers."

Harlem Library
9 West 124th Street
(Bet. 5th Avenue/Malcolm X Blvd.)
New York, NY 10027
(212) 348-5620
Sat. 11:00 AM / 1:00 PM

125th St Branch Library
224 East 125th Street
(Bet. 2nd and 3rd Ave.)
New York, NY 10035
(212) 534-5050
Sat. 11:00 AM / 1:00 PM

A *Tutoring Service* is also provided at the Bedford Avenue Branch Library and targets those students in need of special *one on one homework assistance* in math, science and other subjects.

Bedford Avenue Branch Library
496 Franklin Avenue, Brooklyn, NY 11238 (718) 638-8544

At the structured *Summer Program-Freedom Retreat* children will be instructed in believing and understanding they're African and what are the attendant ramifications and dynamics for their culture in an urban setting such as New York City. The program's design emphasizes motivation, responsibility and reinforces knowledge of the *Nguzo Saba*, where children will learn how to critically and analytically think through the important problems that impact on African-Americans in this country. They'll be having fun in a cultural awareness setting that stresses *pride* though recreational and African centered educational experiences.

FREDERICK MONDERSON

Black Nationalism 232. Chancellor of the University of the Haitian Academy, Madame Marie Rene and Connie Lesold on the institution's grounds in Haiti.

A tenet of the UAM's *Rites of Passage* believes: *In the Child Rearing and the Educational/Socialization Process: Any Group which fails to consciously and systematically frame the parameters in which these processes occur elevates the vulnerability of their young, and promotes underdevelopment of their people and culture.* Therefore, the 1996 *Freedom Retreat/Summer Program* will teach the young to take pride in African culture, understand self-awareness dynamics, and learn they have to develop a sense of commitment and accountability to our community. To encourage high expectations, teachers, elders and administrators have adopted as motto: "Sankofa: Go back and fetch it. The search for Truth."

To accomplish their outlined goals, a *Code of Expectations* was designed to stress timeliness for tasks, cooperation and participation of students in all activities, and involvement in understanding and

BLACK NATIONALISM ALIVE AND WELL

practicing the *Nguzu Saba*. The UAM's program also emphasizes respect for self, parents, guardians and all members of the African families. Parents, on their part are encouraged to practice *Principles of Nguzu Saba* in their homes, join *Parent Network Families*, maintain an *African Heritage Library* in their homes, *pick up kids timely*, and ask questions about assignments and other issues regarding any of these programs.

Black Nationalism 233. The Group, including Dr. Leonard Monroe, in Egypt.

38. Like It is and Imperialism
By
Dr. Fred Monderson

A friend called Sunday March 19, 2006, just around Noon to say, watch *Like It Is*! This wonderfully educational, cultural, historical and intellectually stimulating program featured Adelaide Sandford, Vice-Chancellor, New York State Board of Regents.

Without really digressing, I certainly remember when Dick Clarke's New Year's Rocking Eve celebrated 30 years on air, and with great fanfare. Wow! Thirty years on air! Well, I also remember when Gil Noble's *Like It Is* celebrated 30 years and Elombe Brath held an

FREDERICK MONDERSON

outstanding tribute to him in Harlem attended by Congressman Charles Rangel, Minister Benjamin Chavis Mohammed, Councilwoman Una Clarke, Rev. Calvin Butts, Dr. Lewis the Harlem ophthalmologist and Mrs. Lewis, Jitu Weusi, Publisher Tom Watkins, Dr. Ben-Jochannan, Dr. John H. Clarke and Mrs. Sybil Williams-Clarke, Sonny "Abubadika" Carson, Mrs. Mae Carson, Chief Barkim Parker, Atiim Ferguson, Rasheed Allah, and Mr. and Mrs. Gil Noble and an auditorium filled with thankful and adulating friends of **LIKE IT IS**. They all came to praise a show on air more than 30 years, relating to and covering the Black community in the most unimaginative manner. I also remember the struggles of activists including Dr. James McIntosh and Betty Dopson of **CEMOTAP** who fought to **SAVE LIKE IT IS**. Why, then, adulation for one TV show, entertaining; and, efforts to eliminate the other with same longevity because of its inspiring, educational and ethnic features? Go figure!

Now to return! I turned the TV on just as the program was getting on the way and did not see the title. However, the guest Dr. Adelaide Sandford was responding admirably to the situation.

Apparently, on a recent Regents Examination, High School students were asked to answer two questions, "What were the benefits of Imperialism to Africa?" and on "Imperialism in India" but not mentioning "benefits" in the latter. Dr. Sandford, at her eloquent best; and this program should be re-run; mentioned the letters, phone calls and e-mails she received from parents, children and organizations complaining about the subjective and psychologically detrimental implications the question has had on children, both White and Black, many of whom refused to answer.

BLACK NATIONALISM ALIVE AND WELL

Black Nationalism 234. "Moms Mabley" and cartoon characters created by the Artist Sapp.

The Vice-Chancellor spoke on the loss of confidence in the educational system in New York State. She insisted that to ask students to justify benefits of imperialism in Africa was debilitating, with deleterious effects on both Black and White children. In fact, considering the seriousness of this matter, it was a failure of the people to stand up and demand accountability, she insisted. Dr. Sandford said many children wanted to critique the question but could not for they realized the liabilities of standing up. Insightfully, she indicated that education should provide the freedom and ability to think critically and analytically. The educator pointed out "no people of color who looked at the question" could answer without being upset. Since horrific imperialism and colonialism brutalized people in Africa, to ask the students to "eat from this foul cup," this "gaul," may have long lasting psychological implications, damaging to these young people.

FREDERICK MONDERSON

Black Nationalism 235. Keisha and "Chief" Bryce Green in embrace.

The Host of *Like It Is*, Gil Noble next asked, "What can we do to ensure this type of question does not reappear?" She answered that the remedy will be worthwhile "only if there is sufficient recognition by the Board of Regents of the damage done to the children." Dr. Sandford next addressed the "rage directed to young people." She insisted that "rage is development of a mode of behavior." "Our children turn rage internally." "We are not able to protect our children from physical, emotional, psychological damage because they have no maps, labs, books, as well as the social, human, economic and civil problems, etc., they faced. Still, we don't want to lower the standards for our children. However, we must retain standards and teach and hold accountable the adults who hold the budget strings, who write the exams and who teach our children."

BLACK NATIONALISM ALIVE AND WELL

Black Nationalism 235a. Dr. Fred Monderson poses with Dr. Maulana and Mrs. Karenga, founder of Kwanza and the Nguzu Saba.

Nonetheless, since the very nature of imperialism as a system involves victims and victimizer, conqueror and conquered, with attendant force, killing, intimidation, subjugation and exploitation, there is a price exacted usually in the form of resources. Kwame Nkrumah in *Towards Colonial Freedom* (1973: 13) quotes V.I. Lenin in his *Imperialism: The Highest Stage of Capitalism* who summarized the position thus: "Imperialism is capitalism in that stage of development in which the domination of monopolies and finance capital has taken shape; in which the export of capital has acquired pronounced importance; in which the division of the world by the international trusts had begun, and in which the partition of all the territory of the earth by the greatest capitalist countries has been completed." It also involved humiliation and loss of cultural esteem and destruction of social and other forms of institutions of indigenous people.

FREDERICK MONDERSON

In evaluating the four evils or fundamental causes leading to World War I, viz., nationalism, militarism, international anarchy and imperialism, the latter ranks pretty high among the four, perhaps the most significant driving force, because it was buttressed by colonialism. Therefore, Nkrumah, in recognizing the role of economics at the root of imperialism discusses three fundamental doctrines: (a) the doctrine of exploitation; (b) the doctrine of 'trusteeship' or 'partnership' (to use its contemporary counterpart); and, (c) the doctrine of 'assimilation.' The exponents of these doctrines believe implicitly and explicitly in the right of stronger peoples to exploit weaker ones to develop world resources, and 'civilize' backward peoples against their will." Thus, "imperialism is the policy which aims at creating, organizing and maintaining an empire." Unfortunately, these same "evils" became sledgehammers that cracked the edifice of white supremacy and two decades later shattered the myth of "invincibility of the white man" in World War II and afterwards.

Black Nationalism 236. Marcus Garvey, Mohammed Ali and Stevie Wonder, Black American heroic figures.

This essay therefore seeks to explore some aspects of the interaction between Europe and Africa with the resulting dynamics of imperialism in its "naked," "enlightened," and later "collective" guises with attendant implications for Africans and Africa.

BLACK NATIONALISM ALIVE AND WELL

Europe's First Coming to Africa

Africa experienced two coming of Europe to her soils. The first occurred in the mid-Fifteenth Century and the second in the Nineteenth Century. In the Twentieth Century, "collective imperialism" emerged as an outgrowth of neo-colonialism in response to decolonization and independence. Nevertheless, the initial contact was a part of Europe's mercantile expansion to discover and colonize various parts of the world.

The major development relating to Africa in this first expansion was the Slave Trade. The Slave Trade began in 1441 when Africans were taken to Lisbon, Portugal. It did not end until the Portuguese in Brazil outlawed slavery in 1888, after the French in 1817, the British in 1838 and the Americans had done in 1865. Many nations were involved in the forced removal of African people to the New World. The principal nations involved in the Slave Trade were Britain, France, Portugal, the Danes, Dutch, Brandenbergers (Germans) and of course, Americans. Still, while the Spanish did not carry any Africans they did encourage their removal, through the infamous "Hacienda Treaty," to people their plantations in the Americas! In essence, the Spanish bought slaves rather than remove them from Africa.

Black Nationalism 237. A panoramic view of the mural created by the Artist Sapp on the wall of **Syl's Trophies** on Nostrand Avenue in Brooklyn which has now disappeared. This shows that history not preserved does not exist!

FREDERICK MONDERSON

The mechanism of this removal of Africans was of a two-fold nature. The Triangular Trade represented the effective dynamics of the trade. The Middle Passage represented the affective nature of the experience. Equally too, discussions on the rape of Africa must also mention the work of the abolitionists.

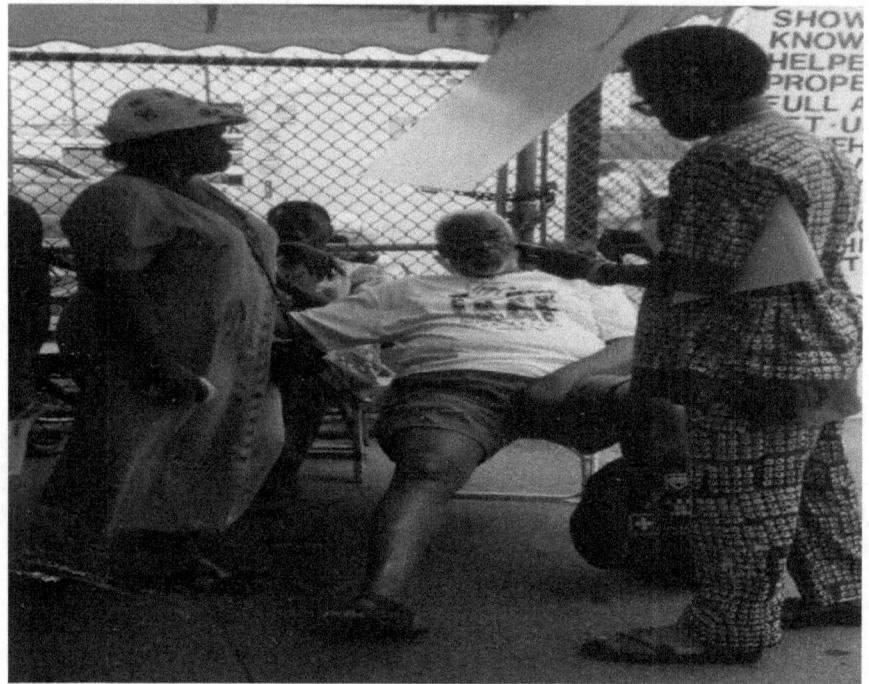

Black Nationalism 238. As Cherise Maloney stands beside Brooklyn Icon Jitu Weusi in a relaxed mood, Basir Mchawi gives a report at the African Street Festival held at Boys and Girls High School, soon to be renamed for Nelson Mandela.

The workings of the Triangular Trade were very simple. European traders would outfit ships trading to African with what is tantamount to junk! This was exchanged on the West coast of Africa for Africans; this, in addition to those being kidnapped, who were then taken to the Americas. Here they would be sold as slaves to do manual labor on the plantations. In the "New World" the sale price

BLACK NATIONALISM
ALIVE AND WELL

was invested in tropical products of cotton, rice, indigo, sugar and molasses. These products were taken to Europe. There, they fetched high prices and provided many jobs. This economic pattern created untold wealth for those nations involved. To meet the needs of expanding trade and industry, European nations created insurance institutions, and began metal industries, banking, cotton and textile manufacturing concerns and industries. They operated sugar refineries and rum distillation factories. Custom duties increased with expansion of boat building, shipping and enlarged ports serving the trade. Equally, rifle and canons played an important part in the Slave Trade.

To supply the demands of the trade it became necessary that ships sailing from Africa to America, on this second leg of the triangle, be loaded with Africans secured in whatever manner. "Get slaves honestly, if you can, if you cannot, get them anyway!" This was an old saying from Liverpool, one of the three principal trading ports in England. The other two were Bristol and London. Manchester and Glasgow were also involved in the trade but on a lesser level. These latter two cities were more interested in manufacturing textile and other commodities to exchange rather than actually carry Africans in slaving ships.

Black Nationalism 239. Journalist Euline Innis beside photographer Lem Peterkin, at an affair held in the Sankofa Academy School on Fulton Street in Brooklyn, New York.

FREDERICK MONDERSON

The Middle Passage was a horrendous experience. The dynamics of the trade exposed the belligerent and exploitative nature of the European traders. The slaving industry wallowed in African defenselessness. The nature of the experience permitted diseases, overcrowding, bad food, hopelessness and cruelty that were a part of the trans-Atlantic experience. Personal abuse of African women and a host of other sicknesses impacted negatively on the psyche of the African personality. The evolutionary process associated with man's development was reversed. The African suffered psychological damage almost beyond repair.

The abolitionists were vocal and keen observers of the Slave Trade. Several courageous Englishmen conducted surveys, recorded statistics of the trade and petitioned Parliament to end the horrendous experience. Some had condemned the practice as robbery not trade! Bu condemning the exploitation in all walks of society and in church, finally the conscience of a Christian civilization was awakened. This was after Europe had reaped untold wealth from enslavement of humanity's African brothers. The Slave Trade was finally abolished among the British in 1807, though slavery was not abolished in the British Empire until 1834 with a 4-year apprentice period until 1838.

The results of the initial contact between Europe and Africa were many. The first and most significant impact was the depopulation of Africa. Figures vary, but Africa is thought to have lost more than one hundred million souls according to the African American scholar W.E.B. DuBois. These include those killed in resisting the slave catchers, those killed in the march to the coast, those killed in the holding pens on the coast, those who died or mutinied and were tossed overboard, those who chose to voluntarily jump overboard, and those who made it to the New World to be sold. Therefore, in addition, there were those taken to Europe to be enslaved there. The psychological emasculation throughout was horrendous. Most important, European nations benefited enormously from the trade. The trade helped to put Europe's economies on a more poised footing to launch the industrial revolution. This movement transformed Europe socially, economically, politically and

BLACK NATIONALISM
ALIVE AND WELL

scientifically. It extended into Europe's military institutions and nature of warfare. Then such weapons and strategy was then unleashed against the Africans.

Black Nationalism 240. Not only did the Artist Sapp have a sense of humor but he was able to show people and animals interacting in joyful moments.

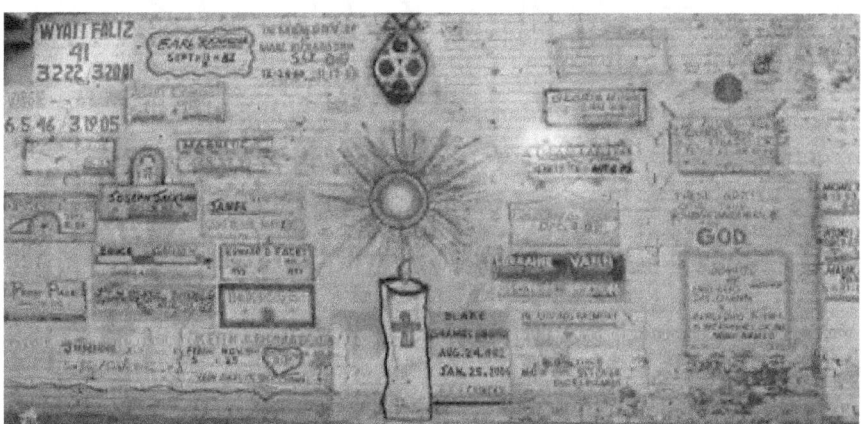

Black Nationalism 241. Remarkable evidence of "Blacks Killing Black," a national phenomenon, but in this case these are actually people who died in the neighborhood. Notice on the left from top to bottom, the names of the three Richardson Brothers, Earl, Keith and Mark Richardson.

FREDERICK MONDERSON

The impact of the Slave Trade on African society is untold. In the depopulation, Africa's growth was eradicated. Her institutions; cultural, social, political and religious suffered tremendously. Unable to develop in a peaceful environment African society was encouraged to stagnate. Fortunately, there is a resilient dynamism in the African spirit and personality. In a way, clinging to the memory of Africa helped her sons and daughters to persevere in their travails abroad and at home. With some nurturing Africa began to grow again.

Lastly, the African captives facilitated European retention and transformation of the New World colonies. This effort generated the impetus to develop and launch the Industrial Revolution in Europe and America. These then, were some of the elements of the "Naked Imperialism" that characterized Europe's first coming to Africa.

Black Nationalism 242. On a trip to Albany to advocate for Health Care, Dr. Fred Monderson stands beside "Read" poster featuring Senator Ruth Hassell-Thompson for New York's Libraries.

Early Exploration of Africa

BLACK NATIONALISM
ALIVE AND WELL

The Rosetta Stone was discovered in 1799 in Egypt and the Frenchman Champollion deciphered Hieroglyphic writing in 1822. These two developments about the ancient Egyptians in Northeast Africa stimulated an interest in antiquarian studies. After this, societies in Europe were formed for exploration of Africa. In great fanfare, the explorers Burton and Speke sought to discover the source of the Nile River. This in turn generated further interest in Egyptian exploration and collection of antiquities. So, as the race to decipher hieroglyphics begun, the science of Egyptology was set in motion. This then encouraged all forms of exploration of the African continent.

Even earlier, after 1600, there was much activity in East Africa. Traffic in the Indian Ocean, contacts with India and China, the role of the Portuguese in search of Prester John, and early trade made this area interesting for discovery and recording of this cultural area. The Arab Slave Trade, for nearly a thousand years in progress, allowed such Africans as Tibbu Tib to make their name in the ghastly trade on that side of the continent.

In South Africa, the British had secured their foothold at the Cape of Good Hope towards the end of the 18th Century. By 1814 they had annexed the Cape. They displaced the Boers who had settled here in 1652. The Boers in turn, had displaced the indigenous Africans they found there when they arrived. As far back as the end of the Fifteenth Century, the Portuguese Bartholomew Diaz and Vasco Da Gama had reported contacts with African "pilots" who assisted in their moorings and passage of the treacherous currents of the Cape of Good Hope at Africa's southern tip.

In West African especially, the most concocted attempts were made at exploration. However, success was dependent on curtailing the Slave Trade. The English Anti-Slavery movement had pressured its government to use naval force, diplomatic persuasions, military pressures, legitimate commerce and missionary propaganda to end the Slave Trade in Africa. Many British missionaries and legitimate

FREDERICK MONDERSON

traders entered West Africa and pushed inland to establish posts that became "spheres of interest," in effort to cut the root off the trade. In this, they persuaded Africans to accept Christianity, legitimate commerce and practice agriculture. The Africans were thus brought into the expanding cash crop reality with demand for raw materials needed in the Industrial Revolution.

To complement their expanding efforts, a number of early explorers converged on the continent. Mongo Park, Hugh Clapperton and Richard Lander came. Walter Oudney, Dixon Denham and Heinrich Barth were also among the early explorers who came to "open Africa." Then there was also Henry Morton Stanley who came to find Dr. Livingston! The *New York Globe* newspaper sponsored his exploration. Private European organizations as well as governments, however, sent most explorers. Hence, the mad dash for African real estate was on!

Black Nationalism 243. Mr. Sapp tried to show African lifestyle in the Congo at 25,000 B.C.

BLACK NATIONALISM
ALIVE AND WELL

Black Nationalism 244. Sporting his "Million Woman March" shirt, Dr. Fred Monderson supports Jeannette Gadsen for Brooklyn Boro President.

These forces converging on Africa in a many-pronged exploration strategy made many discoveries. They secured land concessions and did some scientific experiments. Others surveyed mineralogical possibilities. Still others did ethnological and tropical studies that made the new interest more enlightening. Many propaganda stories were told of exotic and primitive Africa. Newspapers published sensational articles in their "penny press" and "the world simply loved Africa" for its untapped wealth. As such, the Africans were caught up in a new reality. It is interesting; at the 1981 Oxford University Summer Institute held at Exeter College, one of the tutors made an astonishing revelation. He stated, "If in 1900 we knew how truly wealthy Africa was, there would never have been post-World II decolonization and independence."

Early Colonial Settlement

The anti-slavery movement gained momentum in the first decade of the Nineteenth Century. This effort resulted in the British Government outlawing the Slave Trade in 1807. The Americans had raised the question of the Slave Trade in 1787. That year the constitution was drafted. However, a 20-year grace period was given for consideration of the issue. Popular belief held that the Declaration of Independence in 1776 and the revolution had not only freed the nation but also enlightened American thinkers! Some thought slavery was "dying out." Yet, Eli Whitney's *Cotton Gin* in 1793 changed this completely. The *Cotton Gin* revolutionized cotton processing and greater demands for cotton ensued. This innovation required more workers and increased the demand for enslaved Africans.

Now, following the British pattern, the American nation then outlawed the Slave Trade in 1808. It became illegal for Americans to carry Africans into the Americas. Importantly, nevertheless, the institution of slavery remained intact. An internal slave trade developed and was fed from horrendous "slave farms" in the "deep south" where the African woman suffered the most horrendous form of humiliation and degradation in the master's demands that they produce more slave children to enrich himself. This was an especially terrible time for the African spirit. Consequently, many

BLACK NATIONALISM
ALIVE AND WELL

abolitionists felt Africans in America could not get equality in a nation that enslaved significant segments of its population. Many thought of overseas settlement for Africans. They examined the British model in Sierra Leone and approved it.

The Liberian experiment for colonization of American Blacks was considered as a feasible option. It was located in West Africa adjacent to Sierra Leone. Efforts were made to relocate Africans and grant them the wherewithal to begin life anew. This experiment was begun between 1820 and 1822. In commentary on this fiasco, Dr. ben-Jochannan tells, many Black clergy voted one day against colonization; promised to be made Bishops in the church that night; they voted for colonization the next day! Thus, many American Africans were resettled in Liberia, named Libertyville. Its capital Monrovia was named after the US President, James Monroe. Not surprising, the native Africans were visibly upset by this colonization scheme. Several Chiefs sought to wipe out the settlement. It interfered with the slave dealing activities between some African Chiefs and European slavers. Interestingly, provisions were not made for the indigenous inhabitants who became victims of their "American cousins."

More importantly, the settlers adopted an irritating and superior attitude towards the indigenous people. Many of the settlers refused to undertake agricultural enterprise. They preferred to trade which yielded quick profits. These profits were then spent on foreign goods that were bought in the United States.

FREDERICK MONDERSON

Black Nationalism 245. The "Brother" who coined the term "Black Power!" was Stokely Carmichael.

Nevertheless, administration of the settlement became a crucial issue. Though Africans were in the majority, from 1822 to 1841 the colony's officials were white. In 1828, the elective process was introduced. In 1847 the colony got its independence with a Black government. Whites were, however, retained as advisors. This then,

BLACK NATIONALISM ALIVE AND WELL

is how the process of practical colonization in Africa began. By the end of the century with the exception of these two territories, Sierra Leone and Liberia, and Ethiopia, all of Africa was colonized.

The Mineral Resources of Africa

The wide variety of mineral resources in Africa makes it the richest continent on earth. Unfortunately, Africans to this day do not own the principal means of extraction and have very little influence on the world prices for their resources. Many Africans are today indebted to the extractive concerns dating back decades. However, it is safe to say, the Africans are very well aware of this factor. Also, they are concerned enough to use their leverage on extraction and sale of their minerals.

From the earliest days of the Nile Valley civilization, Africa's mineral resources have been worked. This allowed her craftsmen to develop and display their skill in the manufacture of jewelry and ornaments. Gold, copper, tin, brass, lead, silver, iron and many other semi-precious stones have been known and used by craftsmen from antiquity onward.

Gold, iron and copper have featured prominently in the Trans-Saharan trade. The Sub-Saharan Africans exported some 9 tons of gold annually in this trade. These minerals have helped to crown the "Golden Age of West Africa." From 1900 onwards, minerals transformed the South African economy into the continent's powerhouse. According to *Business Study: South Africa*, that nation produced and exported the following minerals. This bonanza also characterized various countries at different levels of production. South Africa has Antimony, Asbestos, Chrome, Coal, Copper, Diamonds, Feldspar, Gold, Gypsum, Iron Ore and Iron Pyrite. There is Lead, Lime, Manganese, Nickel, Platinum, Salt and Silver. Further, Tin, Titanium, Uranium, Vanadium, Vermiculite, and Zinc are also produced. What a tremendous collection of mineral resources!

FREDERICK MONDERSON

Black Nationalism 246. Dr. Fred Monderson stands beside a poster featuring his heroes, "Scholar Warriors," Dr. Leonard Jeffries, Prof. Scobie, Dr. John H. Clarke, Dr. Ben-Jochannan and Prof. James Smalls.

BLACK NATIONALISM
ALIVE AND WELL

Abolitionists newspapers trumpeted the cause of Black dignity and freedom, as their publishers risked physical threat from the many forces that would promote chattel slavery.

The Colored American.

"Righteousness Exalteth A Nation."
Official Motto, *The Colored American*

THE LIBERATOR.

"I am aware that many object to the severity of my language; but is there not cause for severity? I will be as harsh as truth, and as uncompromising as justice."
William Lloyd Garrison, Publisher, *The Liberator*

FREEDOM'S JOURNAL.
DEVOTED TO THE IMPROVEMENT OF THE COLOURED POPULATION.

"We wish to plead our own cause. Too long have others spoke for us. Too long has the republic been deceived by misrepresentations, in things which concern us dearly..."
John B. Russwurm and Samuel E. Cornish, Publishers, *Freedom's Journal*

Black Nationalism 247. "Righteousness Exalteth a Nation" is a Colored Motto for "Freedom's Journal" the first Black newspaper in the nation.

FREDERICK MONDERSON

Black Nationalism 248. The Anti-Slavery Record feature showing Frederick Douglass making his confession: "I prayed for twenty years but received no answer until I prayed with my legs."

The Purpose of Founding Colonies

The last quarter of the Nineteenth Century became the highest stage of European imperialism and beginning of formal colonization in Africa. This distinction was achieved during the period of

BLACK NATIONALISM ALIVE AND WELL

"enlightened imperialism." "Enlightened imperialism" is considered the next stage after "naked imperialism." Ostensibly, the theory enunciates that Europeans help "less fortunate people" of the world. However, in receiving this "enlightenment" these colonial areas must pay for Europe's help by allowing Europeans to exploit the colonial areas' natural resources. In the climate of European geo-political and economic rivalry in the 19th Century, the Berlin Conference was organized and held in 1884-85 to formally divide Africa among European "powers." This meeting helped effectuate the "Partition of Africa" on paper.

Jules Ferrer was a member of the French Chamber of Deputies, that nation's legislative body, earned the nickname "master of imperialist logic." In 1885, in an address to the French Chamber of Deputies he outlined the rationale of the colonial policies of the French government. Hence, he laid down the operational dictum that European nations desired colonies for the following, principally, three reasons.

> RUN away on Monday last, from John Hastier, of this City, Goldsmith, a lusty well-set Negro Man, named Jasper, about 5 Feet 6 Inches high, speaks good English, and understands the Silversmith's Trade. Had on when he went away, a brown Forest Cloth Coat with flat Pewter Buttons, blue Waistcoat, with same Sort of Buttons; a Leather Breeches, with the like Buttons, old Hat, brown Yarn Stockings, and old Shoes. Whoever takes up the said Negroe, and secures him so that his Master may have him again, shall have FOUR POUNDS Reward, and all reasonable Charges paid by
> New-York, May 8, 1758.
> JOHN HASTIER.

"[In New York] I saw more of the foolishness, wickedness, and at the same time the invincibility, of American Negro-hate, than I ever saw elsewhere." – Samuel Ringgold Ward

Black Nationalism 249. Samuel Ringgold Ward's statement is very apropos, "In New York I saw more of the foolishness, wickedness, and at the same time invincibility, of American Negro-hate, than I ever saw elsewhere."

FREDERICK MONDERSON

First, the policy was set in motion, in order that they may have access to the raw materials of the colonies. Europe was experiencing the industrial revolution and mass-produced goods chiefly for export. Europe needed raw materials to feed her industries. Therefore, she needed to effectively control the source of the raw materials. This required an active presence in the colonies.

Second, Europe needed to have markets for the sale of manufactured goods produced at home. These requirements created an insurance, shipping, shipbuilding and maintenance infrastructure to implement the operational policy. In this her missionaries, traders, merchants, marketing and shipping agents and apparatus, and adventurers were consider the "precursors to colonialism." In the colonies, these individuals, considered "imperialist activists" psychologically programmed Africans to need and accept things MADE IN EUROPE. The trade to Africa included clothing, furniture, clocks, radios, and other appliances.

Imagine this scenario! The missionaries' homes were well-stocked with "modern" appliances. They would invite African wives to their "show-room" homes. The wives in turn would say to their husbands, "Honey, we must have 'this' and 'that'" and so began the vicious cycle. The Africans needed to pay for these items in cash. Therefore, they were required to enter the globally expanding cash-economy work-force. Here they earned cash, paid taxes, could purchase goods and made the system work. Unfortunately, however, industry was never encouraged in Africa! It was developed in Europe; African raw materials shipped to Europe and finished products returned to Africa for sale.

BLACK NATIONALISM
ALIVE AND WELL

Black Nationalism 250. Graphic evidence of hatred for the Black man.

Third, colonies were needed as a field for the investment of surplus capital. In a strategic move, Europeans invested their surplus capital in the colonies to construct railroads, roads, and ports and health facilities. The Africans had to underwrite these "development loans." The railroads and roads led to the ports built to accommodate ships bound for Europe loaded with colonial produce of raw materials. In time, port facilities expanded to handle more and expanded mercantile traffic. In many African countries, health facilities built were defensive in nature. They were designed to keep the African healthy and working to support the system. Some critical commentators have argued that hospitals were not truly built as a humanistic concern for the welfare and well being of the Africans. These health facilities were part of the mechanism of enlightened colonial exploitation, the consequences of imperialism.

This was ingeniously thought out, so much so, when Europe was forced to relinquish its colonies, particularly after World War II, after all that transpired, the colonies were considered industrial

FREDERICK MONDERSON

backwaters. They lacked the technological, industrial and manufacturing infrastructure that would enable them to become viable independent nations.

In addition, colonies served as outlet valves for surplus unemployed Europeans at home. Europeans could easily find some sort of employment in the colonies and "lord it over the natives!" In so doing, they transplanted the home culture abroad and thereby propagated and reinforced the myth of "white superiority" or "white supremacy." In order to accomplish this last, they built gulf courses, racetracks, encouraged cricket and built European football or soccer fields and stadiums, tennis courts, etc. They were thus able to live in the tropics with the same amenities of home, even though many could not afford that lifestyle in their native countries.

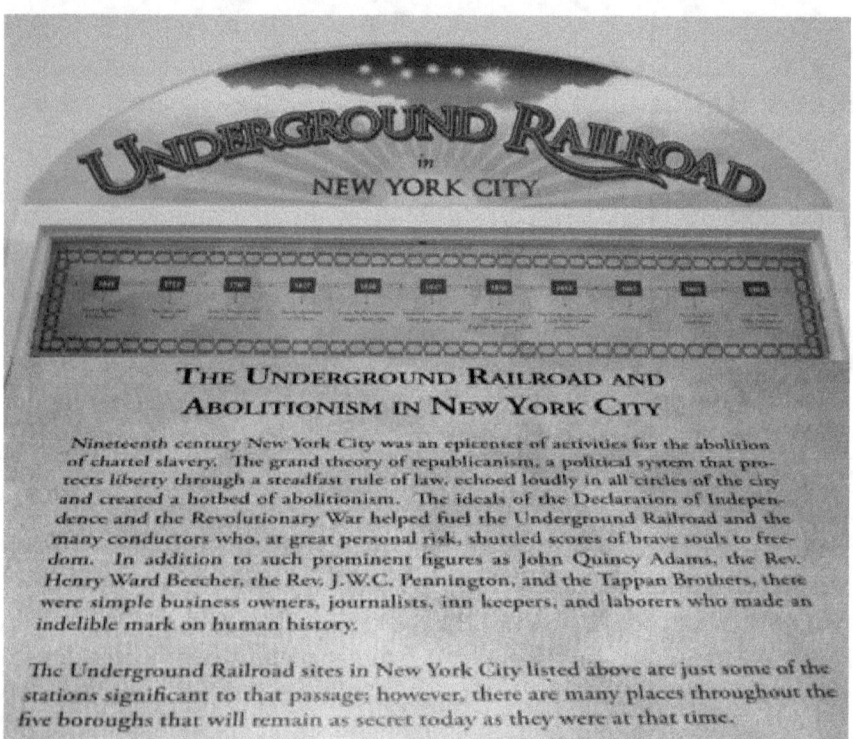

Black Nationalism 251. Evidence of the Underground Railroad in New York City.

BLACK NATIONALISM
ALIVE AND WELL

Lastly, the colonies served as coaling stations to propel Europe's naval and military power abroad. These forces could help to safeguard Atlantic and Indian Ocean shipping sea-lanes. In times of war, the navy engaged in hostilities abroad without returning to their homeports. A good example of the latter was Germany building an enormous transmitter at Yaunde in the Cameroons. When World War I broke out, the German Navy operating in the Atlantic was able to communicate with Berlin using the transmitter as an intermediary. When Cameroons was invaded and conquered it was neutralized.

Therefore, imperialism and colonialism became the practices by which "mother countries" bind their colonies to support them. Through military maneuvers and political ties they were able to assure a primary objective. This is considered the securing and promoting of their own economic advantages. As such, their economic policies and objectives for a favorable balance of trade held that exports must exceed imports in value. In addition, that each colonial power must pursue a strict monopoly of colonial trade. Lastly, these efforts were pursued to build up the national power for the mother country. Colonialism then was designed to help the richer countries get richer and this resulted in pauperizing those areas ensnarled in their colonial empires. These colonial holdings were not really poor because they contained natural resources needed in Europe. They did, however, lack the capital, technology and expertise to exploit their own wealth. This is what the Europeans took advantage of.

FREDERICK MONDERSON

Black Nationalism 252. Dr. James McIntosh welcomes Dr. Jack Felder to the podium at **CEMOTAP**.

Colonial Economics

Any attempt to understand the nature of colonization must deal with the question of colonial economics. In order to comprehend further, a sense of modern western economic history is appropriate. Equally too, an understanding of the stages in the growth of the European economy is also important.

Mercantilism is an outgrowth of Feudalism, the medieval mode of economic production. Mercantilism developed in the commercial expansion of the seventeenth and eighteenth centuries. These were called the "centuries of trade" and the nineteenth century was called the "century of production." Throughout it all, nations were interested in pursuing a "favorable balance of trade." That is, maintaining the relationship of "equilibrium between export and import trade." However, "exports were required to exceed imports."

In order to maintain a "favorable balance of trade," many times governments had to play a major role in their nation's economic

BLACK NATIONALISM
ALIVE AND WELL

system. Even though the West favored "free trade" and "capitalism," the governments intervened through certain economic and political expedients. While encouraging a free enterprise system, government offered incentives as well as directly intervening in economic pursuits.

The first of the economic policies was to "maintain high duties on imports." This discouraged other nations from selling goods in one's domestic market, including the colonies. Domestic production catered to domestic consumption. Equally too, there was a heavy reliance on the export of manufactured goods.

THE BRONX	BROOKLYN
1. MAPES FAMILY FARM (no longer exists) West Farms 180th Street & Boston Road Bronx, NY 10460	4. ABOLITIONIST PLACE Downtown Duffield Street (between Fulton Street & Willoughby Street) Brooklyn, NY 11201
2. MOTT HAVEN DUTCH REFORMED CHURCH Mott Haven 350 E. 146th Street (at 3rd Avenue) Bronx, NY 10451	5. BEREAN BAPTIST CHURCH Crown Heights 49 Dr. Hylton L. James Boulevard (on Bergen Street at Rochester Avenue) Brooklyn, NY 11213
3. CHARLES VAN DOREN VILLA (no longer exists) Mott Haven E. 145th Street and Third Avenue Bronx, NY 10454	6. BRIDGE STREET AFRICAN WESLEYAN METHODIST EPISCOPAL CHURCH (now Wunsch Hall at Polytechnic University) Downtown MetroTech Center Commons 311 Bridge Street (between Tech Place and Myrtle Avenue) Brooklyn, NY 11201

Black Nationalism 253. Churches supporting the Underground Railroad in the Bronx and Brooklyn.

The nation interested in maintaining "a favorable balance of trade" received raw materials from other countries. She in turn exported finished products. Even more, the host nation placed severe restrictions on the export of precious metals. In so doing, she "exalted foreign trade over domestic trade." Everything and everyone was concerned about manufacturing goods to sell abroad.

FREDERICK MONDERSON

This enterprise brought money and precious metals – "specie" - gold, silver, diamonds, etc., into the country. It also ensured full employment at home.

In this economic dynamic, the social and economic infrastructure at home was greatly improved. Better roads were built. Bridges were constructed or improved on. The country's industries and factories expanded and became well organized on the "home front." Schools in Europe trained administrators to govern colonies. On the other hand, schools in the colonial countries developed departments designed to foster better understanding and effective administration of the colonies they acquired. These administrators studied the colonial culture, languages, soil, plant and animal life, rivers, geology and mineral resources. In addition, these "mother countries" stressed the importance of dense home populations. This provided an element of national strength to safeguard foreign trade and provide defense, particularly against competing powers.

7. CONCORD BAPTIST CHURCH OF CHRIST
Bedford-Stuyvesant
833 Dr. Gardner C. Taylor Boulevard
(formerly Marcy Avenue; between Madison Street & Putnam Avenue)
Brooklyn, NY 11216

8. HENDRICK I. LOTT HOUSE
Marine Park
1940 East 36th Street
(between Fillmore Avenue & Avenue S)
Brooklyn, NY 11234-4822

9. LAFAYETTE AVENUE PRESBYTERIAN CHURCH
Fort Greene
85 South Oxford Street
(between Fulton Street and Lafayette Avenue)
Brooklyn, NY 11217

10. PLYMOUTH CHURCH
(now Plymouth Church of the Pilgrims)
Brooklyn Heights
75 Hicks Street (at Orange Street)
Brooklyn, NY 11201

11. SILOAM PRESBYTERIAN CHURCH
Bedford-Stuyvesant
260 Jefferson Avenue
(between Nostrand & Marcy Avenues)
Brooklyn, NY 11216

12. WEEKSVILLE HUNTERFLY ROAD HOUSES
Crown Heights
Weeksville Heritage Center
1698 Bergen Street
(between Buffalo & Rochester Avenues)
Brooklyn, NY 11213

13. WYCKOFF-BENNETT HOUSE
Midwood
1669 East 22nd Street
(between Avenue P and Quentin Road)
Brooklyn, NY 11229

Black Nationalism 254. More evidence of churches and locations supporting the Underground Railroad in Brooklyn, New York.

BLACK NATIONALISM ALIVE AND WELL

Africa in the Nineteenth Century

The Nineteenth Century was the most dramatic in all of Modern African history. It began at the zenith of the Atlantic Slave Trade, while the western region of Africa was particularly ravaged by the mechanisms of "naked imperialism." The century ended with the entire continent divided among the European powers and Africa lay prostrate! That is, with the exception of Ethiopia. In the hundred years of this experience Africa was shocked out of its pristine slumber, never to be the same again.

In 1787 the Colony of Sierra Leone was established by the British to resettle "British-Africans" freed after the Somerset Case of 1772. In this case, Chief Justice Mansfield's decision held" in the interest of "positive law," "English soil is too sacred to encourage slavery." As a result, thousands of slaves were freed in Britain overnight and thrown destitute into the streets. These freedmen were repatriated to Sierra Leone by abolitionists in an agricultural experiment.

Others who had served with the British in the American Revolutionary War of 1776-1783 were taken first to Nova Scotia, Canada. Later they were returned to this West African colony. There they joined the indigenous Africans who lived in the area. In addition, and even more important, slaves who were seized by the British Navy operating off the West African coast after 1807's Slave Trade Abolition were also taken to Sierra Leone. In clarity, while the British outlawed the Slave Trade in 1807, other nations were still involved. Therefore, a potpourri of African peoples settled the Sierra Leone colony. This experiment marked the genesis of African colonization that would later intensify. An interesting observation here is how, a few people, say; the members of the British Parliament were making decisions affecting the lives and destinies of untold Africans in far off places!

FREDERICK MONDERSON

By mid-Nineteenth Century many Europeans encroached upon Africa for a diverse set of reasons. First were the explorers who set out from various points to discover different geographical features such as the source of the Nile, exploration of the Niger region, the Congo Basin and so on.

Others came to trade for tropical products, some were merchants, others were missionaries and then there were others as scientists. Still, there were adventurers who "came to Africa to find themselves." The end result saw the sleeping giant awakened and faced with a new form of exploitation that was economic, cultural and religious, under-girded by imperialistic machinations.

```
MANHATTAN                              16. ISAAC T. HOPPER HOME
                                       (The Women's Prison Association)
14. AFRICAN BURIAL GROUND              East Village
NATIONAL MONUMENT                      110 Second Avenue
Lower Manhattan                        (between E. Sixth and E. Seventh Streets)
Interim African Burial Ground Visitor Center   New York, NY 10003
Ted Weiss Federal Building
290 Broadway                           17. MOTHER A.M.E. ZION CHURCH
(between Duane and Reade Streets)      (former address, identified by a plaque)
New York, NY 10007                     TriBeCa - Plaque erected at:
                                       158 Church Street
African Burial Ground National Monument   (at Leonard Street)
Duane and Elk Streets                  New York, NY 10002
(adjacent to the Ted Weiss Federal Building)
New York, NY 10013                     Current address:
                                       146 W. 137th Street
15. THOMAS DOWNING'S                   (at Malcolm X Boulevard)
OYSTER HOUSE                           New York, NY 10030
(no longer exists)
West Village                           18. THE QUAKER MEETING HOUSE
Former location:                       (now the Brotherhood Synagogue)
Wall & Broad Street                    Gramercy Park
New York, NY 10005                     Gramercy Park South
                                       (between Third Avenue and Irving Place)
                                       New York, NY 10003
```

Black Nationalism 255. Locations supporting the Underground Railroad in Manhattan.

So, by the turn of the century Africans became involved with Europeans in shrinking the globe commercially, industrially, militarily, and geo-politically. Unfortunately, this endeavor was at the expense of the Africans, who however, were quick to learn the nature of the "game of nations." Today we see the early grab for

BLACK NATIONALISM ALIVE AND WELL

Egypt as an extension of the colonization effort. Only in this case, the colonization was of an intellectual nature and the cultural history of ancient Africa can now be considered as a "culture in captivity" held in places like Europe, America, Canada, and even Australia.

The Berlin Conference

From 1850 onwards, Europeans began making incursions into the interior of Africa in search of trading opportunities and to establish contacts with African middlemen. However, by 1870 the creeping encroachment became a flood. The trading concerns and merchants of various European nations operating in Africa carved out "spheres of influence" for their operations. Pretty soon they encountered conflict in trading and securing raw materials with emerging aspirations of Africans. Nkrumah (1973: 13) explained how: "The stage opens with the appearance of missionaries and anthropologists, traders and concessionaries, and administrators. While 'missionaries' with 'Christianity' perverted implore the colonial subjects to lay up his 'treasures in Heaven' where neither 'moth nor rust doth corrupt;' the traders and concessionaires and administrators acquire his mineral and land resources, destroys his arts, crafts and home industries."

In order to solve the problems created by the active competition among them, the European nations called the Berlin Conference of 1884-85. It was held in Berlin, Germany, and attended by 14 European nations, with the exception of Switzerland. An American delegation was given observer status to be appraised of the unfolding developments taking place in the theoretical "Partition of Africa." The end result of this was the Berlin Act of 1885.

This agreement, considered the "Partition of African on Paper," sought to clarify the status of international trade, and acquisition and responsibility for administration of the new colonial territories called "colonial holdings." One of the chief concerns of the nations

FREDERICK MONDERSON

operating in Africa was the status of trade and the question of taxes and import duties of each nation.

The Act made an insistence that all nations notify each other regarding the acquisition of territory in Africa and that such acquisition be recognized as binding! The participating European nations insisted that a special effort should be made to ensure the suppression of the "Slave Trade" in Africa and establish provision to punish those who still so engaged in the traffic.

Black Nationalism 256. Dr. Fred Monderson and Erik beside Dr. James McIntosh (left) and Sister Betty Dopson (right), Co-Chairs of **CEMOTAP**.

The nations agreed that such provisions must be made regarding the protection of the Africans, missionaries, traders and travelers in their territories. Care should also be made to improve and preserve the moral and material well being of the Africans in their territories. Likewise, Christian missionaries, scientists, and explorers, with their

BLACK NATIONALISM
ALIVE AND WELL

followers, property, and collections shall likewise be the objects of special protection.

```
19. DAVID RUGGLES' BOARDING HOUSE        23. MACEDONIA A.M.E. CHURCH
(no longer exists; identified by a plaque)   Flushing
TriBeCa                                   37-22 Union Street
36 Lispenard Street                       (between 37th and 38th Avenues)
(at the corner of Church Street)          Flushing, NY 11354
New York, NY 10013
                                          STATEN ISLAND
QUEENS
                                          24. DR. SAMUEL MCKENZIE
20. THE 1694 FRIENDS MEETING HOUSE        ELLIOT HOUSE
Flushing                                  (now a private residence)
137-16 Northern Boulevard                 Livingston
(between Main & Union Streets)            69 Delafield Place
Queens, NY 11354                          (between Bard and Davis Avenues)
                                          Staten Island, NY 10310
21. BOWNE HOUSE
Flushing                                  25. SANDY GROUND HISTORICAL
37-01 Bowne Street                        MUSEUM
(at 37th Avenue)                          Sandy Ground
Flushing, NY 11354                        1538 Woodrow Road
                                          (between Dexter and Lynbrook Avenues)
22. KING MANOR MUSEUM                     Staten Island, NY 10309
Jamaica - King Park
53rd Street & Jamaica Avenue
Jamaica, NY 11432
```

Black Nationalism 257. More locations supporting the Underground Railroad in lower Manhattan and in Queens and Staten Island.

They further agreed that efforts should be made to protect and favor all religious, scientific and charitable institutions in the territories. The Africans should be instructed to benefit from the blessings of civilization. In this regard, religious toleration was granted to Africans, as well as the right to build places of worship and the right to worship in public.

All parties should be notified of any territory and all Protectorates acquired on the coast of Africa, by any Power outside of their, at the time, present possessions. The acquiring Power was required to establish some form of authority to administer the territory, protect existing rights and guarantee freedom of trade and transit.

FREDERICK MONDERSON

The Berlin Conference II

The Scramble for Africa intensified in the 1870-1884 period. The European nations whose nationals traded in Africa had theoretically partitioned the continent and established "spheres of interest" for trade. Being in active possession, they were awarded these territories at Berlin.

What's significant, however, was the Africans, whose territories were being divided and whose destinies were being shaped, were not aware of any of these developments. They would wake up to find their lands seized, their villages sometimes divided between two European powers and foreigners would afterwards administer them. Thereafter, the implementation of the Berlin Decree thus posed a problem.

The Belgians secured the Congo. The French received significant holdings in North and West Africa, part of the Congo and Rwanda and Burundi. The Portuguese received Angola, Mozambique, Cape Verde and San Thome and Principe. The Germans seized South-West Africa, Tanganyika, today Tanzania, Cameroons and Togo. The Italians got Libya and Eretria. The British were by far the biggest beneficiaries. They received the Gambia, Ghana, Nigeria, Uganda, Kenya, the Rhodesias, and South Africa, and so on. They exercised significant power in Egypt and administered the Anglo-Egyptian Sudan.

BLACK NATIONALISM
ALIVE AND WELL

THE BRONX

The Charles Van Doren Villa provided the northernmost site of Underground Railroad routes going up the Hudson River. Many passengers traveled on the East River to the Hudson, and in the holds of barges traveling up the river. The routes led up Boston, Albany Post, or White Plains Roads to sites in Albany, Syracuse, Troy, Rochester, and onward to freedom. There were a number of taverns, way-stations, and country estates on the route that were affiliated with the New York Vigilance Committee, whose members guided escapees away from the bounty hunters that frequented the area. The Mapes Farm and the Mott Haven Dutch Reformed Church also received runaways on the Long Island Sound route, which led to the crossings over to Connecticut and up to the New England country. After 1827, escapees faced unrelenting hostilities on this side of the Hudson, causing abolitionists to become more vigilant in building new lines north.

QUEENS

The area of Flushing was one of the key routes coming from Weeksville, Siloam, and Berean Brooklyn, up Liberty Avenue or Jamaica Turnpike to this area which led to the water routes out to Long Island Sound. Many stowaways who arrived by ship from Savannah and other ports traveled the canal over the East River into Queens. The 1694 Friends Meeting House and the Macedonia A.M.E. Church were just two of several edifices of freedom that provided safe havens for those traveling to New Bedford and other places north. The Jamaica Convention held in Queens County in 1840 resolved to utilize all legitimate means to obtain redress for Blacks. Early advocates for freedom such as Rufus King spoke against slavery, and the Rev. J.W.C. Pennington and others vowed to protect free citizens and helped promote an oasis in the desert of despair for runaways.

Black Nationalism 258. Tracing the routes of the Underground Railroad in the Bronx and Queens.

FREDERICK MONDERSON

Implementation proved somewhat difficult because many African groups were in the process of nation building themselves. They resented the European claims to their territories. They fought numerous wars of nationalist liberation. However, the well-disciplined and oftentimes ruthless European armies, with their superior firepower, destroyed African resistance.

In West Africa, Samori Toure was building his Mandingo nation and resented the French claim to own his territory. He fought them for two decades. At times he employed scorched earth tactics to hold the French forces at bay. He improvised, made his own weapons and tried diplomatic initiatives to secure his people's independence. This resistance was important. It made a difference between whether the British or French ended up controlling the headwaters of the Nile at Uganda.

In South Africa, the African statesman Moshesh organized his people into a closely-knit state and forced the British into accepting it as a protectorate. This prevented the South African Boers from later incorporating it into their racist apartheid quagmire. In East Africa, in South Africa, in Central Africa, all over the continent all forms of African resistance were crushed in the most un-merciful manner. The ugly intent of imperialism had triumphed!

The Europeans with their disciplined armies, their canons, maxim guns, and repeating rifles systematically reduced the colonies to being appendages of their empires. Let us not forget the role of Native Troops in aiding the colonial imperialists in subduing their fellow Africans. The end result was the establishment of the colonial apparatus characteristic of the various European powers.

What did Europe do for Africa?

Frequently the question is asked: "What did Europe do for Africa?" Admittedly, there is no one answer that could rightfully address such a profound inquiry. Rather, a number of plausible answers would

BLACK NATIONALISM
ALIVE AND WELL

create a better understanding of the unfolding circumstances in the colonial interaction dictated by imperialistic logic, tendencies and practices.

MANHATTAN

The African Free School No. 2 was the first primary school for Blacks in New York. Founded by notable abolitionists Dr. Henry Highland Garnett, Patrick Reason, and James McCune Smith, it was reportedly a site of tremendous Underground Railroad activity. The school also welcomed the revolutionary war hero Marquis de Lafayette to Manhattan as "a friend of African Emancipation." The New York Vigilance Committee stated that more than 400 slaves arrived monthly and were divided among the city's stations, which included the Quaker Meeting House, an active Underground Railroad station until the 1850s.

Mother A.M.E. Zion Church actively participated in the manumission efforts, and opposed passage of the Fugitive Slave Act of 1850, raising monies to purchase the freedom of the first person seized under the new act. Several thousand supporters were said to have stood with the freed man at City Hall Park and escorted him back to his home in Williamsburg. Mother A.M.E. Zion Church was the gathering place of 2,000 Blacks who urged the New York Legislature to declare the Fifth of July "Emancipation Day," a commemoration of New York freeing its slaves in 1827, distinct from the Fourth of July. At Mother A.M.E. Zion Church, the Reverend Hamilton would write, "The Africans are restored! No more shall Negro and slave be synonymous... This day has the state of New York regenerated herself. This day has been cleansed..."

BROOKLYN

The abolition of slavery in New York in 1827 marked an irreversible commitment by many to the guaranteeing of these rights to all of America. The term "inalienable rights" which resounded in the language of the revolutionaries became a clarion call to those who saw New York as a salient point to dissolve this diabolic institution.

Because of its access to rivers and ocean, its roads to Long Island, and its many safe-havens, Brooklyn provided a Jerusalem-like setting for runaways traveling north on the freedom trail. The independent spirit and beliefs of many in this large Dutch settlement created great synergy for the change or total eradication of slavery. The unique socio-economic structure of Weeksville, a Black township, offered a safety net for fugitives, while Brooklyn itself was the Mecca of abolitionist culture, home to several notable anti-slavery pastors, authors, activists, and others who were key to the call for freedom.

Black Nationalism 259. Even more on the Underground Railroad in Manhattan and Brooklyn.

FREDERICK MONDERSON

First, and unmistaken, Africa's mineral wealth was taken out by Europeans and used for Europe's own profit. Gold and diamonds in South Africa, gold and cocoa in Ghana and petroleum in Egypt, Gabon, Nigeria and Algeria, were used to supply European needs. Rubber, tin, diamonds and copper from the Congo, Zambian (Northern Rhodesia) copper and iron, phosphates, cobalt, platinum, etc., from other areas, were all part of the wealth extracted and shipped overseas. The mineral resources of Africa fed Europe's industry and military needs as well as provided personal adornment for the socially well-off.

In many places such as Southern Rhodesia (Zimbabwe), South Africa (Azania), Kenya and Uganda, large tracts of the most fertile lands were appropriated to White settlers. That is, control of colonial legislatures allowed Europeans to cede extensive tracts of land to their fellows. The only criteria for ownership were a White skin and the intent to settle and exploit the land. To encourage Africans to become part of the cash crop economy, tribes were separated and tribal customs and institutions were disparaged, disregarded or destroyed. Taxes were imposed on men, women, children, huts, animals, etc. Many Africans, with subtlety and through force by the Europeans, were made to relinquish their old customs. In the colonial system, they provided European farm labor because they had to earn cash to pay taxes.

In many respects, the colonial countries introduced racial discrimination. The nature and type of this discrimination was totally unknown in Africa before the White man!

BLACK NATIONALISM ALIVE AND WELL

Black Nationalism 260. Erik Monderson in audience to see Senator Barack Obama at Al Sharpton's affair. That's Jeffrey Davis of **Stop the Violence** in brown suit at the rear.

As Europe developed the infrastructure of the industrial revolution, extra-territorial holdings became a necessity. Africa, perhaps more than any other area, felt the full brunt of Europe's assault as mechanisms of the paradigms of imperialism. The emerging European nationalism clashed in efforts to secure colonies, and administer and exploit these lands. The prevailing colonial policy became one of "direct" or "indirect rule." Nations as France, Germany, Portugal and Belgium pursued "direct rule" requiring a greater colonial bureaucracy. This meant more Europeans were employed in the colonial administration. Britain followed an "indirect" policy. The "indirect" policy recognized indigenous or traditional authority as true leaders while the British tended to trade and external relations. If we add other Europeans who were merchants, planers, missionaries, tourists, adventurers, etc., this increased their numbers in Africa. All of these people impacted on the African continent in one way or another, whether in political, military, economic, religious, scientific, agriculture, health, tourism, journalistic or educational perspectives. From this respect, the manner of Europe's impact on Africa can best be viewed.

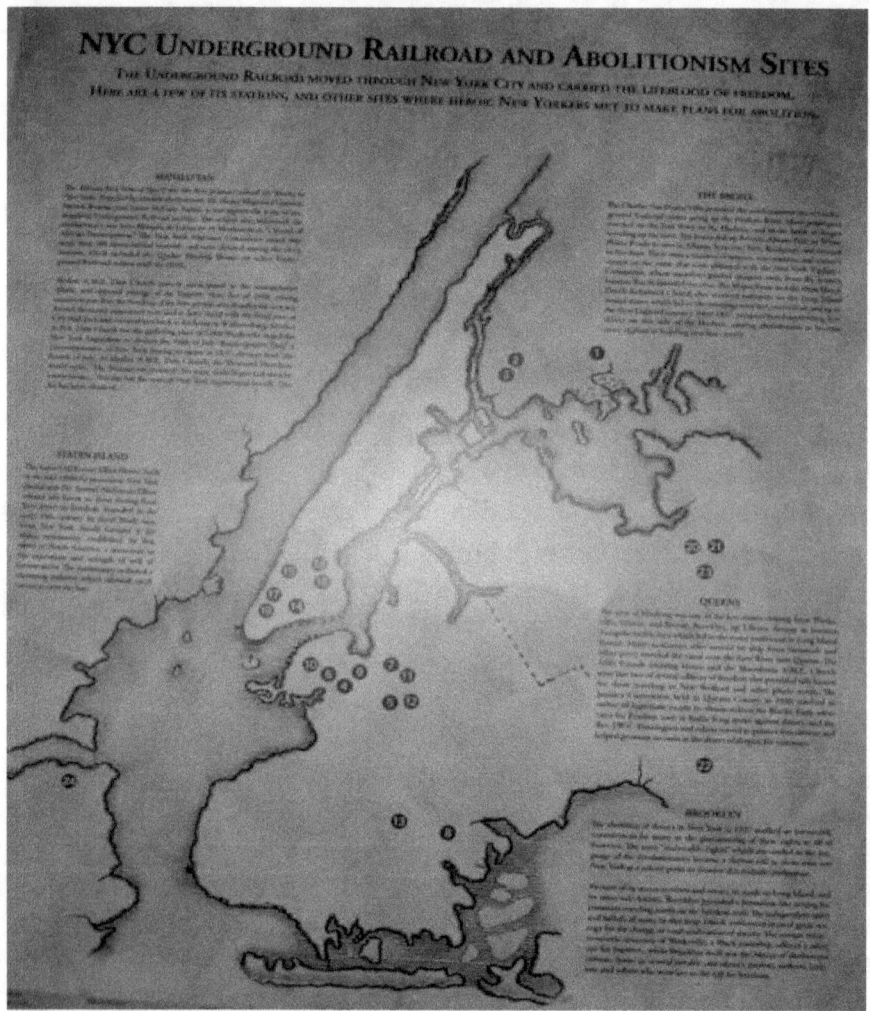

Black Nationalism 261. Underground Railroad and Abolition sites in New York City.

BLACK NATIONALISM ALIVE AND WELL

Among the first things done with colonial possessions was to make geological, botanical, and mineralogical studies of the acquired territory. This done, millions of Africans were hired and trained to operate machines that dug their wealth out of the ground. New roads and railways were built. They led to the ports. Here the wealth was shipped overseas to be processed, pay bills or pay for the administration of the territory.

Ostensibly, hospitals were built to safeguard the health of the nation. However, while they treated Europeans, it has been argued, they were built to keep Africans healthy to ensure work requirements were met on the plantations and government and private service. Schools were built to teach literacy because it facilitated communication between the European powers and residents in Africa and African workers. Other types of buildings were also built, further employing more Africans. Questioned at school, inadvertently, African children by giving up information, unknowingly, were in fact spying on their parents! At first, while the African people were working, paying taxes and buying goods "Made in Europe," the birth and pursuit of the vicious cycle was not obvious. Later colonial agitation, World War I and II, and Pan-African organization as well as unionization at home began to educate the people to the perils of their condition created by European imperialism.

Missionaries helped to build schools in their Christianizing efforts. They also reduced African languages to writing and compiled dictionaries, which helped preserve these languages. Learning European languages assisted reading and comprehending of the Bible, etc. The missionaries also taught the European languages so Africans could communicate better with them. This helped well-to-do Africans to venture to study abroad. Thus, by learning to read and also write, and becoming familiar with basic knowledge of the world, African lives were transformed.

FREDERICK MONDERSON

FREDERICK DOUGLASS
(1818–1895)
Publisher, Orator, Author
& American Statesman

Black Nationalism 262. Frederick Douglass (1818-1895) - Publisher, Orator, Author and American Statesman.

The missionaries were helpful in many other ways. They improved methods of tropical agriculture. Better farming, irrigation and rotation practices increased the wealth, value and production of

BLACK NATIONALISM
ALIVE AND WELL

African soils that fed Europe's needs. The tribal warfare that grew out of the Slave Trade was ended by the work of the missionaries and colonial administrations because this was bad for the emerging business climate. Those Africans educated abroad returned home and helped in further moving their country forward.

Overall, colonial rule did bring some material advantages of western civilization to Africa. There were however, many disadvantages. Firstly, the political structure of traditional Africa was transformed, being replaced by one imported from Europe. This also shifted power from rural to urban centers with attendant benefits and problems in the evolving scenario. Equally too, such things as poverty, illiteracy, and poor transportation infrastructure proved a problem. Many roads remained unpaved, dusty in summer and muddy in the rainy season. In Portuguese controlled areas, such as Mozambique and Angola, there were no universities and in some cases only 1 or 2 indigenous doctors in the whole country. When the colonial power, especially in Angola and Mozambique, withdrew at independence there was either a lack of adequate service or all the Europeans removed "everything" they could get their hands on.

These were some of the factors associated with imperialism and the coming of Europe to Africa, colonial administration and the changing face of Africa. Therefore, when the question is asked, 'What did Europe do for Africa?' These, then, are some of the facts! Let us not forget the many Africans lost in wars against European encroachment; the untold losses and suffering as Leopold's Belgians extracted rubber in the Congo; and, even more, the unending disrespect and psychological dislocation in one's home, land and country. As European nations fought each other in the "Scramble for Africa" and particularly in World War I and II, Africans found themselves fighting on both sides of the divide!

FREDERICK MONDERSON

Black Nationalism 263. Harriet Tubman (c. 1820-1913) - Liberator, Intelligence Agent and Humanitarian.

Notwithstanding, we must never forget, for as Nkrumah (1973: V) puts it: "The aim of all colonial governments in Africa and elsewhere has been the struggle for raw materials; and not only this, but the colonies have become the dumping ground, and colonial peoples the

BLACK NATIONALISM ALIVE AND WELL

false recipients, of manufactured goods of the industrialists and capitalists of Great Britain, France, Belgium and other colonial powers who turn to the dependent territories which feed their industrial plants. This is colonialism in a nutshell."

Finally, in *Neo-colonialism: The Last Stage of Imperialism*, Kwame Nkrumah (1965, 1973: 43) associates the Rockefellers, Morgans, Rothschilds, etc., in the banking interests with oil concerns. In this, he states: "Oil trust reserves run into the billions. Much has been used in investments abroad, America far and away exceeding all others. To financial reserves from oil must be added those amassed from metal and other raw materials' monopolies; from monopoly of food supplies and vast industrial and agricultural empires; from the monopoly network of distribution and distributive agencies; from military preparations and the several wars that have been fought with colonial peoples since the end of the second world war; from the development of nuclear instruments of destruction and the frenzied race for leadership in the realm of space research." Further Nkrumah added: "The European Community, of which the European Common Market is only one aspect, is by no means a new concept. It was foreshadowed by Hobson in his critique of imperialism as 'a European federation of great powers which, so far from forwarding the cause of world civilization, might introduce the gigantic peril of western parasites, a group of advanced industrial nations, whose upper classes drew vast tribute from Asia and Africa, with which they supported great masses of retainers, no longer engaged in the staple industries of agriculture and manufacture, but kept in the performance of personal or minor industrial services under the control of a new financial aristocracy.' It is collective imperialism."

FREDERICK MONDERSON

Black Nationalism 264. Sojourner Truth (c. 1797-1883) Social Reformer, Orator and Humanitarian.

BLACK NATIONALISM ALIVE AND WELL

39. MILLIONS MORE MOVEMENT: I Was There!
By
Dr. Fred Monderson

The reason for my coming to Washington, DC to attend the *Millions More Movement March* was to celebrate the 10th Anniversary of the *Million Man March* of October 16, 1995. On that historic date I was on the bus with some friends, Dr. Jack Felder, Dr. James McIntosh, Dawad Philip and an arm amputee named Sid. When we arrived beside the Capital Building for a few minutes I left for the Library of Congress to deposit a book I had written. Sid said, "I want to make history twice this day" and so accompanied me to the Library of Congress, Madison Building. The book was entitled "19 Letters to O.J. Simpson on Ancient African History" that was deposited in 17 volumes and was designed to be an educational tool of enlightenment for Black people and for all people seeking truth about ancient Africa, the Nile Valley Culture, and ancient Egypt/Kemet. Ten years later like the *Million Man March*, the book has shown historical and creative direction in the intellectual and emotional growth of one individual

Coming to the *Millions More Movement March* in 2005, I brought my daughter Keisha, son Erik and grandson, Bryce, to be part of this historic gathering of their history and the individual and events that have given birth to his new movement of consciousness and direction for Blacks, Latinos, Native Americans and poor people here in America. In addition, the cultural and historical awareness fires lit in the minds of these and many more youngsters were designed to assist their "rites of passage" becoming conscious and strong black-men in America, to be able to live out their destinies. Hopefully, this waxing strength will make them better citizens to make America a better place because our destinies are tied to the

FREDERICK MONDERSON

destiny of this great nation.

Black Nationalism 265. Rev. Henry Highland Garnet (1815-1882) Minister and social activist.

While I do not agree with everything Minister Louis Farrakhan says, and despite what is said about Minister Louis Farrakhan, it was

BLACK NATIONALISM
ALIVE AND WELL

tremendously visionary of Minister Louis Farrakhan to call for the *Million Man March* on October 16, 1995, for now people begin to think in terms of huge gatherings in millions, viz., men, women, youth, moms, families, jobs, coalitions, anti-war advocacy, voter registration, etc. Thus, Minister Farrakhan must be commended for that visionary and historic gathering. When we consider the great parades, marches in America, viz., Columbus Day, Veterans Day, St. Patrick's Day, Firemen, Police and the many ethnic gatherings, someone started these parades/marches years ago and now these groups celebrate with great pride, pomp and gaiety. So, long before a century from now, as we gather on the Great Lawn in Washington, DC., the heritage and legacy of the *Million Man March* will have propelled Martin Luther King's "Dream" that we shall overcome and America will become a true nation of equality for Native Americans, Black men and women, White men and women, Protestants, Catholics, Jews and Gentiles, Muslims and agnostics, atheists, handicaps, gays, straight, you name it. We will know this mid-course correction was designed to help America live out the true meaning of its creed, that all men (and women, people) are created equal. In the meantime we must all work hard for harmony, equality, justice, peace, jobs, dignity, understanding, respect and an end to racism, discrimination and inequality and today's business as usual will be a thing of the past.

FREDERICK MONDERSON

Black Nationalism 266. Michael Hooper (left), Cherise Maloney (center) and Dr. Fred Monderson (right) at the African Street Festival.

The almighty provided optimum weather, a dry, sunny atmosphere that was the first in a long train of success on this marvelous and memorable day. A number of speakers including Dorothy Height of the National Council of Negro Women and Kwesi Mfume, former chairman of the National Association for the Advancement of Colored People believed "racism, discrimination and anti-Semitism are wrong." Even further he continued, "We understand that any bigotry is bad. We also understand that the time for action is now." Jesse Jackson, Benjamin Chavis, Russell Simmonds, Wycliffe Jean, Viola Plummer of the December-12 Movement, Conrad Worrill, Erika Badu, Leonard Jeffries and his wife Roslyn, Ron Walters, the President of the Cuban Assembly, Jamaica's Prime Minister Patterson, congressional and religious representatives, women, Farrakhan's daughter, Amiri Baraka, and a whole lot of others too numerous to mention, spoke at the podium. The Bush Administration was the chief villain for its policies based on arrogance, war mongering, insensitivity to America's poor and minorities and in general poor leadership. Malik Zulu Shabaaz of

BLACK NATIONALISM
ALIVE AND WELL

the New Black Panther Party charged Pres. Bush with several "Crimes" to which the crown responded "guilty as charged." Dr. Yosef ben-Jochannan told the crowd, "look behind you" towards the Washington Monument. He said: "You built that," meaning your ancestors "built the obelisk" (a small pyramid on a high base), which the Washington Monuments represents.

Black Nationalism 267. Rufus King (1755-1827) -Attorney, Politician and Diplomat (left); and, David Ruggles (1810-1849) - Printer, Publisher and Journalist (right).

Rev. Al Sharpton, President of the National Action Network compared Dr. King's 1963 March in which he made his "I have a dream" speech. Sharpton continued that: "What made the 1963 march is that we passed the 1964 Civil Rights Bill, and therefore, the success of this march will be that we take charge of our communities and make a difference in the next [2005, 2006] elections.

FREDERICK MONDERSON

Dr. James McIntosh and Ms. Betty Dopson of **CEMOTAP**, Dr. Blakely, Michael Hardy, Jitu Weusi and his wife Angela, Vincent Emanuel, Carlos Walton, and Kevin Mohammed were some of the people spotted at this event. Wycliffe Jean had people singing on the lawn: "This is not a march, we're building a movement. This is not a march, we're building a movement."

Farrakhan was at his usual best, working the crowd, with a number of anecdotes, humorous, factual, on point. While the numbers probably did not equal the first *Million Man March*, they spoke for themselves. Nevertheless, with the same vibrancy, intensity, electricity in the air, seeking the same hope and promise, the unity and camaraderie, looking for leadership and guidance, the attendees this time were more diverse. Men, women, young people, children, Whites, Asians, Native Americans, some say gays; all represented a beautiful mosaic of motivated individuals from all across America. They were just as peaceful, civil, cooperative, and respectful as ten years ago. Many people from different parts of the country vowed to return to their communities and to do good works. Many saw these marches as good outcomes for Blacks. Many who returned after the first march told of the changes they saw come about because of the intent, honesty and message of that historic time and event.

The closer to the Capital Building where the stage was located, security checkpoints greeted those who ventured this far. As this was a natural security precaution, most people remained on the lawn, sitting on folding chairs, on the grass, on cardboard boxes, milling around, taking pictures, buying buttons, books, T-shirts, CD's, and other souvenirs, making donations in containers passed around by FOI (Fruits of Islam) representatives, buying food, drink, water, ice-cream, etc. and viewing events and listening to the wide screen Jumbo-Trons. There were lots of signs. One read: "Bush lied, people died."

BLACK NATIONALISM
ALIVE AND WELL

Black Nationalism 268. Rev. Henry Ward Beecher (1813-1887) - Minister (left); and George Bourne (1780-1845) - Organizer and Journalist (right).

A most beautiful and far reaching, yet fleeting, moment was to see the Red, Black and Green, pasted against the Capital Building! Unthinkable, that the sons and daughters of former slave-forebears could gather in such numbers on the Capital grounds and to see the nationalist flag of Black-America fly on the Capital Building shows how far we have arrived but only with the intent to challenge racism, discrimination, poverty, adversity, calamity, police brutality, joblessness, the behemoth of the Prison Industrial Complex and most important of all, the tremendous efforts of a well organized and coordinated Movement whose success was very evident this day.

FREDERICK MONDERSON

Black Nationalism 269. Erik Monderson in process of "Knocking Out" Dr. James McIntosh in his headquarters at **CEMOTAP**.

There was talk of forming a new political party, a coalition of Blacks, Latinos, and Native Americans to leverage power within

BLACK NATIONALISM ALIVE AND WELL

both parties, to see which one will give more towards the cause of these constituencies. Fannie Lou Hamer's name was invoked for her role in the Mississippi Democrats. In assisting, Farrakhan urged listeners to visit the Millions More Movement web site, register and make a $20.00 donation or how much you can give. In urging the participants to go home and do constructive things he said: "The measure of this day is not what we do today but the measure of this day will be determined by what we do tomorrow to create a movement, a real movement among our people."

Minister Louis Farrakhan spoke of a time during the Franklin D. Roosevelt Administration when Mrs. Roosevelt invited the great union organizer A. Philip Randolph, to the White House. Mr. Randolph spoke at the dinner about discrimination, racism, black inequality in America, fear and intimidation, lack of jobs, education, health care, and the whole litany of challenges facing African Americans back then. The President listened intently then said: "I recognize what you say. I agree with what you say and the need for change." He sat quietly for a while, passed around cigars then said: "Now go and make me do it." Farrakhan then explained the body of government on whose steps he spoke was very lethargic about the general interests of minorities. They favored special interests and the rich and so have to be prodded through organized numbers empowering Black legislators who could build coalitions, block frivolous legislation from proceeding and move constructive legislation out of committee. That is why we must go home and organize our communities, register people to vote, fight drugs, illiteracy, ignorance, respect the elderly and even more, ourselves. We must recognize that "opposition is as necessary as the wind. Opposition tests our commitment and strength. We can prevail!"

Saying that we cannot let another catastrophe as Katrina occur and not be prepared then what we say can only become flesh if we mobilize street, block, and house and get lots of people on board. Saying that organizing is serious business, and that the rich hate

FREDERICK MONDERSON

anyone who can stimulate the poor, he gave another example of the rich and poor dichotomy. Quoting a biblical analogy using the body as an example he explained how the rich are few and the poor are many. With a head of gold, chest of silver, body of iron and feet of clay, the burden of support rests on the lower extremities while the substance of most value controls the vital regions. This explains how the rich exploits the poor and their antipathy towards anyone who points this out and mobilizes the poor.

Black Nationalism 270. Arthur Tappan (1876-1865) - Entrepreneur and Reformer (left); and, Lewis Tappan (1788-1873) - Entrepreneur and Reformer (right).

Saying that there should be "regime change in Washington" he also indicated: "America is for sale, all she needs is to see more Benjamins" or $100 notes.

BLACK NATIONALISM ALIVE AND WELL

Speaking about Hurricane Katrina, the levees, reluctance to rebuild the 9th Ward (200 B$ for war in Iraq and not 14B$ for New Orleans) and further he spoke of a class action suit for those affected by Katrina. Today there are 75,000 foreign children as sex slaves in America and 2500 children missing in New Orleans. There is need for cooperation and coalition building with Native Americans, Black outreach to Africa and the Caribbean, need for a Caribbean Federation with Venezuela and Cuba, and to aid this he then proposed a 10-Point Plan saying the more organized we are the more demands we can make on this House. Organization begins at home! Here he spoke of POP. "Power of the People, Power of the Poor. We must demand and command what we want. We can demand that America do justice." By organizing, registering and voting this can be done.

Farrakhan then put the following questions to those in attendance, citing the need to create ministries that would cater to the needs of the people. He asked for:

FREDERICK MONDERSON

Black Nationalism 270a. Dr. Yosef ben-Jochannan sits beside Mrs. Gil Noble (center) while Sister Sybil Williams-Clarke sits beside Mr. Gil Noble (right).

1. A Ministry of Health and Human Services. Saying that leadership should build and not be master but servants. He wanted to be able to cater to the social and health needs of his constituency in America that is Black, Brown, Native Americans and the poor. Here he mentioned Fidel Castro's offer of 700 doctors to assist Katrina health recovery and 500 scholarships to study medicine in Cuba that our government, proud, rejected.

2. A Ministry of Agriculture. Saying we must be able to grow what we need to eat and sell the surplus. He pointed out that pharmaceutical companies and other merchants of death, who feed

BLACK NATIONALISM
ALIVE AND WELL

the American people, encourage genetic engineering of foods with chemicals and then turn around to develop medicines that would treat the diseases they engineered. The Native Americans who are considered a nation in this nation want to lease millions of acres for farming so we can control the foods we eat.

3. A Ministry of Education will unite and teach our children history, politics and philosophy so they would be better educated.

4. A Ministry of Defense. Our children are born soldiers but in the wrong war. They kill each other and should be taught to defend, not destroy, our community.

Black Nationalism 271. Rev. James McCune Smith (1913-1865) - Doctor and Author (left); and, John B. Russwurm (1799-1851) - Newspaper Publisher and Abolitionist (right).

FREDERICK MONDERSON

5. A Ministry of Art and Culture should have the responsibility of recording history and encouraging creativity.

6. The Millions More Movement should be involved in Africa and Caribbean trade. These countries will find it hard to exist into the future and hence the need to federate.

7. A Ministry of Justice is needed to solve our legal, social and police problems.

8. A Ministry of Information can create the proper trained reporters who will go and get the right news for us so we don't have to rely on United Press International, Reuters and the Associated Press.

9. There should be **A Ministry of Science and Technology** to keep abreast of fast changing developments in these fields.

BLACK NATIONALISM
ALIVE AND WELL

Black Nationalism 272. The Abolitionist Wall.

10. There should be **A Ministry of Spiritual** needs that combines Christianity, Islam and Judaism to cater to the religious needs of our people.

Finally we must destroy the Willie Lynch Syndrome that has infected and destroyed as well as misdirected our people.

FREDERICK MONDERSON

Black Nationalism 273. National Culture Shame (Center). Political Poster of PNC defaced by supporters of the PPP/Civic Party after they won the National Elections in Guyana. Use of Black paint signifies that Black is Evil.

40. "Greed is good?" By Dr. Fred Monderson

One Citizen said to another, "Well Comrade, the people have spoken!"
The second replied, "What have they said?"
"Well, you know the election results!"
"Greed, is good?"

And so it is! Though the Government in Guyana was accused of being corrupt, in association with criminal elements, death squads, etc., it was returned to power primarily by its enormous ethnic, East Indian base. *Sunday Stabroek*, September 10, p.6, in an Editorial entitled **CHANGE?** in speaking about the election and regarding the obduracy, intransigence and true color of the **PPP/Civic's**

BLACK NATIONALISM ALIVE AND WELL

mask wrote: "And now that everyone knows, the evidence might suggest that Freedom House has not shifted on its axis by a single millimeter. While certainly there are a few new faces who will be governing over us, there too in the complement are members of the old guard, a couple of whom have been warming seats in the cabinet room since the return of democracy all those moons ago, and others of whom are traditional stalwarts even if they haven't been ministers before. Real change, it seems, is simply not what the governing party is good at."

Importantly, and however, perhaps the *Kaieteur News* of Monday September 4,2006, p. 10 in the Freddie Kissoon Column entitled "The day I was ashamed to be a Guyanese East Indian" and Sir Ronald Saunders' "It Can't be business as Usual" *Kaieteur News* Monday September 4, 2006, p.6, as well as A. A. Fenty's column Frankly Speaking article entitled "It's not too late, Mr. President" in *Stabroek News*, Friday September 8, 2006, p. 12 voicing that: "…I say it is not too late for the President to do these things for me. And for many thousands of his fellow citizens: (1) Invite two **PNC-R professionals** into your government; pay them and other non-PPP Cabinet members super-salaries (so-called); imagine Winston Murray or Abiola Wong or Clarissa Riehl in your cabinet Sir. (Dreams of an old man? I can dream, can't I). (ii) Yes, I agree: appoint that person from that critical **NGO!** (iii) I will also welcome the **Chinese-Guyanese** to the cabinet."

None of this happened, for "You can't teach an old dog new tricks" as the new cabinet reflected the same "old boy" or "old gang" syndrome or should I say "old wine in new wineskins" or "new wine in old wineskins" which is the same "business as usual." As such then, these developments equally underscore the intent of this article following the Symposium held on August 25, 2006 at the National Public Library when this author was reminded of his professor's dictum, "Never let a historic situation pass you by without writing about it." At that event, observed were five presenters on the Dais and interestingly there were 3 African Guyanese, 1 Amerindian and

FREDERICK MONDERSON

1 Portuguese. The **PPP/Civic**, a predominantly Indian comprised political party was represented by an African Guyanese and this seemed indicative of the enormous hoodwinking and cons that pervade the strategy of this particular group whose think tank, while pretending to be Marxist-Leninists are more capitalist in their intent, aspirations and desires.

While there were many observers of the recent election in Guyana, from the Commonwealth, Caribbean, OAS, Britain, Canada, USA, etc., who came away with a general consensus that the election was free and fair, though admitting there were a few "hiccups," still others came away with the feeling there were glaring inconsistencies.

Let it first be stated, as a youngster back in 1966, I was chosen along with several others, trained at Carnegie School at High and Durban Streets, to be waiters at the National Banquet celebrating the nation's independence on May 26, 1966. Serving the Queen's representative, perhaps it was Princess Margaret, memory fades after 40 years, though I was commended as the best waiter for my gracefulness and efficiency and recommended to Prime Minister Forbes Burnham who promised me a medal which I never got. So I too am entitled to ask today's leaders, 'What have you done to my beautiful and precious Guyana?'

As a born Guyanese who lived in the United States for nearly four decades, I traveled to the ancestral home to visit relatives coincident with the national elections on August 28, 2006. I observed in the run-up to the elections, the newspapers, principally three in the capital of Georgetown, *Guyana Chronicle*, *Kaieteur News* and *Stabroek News* were replete with articles, letters, reports, advertisements, political cartoons, and there were TV shows, posters, etc., all critical of the government led by H.E. Bharrat Jagdeo, seeming to spell its impending doom. The vultures seemed to be circling overhead as the lonely donkey stumbled with the heavy load it manufactured along the jagged path it had traversed over the recent years.

BLACK NATIONALISM ALIVE AND WELL

Black Nationalism 273a. Dr. and Mrs. Lewis, the Ophthalmologist of Harlem, were in attendance at Gil Noble's tribute.

A political cartoonist, P. Harris in the August 27, 2006, *Sunday Stabroek* emblazoned the word **VACANCY** over an illustration of the national legislature and below this read: "**A Vacancy exists at Parliament Buildings for a governing party**. The successful applicant will be required to govern fairly, firmly and successfully and will be required to protect, serve and improve the lives of a long-suffering, ripped-off, conned, hoodwinked, fcd-up populace. Qualifications required are visionary thinking, strategic and tactical planning and non-racist preferences. Pay will be commensurate with honest, enthusiastic, genuine, unbiased, non-discriminatory governing experience. Send all applications to the

FREDERICK MONDERSON

tired, over-abused, bruised, battered, beaten, bludgeoned citizens of a beautiful, potentially rich country which can do much better."

Black Nationalism 274. Dr. James McIntosh addresses the audience at **CEMOTAP** with Dr. Felder and Betty Dopson in attendance at his rear.

The PPP/Civic asked for peace, they won the election and then indicative of their venom, turned around and defaced a strategically placed poster of the losing party in front of the National Cultural Center. No poster of the PPP/Civic leadership was stated to be defaced anywhere! Fact is; you have to take credit for everything done by your followers, good or bad. Or, are we to believe the PNC/R – 1 Guyana defaced their poster in such a prominent place as the National Cultural Center and also at the juncture where 'back road' intersects with the road from the airport. Perhaps there are others this writer had not seen. A question one should ask regarding this vile act is 'What was the intent and significance of the Black paint?' The villains seem to purposely not choose red paint for this signifies blood, so Black paint! Now, seems in Indian, Hindoo thinking there is a belief that Black is evil and so we ask is this

BLACK NATIONALISM
ALIVE AND WELL

defacement the intent to paint Africans as evil? After all, the Dravidians of India, who are Black, once appealed to Dr. ben-Jochannan of Harlem USA, complaining of the racial prejudices they faced in India and insisted that we never forget that they too are African and equally we in the West must never forget them over there. On the mini-bus one elder responding to the defaced poster said, "They beat me up, kicked my wife, but when they slapped my dog I think they crossed the Rubicon."

Black Nationalism 274a. Elombe Brath, Chairman of the **Patrice Lumumba Coalition** and sponsor of the "Tribute to Gil Noble."

Perhaps the nation should never remove the odious and disgusting defacement in front of the national cultural center for this lets us and the world see the shame heaped on a national monument and the nature of the mindset that would perpetuate this crime against the nation while they are asking for "Peace" or should I say "Piece." Those who forget the past are bound to repeat it. More importantly, the mindset behind this ghastly act may be forgotten and yet fester.

FREDERICK MONDERSON

Years later as we reflect on our history through photographs that shaped the nation, we will see and remember, even the people who did the ghastly act will wish they never did for they shamed us all in the eyes of the world. Nevertheless, these are the people and mindset that will lead the nation for the next five years! Lest we forget all the great revolutions of history, in Rome, France, America, Haiti, were sparked by simple things done by stupid men who trampled upon the aspirations and destinies of people they were supposedly custodians of. Concomitant with this we ask, 'When President Jagdeo boasts of meeting with Presidents of the USA, Britain, Canada, China, we ask why has he not visited Africa once, though he has visited India twice.' There are 50 states in Africa and he may be faced with the pointed question, "Why are you treating our people like that over there?"

Black Nationalism 274b. Drs. James McIntosh and Leonard Jeffries at the Podium in **Clarke House** in Harlem.

BLACK NATIONALISM
ALIVE AND WELL

Black Nationalism 274c. Sonny Carson makes a point standing before the revered Red, Black and Green!

FREDERICK MONDERSON

Nevertheless, since newspapers reflect a nation's history, here are a few samples:

"Vote was peaceful but a few serious incidents" EAB Report in *Stabroek News*, Friday September 8, 2006, Cover, p.13.
Lallman, Vernon V., Jr. "Stop racism, prejudice and discrimination" *Kaieteur News* Friday August 25, 2006, p. 4, Letter to the Editor.
Masdammer, Neil. "Questions that need answers" *Kaieteur News*, Wednesday, June 28, 2006, p. 5. In the aftermath of Roger Khan, "Speaking of questions, what has become of the court case involving fuel smuggling which started since last year? What has become of the court matter involving the murder of a taxi driver at West Demerara for which four youngsters were being tried? Matters such as these simply drop off the radar and no one is aware of their disposition."

Peeping Tom says: "If you find a soul, it may be the PPP's" *Kaieteur News*, June 11, 2006, p. 14. "By turning history upside down, by acting like the proverbial ungrateful dog, the PPP has throughout its fourteen years in power brought nothing but shame and disgrace onto itself, and today stands like a lifeboat gone adrift in choppy waters with no one in sight to come to its rescue."

Kissoon, Frederick, "Luxury Cars and Luxury Homes" in Kaieteur Mailbox in *Kaieteur News*, April 16, 2006, p.5. "The obvious question that arises is how you explain the duty-free cars of PPP members, supporters and sympathizers who haven't contributed one day in labor to the public sector." "When you look at the type of homes and expensive cars most, if not all, PPP mandarins have."

BLACK NATIONALISM ALIVE AND WELL

Black Nationalism 275. Publisher Milton Allimadi at **CEMOTAP**.

We know the story an Indian cricketer, you know, the Rajs and Nawabs, while embracing a West Indian Cricketer refused to accept a ball hit into the stands, collected by a fan who ran on to the field to present it to him. He said to the Indian of Guyanese ancestry, "Put it down!" signaling his contempt for the fellow because he knew it was the dregs of India who were indentured in Guyana. Africans were enslaved in this land and worked for free hundreds of years with no reparations in sight. We were beaten, bludgeoned, shed our blood, murdered, and worked until we died, from sun up to sun down, for our share of this beloved land. Many people refuse to believe that 'Guyana is an Indian Plantation' for slavery was abolished centuries ago. Our people suffered under slavery. Cuffy and the national monument represent the African people's rebellion against slavery and we declared to the world we will never succumb to slavery again, no matter where or under whom. On this matter we will not go quietly into the night! African Liberation Day in May reminds us of the struggle for our freedom. Claude McKay also reminds us in

FREDERICK MONDERSON

his poem, *If We Must Die*, we will face the murderous pack, dying but fighting back!

A close look at some recent development involving the government of Guyana gives some insights into the beast we are dealing with.

It is alleged that in excess of more than 200 contracts were awarded by the government to various contractors mainly of one ethnic group. That same ethnic group got hundreds, perhaps thousands of gun licenses, with relative ease. Interestingly, the scuttlebutt holds even though the police and military were out in force after the election to prevent looting and lawlessness, presumably by Blacks, there were licensed gun holders who were prepared to fire their weapons from rooftops of large building at the masses in the street of downtown Georgetown. So despite the enormous calls for peace, these gun-holding elements were prepared to fire at will. Looting is a criminal offense and looters should be apprehended by law enforcement agents and brought to trial. One has to wonder about vigilantes who could discharge firearms within city limits with impunity or complicity of high officials. Thank God we did not come to that.

In addition, a number of scams perpetuated at the highest level were identified in Guyana such as, "The stone scam;" "The Dolphin and Wild Life scam" involving some $50m Guyana that remains unaccounted for; "remigration scam" of returning vehicles to the country and no one was charged with any wrongdoing; scam regarding raising levels of the Demerara Water Conservancy with a total of $440m that soon collapsed. The same group, B.K. International, given the failed Water Conservancy contract was given most of the Sea Defense Contracts of which many failed equally. Tony Veira's Websites is replete with dirt tied to the ruling PPP/Civic party and government over the last years.

The world watched as improper use and maintenance of pumps and kokers were mainly responsible for failed efforts to combat the recent flooding that devastated many parts of Guyana including the capital.

BLACK NATIONALISM
ALIVE AND WELL

The Constitution says regarding the Consolidation Fund, that all monies accruing from all government activities must be deposited in the Consolidated Fund so that when Parliament approves a budget the spending comes directly from this sum of revenue.

The Lotto system conducted by a Canadian company was licensed to conduct the games for ten years. Yet, they never had the sums of monies deposited in the fund. Some scholars assert the President has violated the law by setting up the President's Youth Initiative and thus used the Lotto monies for projects he deemed were in the best interests of the youth. Still, those monies should have been deposited in the Consolidated Fund. The unregulated spending at will, of this "slush fund" has given the President enormous political capital, particularly when he determines who gets what in which areas.

A particularly poignant observation of this writer has been that most stone that comes from quarries for sale to builders – Toolsie Persaud Ltd.; Bakara Quarries; BK Inc.; and Gafoors, are all owned by one ethnic group which makes it difficult, for contractors of other ethnic groups to proceed with their work. You get stone when they determine!

Paradoxically, upon gaining an election victory, the President and the PPP/Civic received untold congratulatory platitudes despite many of the newspapers, and national and international institutions that had previously been critical of its behavior were now heaping praise for the "new reality." There has been no arrest or indictment for money laundering in this country. Guyanese abroad have weathered the shame of bad publicity as we were told of Cocaine in cabbage and previously cocaine in lumber, molasses, rice, watermelons, fish, pumpkins and coconuts. There was the cocaine connection at JFK, New York, staining the integrity of Guyana abroad. These are the ones that have been caught!

FREDERICK MONDERSON

Black Nationalism 276. Political poster defacement by supporters of the winners of the National Elections. The board stands in front of the National Culture Center. Use of Black paint signifies that "Black is Evil."

Not a traffic light is working in the capital city of the nation and this may be a symptom of the overall chaos that pervades though it is tremendously disguised under extensive cooperation by the people bearing the brunt of the inconvenience. I don't know if it's because I raised this at the symposium but on Monday September 4, I observed two traffic cops directing traffic at Camp and Regent Street and a little further down. This, however, was the first New York Labor Day festivities I missed in 35 years. On Friday September 8, I visited the same spots in the early afternoon and the traffic cops were absent.

This writer attended the first ever national conference at the National Public Library, sponsored by UNDP, in which the first time all the major parties sat down to debate issues bearing on the election. As stated previously, the PPP/Civic was represented by an African Guyanese. Equally on the TV program of 'Parties on Election Issues' hosted by Christopher Ram with associates Kit Nasciemento, David Decaries, etc., one of two representatives from the PPP/Civic was

BLACK NATIONALISM ALIVE AND WELL

also African Guyanese. This strategy seemed to hoodwink the populace since most PPP/Civic votes in the election were cast by Indians.

On way from Cheddi Jagan International Airport we were shown the national stadium being prepared for the 2007 World Cup cricket match. It was understood that a contractor from India would build the structure. However, the subcontracting for stone, sand, and much else fell to Guyanese Indians for they controlled the stone quarries, sand pits, trucks, etc., for delivery. In addition, in the vicinity of the stadium, some 200 new homes as well as a multi-storied hotel are being constructed on what was essentially sugar cane plantation land. Nevertheless, there was never any real public advertisement that the land was for sale, hence another part of the back door and underhand shenanigans bespeaking of the corruption that is associated with the people and party in power that ruin, I mean run, Guyana. Commentary has pointed out 100 of the new homes were being built by the fellow Roger Khan now in US custody for drug trafficking. The other 100 and the hotel are being built by a close associate who five years ago was pretty much no more than of middle-class status. Where did the money come from?

In "Sea, sand and also sex form the region's legacy" *Kaieteur News* April 10, 2006, p. 14 we read: "In an effort to crack down on trafficking, Guyana imposed some of the stiffest sentences in the Caribbean, ranging from three years to life behind bars and forfeiture of property, to full restitution to the victims." Here then is precedence to seize property from illicit gains and the above homes being built should be seized by the government and given to low income families who would welcome them, I'm sure.

FREDERICK MONDERSON

Black Nationalism 277. Radio personality Gary Byrd poses with Erik Monderson at Sharpton's affair for Dr. King.

A few days before the election, I stopped to buy a tray of eggs and the seller wanted $300 for it. A day after the election, he raised the price to $450. In our country, we call this "price gouging" and the government would go after such miscreants. Stopped by the water board to pay a bill and the guard was scanning all entrants into the premises. A woman ahead of me said something and the guard replied, "In the white man's country you obey the law." Then I murmured to myself but there is indeed law and there is a mechanism to seek redress if there is a violation. No government in America would survive being associated with any of the issues mentioned here for there is an investigative press and they expose corruption that is acted upon by the judiciary.

Interestingly, the day of the election, August 28, was as pointed out on TV, a "holy day" in India when people go out and wash themselves in the Ganges River. Ostensibly to prevent violence on Election Day, the national holiday was declared. The hoodwinked never saw that "left hook coming." All the newspapers are

BLACK NATIONALISM
ALIVE AND WELL

controlled by Indians, the Indians who criticized the government and even the Indian columnists never got this. What type of investigative reporting is this or is there complicity? Imagine if it was announced that 'we have chosen this day for the election to reach across the ocean to identify with our Indian heritage.' Then the ethnic sensitivities would have been aroused and the turnout and outcome would probably have been different. One thing is certain, the governing PPP/Civic administration would never have held national elections on the last Saturday in May, African Liberation Day, nor in February, Black History Month!

All this, charges of corruptions, being responsible for joblessness, crime, failure to deliver on human services, allowing one ethnic group to amass an economic stranglehold on the nation, never significantly trying to lift African Guyanese from the poverty level, being associated with drug dealers, money laundering, favoritism etc., and yet the people returned this government to power. They seemed to say, the government may be corrupt, associated with scams and drug lords, etc., but it's ours, or should I say "Ah Wee Own."

Black Nationalism 278. Close-up of political poster of PNCR-1G defaced in front of the National Culture Center by supporters of the PPP/Civic party that won the election. Black paint signifies evil.

FREDERICK MONDERSON

Black Nationalism 278a. Prolific writer and activist, James Baldwin.

Black Nationalism 279. Political Poster of PNC defaced at prominent junction of Airport Highway intersection with West Ruimveldt. Again, Black paint signifies that "Blacks are Evil."

BLACK NATIONALISM
ALIVE AND WELL

Black Nationalism 280. Dr. Fred Monderson on a mission to Haiti after the Earthquake.

FREDERICK MONDERSON

Black Nationalism 280a.   Harlem's Tribute to Harriet Tubman, leader, revolutionary and Underground Railroad Conductor.

BLACK NATIONALISM
ALIVE AND WELL

Black Nationalism 280b. Heroes of the **Haitian Revolution** and the nation's Independence.

Black Nationalism 280c. Rev. Al Sharpton and Stevie Wonder.

FREDERICK MONDERSON

Black Nationalism 280d. Teddy Cubia at work in Middle School.

Black Nationalism 280e. Dave Clarke, Middle School Assistant Principal poses as Hannibal for Budweiser African Series.

BLACK NATIONALISM ALIVE AND WELL

41. THE ROAD AHEAD
By
Dr. Fred Monderson

Mr. Williams offered me the opportunity to speak to graduating young people on this their auspicious day, the first day of their new life going forward, which I would like to call **THE ROAD AHEAD**. I say if you keep your eyes focused on the road, avoid distractions and be diligent, and creative and steadfast in your work, even you can be surprised in the outcome of your final destination.

Dr. Ben Jochannan, my friend and teacher has always said the child should not celebrate a birthday, as only the mother, who did all the work, should get the credit because the child simply arrived. So, we should thank our parents for their support on this important day. Let us give the parents a hand. Let's also remember, "It takes a Village to raise a child" and in that context, the village is this organization. So, let's give them a hand. Last, but certainly not least, let's give the graduates themselves a big hand.

1. Dr. ben-Jochannan is a famous Harlemite. I was one of his students. There is a buffet restaurant on Lenox Avenue and 134th Street where he eats regularly. You will see an old man in a mobile chair with an attendant. He is about 94 years old. One day in the 1980s he took 2000 people to Egypt! It was like 50 tour buses on the road at one time. This was never done before or since. He made his Name! So, you can never tell who may be sitting next to you. I will also tell you about me.

FREDERICK MONDERSON

Black Nationalism 281. The flag of Red, Black and Green with 50 stars for fifty African countries.

I am not a Biblical scholar. I am an Egyptological scholar. Malcolm X said he had read something passingly. I too read passingly somewhere in the Bible, "You have to be wise as a serpent and harmless as a dove." Certainly wise as a serpent!

The famous quote I like from the Renaissance political philosopher Machiavelli is, "Any man who wishes to make a profession of goodness must naturally come to grips with people who are not good. So you must learn how to be good and not be good, and use and not use this skill according to the situation." But most important,

BLACK NATIONALISM
ALIVE AND WELL

you must be wise because if you're not wise you will easily be swept away.

Let me give you an example from my experience. Some two Saturdays ago I was standing in the left rear door of my car cleaning some junk from the back seat. I felt a bump and looked out. The car in front of me was pulling out and backed into me. Normally I would have no reason to approach the driver. Nevertheless, I went to the car to enquire. I saw a couple, an older man and a younger woman. I told him about the bump. They both got out. Immediately he started cursing me. "I didn't hit your "F-ing" car and so on. I did learn some things from watching my son practice Karate. He was a big guy and I figured, if he came any closer I would have to drop to my knees and punch straight into his scrotum. That should bring him down.

Black Nationalism 282. City Councilman Al Vann and education activist Jitu Weusi stand with a young man to receive an award for exemplary citizenship. Note Jitu's cameras.

Fortunately I started thinking. I had just uploaded a 626 page book to Amazon.com entitled **BARACK OBAMA: MASTER OF WASHINGTON, DC**. I had read last year there were some 50 books written about Barack Obama that were negative. I intended my book would show the positive side of the man. I have written a third, **Obama: Master and Commander**. So what was I

FREDERICK MONDERSON

doing brawling in the street with this stupid Negro! Considering where I came from! I was born in Guyana and came to New York some 43 years ago. My mother had 8 children with my father. He was a gold and diamond miner and never there. She raised us all as a single mother without any help.

I have 7 college degrees, six with the City University of New York. This was my second book on President Obama but the most extensive one. So, to these young graduates, you will meet these clowns who will pull you off the road ahead of where your destination is to become a professional and respectful citizen, not languishing in some prison, because you did not take a step back and think. So you must be wise! You must be wise in all facets of your life because the way ahead is strewn with traps but you don't have to be entrapped.

Mourners follow funeral cortege of legendary human rights activist Sonny Carson as it proceeds along Fulton Street in Brooklyn last week. Carson died December 20. See Story on Page 7
Photo by Kwame Brathwaite

Black Nationalism 282a. The Funeral Cortege of Sonny Carson makes its way down Fulton Street as seen in Caribbean Newspaper.

After 9/11 Vice-President Chaney said we have entered the age of the "New Normal." You see that all the time. Everywhere you go they have got cameras that pick up your every move. If you have a backpack in the subway they want to search you. At the airport you

BLACK NATIONALISM
ALIVE AND WELL

go through a thorough screening. Soldiers with guns patrol Am Track and Grand Central Stations. Jobs have random drug testing policies. We have the Patriot Act that keeps tabs on everyone.

There are people who come on the job, befriend you, smoke or drug with you, then tell the boss, Smith, Jones, uses drugs. You lose your job. Sometimes it's easy to get a job but hard to keep it.

Back in 2002 when I was Chairman of Kings County Hospital Advisory Board and the Behavioral Health Committee the doctors would report to my committee on a monthly basis. There was a Spanish professional who would come to report. In one conversation he said to me, "Dr. Monderson, I was the first Puerto Rican to hold this job and have held it for 26 years." I said, "You must have seen a lot in that time." He replied that he did. Then I thought, wow! For 26 years, every two-week this guy would get a paycheck. He could raise a family. Purchase a house and pay on his mortgage and do many things, because he was wise enough to hold on to his job. So getting the job is one thing. Holding on to it is another.

Black Nationalism 282b. Atiim Ferguson, Sonny Carson's Chief of Staff, in a very pensive mood at Sonny's funeral.

FREDERICK MONDERSON

2. How many people can tell me what the Washington monument looks like?

Black Nationalism 283. Urban art produced by young people and decorating a wall in Downtown Brooklyn.

That is what we call historic memory.

Who can tell me who was the first President of this country?
Jim Hanson, a Black man.

Who was the first and most celebrated poet in the United States?
Phyllis Wheatley. A Black woman.

Who was the world's first scientist?
Imhotep. He was the world's first multi-genius. A poet, physician, architect, administrator, priest and philosopher. He said, "Eat, drink and be merry for tomorrow we die!"

BLACK NATIONALISM ALIVE AND WELL

Black Nationalism 283a. Mitch Penn, Kashida Maloney hugging Cherise Maloney and Santana Payton with others outside the Institutional Church on Adelphi Street awaiting the "Bones of Samuel Carson" on way to Ghana.

Black Nationalism 284. Sister Betty Dopson, Co-Chair of **CEMOTAP** at the Podium with Dr. James McIntosh seated and listening attentively.

FREDERICK MONDERSON

3. Do you know as minorities you are, for most part programmed to fail. In fact, in this instance, your teachers have provided you with the wherewithal to succeed but it is up to you.

Do you know 32 percent of all high school students will not Graduate? And the numbers are higher for minorities!
Do you know 70 percent of all high school graduates are not ready for college? But, because of the confidence with which you are starting this day, your success is possible. When you do go to college and succeed, you must come back and convince some of the knuckleheads who will be passing through this is the way to go.

I think it was my second graduation at Hunter College. This gentleman gave the Commencement Address. He was tall and said, "When I went to college they gave me a basketball and told me to play. I responded that I came to study Biology not Basketball."

But, do remember. You are not going to college to get a job. Today there are no jobs! You are going to college to learn a skill, learn how to think, learn how to be industrious on your own behalf. There are no shortcuts. Shortcuts can turn out to be the long way!

Aristotle said "Knowledge is power." I say, knowledge is freedom. Knowledge is the power and freedom to make your dreams a reality. Knowledge is the power to be wise! Being wise is being prepared!

I once listened to Shekur Ur Shekum. He is a Black Muslim. I have never forgotten his words. He said: "If you work for the man from 9-5, then go home and work for yourself from 5-9." Over a period of time you will have something going for you. That is, the art of being wise. Remember, this world is not for stupid people!

BLACK NATIONALISM
ALIVE AND WELL

Black Nationalism 285. New York City Mayor David Dinkins presents an award to a well deserving citizen.

Black Nationalism 286. Frederick Douglass, the great orator, abolitionist and freedom-fighter who escaped from slavery and founded the North Star newspaper.

FREDERICK MONDERSON

4. How many people have heard of the *Daily Challenge*, a Black newspaper in Brooklyn? In 15 years I wrote over 1000 articles for them, all *Pro Bono*. That is what you missed if you have never heard of that paper.

I wrote nearly 100 articles for the *Challenge* on Barack Obama. In **BARACK OBAMA: MASTER OF WASHINGTON, DC**, I included 75 articles of these. I took more than 450 photographs of the buildings in Washington DC and then I added some quotations from the President himself. In a Speech on June 16, 2006, as a young Senator from Illinois, he said: "It is only when you hitch yourself to something larger than yourself that you will realize your true potential."

And so, what is your true potential young graduates? It should be, to be the best you can be! That is useful, functional, law abiding citizens. We must recognize the Police are a major force in our communities. To deal with them you must have credibility. You must be wise. Even then, but you must still have credibility. How do you do that? By being constructively busy.

In 1976, I won a scholarship from Hunter College to attend Summer School at Exeter College, Oxford University. In the Bodlian Library I would often meet my Tutor. Every time I tried to engage him in conversation, he would say "I'm busy." At first I thought he did not want to speak with me but quickly I realized I needed to get busy myself. You need to get busy yourself!

One way to be that useful citizen and busy is to get on the Community Planning Board of your area. Most of the slots are held by Seniors. They need young blood! Contact your City Council Person or the Boro President and ask to be appointed to the Community Planning Board. Then you will have an understanding of what's really happening in your community. Get on one of those Committees – Housing and ULURP; Economic Development; Youth

BLACK NATIONALISM ALIVE AND WELL

and Culture; the Aged; Police; Fire Services; Environment and Sanitation; Parks and Recreation; or Transportation and Traffic.

I'm the Chairman of Transportation and Traffic in my board. Membership on the Community Planning Board is a 2-year appointment. I have been a member for 26 years. I worked my way up from Chairman of Sanitation, then Environment, and Co-Chair of Parks and Recreation. I'm responsible for advising on my Committee's Expense and Capital Budget; understanding the dynamics of trains and buses that pass through my district; erecting bus shelters; street resurfacing; street lights; traffic signals, bike lanes; street Co-naming, and a whole lot more. I have Co-named 14 streets in my district for Black heroes.

Harlem Hospital is right there! Ask to be put on the Hospital Community Advisory Board. Ask the Boro President or the Chairman of the Community Planning Board. Now, I've done 20 years on Kings County Community Advisory Board. Now I serve on both Kings and Dr. Susan Smith McKinney Boards. I'm also a member of the Health and Hospital Corporation's Board, 125 Worth Street, NYC that oversees health care for all the public hospitals and their satellites in the City of New York.

Something even bigger than all is the study of ancient Egypt which Dr, ben-Jochannan introduced me to. You don't have to become a specialist in this field, but it is something you could study for the rest of your life as a past-time hobby and hardly touch the surface. You should simply buy books and read. Visit Egypt to see its wonderful pyramids, temples, tombs. Create a library for your children and teach them the right way. This is the way to go!

FREDERICK MONDERSON

Black Nationalism 287. Urban art decorating a wall in downtown Brooklyn.

So my friends, I say to you today, the road ahead may be difficult but it could be very enlightening and rewarding. This school, this program, your parents, your families, has brought you along. It's like riding a bicycle. They have shown you the basics and feel confident you can tackle the challenges. Be Wise! Plan ahead and keep your eyes on the prize that you want to achieve. From one generation to the next. From one level to the next. Be successful. Thank you.

BLACK NATIONALISM ALIVE AND WELL

Black Nationalism 287a. Sonny Carson (center in glasses), Prof. Patterson, Funeral Director Gafney, Bishop Shivers, and others including Ofori Payton in shorts waiting on the Bones **of the Runaway Samuel Carson** on way to Ghana to a site of pilgrimage.

42. Black Nationalism: Alive and Well
By
Dr. Fred Monderson

Upon arising this morning, the last day of **Black History Month**, February 28, 2011, I began my day perusing an old newspaper article entitled "Marcus Garvey and the UNIA" (*Daily Challenge*) and luckily on the obverse page was an ad announcing a March in Harlem commemorating the 122 Birthday of Marcus Garvey. I could not envision what a glorious day it would turn out to be. While it rained and "I walked between the raindrops," I stopped, to purchase *The New York Times* newspaper. Beyond surprise, I was shocked to see a Red, Black and Green flag atop a Libyan tank on the front page of *The Times*. Flabbergasted, I instantly called a

FREDERICK MONDERSON

friend, who perhaps had not yet seen the day's paper, informing him of the strange occurrence. This time, however, there was a white sickle on the flag which was not at first noticeable in the *Times* photograph.

Sure, *The Times* had pictured Tiger Woods wearing his customary red shirt and black pants on the Masters' 18th Hole Green when he won that tournament. That, however, was an entertainer in action and far removed from the political, revolutionary and liberation implications, that today's international lead conveyed to the world, particularly for people who knew the significance of the Red, Black and Green!

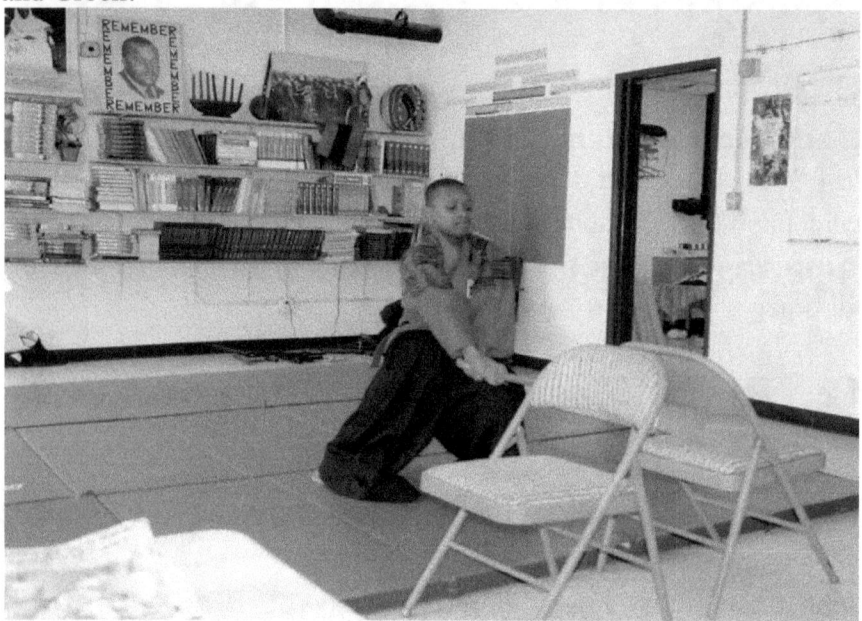

Black Nationalism 288. Erik Monderson working out as a Brown Belt in Karate.

For some clarification, amidst the Harlem Renaissance and the birth and expansion of the Universal Negro Improvement Association (UNIA), Marcus Garvey advocated liberation, freedom, equality and unity of African people worldwide when he was proclaimed Provisional President-General of Africa. In this, he claimed, to represent some 400 million Africans worldwide. In the dynamics of

BLACK NATIONALISM ALIVE AND WELL

that age when Black men worldwide, particularly emanating from Harlem, struggled to assert their humanity and dignity in an age of global colonialism, imperialism, lynching and racial discrimination, Marcus Garvey issued his shibboleth of "One God, One People, One Nation, One Destiny" and established the Red, Black and Green flag as the motif of African liberation. The world is now aware of the infiltration of his movement and persecution and betrayal of this great liberator who not only lit a fire among African people, but highly incensed imperial powers that trampled upon the dignity and aspirations of a subjugated African people. The powers that be in this country sought to ridicule and destroy Mr. Garvey's movement by falsely accusing him of a litany of trumped up charges fabricated with the assistance of "Negroes" whose "leadership" Garvey challenged because he offered substance to their empty rhetoric. On way to the Atlanta Federal Prison, a manacled Garvey proclaimed to his followers, "Look for me in the whirlwind!" and to his oppressors he said, "You have caged the lion but the cubs are now running loose out there."

In that time of nationalist expression, Mr. Garvey created the Red, Black, and Green motif among other major achievements of Black Nationalism. Establishment media scorned the flag and Mr. Garvey, because, perhaps in their view, such a motif would give legitimacy to the movement of African liberation. Nevertheless, Marcus Garvey was imprisoned, his movement fractured, saddened and defeated he died a "failed leader" in 1940. However, this was not really true! Like all experiments genuinely grounded in liberation of the minds, hearts and well-being of the people, a dormant movement lived on in the aspirations of the next and subsequent generations of African American "cubs." Garvey's influence began to impact the Pan African movement nurtured by W.E.B. DuBois, George Padmore, Rev. Shutllesworth, Harry Belafonte and the indomitable Queen Mother Moore, Paul Robeson and Thurgood Marshall and even Sonny Carson in this country; Kwame Nkrumah, Namdi Azikwi, Julius Nyerere and Albert Luthuli in Africa, and Sylvester Williams

FREDERICK MONDERSON

among others from the Caribbean, all had their aspirations lit by Mr. Garvey's influence.

Black Nationalism 289. Urban art created by youths and adorning a wall in downtown Brooklyn.

Black Nationalism 289a. Mitch Penn (backing camera), Ofori Payton, Sonny Carson, Prof. Patterson, James Smalls, Santana Ofori, "Chief Barkim Parker" (partly hidden) and other ladies outside Institutional Church on Adelphi Street.

BLACK NATIONALISM ALIVE AND WELL

The master organizer and theoretician's ideas set forth in his exemplary book, **Philosophy and Opinions of Marcus Garvey** had a profound impact on Kwame Nkrumah who chaired the 5th Pan African Congress at Manchester, England in 1945.

From these beginnings the Red, Black and Green became the standard for African Liberation and Black Nationalism; and to this day, the last week-end of May, African Liberation Day weekend and at the African American Day Parade, the flay is very prominent. Equally in the village of Harlem the Red, Black and Green is the official flag of this Black World capital. Therefore it is quite surprising to see *The New York Times* prominent display of this flag. Even more significant, the people of Libya, seeking genuine liberation had long recognized the significance of this symbol and reached across the ocean to choose such and show solidarity with long held Black aspirations. So much so, *The New York Times* has come full circle in recognizing the potency of this motif as today Marcus Garvey is vindicated. Can you hear him laughing from his grave as the world has come to recognize African aspirations through Black Nationalism is alive and well.

Black Nationalism 290.   Urban art created by young people and adorning a wall in downtown Brooklyn.

FREDERICK MONDERSON

Black Nationalism 290a.   Bringing out the **Bones of Samuel Carson** from Institutional Church on Adelphi Street.

43. Who were the Ancient Egyptians?
By
Dr. Fred Monderson
Introduction

Today, most books on Western Civilization begin with a chapter on Ancient Egypt. Previously they began with a chapter on Greece and Rome. They all say unmistakably "the ancient Egyptian were Caucasians" which is a position held by many books on Egypt. The position of these books, the writers and publishers, even museum displays, ignore the constructive new analyses of the African world's methodology depicting the falsity of such assumptions most people are fed with. Thus, in the search for the truth about the ancient Egyptians, we must not simply look to history, but also to archaeology, anthropology and art as well as a number of other specializations such as mathematics, science, medicine, philosophy, religion, hematology, biometrics, and more. Nevertheless, anyone who still believes the ancient Egyptians were Caucasian is either a moron, mis-educated or perniciously supports the notion of "White

BLACK NATIONALISM ALIVE AND WELL

Supremacy," which is in itself a fallacy! Prof. Diop admonished, Africanists must live and die on the battlefield of African historiographic reconstruction consciousness. This means, whether you're in the front-line trenches or on the periphery of the struggle, you must have all the available information. You must know who is saying what about the culture of ancient Africa, the Nile Valley and Egypt and Ethiopia.

In this respect and in an important work entitled, *Predynastic Origins of Egyptian Hieroglyphs*: *Evidence for the Development of Rudimentary Forms of Hieroglyphs in Upper Egypt in the Fourth Millennium*, B.C. William S. Arnett (University Press of America, 1982) in his wide-ranging critique of the literature has written: "In reference to Dr. Diop's theories, this writer would like to say that he agrees with the latter's refutation of the efforts to define the 'Dynastic Race' as being 'white,' but finds his efforts to prove that the ancient Egyptians were black 'unconvincing." In as much as Mr. Arnett has done a credible job assessing some of the literature regarding the origins of the ancient Egyptians, he certainly got it wrong regarding Dr. Diop's position! In fairness, he did not challenge Wortham's statement in *Genesis of British Egyptology* statement that the Egyptians were "Caucasians!" Still, while this falsity has attracted many disciples, it has really been proven to be just that! Falsity! Consider that Diop in "Origin of the Ancient Egyptians in Van Sertima's *Egypt Revisited* (1991: 14) lays it out; not on speculation; a la "for some unknown reason;" clearly in uncontroverted facts; stating: "In the tomb of King Ka (first dynasty) at Abydos Petrie found a plaque showing an Indo-European captive in chains with his hands behind his back. Elliott Smith considers that the individual represented is a Semite. The dynastic epoch has also yielded the documents illustrative in Pls. 1.9 and 1.14 showing Indo-European and Semitic prisoners. In contrast, the typically Negroid features of the Pharaohs (Narmer, first dynasty the actual founder of the Pharaonic line; Zoser, third dynasty, by whose time all the technological elements of Egyptian civilization were already in evidence; Cheops, the builder of the third Great Pyramid, a

FREDERICK MONDERSON

Cameroon type; Mentuhotep, founder of the eleventh dynasty, very black; Sesostris I; Queen Aahmose-Nefertari, and Amenophis I show that all classes of Egyptian society belonged to the Black race."

Black Nationalism 291. Amon-ra enthroned among other gods in a chapel at Medinet Habu, no longer open to visitors.

BLACK NATIONALISM
ALIVE AND WELL

Thus, and principally, in iconoclastic refutation of Indo-European claims, Diop argued in *The African Origins of Civilization: Myth or Reality*, that "though the branches of his tree could use some pruning, the roots and trunk are fundamentally strong." That is, even while "*African Origins*," an original Doctoral Thesis may have had some flaws, Diop's maturity was proven in the 1974 Cairo Conference when he and Theophile Obenga outdistanced the pedestrian competition in his classic presentation of the "Origin of the Ancient Egyptians" that formed the basis of UNESCO's final report affirming the "fundamental blackness of ancient Egypt."

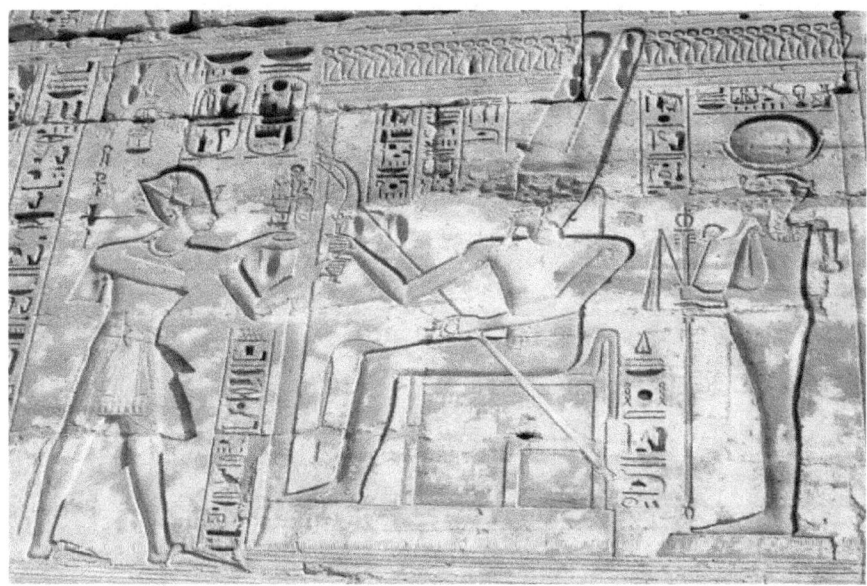

Black Nationalism 292. With Moon God Khonsu at his rear and in his shrine (uraei overhead), enthroned Amon-Ra in plumes or feathers offers the curved sword to Rameses III who in turn presents the symbol of eternity to the god.

The "great researcher" Danny Kaye in his monumental and groundbreaking work *The King's New Clothes* eloquently articulated and identified that the king was not wearing anything as he paraded

FREDERICK MONDERSON

before the people. He was embarrassingly naked! Equally, Baron de Montesquieu, author of the *Spirit of the Laws*, has argued that man should 'act as if your actions,' and in this case, writings, 'can become a universal law.' Now, when we examine some early writings on Egypt, what by today's standards, we can easily call pseudo-scientific writers; in view of historical revelations, their work certainly emerges as questionable and pejorative at best. At worst, it appears somewhat dishonest, vindictive and mean-spirited, some say racist! Prof. John H. Clarke, in his "Introduction" to Anthony Browder's *Nile Valley Contributions to Civilization* (1992: 9) puts it best in the statement: "Except for Egypt, African people have been programmed out of the respectable commentary of history. Europeans have claimed the non-African creation of Egypt in order to downgrade the position of African people in world history. They have laid the foundation of what they called Western civilization on a structure that the Western mind did not create. In doing so, they have used no logic!" Let us also remember, Prof. John Clarke pointed out, "The people who preached racism colonized history," and reminded "When Europe colonized the world, it also colonized the world's knowledge!"

Black Nationalism 293. At the Temple of Edfu Horus, with Isis aboard, spears his evil uncle Seth in the war for the Osirian succession.

BLACK NATIONALISM ALIVE AND WELL

Let us first not forget, modern interpretation of the culture of ancient Egypt/Kemet in contemporary times has been oriented as Europeans ascended the Nile from north to south as opposed to the flow of the river and culture from south to north and therein lies the conundrum; some say misinterpretation, some say racist, view of ancient Egypt and its relationship with Africa or should we say, Africa's relationship with Egypt, "Ethiopia's eldest daughter." As an example, we know the Tigris-Euphrates Rivers flowed from north to south. The comparative view would be to argue civilization ascended that river valley by an invading force that created the culture. This is the type of argument being presented in the European conception of culture ascending the Nile River.

Conversely, because of its relation to the Nile, at its headwaters, the ancients believed the Ethiopians influenced Egypt. In ancient times all Black Africans were thought to be Ethiopians. The Ethiopians, in fact, have held they colonized Egypt, since the peoples of the Nile were the same, being only shades of difference in color. This is a very plausible argument. Culturally, many modern scholars not only read the ancients but also saw the resemblance or "Negro mold" of Egyptian statues and depicted such in their works. Khamit Indus Kush in his book, *The Missing Pages of "His-Story"* (1993: 42) quotes several people regarding the connection between Egypt and Ethiopia. First, Basil Davidson in "The Ancient World and Africa, Whose Roots?" (*Race and Class*, XXIX, Autumn 1987, No. 2, p. 2) wrote: "The ancient Egyptians were black (in any variant you may prefer) - or, as I myself think, it more useful to say, were African, is a belief which has been denied in Europe since about 1830" not generally before. It is a denial, in short, that belongs to the rise of modern European imperialism, and has to be explained in terms of the 'new racism' specifically and even frantically an anti-black racism, which went together with and was constantly nourished by that imperialism. I say, 'new racism' because it followed and expanded the older racism which spread around Europe after the Atlantic slave trade had reached its high point of 'take off' in about 1630." That is to say, the 'old racism' was part of the 'naked

FREDERICK MONDERSON

imperialism.' The 'enlightened imperialism' was justification for exploitation of material and intellectual resources; while the 'new racism' supported the methodology of administration and exploitation, particularly as it related to "intellectual imperialism."

Black Nationalism 294. In his temple to Osiris at Abydos, Seti I offers a platter to enthroned Isis.

However, as Kush has argued, despite the emerging and solidifying falsity, the American Egyptologist George Gliddon in *Ancient Egypt: The New World* (1843: 59) pointed out in contrast: "The advocates of

BLACK NATIONALISM ALIVE AND WELL

the African origin of the Egyptians cling to the superior antiquity of the pyramids of Meroe as a proof of the origin of civilization in Ethiopia, and its consequent descent into Egypt." Again, according to Kush, despite the "New Aryan model," Professor Rossellini, "accepts and continues the doctrine, of the descent of civilization from Ethiopia and the African origin of the Egyptians." Prof. Naumann equally believed: "We will first deal with the Ethiopians, as they are the nearest neighbors of the Egyptians, and further because it is historically affirmed that the latter originally migrated from Ethiopia. Indeed, the music of the Ethiopians offers strong internal evidence in support of the assertion." In *Prehistoric Nations* (New York: 1898, p. 276), John D. Baldwin wrote: "Diodorus Siculus adds to his statement that the laws, customs, religious observances, and letters of the ancient Egyptians closely resemble those of the Ethiopians, 'the colony still observing the customs of their ancestors.'"

And on and on!

Now, in aftermath of the decision to build the Aswan High Dam, **UNESCO** appealed to nations with a history of excavation in Egypt to help rescue Nubian monuments that would be lost with the creation of Lake Nasser.

The discoveries done by the University of Chicago team headed by Kurt Sethe at Qustol in Nubia revealed important artifacts that were collected and deposited in the Museum's archives. No report was filed! In his in-house researches, a graduate student, Bruce Williams, uncovered evidence of Pharaonic regalia, viz., white crown, 3 sailing boats, enthroned king, scepter and flail, incense burner, palace facade, etc., dated at c. two hundred years (3400-3200 B.C.) before such appear in Egypt. Underscoring this discovery, Dr. Clarke previously had reminded the Tasians, Badarians, the people from Merimde and Badari, all prehistoric Egyptians, were Negroes! In fact, he said, the Egyptian civilization was "rehearsed in Ethiopia before it made its debut on the stage in Egypt."

FREDERICK MONDERSON

Black Nationalism 295. At the Temple of Isis at Philae, now on Agilka Island, enthroned Nephthys receives a gift from Pharaoh.

Significantly, the reason for the great hunger for Egypt is best explained in a quote from W.J. Perry in *The Growth of Civilization*, Penguin Books (1924) (1937: 48-49) where he quotes G. Elliot Smith in *The Ancient Egyptians*. It reads as follows: "The Egyptians did a great deal more than merely invent agriculture and devise the earliest statecraft and religion. Not only did they devise the methods of working wood and stone and the art of architecture, they seem also to have been the inventors of linen and of the craft of weaving, of the use of gold and copper, and the making of metal tools and implements. They were the first people to measure the year and to devise a calendar, and later on to substitute for the rough calculation based upon the date the observation of the sun's movements. They also invented shipbuilding and constructed the first sea-going ships.

BLACK NATIONALISM ALIVE AND WELL

In a thousand and one of the details of our common civilization the originality of Egyptian civilization is revealed. The art of shaving, the use of wigs, the wearing of hats, the invention of the kilt and of the sandal and subsequently of a variety of other articles of dress, many of our musical instruments, chairs and beds, cushions, jewelry and jewel-cases, lamps - these are merely a few of the items picked at random out of our ancient heritage from the Nile valley."

Interestingly, however, when he uses the term "our" he means Europeans, not all of humanity or Africans. This, then, is what is at stake and must be corrected in unrelenting challenge!

In the reality of the Slave Trade and Slavery, the western world could not admit at the back of their civilizations of Greece and Rome, were the creations of the people they were enslaving. In fact, this is what Count Volney affirmed in his *Ruins of Empires*, p. 16.

Notwithstanding, and commenting on the significance of ancient Egyptian contribution to civilization, Margaret Murray in *The Splendor that Was Egypt*, New York: Hawthorn Books, Inc., (1949) (1969: xvi) offers the following, reinforcing the view previously expressed and attributed to G. Elliot Smith: "For every student of our modern civilization Egypt is the great storehouse from which to obtain information, for within the narrow limits of that country are preserved the origins of most (perhaps all) of our knowledge. In Egypt are found the first beginnings of material culture - building, agriculture, horticulture, clothing (even cooking as an art); the beginnings of the sciences - physics, astronomy, medicine, engineering; the beginning of the imponderables - law, government, and religion. In every aspect of life Egypt has influenced Europe, and though the centuries may have modified the custom or idea, the origin is clearly visible. Centuries before Ptolemy Philadelphus founded his great temple of the Muses at Alexandria, Egypt was to the Greek the embodiment of all wisdom and knowledge. In their generous enthusiasm the Greeks continually recorded that opinion; and by their writings they passed on to later generations that wisdom of the Egyptians which they had learnt orally from the learned men of the Nile Valley." Arnett's denial nevertheless and contrary to Murray's mentioning "the Greeks," Diop names the classical commentators and enumerates their views!

Black Nationalism 296. The Khepre beetle, in his most colorful form, performing the function of pushing the sun across the sky.

Further, in her explanation, Murray (1969: xvii) revealed: "Egypt was the supreme power in the Mediterranean area during the whole of the Bronze Age and a great part of the Iron Age; and as our present culture is directly due to the Mediterranean civilization of the Bronze Age, it follows that it has its roots in ancient Egypt. It is to Egypt that we owe our division of time; the twelve months and three hundred and sixty-five days of the year; the twelve hours of the day and the twelve hours of the night are due to the work of the Egyptian astronomers. The earliest clocks, the clepsydra, were the invention of Egyptian physicists. The earliest known intelligible writing is the

BLACK NATIONALISM ALIVE AND WELL

Egyptian, so also are the earliest recorded historical events. It is due to the passion of the Egyptians for making records that so much has been preserved of their history and their literature, of their religious beliefs and their religious ritual. This passion for writing made them invent the first actual writing materials - pens, ink, paper - materials which could be packed in a small compass, were light to carry, and easy to use."

Murray (1969: xvii) continued highlighting Egyptian contributions even more, by contrasting this earliest culture with subsequent civilizations in the human drama and pointing out how Egyptian accomplishments have left them in the distance. She wrote: "The splendor of Egypt was not a mere mushroom growth lasting but a few hundred years. Where Greece and Rome can count their supremacy by the century, Egypt counts hers by the millennium, and the remains of that splendor can even now eclipse the remains of any other country in the world. According to the Greeks there were Seven Wonders of the World; these were the Pyramids of Egypt; the Hanging Gardens of Babylon; the statue of Zeus at Olympia; the Temple of Diana at Ephesus; the Tomb of Mausoleum; the Colossus of Rhodes; and the Lighthouse of Alexandria. Of all these great and splendid works, what remains to the present day? Babylon and its gardens are a heap of rubble, as ruined as a bombed city; the statue of Zeus was destroyed long ago; the Temple of Diana is utterly demolished, leaving only a few foundations; fragments of the Mausoleum are preserved in museums where they are a source of interest to experts only; the Colossus of Rhodes survives only in legend, so completely has it disappeared; the Lighthouse of Alexandria has perished almost without a trace. Of the Seven Wonders the Pyramids of Egypt alone remain almost intact, they still tower above the desert sands, dominating the scene, defying the destroying hand of Time and the still more destructive hand of Man. They line the western shore of the Nile for more than a hundred miles, and are the most stupendous and impressive as they are the most ancient of all the great buildings of the world."

FREDERICK MONDERSON

Black Nationalism 297. One of the two "Eyes of Horus."

Equally too, Lester Brooks in *Great Civilizations of Ancient Africa* (1971: 28) confirms: "From the cemeteries dating back before 3200 B.C., anthropologists have identified remains they label 'Eurobond' (indicating those of Cro-Magnon types), "Negroid" and some Asian types, with the 'Europoids' predominating in the north and the 'Negroids' predominating in the south. As one expert puts it, 'the races were fused on the banks of the Nile well before Pharaonic civilization came into being. These people were black by the operating definition of skin color as well as by the general physical characteristics they had then.'" Even more, Brooks (1971: 28-29) continued: "The Greeks were surprised twenty-five hundred years ago to discover that the Egyptians were the darkest-skinned peoples of the so-called Near East. Typically they were - and are today - not homogeneous. Their skin color ranges from red-black to yellow. Their hair is black and wavy, curly or wooly; their eyes are bright

BLACK NATIONALISM ALIVE AND WELL

and black; their bodies are lean and muscular, generally tending to tallness. Egyptian noses usually are large and straight, but frequently aquiline; their jaws generally tend to thrust forward with fleshy lips, often curled back. We can say without the slightest hesitation that the ancient Egyptians would have been considered Negroes by American standards, and until the passage of the **Civil Rights Act of 1964** not one of the Egyptian Pharaohs could have bought a cup of coffee in a white drug store in the southern states of the U.S.A."

Still, and again, contrary to Arnett's contention; in his "Argument for A Negro Origin" in *The African Origin of Civilization*: *Myth or Reality*, Cheikh Anta Diop (1974: 134-155) cites "Totemism," "Circumcision," "Kingship," "Cosmogony," "Social Organization," "Matriarchy," "Kingship of the Meroitic Sudan and Egypt," "Cradles of Civilization Located in the Heart of Negro Lands," and "Languages," as evidence for his position. His two-cradle theory for "ice" and "sun" environments and their influences, and patriarchy as opposed to matriarchy, viz., Europeans in the North and Africans in the South, were very convincing. Brooks (1971: 29) equally too sheds more light on this situation, writing: "What African elements can be discovered in the extremely sophisticated civilization of Egypt? Among others, the complicated religious beliefs wherein tribalism, animism and taboos had extraordinary force - with special rites for the major activities such as planting, harvesting, fishing, hunting and war, in addition to the *rites du passage* – birth, marriage, death." Further he points out: "We think of African witch doctors with fantastic, colorful costumes. Look again at a formal portrait of a Pharaoh. Note that, he wears an enormous headdress. From his 'double crown' sprout the head of a vulture and the 'fire-spitting' flamed head of a female hooded cobra, supposedly capable of consuming rebels in flames. The pharaoh was the son of the falcon-god, and was considered a falcon himself, endowed with magical powers and an all-seeing eye. From his waist hangs an animal tail; on his shaven chin he wears a false beard, which is, itself, considered a god. In his hand he carries a scepter with the head of the god Seth atop it - recognizable in the curious curved snout, long, straight ears and almond-shaped eyes."

Black Nationalism 298. Another of the "Eyes of Horus;" this time with a little variation in subliminal message.

Adding even more to this fanfare, Brooks demonstrates further: "In processions, banners are carried before the king. These banners bear the symbols of the many powerful brother gods who have blessed him and whose aid is his to command." Of course pharaohs also wore jewels of arm bands, a necklace, rings, a girdle or apron with Uraeus, sandals and carries a dagger, a flail, and either a mace or bow and arrows, with which to slay his enemies, who as a god and superhuman on the battlefield could slay 'hundreds of enemies at a stroke all by himself.' 'His eyes scrutinize the depths of every being.' Nothing is impossible for him: 'Everything which he ordains comes about.'"

BLACK NATIONALISM ALIVE AND WELL

In this respect then, the answer to the question of "Who were the ancient Egyptians?" should not have done so, but still has baffled, confused, contradicted and often been obfuscated by modern scholars, viz., historians, journalists, archaeologists, anthropologists, and every other form of commentator particularly those moderns who use the film and video medium as well as persons involved in printing, dissemination and distribution of information relative to Egypt. All this has left many scholars, students, and average citizens in a state of confusion. In fact, these end up engrained in the fallacy. Quite frankly, these latter may have been misinformed intentionally or even unintentionally because of the falsity fed by the previous generations upon whose "facts" they had come to rely. Truthfully, and upon close examination, generation after generation of scholars and lay people, have been misinformed regarding the origin of the ancient Egyptians. Much of this, some have argued, has been intentional and when it has not been so, it has been due to ignorance. Some of it is traceable to Wilhelm Hegel and other German scholars, who held, for much of the 19th Century that 'Africa was outside the realm of history,' and by extension the Egyptians were an Asiatic people in the "Middle East" being part of the "Fertile Crescent." As Dr. Carruthers has explained, "Hegel took Africans out of Egypt and then Egypt out of Africa." C.G. Seligman in *The Races of Africa* (1930) wrote: "The civilizations of Africa are the civilizations of the Hamites." Davidson clarifies, "These are Caucasian, i.e., they belong to the same branch of mankind as almost all Europeans." This position has been buttressed by others subscribing to this same view as Carl Meinhof, a German, who in 1912 wrote, "Hamitic peoples subjugated and governed dark pigmented Negroes," and in the 1920s, Reginald Copeland also wrote as if parroting Hegel, "Africa proper had no history. The heart of Africa was scarcely beating." Equally, the Oxford Don, Hugh Trevor Roper expressed the view, "There is no history of Africa, only a history of Europeans in Africa." Thus, in the European nationalist, imperialist, colonial climate of the 19th and early 20th Century mentality, coupled with the age of rapid publication of archaeological discovery, these efforts ossified the false notion of who the ancient Egyptians really were.

FREDERICK MONDERSON

But objectively speaking, the new information demolishes the falsity but as "old ideas die hard" Europeans still want to take credit for initiating all forms of knowledge! The conundrum with such a position, as Molefi Asante has held, "There is a problem when you occupy all the space and no one else gets any!"

Even more significant, it is understandable the position of "white supremacy" was enunciated during the greatest humiliation, degradation and inhumanity practiced against Africans, that is at the height of the slave trade, slavery, the emergence of the abolition movement to outlaw the slave trade, and in aftermath of the American, French and Haitian revolutions and the discovery of the Rosetta Stone. Millennia prior to that most people believed the Egyptians were Africans and black! However, in unfolding world history and after the discovery of the Rosetta Stone in 1799, Champollion, DeSacy, and Young became involved in the process of decipherment of the hieroglyphic script, which the ancient Egyptians had named *Medu Netcher*. Of these great intellects, Champollion was the most successful deciphering hieroglyphics in 1822. This linguistic break-through gave birth to the discipline of Egyptology and an effervescence of societies were founded fueling an aggressive antiquarian movement. Diop has pointed out his brother Champollion-Figeac falsified the older antiquarian pioneer's intent, based on his studious observations; and others such as Herodotus' observations about the ancient Egyptians, have conveniently been ignored. Following Champollion's observations and work, the mad dash for antiquities resulted in what Brian Fagan later dubbed "The Rape of the Nile." That is, he chronicled the unchecked, unscrupulous and nefarious activities in which individuals secured artifacts to supply museums and private collectors with the bases of their wonderful collections of ancient Egyptian memorabilia.

BLACK NATIONALISM
ALIVE AND WELL

Black Nationalism 299. Another more colorful depiction of the Khepre beetle doing his function of pushing the sun across the horizon.

As such then, when it comes to the ancient Egyptians there is an unbridgeable chasm, because most White people believe the ancient Egyptians were White, and most Blacks with any sense of historical understanding believe the ancient Egyptians were Black! Nevertheless, a lot of ink has been spilled on the color of these early Egyptian Africans. This is particularly so of the "red color" of the Egyptians. At the Cairo conference, Dr. Diop took to task Prof. Vercoutter's claim the Egyptians were "black skinned white men!" However still, while we have heard of "white, white men," "red, white men," and "black, white men," one thing is certain, the ancient Egyptians were really not white! Importantly, however, David O'Connor, a Curator at the Philadelphia Museum has expressed such to this author! That is not to say others have not also done so! The

FREDERICK MONDERSON

point is, if this "mainstream White scholar" could say the "Egyptians were not white!" then the issue should have been evident and put to rest long ago, but it is not! Let us not forget, if there were any painted evidence of white Egyptians, it would have been magnified many times. However, while the ancient Egyptians were painted red, they were also painted black; and even Osiris often painted Black, was also painted green but Egyptians were never painted white! Blue was a form of black and even green was black.

In regards the color red. From the time of the Stone Age, man has had a penchant for red as his favorite color and this led us to believe the Egyptian, followed in this vein, and painting of himself in the color red, is simply to demonstrate love for this color. However, in creation of the falsity surrounding the ancient Egyptians, European scholars argued for a race of red men and held that these were "Red white men!" In clarification, Gay Robbins has informed, the Egyptian believed red and even gold had a solar connection and as a people who believed they were divinely chosen, they used red to depict themselves. They, however, also used black to depict themselves, (Thutmose I, Aahmes-Nefertari, Tutankhamon, among survivals) though they never used white for such a depiction! Cheikh Anta Diop said the Egyptians painted themselves red to distinguish themselves from other Africans since they considered themselves special! Henry Lhote in "Tassili Frescoes" and Mary Leakey on "East African Stone Age Art" paintings speak of the "predominant red" used by these Negro painters. Were they Egyptians? In October 2011, *The New York Times* published the discovery of a paint factory find in South Africa and dated to 107,000 years ago exhibiting surviving evidence of mixed "red paint" found in a container. It also indicated this process of paint mixing "pushed complex African thinking far back in time!"

In September 2005, a young female guide in the Cairo Museum, in referring to the statue of Mentuhotep II found in his Middle Kingdom temple at Deir el Bahari, told this writer: "He was painted black because he was dead." Obviously she did not know, and is being taught to falsely propagate such by saying 'My Professor told

BLACK NATIONALISM
ALIVE AND WELL

me this at the American University in Cairo!' Interesting, though found in 1904, untold commentators wrote and spoke on Egypt without ever mentioning Mentuhotep II's color, until in 1958, he was described by E. Stephenson Smith in *The Art and Architecture of Ancient Egypt* as having "black flesh!" The guide even told this researcher she never saw Osiris, God of the Dead, painted black! So I searched him out in the Museum and found numerous examples of papyrus and wood, not just of Osiris but others as well. We must also remember; these wooden models particularly are what have survived the destructive elements of time and man! Just as the two wooden statues in Tutankhamon's burial chamber were painted black to represent him, this was a standard practice. With all the destruction and many tombs not found intact, such evidence was lost. However, many tombs, thoroughly excavated and catalogued in the Valley of the Kings, record scattered fragments of painted black wood presumably used in similar internments.

Black Nationalism 300. Still another colorful depiction of the Khepre beetle.

FREDERICK MONDERSON

On the second floor in the Cairo Museum, Number J 95,655 Osiris in White Crown is painted green. However, in JE 36,465 Osiris is painted black; JE, 95,645 Osiris is black; J, 26,228 Osiris is black; J, 35,669 Osiris is black; Papyrus B 24 Osiris is black. This is a lengthy papyrus depicting a winged snake with 4 feet; as 4 goddesses ride 4 uraei with double heads. Then 7 goddesses ride a lengthy snake crossing a river while 6 goddesses pull the snake's tongue as it stands behind a line of 6 goddesses and 6 gods led by Khepre towards the deceased, who has his back towards Nephthys and Isis standing behind an enthroned Black Osiris who greets the deceased who in turn offers a plant.

In Room 12 is housed funerary furnishing from royal tombs.

Statue No. 2374 - made of wood, Osiris is painted black.
Statue No. 2372 - made of wood, Osiris is painted black.

In this room, Case GL contains 9 large Afro wigs. These were discovered in the "Deir el Bahari Cache" in 1881.

Wooden statues Numbers 3827, 3836, 3834, 3832, 3824, are all painted black. The wooden duck Number 3838 and a wooden panther No. 3840 and wooden panther No. 3842 are all painted black. In front and outside Room 12 large wooden statues 3834a and 3834b are painted black.

In room No. 22, 9 wooden statues, painted black, are placed above Case J.

4 wooden statues are above Case I
4 wooden statues above Case O
4 wooden statues above Case P
7 wooden statues above Case R
7 wooden statues above Case T

These are all painted black. Still, who knows what is in the basement! We must remember the place cards for much in the Museum was done by Gaston Maspero. He, incidentally as Curator

BLACK NATIONALISM ALIVE AND WELL

of Antiquities, in the 19th Century, described Prince Mahepra as "Negroid but not Negro!" He probably did not even use capitals! However, contemporary with Maspero biographers of the musical genius Beethoven described him as "black," "swarthy," "Negroid," "Negro," etc. I ask that you to do the math!

Conversely, Dr. Yosef ben-Jochannan said the Egyptians were painted "red" because they were dead. Even further, that the Henna plant is used to paint particularly young Nubian brides red, as part of a cultural ceremony. Now, in the Tomb of Vizier Rekhmara, the numerous individuals are all painted red, though some are shown making a black figure. All this notwithstanding, there are pictorial "survivals" of Egyptians and gods painted black, viz., Amon, Min, Thutmose I, Tutankhamon, Ahmose-Nefertari, wife and sister of Ahmose and their brother Kamose whose mother Ahotep and her father Sekenenra Tao must have been black to have produced their "coal black Ethiopian" daughter. Let's face it, in *Red Land, Black Land*, red represented barrenness of the desert; and blackness represented fertility of the cultivable land. Osiris was black, so he represented resurrection and eternal life! In fact, Osiris was called "the Great Black!" Egyptologist Theophile Obenga has reminded all, Kemet or the "black land" referred to the people not the land itself!

Rameses II's wife Nefertari was Nubian. Yet she is painted red in her tomb in the Valley of the Queens. In December 2005, someone called this writer to look at a program on the History Channel entitled *Black Pharaohs* about the 25th Dynasty who were Nubian and black. In a fleeting glance the camera showed an image of Tanutemon, one of these black pharaohs and lo and behold, this ruler was painted red in the tomb! Let us not forget also, images in the tomb of the nobles at Aswan also show these southernmost Egyptians, where Nubia interacts significantly with Egypt and who were essentially black, also painted red. At the Nubian Conference on October 1-4, 2012, the Black Nubian 25th Dynasty individuals are also shown painted red. Even that piece done in National

FREDERICK MONDERSON

Geographic showed the Nubians as painted red! What does all this mean? It means the Egyptians were African not European or Asiatic, black not white and Egypt was and is still located in Africa not the Middle East or Asia. Now what is the evidence for all of this?

Thus, this presentation will focus on a chronological approach showing how principally eyewitnesses portrayed the ancient Africans of the Nile Valley, Egypt; first, and as interest intensified in modern times, how Egypt was viewed particularly in the 19th and 20th Centuries of our era. One thing is certain as European writers, historians and antiquarians first encountered Egypt following Napoleon's discovery and decipherment of the Rosetta Stone by the Savant Champollion, many "colored" their reports to appease a reading and rapidly emerging appreciative public in Europe. With time, African scholars did significant research unearthing the distortions, omissions, and misrepresentations revealing what they had found. Despite profound scholarship by these Blacks, European writers and their American cohorts have found it difficult to accept the revealed facts or have refused to deal with the issue, side-stepping it. African research has been attacked in the most inclandestine and vituperative manner; minutely scrutinized and dismissed in the most unprofessional method. It's as if such efforts were grounded in malice. Those Europeans who bucked the trend and wrote otherwise of the distortion, were ostracized and their works equally subject to the most insidious criticism.

BLACK NATIONALISM
ALIVE AND WELL

Black Nationalism 301. The "Great Cackler" or "Great Goose," an earthly manifestation of Amon-Ra, Theban great god!

For example, much confusion has been created as European scholars, not finding any evidence of "White Egyptians" have emphasized "Red Egyptians" as being "Red Egyptian White men." Even Vercoutter remarked essentially they were "white men in black skin!" Let me give this example and pose a question before we begin. Murnane (1983: 231) in discussing the Sanctuary area of the Temple of Karnak where the god Amon-Ra dwelt, wrote: "The walls are covered with scenes illustrating the episodes of the offering rite with Amun appearing in his usual anthropomorphic guise and also in the ithyphallic form he shares with Min, the god of fertility." Further, another writer Michael Haag's Cadogan series in *Cairo, Luxor, Aswan* (2000: 212) adds: "On the north side of the sanctuary, where there was much rebuilding a wall erected by Hatshepsut was found concealed behind a later wall of Thutmosis III, thus preserving the original freshness of the coloring. The wall has now been

FREDERICK MONDERSON

removed to a nearby room, and shows Amon, his flesh painted red and with one foot in front of the other, and also Amon in the guise of the ithyphallic Min, a harvest god, often amalgamated with Amon, his flesh painted black." Let us remember, while Amon is here represented with "his flesh painted red," in the back room at Medinet Habu, he is shown enthroned and his skin is painted black. He is also painted blue here and at Karnak beside the *Akh Menu*!

Now the serious first question is: "Why would white red men be worshipping black Gods or painting their gods black?" Also, why would Central Africa be considered "God's Land?" Equally too, another question is, "Why did Murnane not refer to the color of Amon, as Min, being black?" Elsewhere, in the *American Journal of Archaeology* of 1931 Amon has been described as "so black, he was blue!" Many writers have a tendency to skillfully dance around the question of the race of the Egyptians, particularly when evidence indicates they were black! It's all part of the conspiracy against ancient Egypt! Much further, when evidence surfaces depicting Egyptians "painted black," the logical explanation given is they were painted black because either they were dead or for the death ceremony. Yet still, while Diop extolled the cultural accomplishments, of the first dynasties in the Old Kingdom and affirmed their blackness, Arnett discounts this saying the archaeological evidence cannot prove the blackness of the ruling elite. Of course, the same evidence was used to prove the whiteness of Egypt more than a century ago still persists! That is, while *no evidence exists to show Egyptians white*, yet the *assumption and propagated falsity is that they were white*! Again, a very good reason the white writer affirmed to this researcher "The Egyptians were not white" is simply because today men of reasonable intellect know the falsity of a "white Egypt" is just that, falsity and must be challenged.

Now, let us begin!

BLACK NATIONALISM ALIVE AND WELL

Black Nationalism 302. Still another colorful depiction of the "Great Cackler," one of many manifestation of the Theban deity Amon-Ra.

II. Classical Writers

In assessing the classical writers' contributions, Diop wrote: "To the Greek and Latin writers contemporary with the ancient Egyptians, the latter's physical classification posed no problems. The Egyptians were Negroes, thick-lipped, kinky-haired and long-legged; the unanimity of the authors' evidence on a physical fact as salient as a people's race will be difficult to minimize or pass over."

a. Homer - Most scholarship seems to date Homer to about 800 B.C. However, this may be incorrect, even though we know he is "credited" with writing the *Iliad* and the *Odyssey*. Several things need to be looked at in relation to dating of Homer and even questioning his originality. First, we are told that Abu Simbel temple of Rameses II has the earliest examples of Greek writing and this writing is dated to the 7th Century B.C. Now, if Homer wrote the *Odyssey* and *Iliad* then it cannot be 800 B.C., as previously thought. Second, Cheikh Anta Diop says, if Homer visited Egypt it had to be in the 8th Century during the time of the Twenty-fifth Ethiopian Dynasty and much of his descriptions may be representative of earlier events in Egypt. Interestingly, Murray's *Handbook for Egypt* (1888) informs, "In the Ramesseum, North face of the South East Wall of the 2nd area is a scene of combat that very much resembles what Homer tells us of his *Odyssey*!"

b. Herodotus 480-425 B.C. - Herodotus visited Egypt around 450 B.C. and wrote his *Histories* devoting Book II *Euterpe* to Egypt. Diop (1989) argued in "Origins of the Ancient Egyptians" in *Egypt Revisited*, Edited by Ivan Van Sertima, and quotes the "father of history" in regard to the *Origins of the Colchians*, where Herodotus stated, "It is in fact manifest that the Colchidians are Egyptians by race ... several Egyptians told me that in their opinion the Colchidians were descended from soldiers of Sesostris. I had conjectured as much myself from two pointers, firstly because they have black skins and kinky hair (to tell the truth this proves nothing for other peoples has them too) and secondly and more reliably for the reason that alone among mankind the Egyptians and Ethiopians have practiced circumcision since time immemorial." Herodotus says further, the Egyptians have "thick lips, broad noses and are burnt of skin," meaning they are black! Practically everything else Herodotus wrote about was accepted by moderns as observed fact other than that the Egyptians had "wooly hair, thick lips, broad noses and were burnt of skin." We must realize, much of what he heard or theorized could be considered conjecture, but his observations cannot be disputed. Naturally, he never said black as compared to what or whom!

BLACK NATIONALISM ALIVE AND WELL

Black Nationalism 303. Still another colorful depiction of the "Great Cackler," Theban deity of the Middle and New Kingdoms.

c. Aristotle 384-322 B.C. - Aristotle in his work *Physiognomy* made a somewhat controversial statement regarding the ancient Egyptians. He says: "Those who are too black are cowards, like for instance, the Egyptians and Ethiopians. But those who are excessively white are also cowards as we can see from the example of women, the complexion of courage are between the two." He was seeking to affirm that the "middle ground," perhaps a "Mediterranean Race" type was the ideal. Now, while his science of cowards was wrong, for we know as proven by the many wars Africans in particular have fought; however, his description of the Egyptians and Ethiopians is essentially correct. This is one incidence in which this great philosopher and scientist was both wrong and right on the same issue. Are we to believe these ancients' observations or moderns' racist interpolations?

FREDERICK MONDERSON

d. Lucian the Greek writer 125-190 A.D. speaks to Lycinus, "The boy is not only black; he has thick lips and his legs are too thin …."

e. Apollodorus, first Century Greek philosopher said, "Aegyptus conquered the country of the black-footed ones and called it Egypt after himself."

f. Aeschylus, Greek tragedian in *The Supplicants* describes the Aegyptaids in their vessels: "I can see the crew with their black skins and white tunics."

g. Diodorus **Siculus** of Sicily 63-14 B.C. - Diodorus held to the view that Ethiopians colonized Egypt. Diop says, according to Diodorus: "The Ethiopians say that the Egyptians are one of their colonies, which was led into Egypt by Osiris. They claim that at the beginning of the world Egypt was simply a sea but that the Nile, carrying down vast quantities of loam from Ethiopia in its flood waters, finally filled it in and made it part of the continent. They add that the Egyptians have received from them, as from authors and their ancestors, the greater part of their laws." Inadvertently Diodorus tells us the origin of Osiris as being Central African, a view affirmed by the *Papyrus of Hunefer*!

h. Diogenes Laertius says of **Zeno**, founder of the Stoic school 333-261 B.C., that he was "tall and black" and "people called him an Egyptian vine-shoot."

i. Ammianus Marcellinus the Latin historian of 33-100 A.D. notes that the "men of Egypt are mostly brown or black with a skinny and desiccated look." He says further that the Colchians were "an ancient race of Egyptian origin." The mummy of the *Gentleman Magazine* article of 1820 and the mummy of Rameses II were also brown!

BLACK NATIONALISM
ALIVE AND WELL

Black Nationalism 304. Yet another colorful ceramic depiction of the "Great Goose" or "Cackler," a manifestation of Amon-Ra, Theban deity.

j. Count Volney, one of the Savants who followed Napoleon to Egypt at the end of the 18th Century, made the following statement regarding the ancient Egyptians from observations of the Copts. According to Diop (1989) Volney wrote: "All of them are puffy-faced, heavy-eyed and thick-lipped, in a word, real mulatto faces. I was tempted to attribute this to the climate until, on visiting the Sphinx; the look of it gave me the clue to the enigma. Beholding that head characteristically Negro in all its features, I recalled the well-known passage of Herodotus, which reads: 'For my part I consider the Colchoi are a colony of the Egyptians because, like them, they are black-skinned and kinky-haired.' In other words the ancient Egyptians were true Negroes of the same stock as all the autochthonous peoples of Africa and from that datum one sees how their race, after centuries of mixing with the blood of Romans and Greeks, must have lost the full blackness of its original color but retained the impress of its original mould. It is even possible to apply this observation very widely and posit in principle that physiognomy is a kind of record usable in many cases for disputing or elucidating the evidence of history on the origins of the peoples ...."

Even further Volney noted: "By reverting to Egypt, its contributions to history afford many subjects for philosophic reflection. What a subject for mediation is the present-day barbarity and ignorance of the Copts who were considered, born of the alliance of the deep genius of the Egyptians and the brilliance of the Greeks, that this race of blacks who nowadays are slaves and the objects of our scorn is the very one to which we owe our arts, our sciences and even the use of spoken word; and finally recollect that it is in the midst of the peoples claiming to be the greatest friends of liberty and humanity that the most barbarous of enslavements has been sanctioned and the question raised whether black men have brains of the same quality as those of white men."

III. To the Mid-19th Century

In a chapter entitled "Modern Falsification of History" Cheikh Anta Diop's *The African Origin of Civilization: Myth or Reality* discusses Domeny de Rienzi's contention that: "It is true that back in the distant past, the dark red Hindu and Egyptian race dominated culturally the yellow and black races, and even our own white race then inhabiting western Asia. At that time our race was rather savage and sometimes tattooed, as I have seen it depicted on the tomb of Sesostris I in the valley of Biban-el-Moluk at Thebes, the city of the gods."

This is interesting, for if we believe the Egyptians were white and migrated to Africa leaving no evidence of the prototype of Egyptian culture in their place of origin in Western Asia, how did Thebes in Upper Egypt become the "city of their gods." Equally, any claim of

BLACK NATIONALISM ALIVE AND WELL

a western Asian origin of the Egyptians ties them to the white race. Yet, the Egyptians have no recollection or record of an Asiatic past! However, let us not forget, Nubia and Central Africa was considered "God's land." Again, we are also faced with the absolutely absurd conclusion that whites from western Asia considered Africa as their "God's land!" We can interject here that Toby Wilkinson identified the first god in history as Min in feathers and his emblematic form!

Black Nationalism 305. The peregrine falcon, a manifestation of Horus of Edfu, who defeated his wicked uncle Seth and succeeded to the throne of his murdered father Osiris, who reigns as "Judge of the Dead" or the "Underworld."

We should be aware, every people who migrated from one place to the next, retained some reference to their ancestral home. Contrary to popular western prognostication, the Egyptians never associated Mesopotamia or Southwest Asia with their origins. In fact, the

FREDERICK MONDERSON

record seems to indicate only one surviving reference to origins and this was made by Hunefer, 19th Dynasty priest of Seti I, whose papyrus, *Papyrus of Hunefer*, now in the British Museum, states: "We came from the foothills of the Mountains of the Moon where the God Hapi dwells." This area is the plains of the East African mountain range. Inadvertently, he also identified the place of the origin of Osiris also called Hapi, equally a god of the Nile. As Wortham submitted one modern 1825 mummy dissection to prove the ancient Egyptians were Caucasian how then would we regard the ancient Egyptian Hunefer's and the Roman Diodorus' contentions as to the origin of Osiris (Hapi) and the Egyptians? It is amazing, an ancient Egyptian proposes the place of his origins which is disputed; but, moderns places his origins and this is believed!

a. Jean Jacques Champollion the Younger set to work and was successful in deciphering the hieroglyphic script, as we know, in 1822. Within ten years he was dead from overwork. However, his extensive work did unleash an interest in antiquarian studies. Diop quotes Champollion from a letter to his brother Champollion-Figeac, who twisted his brother's words, thus helping to bring about the falsification of Egyptian history and the continued removal of Africans from this important part of African history. He mentions a group of four people starting with the Egyptians shown with a dark red color. "There can be no uncertainty about the racial identity of the man who comes next: he belongs to the black race, designated under the general term *Nahasi*. The third represent a very different aspect; his skin color borders on yellow or tan; he has a strongly aquiline nose, thick, black pointed beard, and wears a short garment of varied colors; these are called *Namou*. Finally, the last one is what we call flesh-colored, a white skin of the most delicate shade, a nose straight or slightly arched, blue eyes, blond or reddish beard, tall [in] stature and very slender, clad in a hairy ox-skin, a veritable savage tattooed on various parts of his body; he is called *Tamhou*." He wrote elsewhere: "We find there Egyptians and Africans represented in the same way." Let me also point out, the origin of the term Negro to describe Africans is 16th Century A.D. and any use

BLACK NATIONALISM
ALIVE AND WELL

of the word in reference to ancient Egypt is modern, false and tainted in racism.

Even more striking, Diop argues in comparison with many West African blacks whom he names and finally states: "If the Egyptians were white, then all these fore-mentioned Negro peoples and so many others in Africa are also whites. Thus we reach the absurd conclusion that blacks are basically whites." Even further, he writes: "On these numerous bas-reliefs, we see that, under the Eighteenth Dynasty, all the specimens of the white race were placed behind the blacks; in particular, the 'blond beast' of Gobineau and the Nazis, a tattooed savage, dressed in animal skin, instead of being at the start of all civilization, was still essentially untouched by it and occupied the last echelon of humanity."

Black Nationalism 306. Another version of Horus of Edfu, son of Isis and Osiris.

FREDERICK MONDERSON

b. Karl Lepsius - Diop states further, Karl Lepsius offered a "Canon of proportion" in his *Discoveries in Egypt, Ethiopia and the Peninsula of Sinai in the Years 1842-1848* (London: 1852) that denotes: "The proportions of the perfect Egyptian body; it has short arms and is Negroid or Negritian. From the anthropological point of view, the Egyptian comes after the Polynesians, Samoyeds, Europeans, and is immediately followed by African Negroes and Tasmanians. Besides, there is a scientific tendency to find in Africa, after excluding foreign influences, from the Mediterranean to the Cape, from the Atlantic to the Indian Ocean, nothing but Negroes or Negroids of various colors. The ancient Egyptians were Negroes, but Negroes to the last degree."

c. Garner Wilkinson – An English nobleman, spent several years in Egypt, particularly Thebes, during mid-19th Century. He did extensive research and produced significant works on the Egyptian culture that is still consulted by experts in the field.

IV.   To 1900

a. Auguste Mariette – Was of an age when great interest in Egypt very early attracted many scholars from different countries, in the aftermath of Napoleon's discovery of the Rosetta Stone and Champollion's decipherment of the language. However, his vision seemed different from most of his age principally bent of antiquities acquisition. Ruffle (1977: 8-9) best puts the man and his time in perspective. "With funds from King Friedrich Wilhelm IV of Prussia, Richard Lepsius made a great survey of the monuments (published in a mammoth twelve-volume work) and collected many objects, which formed the basis of the great Berlin collection. The increasing scholarly interest highlighted the need for orderly and controlled excavation. Auguste Mariette, who was sent by the Louvre to collect antiquities in Egypt, realized this. With the support of the Khedive he founded the Egyptian Museum and Antiquities Service and became its first director, often pushing through his

BLACK NATIONALISM
ALIVE AND WELL

scientific policies in the teeth of opposition from other European Egyptologists."

"Mariette's concern was matched by the painstaking methodology preached by William Matthew Flinders Petrie, grandson of the explorer of Australia and the first person to hold a chair in Egyptology [in England] - University College, London. This chair had been founded by Amelia Edwards whose un-intentional Nile cruise - she had gone there when a sketching holiday in France was rained off - had filled her with an enthusiasm for Egypt that led her to found not only Petrie's chair but also the Egypt Exploration Fund. Other learned societies were also formed - notably the *Deutsche Orient Gesellschaft* in 1888 and the *Mission Archaeologique Francaise* in 1880, later the *Institut Francais d'Archaeologie Orientale*."

Black Nationalism 307. Yet another colorful representation of Horus of Edfu.

b. Brugsch-Bey - Karl Heinrich Brugsch-Bey in his *Egypt Under the Pharaohs* (London: John Murray, 1902: 2-3) has argued: "Suffice it to say, however, that, according to ethnology, the

FREDERICK MONDERSON

Egyptians appear to form a third branch of the Caucasian race, the family called Cushite; and this much may be regarded as certain, that in the earliest ages of humanity, far beyond all historical remembrance, the Egyptians, for reasons unknown to us, left the soil of their early home, took their way towards the setting sun, and finally crossed that bridge of nations the Isthmus of Suez, to find a new fatherland on the banks of the Nile." For argument sake, immigrants to Australia and to America knew of the land, had fellow citizens there and so migrated to settle bringing and retaining their cultural traits. However, Brugsch-Bey's Caucasians probably didn't know of Egypt and thus can't say they had citizens there which would mean they did more than one migration. Nevertheless, many of these individuals generally argue on speculation and offer no facts to support their contentions because none exists!

c. Adolf Erman - German scholar extraordinaire. It's been argued Erman was probably the only modern who understood exactly what the Egyptians meant in their language. Nevertheless, Charles Finch writing "Black Roots of Egypt's Glory" in *Great Black Leaders*: *Ancient and Modern* (1988: 140-141) edited by Ivan Van Sertima has written: "As the 19th century wore on, German scholars began applying their meticulous methods of research to the study of ancient Egyptian language. Finding many similarities in words and syntax between Egyptian and the Semitic languages, the Germans unhesitatingly proclaimed Egyptian to belong to this group. As a result, their leading Egyptologists Eber, Erman and Brugsch - concluded that the impetus for Egyptian civilization itself came from a western Asiatic or Semitic source. Like others, they saw in the human figures on the Egyptian monuments - many colored a reddish-brown - evidence of a non-African 'Mediterranean race.' Anthropologically speaking, no such race ever existed, but that did not trouble them overmuch and the term has remained in vogue to this day." Obviously, there was somewhat of a turn around because Erman later wrote in *Life in Ancient Egypt* (New York: Macmillan, 1894: 32) confirming: "The inhabitants of Libya, Egypt and Ethiopia have probably belonged to the same race since prehistoric times. In

BLACK NATIONALISM ALIVE AND WELL

physical structure they are still Africans." Otherwise he implied they were all white! Let me also add, Brugsch is different to Brugsch-Bey!

d. Gaston Maspero – A French Egyptian expert, as Director of Antiquities in the late 19th Century had written extensively on the history and culture of Egypt. However, his take was that the ancient Egyptians were of European origin, crossed over to North Africa and entered Egypt from the west. What a pity! Lhote in "Tassili Frescoes" identified Negroes in the Sahara between 7000 and 6000 B.C. Why could these blacks not be able to enter the Nile Valley from the Sahara but whites could cross over to North Africa from Europe and then follow essentially the same route into the Valley? However, this western entry has gained greater credence with publication of Brophy and Bauval's *Black Genesis* proclaiming the Negroes of **Nabta Playa**, further south and west of Abu Simbel, migrated from there to the Aswan area and became the predecessors of the pharaohs.

FREDERICK MONDERSON

Black Nationalism 308. Still another more colorful representation of Horus of Edfu.

e. William Matthew Flinders Petrie (1853-1942) - The "Father of modern archaeology," did extensive research in Egypt and was one of the most prolific writers of his day, influencing a great many people with his still, now considered, racist views. Stuart Tyson Smith's "Race" in Donald B. Redford's Edited *The Oxford Encyclopedia of Ancient Egypt* Vol. 3, (2001: 111) has written: "The origins of the modern conception of race derive from the work of nineteenth-century anthropologists like L.H. Morgan and E.B. Taylor, who developed 'scientific' unilinear evolutionary theoretical models for the development of human beings from 'Savagery' to 'Civilization.' Racial groups were ranked by evolutionary categories, linked to intellectual capacities, based on elaborate cranial measurements; supposedly, this provided causal links between phenotype (observable) traits, mental capacities, and socio-political dominance. This model not coincidentally reinforced the existing European-American domination of third-world peoples with

BLACK NATIONALISM ALIVE AND WELL

the claim of scientifically 'objective' methodologies based on race and evolution." Even further Smith continued: "The unilinear evolutionary model did influence some early Egyptologists. W. M. Flinders Petrie used it to develop his notion of the 'Dynastic Race,' to explain the rapid development of Egyptian civilization. In part this was based on prevailing models of culture change that emphasized migration as an explanation for cultural change, but, ultimately, racist notions drove the model. The implication was that Egypt had a 'white' or 'brown' ruling class dominating a native 'black' African underclass who supplied the labor to build Egypt's great monuments. The Egyptological community as a whole never enthusiastically accepted Petrie's model, although the idea persisted through a few enthusiasts." James Henry Breasted echoed the sentiments of most contemporary Egyptologists in seeing the Egyptians as indigenous, but as a brown rather than black race, related to other northeastern Africans. It is interesting to note that for Breasted the Egyptians became 'White' for a classroom textbook, presumably reflecting the racism of the day. The last serious argument in support of the Dynastic Race theory appeared in Walter Emery's *Archaic Egypt* (New York 1961)."

f. Ernest Alfred Wallis Budge - Wallis Budge was Keeper of Egyptian and Assyrian Antiquities at the British Museum and a prolific writer who wrote about *The Gods of the Egyptians*, *The Mummy*, *Egyptian Magic*, produced an *Egyptian Hieroglyphic Dictionary*, and a whole lot more. Regarding Budge's work, Finch (1988) states, though: "Unusual for an Egyptologist, he had conducted extensive research among the peoples of the Sudan and Ethiopia - encountering cultural practices, religious ideas and languages which showed clear and identifiable linkages to ancient Egypt. It became clear to Budge that everything about ancient Egypt could be understood only by reference to Africa; there was nothing fundamentally Asiatic about Egyptian culture. In 1920, in his massive and erudite *'Egyptian Hieroglyphic Dictionary,'* Budge,

FREDERICK MONDERSON

reversing a 100-year trend and his own earlier opinion, classified Egyptian as an African rather than a Semitic language."

Black Nationalism 309. Yet another manifestation, "The Ram," of Amon-Ra, Theban deity.

Then again, we know the Egyptian religious writing is the oldest in the world. By the First Dynasty, the *Book of the Dead* was a compilation of much earlier works, which means Egyptian writing certainly took some time to develop into that state. Arnett traced these beginnings to the 4th Millennium, 4000-3000 B.C. How come the people from Asia or wherever they came from never invented Hieroglyphics in their point of origin, nor probably had any writing until they came to the Nile Valley? Even when they did, they wrote on stone in their original home. Imagine a student carrying a bag full of stone tablets! The answer debunks Brugsch-Bey! Certainly Diop, Arnett and even Winkler show the development of rudimentary forms of Hieroglyphs in the Upper Nile region dating as early as 4000 B.C. However, while Diop and Arnett see them as indigenous,

BLACK NATIONALISM ALIVE AND WELL

Winkler holds to Mesopotamian origins. However, Wilkinson shows evidence Winkler's ideas are at least a thousand years before his "Mesopotamians came."

g. Canon George Rawlinson, in the *Story of the Nations: Egypt* (1893: 23-24) stated: "It is generally answered that they came from Asia; but this is not much more than a conjecture. The physical type of the Egyptians is different from that of any known Asiatic nation. The Egyptians had no traditions that at all connected them with Asia. Their language, indeed, in historic times was partially Semitic, and allied to the Hebrew, the Phoenician, and the Aramaic; but the relationship was remote, and may be partly accounted for by later intercourse, without involving original derivation. The fundamental character of the Egyptian in respect of physical type, language, and tone of thought, is Nigritic. The Egyptians were not Negroes, but they bore a resemblance to the Negro, which is indisputable. Their type differs from the Caucasian in exactly those respects which when exaggerated produce the Negro. They were darker, had thicker lips, lower foreheads, larger heads, more advancing jaws, a flatter foot, and a more attenuated frame. It is quite conceivable that the Negro type was produced by a gradual degeneration from that which we find in Egypt. It is even conceivable that the Egyptian type was produced by gradual advance and amelioration from that of the Negro."

FREDERICK MONDERSON

Black Nationalism 310. Anubis, Egyptian "God of the Dead," who embalms the deceased and guards the way to the sepulchral chamber.

h. M. le Vicomte J. de Rouge is mentioned in an article in *American Journal of Archaeology*, Vol. 1 (1897: 393-95) where he raises the question of "The Origin of the Egyptian Race" and attempted to "prove the theory of the Asiatic derivation." Emphasizing statues found belonging to the third, fifth and sixth dynasties, he stated: "The types of the faces do not belong to the later Egyptian style, but possess elements of the more refined Semitic organization; and this fact is used by the writer as a proof of the importation of a fully developed civilization into Egypt." Where did it come from? Essentially, the article argued there are three theories as to the origin of the Egyptian race: (1) that the entry of the population into Egypt was made by way of Asia, passing through the Isthmus of Suez; (2) that Egypt became occupied by a colony which came in part from Asia, but passed through Ethiopia; (3) that the majority of the Egyptian population had its origin in Africa and passed into Egypt by the west and southwest." This last is "a more

BLACK NATIONALISM
ALIVE AND WELL

recent theory which has been in a measure accepted by M. Maspero, and is supported by a large number of students of natural history and of ethnology, while the theory of the Asiatic origin is based on linguistic comparisons and a study of the monuments, especially the primitive monuments of Babylonia."

He says further: "The Egyptians seem not to have preserved any tradition or indication, or even memory, of their foreign origin, for they consider themselves as autochthones, and regard their country as the cradle of the human race." In addition, he argues: "The most ancient monuments discovered up to this time appear to belong to the third dynasty, such as the recently discovered bas-relief of King Sozir; that of Prince Ra-hotpu and of Princess Nofrit, etc. The statues of the two last mentioned royal personages show that the art of sculpture was already in an advanced stage of development, and the types of the faces, with their aquiline noses and thin lips, recall the Semitic race rather than the Egyptian. The great sphinx of Ghizeh, which is perhaps the most ancient relic of Egyptian art, is also anterior to the fourth dynasty." He never says anything more regarding the "Negro features" of the Sphinx. Of course, Dr. ben-Jochannan, the master-teacher, extols Hunefer, a priest of King Seti I, during Ramesside times; who, in *The Papyrus of Hunefer*, noted "We came from the headwaters of the Nile, at the foothills of the mountains of the moon where the God Hapi dwells." This area is in the East African region of Mounts Ruwenzori, Kenya and Kilimanjaro near Uganda and Kenya. Importantly also, it places the origin of Osiris in Central Africa!

FREDERICK MONDERSON

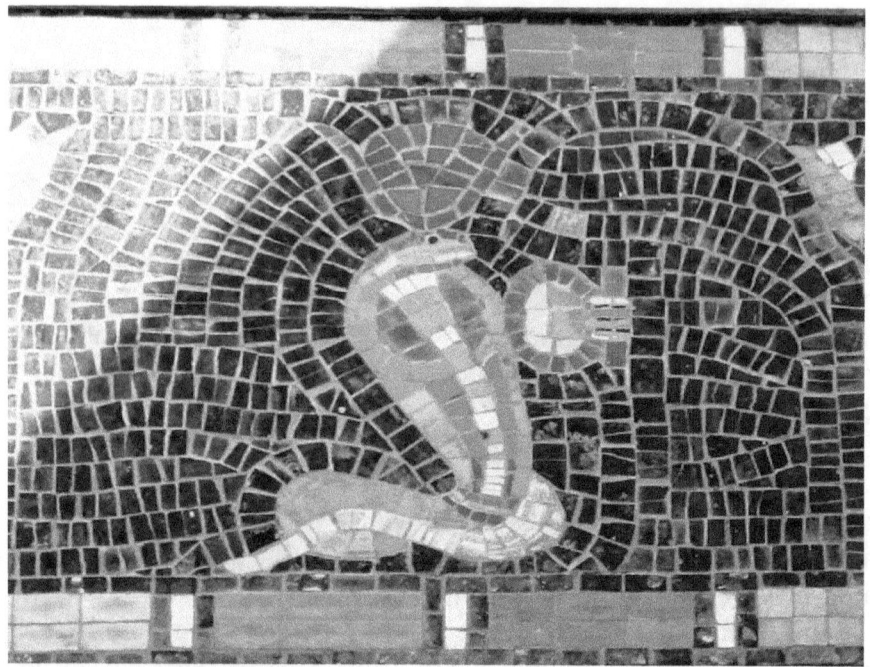

Black Nationalism 311. Uraeus, protector of Pharaoh, wearing horns and sun-disk.

i. Edouard Naville, a Swiss Archaeologist, cleared the two Deir el Bahari complexes of Hatshepsut (18th Dynasty) and Mentuhotep (11th Dynasty). The *American Journal of Archaeology* XVIII (1913: 202) reported Edouard Naville presented a paper on "The African Origin of Egyptian Civilization" in *R. Arch* XXII (1913, pp. 47-65) that states essentially: "The rise of Egyptian civilization after the Neolithic period was due to conquest by an African people from the South, called Anou. The people who caused the changes when the Thinite period ends and the Memphite period begins may have been Asiatic but they brought in no important new elements, - they merely gave a new impulse to the existing civilization." This means these Asiatics comprised the third and fourth dynasties ruling at Memphis and all they brought were their "pretty white selves." However, Petrie mentioned the founder of the third dynasty was Ethiopian from observing his features in the Sinai.

BLACK NATIONALISM ALIVE AND WELL

Notwithstanding, from their images, Snefru of the third and Khufu, Khafre and Menkaure, builders of the fourth dynasty Ghizeh Pyramids, were, by operating definitions, black or Negro! This is mentioned earlier by Cheikh Anta Diop.

j. On the subject, **G. Elliot Smith** in *The Ancient Egyptians and Their Influence Upon the Civilization of Europe* (London and New York: Harper and Brothers, 1911: 32-39) informs: "Even such eminent scholars as de Rouge, Heinrich Brugsch, and Ebers, among many others, claimed that Egypt derived her language as well as much of her culture and knowledge of the arts from Asia; and Hommel and others went much further, and claimed that the whole Egyptian civilization was Babylonian in origin …."

Even more, Smith continued: "De Morgan and his collaborators claim that the Ancient Egyptian language and mode of writing, the importation into Egypt of the knowledge of metals, and of such crafts as brick-making and tomb-construction, and even the fauna and flora of the country in ancient times, all point to Babylonia as the place where the roots of Egyptian civilization should be sought." More so, however, "But, under Dr. Reisner's critical analysis of the foundations upon which these speculations were supposed to have been based, practically the whole of the elaborate edifice has tumbled to the ground. As Eduard Meyer has said, 'the suggestion that a culture, or even its chief elements, can be derived from another people is unthinkable and historically false: but influences must have been at work, and the Egyptians and Babylonians must have given and taken.'"

Still more, Smith wrote: "Dr. Reisner has proved the indigenous origin of Egyptian civilization in the Nile Valley, and has revealed the complete absence of any evidence to show, or even to suggest, that the language, mode of writing, the knowledge of copper, or the distinctive arts and crafts were imported."

FREDERICK MONDERSON

"Schweinfurth argued that the 'invaders' of Egypt - the stereotyped phrase used by so many writers, tacitly assuming as a fact the idea of an immigration into Egypt - came from Southern Arabia (Sabaea or Hadramut), across the Straits of Bab el-Mandeb, thence through Abyssinia and the eastern Desert into Nubia, from which they spread along the banks of the Nile into Egypt ...." In essence, these people passed through Nubia heading down-river. One has to wonder whether Nubians standing on the river banks cheered them on! On the other hand, "Lortet and Gaillard, the most recent writers to discuss the fauna of Ancient Egypt, protest against the conclusions of Duerst that certain of the domestic animals of Ancient Egypt were brought from Asia; and they tell us that the animals known to have lived in Egypt at the time of the Ancient Empire were all African, that is, local in origin ...."

Referring to previous statements, and that preceding his book by almost a century, "Blumenbach began the serious study of the physical characters of the Ancient Egyptians. Since then a considerable number of scholars have contributed to the discussion of the significance of the anatomical evidence - in America, Nott, Gliddon, and Meigs might be mentioned as pioneers; in France, Perrier, Pruner, Broca, Quatrefages, Hamy, Fouquet, Zabarowski, Cantre, Lortet, and Verneau have made contributions of varying importance; in German-speaking countries, Carus, Czermak, Virchow, Hartmenn, Emile Schmidt, Stahr, and Oetteking may be mentioned; in England, Bernard Davis, Huxley, Owen, Petrie, Garsin, Randall-MacIver, Thomson, Macalister, Karl Pearson and his school of biometricans, Myers and Keith represent some of the outstanding names of those who have written about the craniology of the Egyptians; and last, but by no means least, Italy has added the important and highly suggestive writings of Sergi, Biasutti, and Giuffrida-Ruggeri."

G. Elliot Smith, the anatomist from the University of Manchester examined the royal mummies and is the author of the "Diffusionist theory" that Egyptian culture spread far and wide influencing many people with its contributions to human civilization development. His book, *The Ancient Egyptians and Their Influence Upon the*

BLACK NATIONALISM ALIVE AND WELL

Civilization of Europe is a classic. Some guides have commented on his bitterness; however, for, after having examined the mummies and washing his hands, he was ushered from the room without his notes, paid and barred from re-entry. This may have led to some enmity towards the ancient and modern Egyptians.

Black Nationalism 312. Majestic and colorful bird in flight.

V.   To 1950

a. Randall MacIver did a study in 1905 and came to the conclusion that there were two peoples living in Egypt, side by side, Africans and Europeans. His position has been; whites were in occupation in the north and blacks in the south. There was much discussion about this but it forces us to wonder how the critics in

FREDERICK MONDERSON

Europe, England especially, could have come to agreement on this so later disputed fact.

b. Arthur Weigall – Young and impetuous, he was an Englishman who first studied with Petrie at Abydos. He wrote a book entitled *Flights into Antiquity* in which he entitled a chapter, "Exploits of a Nigger King," dealing with the XXV Dynasty. The title of this chapter signals his contempt for Africans and thus he would not have seen Egypt as African and black. He is the writer who claimed Rameses II was Syrian, which was a popular refrain for any Egyptian of substance was so labeled, "He was Syrian." Which begs the question, 'Why would Rameses, in the Battle of Kadesh, call on an African god, Amon, saying his ancestors had worshipped the god for time immemorial, and sought his help at that crucial and challenging time.' Imagine a Syrian, Asiatic, calling upon an African god while doing battle in Asia! Further, imagine this same Syrian calling upon and even worshipping an African god whose alter ego, Min, was black! We also know Amon was black. This also raises the absurd contention as to why Ptah, one of Rameses II's favorite deities, a bald-headed pygmy could be so endeared. Fact is the straw men arguments easily fall apart! Remember, after Ra had created the world, the "first people he made were Nubians."

c. James Henry Breasted, pioneering American Egyptologist - Charles S. Finch III again in "The Black Roots of Egypt's Glory" takes to task James Henry Breasted who wrote: "Unfitted by ages of tropical life for any effective intrusion among the White Race, the Negro and Negroid people remained without any influence on the development of civilization."

It is amazing that people of Breasted's hue could write about such significant historical issues with such profound racial venom. Breasted's *History of Egypt, Ancient Records of Egypt, Ancient Times* and *The Development of Religion and Thought in Ancient Egypt* are classic "primary sources of the primary sources" of ancient Egypt. The thought of a German American writing about a people of

BLACK NATIONALISM ALIVE AND WELL

ancient Africa and could entertain the above quote raises a whole series of questions about integrity, intent and influence. We need never forget, Goethe believed, "Wherever Germans went, they corrupted whatever culture they found!"

You mean to tell me, while writing his *Records of Ancient Egypt* in 1905, by the time his *Ancient Times* was published in 1916 where he described the Egyptians as "brown people," he did not know Mentuhotep II of the 11th Dynasty had "black flesh" even though his statue was discovered in 1904. Perhaps also, the later discovered gold of Tutankhamon blinded Breasted to the young king's black skin. In his *Ancient Times* published in 1916, Breasted described the ancient Egyptians as "brown people." However, when he re-issued the work in 1935, he only dealt with "the great white race." Some have argued, because Rockefeller gave monies to fund his Oriental Studies Program, this turn-around was the 'quid pro quo.' Again, nowhere does Breasted refer to Mentuhotep's "black flesh."

Nevertheless, it is well known that the resurrection and reclamation of ancient Egypt occurred in the later part of the 19th Century and early part of the 20th Century. That is, c. 1870-1930 has been labeled the age of the "ancient records of the ancient records." However, in this period of "The Rape of the Nile" there was a consistent cry about destruction of the ancient culture both by natives and European plunderers seeking treasure and collectibles. Often reports would be made that natives were destroying sites whether for purposes of fuel or in order to secure and sell antiquities to anyone who would buy them. Generally Europeans who wanted to draw attention to the problem and help to preserve the ancient record made these reports. However, very seldom did the finger get pointed or identify European plunderers and all that is said is that this or that site or antique was damaged. Who knows what was destroyed purposely or by "accident?" Certainly, "strongman Egyptologist" Belzoni unquestionably did his share of destruction in 1818-1819.

FREDERICK MONDERSON

Black Nationalism 313. Another version of the colorful bird in flight.

Still, one certainly has to entertain a credible question, with today's hindsight, which is, 'How accurate is the work of the Breasteds?' or, 'Has there been any distortion, omission or exclusion in the work of early 20th Century European and American scholars?' In the reconstruction of the role of Blacks in ancient Egypt, evidence has to be gleaned from fragments and from the honest reports of men of good will, simply because much of racially relevant material has been destroyed in the trampled-over state. However, as more and more research focuses on these fragments they emerge larger than originally thought, for "truth crushed to the earth shall rise." In this, the work of racist and pseudo-scientific writers and historians are highlighted and the smoke and mirrors they constructed around the historical truth are now being blown away; and the true and marked naked prejudice of their writings and thinking that have misinformed for so long, are finally being blown away. And there they stand,

BLACK NATIONALISM ALIVE AND WELL

"naked, without clothes" in a world of political and historical correctness.

d. T. Eric Peet was an Oxford scholar and part of the Egypt Exploration Fund staff. He was critical of Akhnaton in an article entitled "The Problem with Akhnaton." While doing important work in the reclamation of Egypt, he too entertained the same false conception that the Egyptians were white! To wit, in 1888 *Murray's Handbook for Egypt* mentions similarities among the 4 figures at entrance to Seti I and Rameses III's tombs, arguing Nubians and Egyptians were pictured same, Black! In 1911, in *Antiquities of Upper Egypt*, Arthur Weigall omits this reference and so do does *Baedeker* on 1929.

VI. The Black Challenge To 2000

a. W.E.B. DuBois began *The Negro* (Oxford University Press (1915) 1970: 140) by affirming Negro blood ran in the veins of the Egyptians, but held they were mulatto! He wrote: "With mulatto Egypt Black Africa was always in close touch, so much so that to some all evidence of Negro uplift seems Egyptian in origin." He continued this in his *The World and Africa* but could not fully defend the argument of a Black Egypt! Yet, in *The World and Africa* (1946) (1971: 91-92) as some Afrocentrists have argued, he yet quotes Palgrave who says: "As to faces, the peculiarities of the Negro countenance are well known in caricature; but a truer pattern may be seen by those who wish to study it any day among the statues of the Egyptian rooms in the British Museum: that large gentle eyes, the full but not over protruding lips, the rounded contour, and the good-natured, easy sensuous expression. This is the genuine African model; one not often to be met with in European or American thoroughfares, where the plastic African too readily acquires the careful look and even the irregularity of the features that surrounded

FREDERICK MONDERSON

him; but which is common enough in the villages and fields where he dwells after his own fashion among his own people; most common of all in the tranquil seclusion and congenial climate of Surinam plantation. There you may find also, a type neither Asiatic nor European, but distinctly African; with much of the independence and vigor in the male physiognomy and something that approaches, if it does not quite reach, beauty in the female. Rameses and his queen were cast in no other mould." Such a claim flies in the face of those museum displays that misrepresents in catering to please European and American visitors.

Black Nationalism 314. Four colorful amphora vases used for storage.

b. Carter G. Woodson, the "father of Black History" in *The Mis-Education of the Negro* (Trenton, New Jersey: Africa World Press, 1993: 154) reminded all: "We should not underrate the

BLACK NATIONALISM ALIVE AND WELL

achievements of Mesopotamia, Greece and Rome; but we should give equally to the integral African kingdoms, the Songhay empire, and Ethiopia, which through Egypt decidedly influenced the civilization of the Mediterranean world."

c. J.E. Harris (Editor) of *Pillars in Ethiopian History* (Howard University Press) (1981: 6-7) has discussed the work of William Leo Hansberry, who, at Howard University began teaching about Negro Civilizations of Ancient Africa and developed the following courses:

1. NEGRO PEOPLES IN THE CULTURES AND CIVILIZATIONS OF PREHISTORIC AND PROTOHISTORIC TIMES. This was a survey course based on the latest archaeological and anthropological findings concerning the Paleolithic and Neolithic cultures of Africa, the pre-dynastic civilization of Ancient Egypt, and relations to the proto-historic and early historic civilizations of the eastern Mediterranean, and western and southern Asia.

2. THE ANCIENT CIVILIZATIONS OF ETHIOPIA. This course was a survey from about 4000 B.C., covering the general areas encompassed by the present-day countries of Sudan and Ethiopia. Hansberry relied on Egyptian, Hebrew, and Greek sources as well as archaeological and anthropological data from several expeditions, including Harvard-Boston Expedition at Kerma, Napata, and Meroe.

3. THE CIVILIZATIONS OF WEST AFRICA IN MEDIEVAL AND EARLY MODERN TIMES. This course surveyed the political and cultural development of Ghana, Mali, Songhay and Yorubaland as portrayed in Arab chronicles, and the archaeological and anthropological evidence in English, French and German investigations.

FREDERICK MONDERSON

d. Prof. John H. Clarke in John G. Jackson's *Introduction to African Civilization* (1970: 12) says "the 19th Century German scholar Arnold Herman Hereen" in discussing trade between the Carthaginians, Ethiopians and Egyptians, "gave more support to the concept of the southern African origin of Egyptian civilization."

e.   Yosef A.A. ben-Jochannan wrote extensively and very early began carrying people to Egypt to experience the monuments as he meticulously pointed out disparities in reporting by Western, European and American writers. He made a special effort to point out, in the Cairo Museum, the role Gaston Maspero played in shaping the interpretation of ancient Egypt by creating the "Place Cards" of the display cases. He particularly pointed to Maspero's determination that Mahepra, a prince, was "Negroid but not Negro." This was tremendously important because Mahepra's was of that age of Hunefer whose papyrus specifically points out the place of "Origin of the Egyptians" and from whence the God Hapi (Osiris) came.

f.   J.A. Rogers in *Sex and Race* Vol. I (1967: 42), echoing sentiments similar to Diop's contention that "The true Negro is nothing more than a cigar-store concoction," says essentially Herman Junker, who had written about "The First Appearance of the Negroes in History" *Journal of Egyptian Archaeology* (1924) was mistaken in looking for Negro traits in the graves of 5000 to 3600 B.C. "The Ethiopians, or Nubians, who were described by Herodotus, Diodorus Siculus, Ammianus and others as black and woolly-haired, were Hamites, he declares." Rogers continued: "It is no wonder he did not find any of that type, however, because the kind of Negro created by the right-wing ethnologists is a rarity. It is no more characteristic of the race than the ape-like creature of the bogs that was once used to represent the Irish was true of all Irishmen." We must remember, the 19th Century English writer Winwood Reade noted: "The typical Negro is a rare variety even among Negroes."   Frobinus says also, "Open an illustrated geography and compare 'The Type of the African Negro,' the bluish-

BLACK NATIONALISM
ALIVE AND WELL

black fellow of the protuberant lips, the flattened nose, the stupid expression, and the short curly hair with the tall, bronze figures from Dark Africa with which we have of late become familiar, their almost fine-cut features, slightly arched nose, long hair .... In other respects, too, the genuine African of the interior bears no resemblance to the accepted Negro type.'"

Black Nationalism 315. This time, three amphora vessels made of ceramic.

Even further, Rogers mentions: "Livingstone said that the Negro face as he saw it reminded him more of that on the monuments of ancient Assyria than that of the popular white fancy." Sir Harry Johnston, foremost authority on the African Negro noted: "The Hamite, that Negroid stock which was the main stock of the ancient

Egyptians, is best represented at the present day by the Somali, Galla, and the blood of Abyssinia and Nubia. Sergi compares pictorially the features of Rameses with that of Mtesa, noted Negro king of Uganda, and shows the marked resemblance. Sir M.W. Flinders Petrie, famed Egyptologist, says that the Pharaohs of the X dynasty were of the Galla type, and the Gallas are clearly what are known in our day as Negroes. He tells further of seeing one day on a train a man whose features were 'the exact living type' of a statue of ancient Libya, and discovered that the man was an American mulatto."

g. Ivan Van Sertima in his "Race and Origins of the Egyptians" in *Egypt Revisited* has argued: "The African claim to Egyptian civilization rests upon a vast body of evidence. Some are cultural (ritual practices of the ancient Egyptian can be traced to the African - his totemism, circumcision, form of the divine kingship are distinct from that of the Asian); some are linguistic (Diop demonstrated convincingly at the **UNESCO** debate in 1974 that the Egyptians belonged beyond question to the family of African languages); some indicate a shared techno-complex (the forerunners of mummification and pyramid-building are found south of Egypt in pre-dynastic times). Most important, however, are the physical evidences. The Greeks saw the Egyptians and described the typical Egyptian circa 500 B.C. as dark-skinned with wooly hair. Studies in ancient Egyptian crania by Falkenburger tried to prove that only one-third of the Egyptians were of the classical Negroid type and that most of them were Euro-African or, to use the term invented by Sergi "the brown Mediterranean race" classification. Chatterjee and Kumar in a 1965 study ... analyzed crania from pre-dynastic Egypt and compared them with skulls of the Old Kingdom as well as the much later Middle Kingdom (12th and 13th dynasties) and found that all these skulls in respect to 'long head, broad face, low orbit and broad nasal aperture have the same characteristic features of the Negroid type.'"

BLACK NATIONALISM
ALIVE AND WELL

Black Nationalism 316. Colorful uraei sporting sun-disk alongside feather, symbol of Ma'at.

In *Egypt: Child of Africa* (1990: 20) Ivan Van Sertima again writes: "There was probably no civilization in the world, be it African, European, or Asian, that was entirely pure and homogeneous. The great Roman historian Pliny, who first saw the Briton in the second century A.D., describes some of them as having complexions as dark as the Ethiopian. Claudian, reporting the victory of the Roman general, Theodosius, over the English, mentions a good number of 'nimble blackamoors' among them. The Chinese themselves recorded that there were men of black skin among the rulers of the Shang dynasty (1766-1100 B.C.). They actually speak of them as *Na-Khi* (*Na* in Chinese means black and *khi* means man). Schliemann and Evans, who excavated Minoan Crete, also tell us of the black skins of many of these Cretans who entered Greece in great numbers at an early time. Yet nobody would dare to pose questions such as: Were the ancient Chinese Black or yellow? Were the ancient Greeks or the ancient Britons White or Mixed? No. No. No. No. No."

II. So Here We Are! – Whether in scholarly debate or layman parlance, we must affirm, articulate, teach, preach and fight to defend Egypt as African and Negro or Black. This is essentially what our intellectual ancestors, researchers, historians, lecturers, writers and activists, who, after their many years, sometimes more than thirty years of research have discovered, as being omitted and distorted regarding the history of the Ancient Egyptians.

VIII. Conclusions

As more and more evidence is unearthed and equally more Afrocentric scholarship unmasks untruths, distortions and omissions through vigorous analytic examination, the effort of African historiographic reconstruction will not only correct the historical record but also expose the prejudice and vindictiveness involved in earlier writers' works. Some years ago, while a student at Oxford University I met a Black Englishman who, in discussion, told me, 'In any debate between a Black Historian and a White Historian, the Black will always win. All he has to do is to show what white men have been doing all around the globe, and with any sense of conscience the White man has to back-pedal.' Hence, despite efforts to 'hold back the dawn,' unmistakable truths are changing the minds of some while others 'prefer not to discuss such.' They simply skirt around the issues, and with today's knowledge and vision, are ashamed that their mentors, teacher and predecessors had been wrong and prejudiced in reporting the history of Black men and women who began humanity along the civilization pageantry of art, architecture, medicine, science, agriculture, astronomy, religion, knowledge, period! It is reassuring to show that despite Breasted's venom, Black men and women have given and continue to give knowledge and enlightenment to all who seek the truth!

BLACK NATIONALISM ALIVE AND WELL

Black Nationalism 317. Beautiful hieroglyphic symbolism.

IX. References

Brooks, Lester. *Great Civilizations of Ancient Africa*. New York: Four Winds Press, 1971.
Browder, Anthony. *Nile Valley Contributions to Civilization*. Washington, D.C.: The Institute of Karmic Guidance, 1992.
Clegg, Legrand H.H. "Black Rulers of the Golden Age" in *Nile Valley Civilizations*. Edited by Ivan Van Sertima (1985) (1986: 39-68).
Diop, Cheikh Anta. *African Origin of Civilization: Myth or Reality*. New York: Lawrence Hill and Company, (1967) 1974.
_____. "Origin of the Ancient Egyptians" in *Egypt Revisited*. (Edited by Ivan Van Sertima) New Brunswick, New Jersey: Transaction Publishers, (1989: 9-37).
Du Bois, W.E.B. *The Negro*. New York: Oxford University Press, (1915) 1973.

FREDERICK MONDERSON

_____. *The World and Africa.* New York: International Publishers, (1946) 1971.
Erman, Adolf. *Life in Ancient Egypt.* New York: Macmillan, 1894.
Finch, Charles S. "Black Roots of Egypt's Glory." *Great Black Leaders*: *Ancient and Modern.* Edited by Ivan Van Sertima. Transaction Books, (1988: 139-143).
Harris, J.E. *Pillars in Ethiopian History.* Washington, DC: Howard University Press, 1981.

Black Nationalism 318. Two pyramids over water contained in a basket with handle.

Jackson, John G. *Introduction to African Civilizations.* Secaucus, - New Jersey: Citadel Press, 1970.
Kush, Khamit Indus. *The Missing Pages of "His-Story."* Laurelton, New York: D and J Books, 1993.

BLACK NATIONALISM
ALIVE AND WELL

Black Nationalism 319. Urban art by young people.

Murray, Margaret A. *The Splendor That Was Egypt*. New York: Hawthorn Books, Inc., (1949) 1969.
Perry, W.J. *The Growth of Civilization*. Hammondsworth, England: Penguin Books, (1924) 1937.

Black Nationalism 320. Ankh within the Sun-disk atop a pyramid.

FREDERICK MONDERSON

Rawlinson, George. *The Story of the Nations*: *Egypt*. London: T. Fisher Unwin, 1893.

Rogers, J.A. *Sex and Race Vol I.* New York: Helga M. Rogers, 1967.

Van Sertima, Ivan. "Race and Origin of the Egyptians" in *Egypt Revisited*. Edited by Ivan Van Sertima. Transaction Publishers. New Brunswick, New Jersey, (1989: 3-8).

_____. "African Origin of the Ancient Egyptian Civilization" in *Egypt*: *Child of Africa*. Edited by Ivan Van Sertima. New Brunswick, New Jersey, (1994) 1995.

Woodson, Carter G. *The Mis-Education of the Negro*. Trenton, New Jersey: Africa World Press, (1990) 1993.

Black Nationalism 321. Dr. Fred Monderson (left) sits beside Dr. Runoko Rashidi.

BLACK NATIONALISM ALIVE AND WELL

Black Nationalism 321a. Prof. Joycelynne Loncke, Chairperson of the **Guyana Branch of the Pan-African Movement**, announces the opening of the **Dr. Fred Monderson Reading Room and Library at the Ethiopian Society** in Georgetown, Guyana.

FREDERICK MONDERSON

Black Nationalism 321b. Brooklyn District Attorney Thompson poses with Civil Rights icon John Lewis at Congressman Major Owens' funeral at First Baptist Church in Crown Heights, Brooklyn.

BLACK NATIONALISM ALIVE AND WELL

44. CELEBRATING DR. IVAN VAN SERTIMA
By

Dr. Fred Monderson

In ancient Egypt, the king celebrated his Heb Sed Festival of rejuvenation after 30 years of rule, which was a significant achievement then, as is any such lengthy accomplishment, now. Its public knowledge, when Dick Clark, the TV personality, celebrated 30 years of New Year's "Rocking Eve," this was greeted with much hoopla and congratulatory accolades from print, radio and television media; emphasizing his longevity and how significant this milestone really was. Granted this was so! However, after Gil Noble the public service news reporter reached the same milestone with his TV Show, **LIKE IT IS**, ABC, Channel 7, New York, moved to cancel this program. Fortunately, the community and such groups as **CEMOTAP** under the distinguished leadership of Dr. James McIntosh and his co-Chair Betty Dopson dispatched a forceful rebuke in defense of this important program. Both sides recognized the significance and ramifications of the public service message this important show presented, as demonstrated by the interest generated over the longevity of its duration. As a result, the Gil Noble show continued telling it "Like It Is" and on to an international audience. Unfortunately the show's host became ill and then it changed name and focus.

FREDERICK MONDERSON

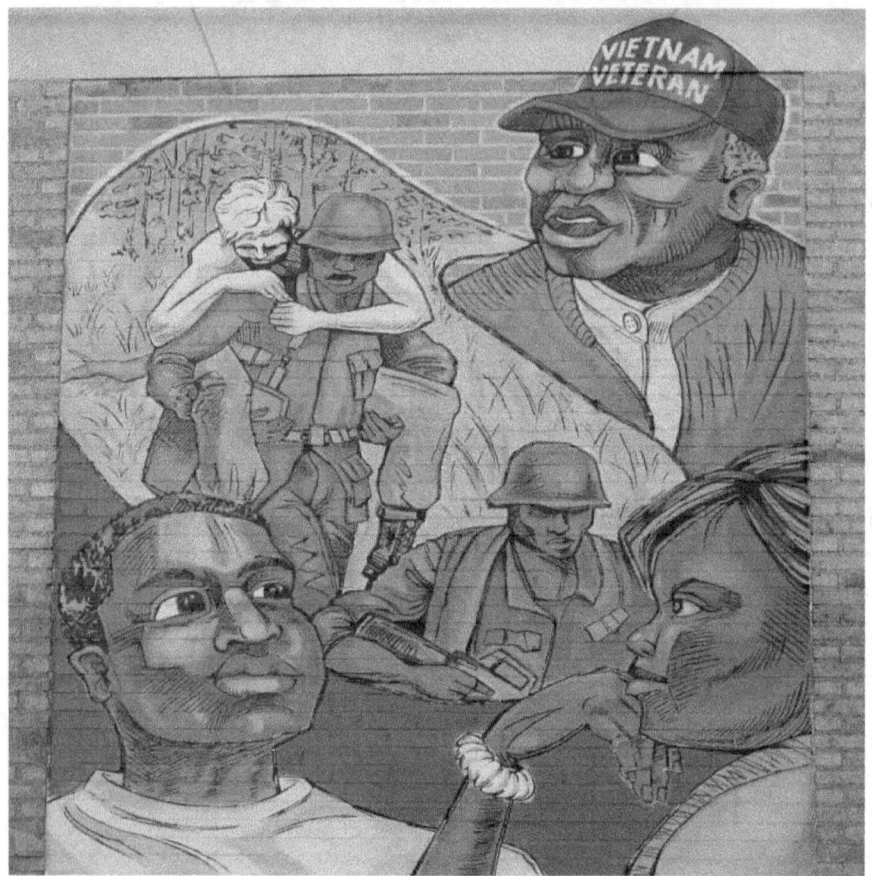

Black Nationalism 322. Black Veterans who served.

This April 2009, marks the 30th Anniversary of the *Journal of African Civilizations* founded by Dr. Ivan Van Sertima of Rutgers University. This writer, historian, anthropologist, teacher, humanitarian and scholar extraordinaire has produced ground-breaking scientifically based, accurate and historically truthful, research depicting people of African ancestry, as subjects not objects of historical phenomena. Van Sertima's initial emphasis has been on Blacks in ancient Egypt and expanding into a historical "catch-basin funnel" to include Africa and the Diaspora's involvement and investigations in science, mathematics, medicine, metallurgy, aerodynamics, linguistics, building, agriculture, and most importantly, history.

BLACK NATIONALISM ALIVE AND WELL

Black Nationalism 323. Mzee Moya, "the Brother from **The East**" (left); Michael Hooper of "**Roots Revisited**" (right).

Black Nationalism 323a. "Abubaca," longtime Black Nationalist, Community Activist and confidant of Sonny Carson.

FREDERICK MONDERSON

Through the work of this visionary with enormous potential, that quintessential organ, the *Journal of African Civilizations*, became a major source in Egyptian, African and African American history. Undaunted by criticisms, the *Journal's* coverage expanded to give agency to enormously credible scholarship. Its content was well researched and provided laudable credence to an enormous body of scientifically based, factually revealing, information on Africans in Africa, Europe, Asia, and the Americas.

Black Nationalism 324. Efforts and experiences of "Our People," "Span the Brooklyn Bridge."

BLACK NATIONALISM
ALIVE AND WELL

This ground breaking approach and its results made the world stand up and take notice of significant Black contributions across the wide spectrum of knowledge, from ancient through modern times. In view of these amazing revelations, one has to wonder how credible non-African scholarship had not been able to make the same discoveries and report such. Naturally, this new information, once revealed by the *Journal of African Civilizations*, was thereafter put to tremendous scrutiny to authenticate its findings. This was expected for much of these new revelations threatened the pillars that supported the foundations of a questionable, articulated world history whose structural integrity, it has now come to be known, propagated the false notion of "all the history that's printed to fit," rather than "all the history fit to print." Therefore, kudos goes out to Dr. Ivan Van Sertima, a pioneer who deserves qualitative recognition for the legacy he bequeathed. His steadfast and consistent ferreting out important cultural data, placed African people at the nucleus of knowledge advancing the cause of humanity's progress along the historical continuum. In this he struck a major blow to "global White intellectual supremacy!"

Black Nationalism 325. That "Frederick Douglass is my ancestor" is a very good refrain!

FREDERICK MONDERSON

Black Nationalism 326. Restoration, in the heart of Bed-Stuy, where Sonny Carson "Held Court" with **The Committee to Honor Black Heroes** and gave us **Marcus Garvey** and **Malcolm X Boulevards** and **Harriet Tubman Avenue**, the **Malcolm X School**, and was very instrumental in forcing the naming of a school for **Toussaint L'Ouverture**.

The *Journal of African Civilizations* began as a Quarterly that was ground-breaking in its revelations as a tremendous reservoir of factual information; and this contributed to its success in appeal for academic and grass-roots support. The present writer was glad to have purchased the first two gold-covered issues in 1979; that in their own-right consisted of "gold-loaded new and revolutionary information." The standards of his unparalleled scholarship, impeccable in their nature, copious nature of his sources, not only stunned but attracted a reading public ecstatic with the new and high level of quality historical recordings. This organ never let up as the vision and focus of its creator masterfully commanded the academic and intellectual stage of knowledge. This new approach at African historiographic reconstruction sought to correct distortions and include omissions within the corpus of African and African American history, science and culture, systematically manipulated by pseudoscientific writers and historians from Europe and America who, ultimately for one reason or another could not countenance the significance of Dr. Van Sertima's prodigious production.

BLACK NATIONALISM
ALIVE AND WELL

Black Nationalism 327. Jitu Weusi sits surrounded by Councilwoman Una Clarke (right), Assemblyman Al Vann (Center) and a friend, Preston Wilcox (right).

As with all such iconoclastic work, Dr. Van Sertima's scholarship was naturally subjected to the most intense scrutiny to check and challenge his findings; but, alas, his scholarly approach and ferreting techniques were unparalleled. Thus he was able to produce such remarkable results that have withstood the vicissitudes of pernicious challenges to his integrity and the impeccable nature of his scholarship and the results.

FREDERICK MONDERSON

Black Nationalism 328. To shake the hand of a great actor as Ossie Davis (right) and stand beside Gordon Parks (left) is indeed a tremendous honor for Melvin Van Pebbles.

As an intellectual visionary, this outstanding iconoclastic scholar thus unleashed a cascading avalanche of scientific revelations that coupled with his lectures, shattered prevailing falsity regarding African history which easily struck a blow against the falsity of "global White supremacy." **NASA** recognized the potency of his work and welcomed his unparalleled scientific scholarship. His scholarly ground-breaking, *They Came before Columbus* is a seminal work in African and African American history detailing Africans in the Americas before Columbus. The irrefutable revelations therein heralded the reservoir of knowledge Van Sertima unleashed in the masterful presentations later produced in its metamorphism from Journal to consistently voluminous and scholarly monograms.

BLACK NATIONALISM ALIVE AND WELL

Black Nationalism 329. Urban art and poetry decorate this wall.

With Ivan Van Sertima as Editor, the *Journal* boasted an Editorial Board consisting of Godfrey C. Burns, MD; Leonard Jeffries Jr.; John Henrik Clarke; Edward Scobie; Legrand Clegg II; and Clyde-Ahmad Winters. Sylvia Bakos was Art Editor and Sandra Schell, Secretarial Assistant.

The East Coast Board consisted of Godfrey C. Burns, MD; Ida Lewis; Gil Noble; John A. Williams; Leonard James. The West Coast Board comprised Legrand Clegg II; Asa Hillard; Clara Mann. Mid-West consisted of Ismay Ashford; Celeste Henderson; and Roger K. Oden; while New England and the South were Willard R. Johnson and Ernest Withers, Jr., respectively.

FREDERICK MONDERSON

Black Nationalism 330. Revered nationalist Jim Cuffe sits in his chair flanked by Atiim Ferguson and Ofori Payton, partially obscured.

This tremendous brain thrust was thus a dynamo that encouraged and supported Dr. Van Sertima as he blazed the trail of remarkable revelations changing the whole dynamic of historical discussion regarding African peoples' contributions to the advancement of knowledge.

As an example, Volume 1, No. 1 April, 1979 of the *Journal of African Civilizations* consisted of:

Section 1: EARLY EGYPT

"Early Egypt: A Different Perspective"
Excerpts from WAB.C.-TV documentary "Tutankhamun: A Different Perspective" produced by Gil Noble, with John Henrik Clarke and Josef Ben-Jochannan.
Cheikh Anta Diop and Freddie L. Thomas: "Two Philosophical Perspectives on Pristine Black History" – James G. Spady.
"The Black Image in Egyptian Art" – Jules Taylor.

BLACK NATIONALISM ALIVE AND WELL

"Ancient Cataclysmic and Tectonic Change: Their Impact on the Peopling of Egypt" – John A. Williams.

Section 2: EARLY AFRICAN SCIENCE

"Editorial Introduction" – Godfrey C. Burns, M.C.

"Complex Iron-Smelting and Prehistoric Culture in Tanzania" – Peter Schmidt and Donald H. Avery.
"Namoratunga: The First Archeoastronomical Evidence in Sub-Saharan Africa" – B.M. Lunch and L.H. Robbins.

Section 3: EARLY AMERICA

"They Came Before Columbus: New Developments and Discoveries" – Ivan Van Sertima
"Mandingo Scripts in the New World– Part I" – Clyde-Ahmed Winters.
"The First Americans" – Legrand Clegg II
Biographical Note on Contributors.

Journal of African Civilizations Vol. 1, No. 2 November 1979

Editorial: Ivan Van Sertima

FREDERICK MONDERSON

Black Nationalism 331. Let the good times roll!

Section 1: AFRICAN SCIENCE

"African Astronomy"
"African Astronomy: African Observers of the Universe: The Sirius Question" – Hunter H. Adams III.
"African Mathematics"
"The Yoruba Number System" – Claudia Zaslavsky
"African Navigation"
"Traditional African Watercraft: A New Look" – Stewart C. Mallory.
"African Metallurgy"
"Independent Origins of East African Iron-Smelting" – Clyde-Ahmed Winters

BLACK NATIONALISM ALIVE AND WELL

Black Nationalism 332. City Councilwoman Una Clarke and her daughter Councilwoman, later Congresswoman, Yvette Clarke, who is flanked by Kwame, brother of Rasheed Allah, and El Hombe Brath with unidentified others.

Section 2: "AFRICAN SCIENCE AND INVENTION"

"Black Americans in the Field of Science and Invention" – Robert C. Hayden.
"Lewis Latimer, Bringer of the Light" – John Henrik Clarke.
"African Americans in Science and Invention: A Bibliographical Guide" – John Henrik Clarke.

Dr. Cheikh Anta Diop was so impressed with the path Dr. Ivan Van Sertima had undertaken; in the second issue of the *Journal* he wrote a letter to the Editor, detailing his observations regarding the mummy of Pharaoh Rameses II. The mummy of this "Great" king was in a state of decay and was rushed to Paris to undergo "corrective surgery" to stem its deterioration. The Senegalese, Cheikh Anta Diop, was the only black African scholar of sufficient

FREDERICK MONDERSON

Egyptological proficiency permitted to be part of the reconstruction team. This inclusion enabled him to observe and report "New World Tobacco" was found in the intestines of Rameses II. In the revealing tradition of the *Journal*, Dr. Diop, himself a researcher of tremendous potential, theorized and postulated the view, Rameses II of the 19th Dynasty, 13th Century Before Christ, had dispatched seafarers to the New World who brought back tobacco which he smoked before he died. Much ink was spilled to prove it was "Old World Tobacco," but to no avail. Thus, Dr. Diop through the auspices of Dr. Van Sertima's *Journal* proved Africans were in the Americas nearly 2800 years before Columbus. Much of this, however, was in keeping with Dr. Van Sertima's contention that *They Came before Columbus*. Hence, Dr. Diop's postulation added to Van Sertima's arguments before Columbus.

Black Nationalism 333. Evidently, Spanish men of distinction.

This incredible scholar was therefore able to begin and produce a tremendous body of scholarly work including the following:

Blacks in Science: Ancient and Modern. New Brunswick, New Jersey: Transaction Books, 1983.
Black Women in Antiquity. New Brunswick, New Jersey: Transaction Books, (1984) 1985.
Nile Valley Civilizations. Journal of African Civilizations, (1985) 1986.

BLACK NATIONALISM ALIVE AND WELL

African Presence in Early Europe. New Jersey and London: Transaction Books (1985) 1996.
Great African Thinkers: *Cheikh Anta Diop.* New Brunswick, New Jersey: Transaction Books, (1986) 1987.
Great Black Leaders: *Ancient and Modern.* New Jersey: Transaction Books, 1988.
Egypt Revisited. New Jersey: Transaction Books, 1989.
African Presence in Early America. New Brunswick, New Jersey: Transaction Publishers (1992) 1995.
Egypt: *Child of Africa.* New Brunswick, New Jersey: Transaction Books, (1994) 1995.
Early America Revisited. New Brunswick, New Jersey: Transaction Publisher, 1998.
African Presence in Early Asia. New Brunswick, New Jersey: Transaction Publishers (1985) 2004

Black Nationalism 334. Frederick Douglass and Marcus Garvey, outstanding African nationalists, influential in the 19th and 20th Centuries.

The above sources indicated here do not exhaust that outstanding scholar's prodigious production of a reservoir of knowledge that now arms the young, teachers and students engaged in rectifying the role of African people in the intellectual development of humanity's cultural and historical legacy and social accomplishments. Such an outstanding production places Dr. Van Sertima on par with the likes of Dr. Yosef A.A. ben-Jochannan,

FREDERICK MONDERSON

Dr. John Henrik Clarke, Dr. Molefi Asante, Dr. Carter G. Woodson and J. A. Rogers. For this we give praise to a great African American mind whose name will forever echo in the pantheon of Black heroes and be remembered as arming his people for the challenges to their intellectual and cultural integrity and accomplishments. For this enormous gift of Africa to the world, we say, God Bless and Thank God for Dr. Ivan Van Sertima.

Black Nationalism 334a. Newspaper publisher Milton Allimadi sits in quiet contemplation at one of many Forums defending Blacks.

BLACK NATIONALISM ALIVE AND WELL

Black Nationalism 335. Ali Lamont (left) of **The Committee to Honor Black Heroes**, founded by Sonny Carson, and Assemblyman, later Councilman Al Vann (right) at his side.

45. BLACK SPENDING HABITS
By
Dr. Fred Monderson

On Tuesday August 6, 2013, the noted radio personality Bob Law, joined by Rev. Calvin Butts moderated a program at First Church of God in Christ on Kingston Avenue and Park Place in Brooklyn, regarding black earning power, the potentialities of their spending practices and the capabilities of an organized economic effort that maximizes this spending potential as well as insisting where to invest with the greatest economic benefit to African people.

Mr. Law pointed out; this new movement is a national effort supported by Rev. Ben Chavis, Conrad Mohammed, Sister Souljah, Rev. Dr. Calvin Butts of Abyssinian Baptist Church and a number of

FREDERICK MONDERSON

politically and economically conscious individuals across the national spectrum. Reminding that "Jesus came specifically to his own," Bob Law told the nearly three hundred individuals gathered to receive his usually highly informative message. He wanted them to join his effort because a great deal was at stake. He wanted them to assess the situation and redirect their spending habits to really get the most "bank for their buck."

Black Nationalism 336. Without question, two serious brothers committed to the cause of African Liberation!

For one thing, a plague has infested the Black community that beyond economic considerations has implications for health concerns with even a tremendous impact on the family structure. This is exacerbated because many families, individuals, are struggling in the bowels of our community and they don't even realize the true impact of this "sweet tasting plague." Even more important, they are at a disadvantage because of the inability to control their spending habits, then as an analogy he delved into the impact of the Montgomery Bus Boycott of which Rev. Augustus Jones and Rev. Wyatt Tee Walker were a part and how this strategy undergirded the effectiveness of the Civil Rights Movement within

BLACK NATIONALISM
ALIVE AND WELL

the context of Adam Clayton Powell's admonition, "Don't buy where you do not or cannot work!"

Black Nationalism 337. Cherise Maloney (left); George Murden (center); and Jitu Weusi (right); attend the **African Street Festival** at Boys and Girls High School, soon to be named in honor of the South African leader Nelson Mandela.

As such, Mr. Law delved into the "preponderance of fast food joints" that saturates the Black Community." This reality creates a moral and social dilemma of dependence with lasting implications not simply for economic matters of spending, but health and the inability to pay full attention to one's eating habits. This is especially so because of the lack of fruits and vegetables in the African American diet. This significant unavailability of fruit and vegetable establishments in the Black Community has given way to that preponderance of Fast Foods that call into question health issues as diabetes, cancer, heart attacks, strokes at a time when health care is more and more expensive and hospitals that serve the Black community are being closed en masse. Case in point in Central Brooklyn alone we count how many hospitals are closed or closing. Brooklyn Women's Hospital, Caledonian, Brooklyn Jewish, St.

FREDERICK MONDERSON

Mary's, and Long Island College and Interfaith are on life support. Robert Cornegy, subsequently elected to the New York City Council, spoke about Interfaith Hospital being on the chopping-block for closure. Connie Lesold, a longtime advocate for this hospital and many social issues of the Black community was in the audience.

Black Nationalism 338. Harry Belafonte (left) and associates entertaining during the March on Washington in 1963.

The state of affairs prompted this reporter to investigate this matter further. As such, I chose the "**Nostrand Avenue Corridor** from Fulton Street to Eastern Parkway in Brooklyn." This is a good representative sample, of the Black Community, and while the results are not exactly a duplicate elsewhere, they can, however, serve as a pretty good barometer to assess the significance of the problem. Well, what did this inquiry find?

BLACK NATIONALISM ALIVE AND WELL

Black Nationalism 339. Carlos Walton, Dean of Students at MS 61 (left); a sister teacher (center); and Mr. Gerald Joshua (right), "been everywhere" and now passed on to "Ancestor Glory."

There are "23 Fast Food Establishments" not counting the nearly 12 or so Delis in this 12-block stretch along Nostrand Ave from Fulton Street to Eastern parkway. There are 4 at Fulton Street and Nostrand avenue alone and 1 or sometimes up to 3 on each block as you approach Eastern Parkway. As such, in this and other instances, Bob Law wanted to redirect spending habits, because we represent these establishments' "margin of profits." When "they lose that margin of profit" they respond to the demands of the Black Community. One way to get this nation to respond to our concerns is the economic boycott and it becomes more effective if conducted on a national level across city after city, state after state, with religious institutions spearheading the effort.

FREDERICK MONDERSON

Black Nationalism 339a. Kwame Ture (Stokely Carmichael), the quintessential Black Nationalist (left); and Dr. Carlos Russell, founder of Black Solidarity Day (right).

Black Nationalism 340. Rudy Giuliani, later Mayor of New York City interviews Rosa Parks.

BLACK NATIONALISM
ALIVE AND WELL

Black Nationalism 341. Justice Thurgood Marshall and Nationalist Malcolm X.

Next Reverend Butts began to elaborate on the problem. Reminding that "We represent the margin of profit" then if "We stop buying a product" the makers suffer and begin to listen to our concerns! This strategy has had the greatest success backed by the Black Church, whether it's the African Methodist Episcopal, the Christian Methodist Episcopalian, or the Church of God In Christ. The Montgomery Bus Boycott was effective because of the role of the church! Adam Clayton Powell's mantra, "Don't buy where you can't work" was not "Burn Baby Burn" but "Economics Baby Economics." We must remember Marcus Garvey and Elijah

FREDERICK MONDERSON

Mohammed encouraged our people to "Do for self!" The Black Churches were built by people pooling their money. Bishop McCulloh and Sweet Daddy Jones were able to establish banks, insurance companies, foundations with people pooling their money. "When you begin to amass economic strength you gain respect in this nation. We can focus our economic strength."

Black Nationalism 342. Attorney Johnny Cochran appearing at Rev. Sharpton's **National Action Network** (at the Madison Avenue location) where he spoke on behalf of Abner Louima (seated left) after Officer Volpe had assaulted him with a plunger.

"We have the right to read, own property, save our money. We spend crazy with people who really don't care about us. They don't employ us and take our monies out of our community. We can make a difference." Remember, "a little bit of salt changes the flavor of food. We must shop at Black establishments. We must respect ourselves and we must spread the word! We must remember radio stations such as KISS and WLIB do not program in our best interest. TV is not of any substance. We must spread the word through our churches, civic organizations, and fraternities. We must become

BLACK NATIONALISM ALIVE AND WELL

Black Nationalism 343. Sitting beside Queen Mother Moore, Rosa Parks receives a Citation of Honor.

Bob Law again addressed the gathering. He introduced Bishop Jerry Seabrook. The Bishop referenced a recent episode. The streets of Detroit looks like a war zone. The City is in default. Yet, poor folks raised $18,000.00 in a free-will offering for a pressing cause. This was pocket money understandably. People protesting and marching were outraged because of Zimmerman, Randy Evans shot by Officer Torsney who was declared not guilty because of a temporary

FREDERICK MONDERSON

insanity plea. Then there was Eleanor Bumpers in the Bronx. These all claimed police feared for their lives when they shot these people. It is clear from the Dred Scott 1857 Decision to now, we are still denied justice! A national coalition is formed around this issue. Let us begin to use the leverage we have in our community which is our economic strength in our spending habits.

Black Nationalism 343a. In Stan Kinnard's candidacy for state Assemblyman, Sonny Carson, Al Sharpton and Michael Hardy came out to campaign for him.

We spend over one trillion dollars annually! Blacks outspend everyone else. We spend more money on everything than everyone else! Revlon! Nobody respects us! Everybody takes us for granted! When the Russian Prime Minister said something derogatory about Gays, these people called in the "Vodka lords" and told them "We will stop buying your Vodka unless you say and do something!" That is clout! "Economics is one of the ways we have power." Remember Emmett Till. It was not stand your ground in St. Louis, New York, Mississippi, Florida. It is the institution of racism.

BLACK NATIONALISM
ALIVE AND WELL

Institutional Racism. "What's in your hand?" "Over One Trillion Dollars!" "Hold on to your dollars! Give to constructive organizations that are working in our best interest. Give your 'Burger and Fries' monies to Sankofa Academy or the Learning Tree School."

African Americans consume more fast food than every other group. The location of fast food establishments is determined by race. Racial profiling is conducted on every level. There are 6 times as many fast food restaurants in the Black Community than in any other communities. We must remember 80 percent of processed food in the United States is already banned in other nations because of the preservatives put in them to extend shelf life. Burger King, Wendy, Kentucky Fried Chicken all take out money from our community but don't support anything we do for social justice. The Fast Food industry depends on our money! We must push back and not allow our community to be systematically pulled from under us. We must never forget police lynch mobs murder our people and are acquitted.

The Cola industry and Craft and Mac and Cheese are making millions. We must be a part of this national movement. Remember, John Killins, Lorraine Hansberry, James Baldwin all, for the longest, spoke against this issue. Yet, we are still denied justice and freedom.

FREDERICK MONDERSON

Black Nationalism 344. Shirley Chisholm (left); and Harriet Tubman (right); stalwarts of African uplift.

Then Mr. Law mentioned Rev. Leon Sullivan in Detroit. He was trying to get to some big wig in the auto industry to say we need jobs. The man outright said "I don't have time to speak with you." That was Wednesday afternoon. Rev. Sullivan got the word out to 72 pastors. On Sunday morning word got out from these church pulpits "Don't Buy his product!" By Tuesday morning, the man called Rev. Sullivan stating, "When are you available to meet with me!" Leadership has traditionally come from the church. Systemic racism is condoning and supporting institutional racism. They are closing hospitals, close over one hundred schools. So, "We Must Stand Our Ground: Turn Black Spending into Political Power!" We must use our money to influence policy! We must have an intelligent policy that is used effectively.

We don't have to stop all Black folks from buying fast food. Just 8 percent need stop buying fast food. This is indeed a national

BLACK NATIONALISM ALIVE AND WELL

movement. Chukwu Lumumba in Mississippi and Maulana Karenga in Los Angeles are part of this movement. Then he admonished, "Can you hold back some of your Fast Food Spending. Your Burger and Fries Money."

Bishop Seabrook called for a self-assessment. These fast food establishments are not hiring anyone from our community. Chinese, Hispanics, Koreans not hiring anyone from our community! Someone offered, "Have you seen a Chinese restaurant go out of business?" Then he addressed Black on Black crime.

Black Nationalism 345. "Coach" George Murden escorts Cherise Maloney as Jitu Weusi stops for a quiet conversation and his wife Angela Weusi looks towards the stage at the **African Street Festival**, held at Boys and Girls High School in Brooklyn.

"We rally around other people killing us but nor rally around us killing us. If we come together in unity we could stop some of this injustice. Burger King is a Florida Based Fast Food company."

We must remember we spend between 900 billion and one trillion dollars. We spend 321 billion on books, 714 billion on beauty and hair products. All the while 24 schools were closed with 19 more on

FREDERICK MONDERSON

the block. 34 schools must be replaced. 23 schools were closed in Philadelphia. All the while 420 billion are spent on prisons.

Ollie McClean, Founder and principal of the Sankofa Academy, nearly 30 years in existence, next related the positive curriculum taught in the school. She delved into some of the activities the young people are a part of and the percentage who go on to college. This, then, is a good example why Bob Law suggested, "Hold Back the Burger and Fries" small change and give to such positive organizations as Sankofa and the Learning Tree. Meanwhile we will coordinate economic strategy boycott across the country!

Black Nationalism 346. Rev. Al Sharpton introduces Senator Barack Obama (with black hair) when he visited National Action Network in 2008 as he campaigned to become President of the United States.

BLACK NATIONALISM ALIVE AND WELL

Black Nationalism 347. Senator Obama responds while Rev. Sharpton listens attentively from his seat.

46. "HEAVEN IN AN UPROAR"
By
Dr. Fred Monderson

From the time the great labor leader and political tactician William ("Bill") Lynch had "gone to glory" and arrived at the "Pearly Gates" a bee-hive of activity began to unfold regarding his entry into the "Kingdom of Heaven." After the "drums" announced Bill was on his way, not only was there consternation here on earth among those he befriended, worked with, influenced and mentored including such political luminaries as John Liu and Bill De Blasio; yet, ancestral angels in train of Sonny Carson, "over there," insightful as he has always been, supported his theory, there would be static at the gate where St. Peter was mandated to do his examination. Sonny thereupon called upon associates Jitu Weusi, Afori Payton, Hodari the "Fire man," then sent word to Malcolm X, Dr. John Henrik Clarke, W.E.B. DuBois and Martin Luther King with instructions to call upon the oldsters Paul Robeson, A. Philip Randolph, and Marcus

FREDERICK MONDERSON

Garvey to meet him at the Gates for a show of Black Solidarity and to welcome "Brother Bill" into the majesty of heaven!

Black Nationalism 347a. At the African Street Festival at Boys and Girls High School, Prof James Smalls makes nice with Cherise Maloney while Sonny Carson and a friend mugs for the photo.

Since state of mind has a tremendous impact on well-being, and as much as Bill had been preparing in his journey heavenward, leaving a wife, son and daughter behind; as he approached that revered existence, and sensing some kind of commotion from the people massed in and outside the fence; Mr. Lynch stood up from his chair!

BLACK NATIONALISM ALIVE AND WELL

He approached the table where sat an elderly but vibrant gentleman with a long white beard. Realizing the consternation unfolding in the opposing gatherings for a potential war in heaven, St. Peter donned his Inquisition hat and exhorted, "Mr. William Lynch, What are your qualifications for entry into this gloriously hallowed and blissful existence?"

Black Nationalism 348. Isaac Hayes, entertainer often regarded as "The Black Moses" (left); and Bernie Mac, actor and comedian (right); both now deceased.

Bill responded, "Pardon!"
"What have you done?"
"Your book is a record!"
"No, you tell me!"

Bill Lynch responded: "I am a Harlemite born to a Long Island potato farmer!"

FREDERICK MONDERSON

"I served in the United States Air Force and on the Children Defense Fund."

"I managed David Patterson's campaign for New York State Senator in 1985."

"I was Chief of Staff for David Dinkins when he served as Manhattan Borough President."

"I helped bring the 1992 Democratic National Convention to New York City and was Bill Clinton's 1992 New York State Campaign Manager."

"I became David Dinkins' Campaign Manager and engineered his victory to become New York City's first Black Mayor in 1989."

"In that administration I served as Deputy Mayor or Inter-Governmental Relations."

"Upon Nelson Mandela's 1990 release from Prison in South Africa, I engineered his visit to New York City, coordinated speaking events in Harlem and Yankee Stadium and arranged a Ticker Tape Parade down the New York City's "Canyon of Heroes."

"I served as Director of Legislation and Political Action for District Council 1701 of AFSCME."

"I was adviser to Jesse Jackson's and Walter Mondale's presidential campaigns.

"I served as advisory Vice-Chairman to the Democratic National Committee in 2004.

"I was also Deputy Campaign Manager to Senator John Kerry's 2004 Presidential Campaign.

"I sat on several Boards to aid the cause of my fellow man. Is all this necessary? What does your book say?"

BLACK NATIONALISM
ALIVE AND WELL

Black Nationalism 349. Revs. Jesse Jackson and Al Sharpton, his mentee, at the "Million Man March" in Washington, DC, 1995.

Black Nationalism 349a. Rev. Al Sharpton introduces Senator Barack Obama during his first campaign for the Presidency.

FREDERICK MONDERSON

Turning to his official record, St. Peter realized "I'm dealing with a man of superior mentality, who is courageous with a strong sense of commitment in his fight for Civil Rights and social and racial justice." He noted former Mayor David Dinkins sorrowfully confessed, his friend Bill Lynch "had a unique capacity to pull together bright young women and men who are dedicated to doing good things." In fact, Mr. Dinkins added: "Over eight years, four as Manhattan borough president and four as mayor, much that was accomplished was because of Bill Lynch. It was he who persuaded me, in 1989, to run for Mayor, and I shall be eternally grateful for that which he helped me accomplish. Bill, who was sometimes referred to as the 'rumpled genius,' was the architect of so much that I'm credited with having accomplished during our administration. He had a genius for connecting people of common interests and goals, and for the political game and behind-the-scenes strategy. He was a genius but, more than that, he was a dear friend and I will miss him dearly."

Black Nationalism 350. Minister Louis Farrakhan (organizer of the "**Million Man March**," October 16, 1995) (left); and Washington, DC Mayor Marion Barry (right); among throngs at the "**Million Man March**."

BLACK NATIONALISM ALIVE AND WELL

Equally, St. Peter realized many important people had been touched by the meaningful life of this giant in New York politics. Many with similar standings had instantly responded in praise of the genius whose accomplishments changed the New York political landscape. Among those, former President Bill Clinton and his wife Hillary Clinton had pointed out, "Bill Lynch always put people first. He had a heart even bigger than the city he served."

However, feeling somewhat embarrassed by the "third degree," amidst the clamor of the demonstration and the counter demonstration, St. Peter's further read the Clintons' comments stating, "Bill Lynch was a friend to both of us over many years. We admired his integrity and his generosity, including his support for scores of community organizations. New York has lost a champion!"

Black Nationalism 351. Minister Clemson Brown, photographer and Black History archivist.

FREDERICK MONDERSON

Black Nationalism 352. Notorious "Biggie Smalls" (left); and TuPac Shakur (right).

St. Peter, on the other hand, wants the best for a tranquil and harmonious heavenly existence, thought, "Perhaps Bill could save heaven from foolish people, who put this sacred place in a rage." Further, St. Peter's record showed, New York City Mayor Michael Bloomberg also made the statement that Mr. Lynch, "sought to better our city by bringing people together and served as Deputy Mayor because he wanted to make a difference for New Yorkers. He spent his life passionately pursuing his ideals – civil rights and social justice. Many of the most influential political leaders – here in the city and also on the national level – sought his counsel. He lived a remarkable life, and my thoughts and prayers are with his family."City Council Speaker Christine Quinn, expressed, "Today, we mourn the loss of a true champion for progressive causes and one of the sharpest minds that New York government and politics has ever seen. Bill Lynch dedicated his life to making New York City a better place. As a Deputy Mayor under Mayor Dinkins, Bill played a critical role in facilitating Nelson Mandela's historic visit to New York City in 1990. Bill was a fighter for equality and the

BLACK NATIONALISM
ALIVE AND WELL

embodiment of a New Yorker: tough, smart, and fiercely loyal to the City he loved. Bill was my friend - he was a one of a kind New Yorker, and he will be sorely missed."

Former Controller Bill Thompson confessed: "I lost a friend today. And the city lost a giant. Bill Lynch was a brilliant strategist and thinker - that was unmistakable from the moment he entered a room. And his body of work, including his tireless effort to help elect political leaders across New York City, most memorably David Dinkins, tells his powerful story. But Bill always understood that politics is about people. He didn't just help elect leaders full of heart and vision and know-how, Bill served. He had a deep belief that government could be a tool to improve the lives of New Yorkers. Bill Lynch lived by that belief. No matter what the challenge, he persevered. Even though he left us today, Bill and his voice will continue to guide our city and its people to a better place."

Black Nationalism 353. Rev. Jesse Jackson shakes hands with Dr. Roscoe Lee Brown, famed "Tuskegee Airman."

FREDERICK MONDERSON

The Rev. Al Sharpton: "National Action Network and I are heartbroken over the passing of Bill Lynch. We lost a brilliant political strategist and the 'Godfather' of the Harlem political establishment. Bill was not only one of the most astute political minds in the country, he was a political father to many and worked with National Action Network for over twenty years on some of the most pertinent issues of our time. Bill believed in mentoring young people and it came easy for him because he believed in putting people and community first and said: 'When you do that, you always win.' Bill Lynch personally mentored countless young strategists who now hold key positions including National Action Network's own National Field Director LaMon Bland. Bill has been a revered advisor to some of the great humanitarians and elected officials of our time."

Black Nationalism 353a. Stan Kinnard brings out "heavyweights" to support his candidacy for Assemblyman.

Hector Figueroa, President, 32BJ/SEIU noted: "32BJ joins the many others across the country saddened by the passing of our brother, comrade, and friend Bill Lynch. Our movement lost a singular

BLACK NATIONALISM
ALIVE AND WELL

warrior today. Bill's years of visionary work with labor, political leaders and the Black community are unparalleled, and the fruits of his many endeavors will live far beyond him. Bill believed in the transformative powers of democracy and political engagement and was an unwavering champion in the ongoing fight to get unheard voices heard. Our deepest sympathies go out to his family and loved ones. Bill, we will miss you."

Black Nationalism 354. Dr. Benjamin Chavis (center); Dr. Delores Blakeley ("**Queen Mother of the Slave Trade**") (left); Prof. James Blake in glasses at rear, and Minister Conrad Mohammed, etc.

Bertha Lewis, President, **The Black Institute wrote**: "I am heartbroken. Today, a great man has passed and I am deeply saddened by the loss of yet another mentor and friend to our community. A lot of what I know about Politics and Organizing, I learned from Bill Lynch. He was undoubtedly one of the greatest political minds of our era, and will forever be known as a giant in

FREDERICK MONDERSON

politics. He was a legend on the gridiron and on the gritty streets of Harlem and his passing creates a huge chasm in our City and our Nation's political fabric. I am honored to have known, learned and worked with him. Bill was a master political architect who was a key link between the Civil Rights Movement and electoral politics. The effects of his genius touched as far as South Africa and its abolishment of Apartheid and the world mourns his passing. The hearts and minds of **The Black Institute** are with his family and our friends at Bill Lynch Associates."

Having assessed some such statements, St. Peter then realized humanity had indeed lost a champion, for Bill had always believed, "Good government is good politics." After that, St. Peter began to ponder his decision!

Black Nationalism 355. Haitian President Bertrand Aristide receives an award in the Oval Room at the World Trade Center.

On Bill's part, awaiting the verdict, he finally turned and affixed his gaze on the group outside the gate who had been most vocal. He could make out a well-dressed gentleman in a white suit with a hood turned backwards over his shoulder. Then he realized, "Heaven is also beset by the great issues of earth!" There were others whose faces he could not make out.

BLACK NATIONALISM
ALIVE AND WELL

Black Nationalism 356. Sonny Carson is flanked by Reverends Al Sharpton (left); and Wyatt Tee Walker (right); President and Chairman of the **National Action Network**.

Inside, a band of singers comprising Sam Cooke, Baby Huey, Charlie Parker, Michael Jackson, James Brown, Ella Fitzgerald, Bob Marley and Luther Vandross were singing "A Change is going to come" and their melodic voices were harmoniously blended with the sweet instrumentation of Louis Armstrong, Dizzy Gillespie, and Hasan Roland Kirk. Just then the Jubilee Singers arrived on a flatbed truck and joining the others they began singing "When the Saints Go Marching In, when the Saints go marching In, I want to be in that number, When the Saints goes marching in." Then hearing these heavenly chimes, Mr. Lynch finally broke into a smile and really noticed the individuals in that group. "All this and heaven too," he thought. The more familiar faces of Carson, Weusi, Malcolm, Marley, Martin, Nkrumah, Sekou and Kwame Toure, and Robeson he easily recognized. Also there in the welcoming crowd were John Brown, William Lloyd Garrison, Charles Sumner, the Kennedy

FREDERICK MONDERSON

Brothers, and while Betty hugged Malcolm, Coretta grabbed Martin's arm. Bill also recognized Queen Mother Moore, standing beside Mary McCloud Bethune. Much further back and peering over the crown was Booker T. Washington, George Washington Carver, Medgar Evers and Rev. Shillingsworth, all standing behind Yaa Asantewaa, Bottom Belly, Queen Mary, Rosa Parks, Sojourner Truth, Fannie Lou Hamer and Harriet Tubman. These brothers and sisters were serious about Bill Lynch entering heaven as a member of the great and blessed pantheon of black hero saints. However, in a note to Sonny, Denmark Vesey, Nat Turner and Samuel Carson had informed, "We can't get there today but we're with you in spirit!"

Black Nationalism 357. Comedian and actor Redd Foxx (left); and singer and entertainer James Brown (right).

As all this unfolded, Bill was really surprised, that at such short notice Sonny Carson was able to contact so many and organize such a meaningful welcoming committee; all expressing a determination to have him share in the joys of heaven, where the light of righteousness forever shines. Sonny, for his part; and knowing that

BLACK NATIONALISM ALIVE AND WELL

Bill Lynch was a tireless champion for New York; was thinking, we could really use Bill's organizational and planning expertise, his coalition building acumen and his ability to forge consensus on issues.

Now in a quandary, Saint Peter turned to Bill Lynch and said, "Mr. Lynch you must understand, I have a job to do. My boss, the gentleman with the 'lamb's wool hair,' did insist everyone, no matter whom, must be rigorously examined to enter this eternal realm. You have passed with flying colors, particularly because of your concern for doing good." With that he handed Mr. Lynch the "keys to heaven" and bid him enter the realm of the sacred and blessed.

Instantly as the "rumpled genius" entered the realm of spiritual existence, the tactician and strategist that he has always been, immediately forced Mr. Lynch to believe he must contribute to making heaven drowsy with the tranquilizing harmony of love and cooperation. Still, he demanded an assessment of the state of things, to which Mr. Carson instantly handed over a list that included the following demands:

Black Nationalism 358. Dr. Leonard Jeffries makes a point at a Black United Front Celebration as he upholds Prof. Amos N. Wilson's book *Blueprint for Black Power*.

FREDERICK MONDERSON

An end to segregation; an end to racial profiling; no more stop and frisk; meaningful programs for seniors; meaningful programs for youth; freedom of expression and freedom from fear; the need for jobs, meaningful jobs, even here in heaven; the need for our people to be more organized; better educational opportunities; and equal compensation for the same work.

Just then Mr. Lynch realized his work was cut out for him. Sensing the heavenly waters were not all tranquil, he realized his was a role to bring these blessed souls together through organizational and unifying leadership. He had to help create a new heaven that would lay the ground work for a better earth. Thus, he felt confident with the litany of blessed ancestors present; his skills will be even more meaningful. Just then he thought, "I have got a lot of work to organize this place. I must continue to work to make all peoples' expectations of heaven a blissful reality!

Black Nationalism 359. Richard Pryor - actor, entertainer and comedian.

BLACK NATIONALISM ALIVE AND WELL

47. DR. JOHN HENRIK CLARKE: "Failure is not an Option in 2013!"

In keeping with its tradition of excellent presentations, on Sunday July 28, 2013, **CEMOTAP** paid tribute to Dr. John Henrik Clarke on the 15th anniversary of his passing. In a tremendous show of appreciation and gratitude for his extraordinary contribution to the intellectual and educational advancement of African people worldwide, guided by his revolutionary consciousness, some 300-400 people packed the Boys and girls auditorium to hear Gary Byrd and Lisa Noble, daughter of Gil Noble of '**Like it Is**' fame, announced a litany of scholars, activists, people of goodwill who came to praise, salute and thank Dr. Clarke for his wisdom, counsel, symbolism and steadfast and tenacious fortitude in praising, defending and uplifting African people at home and abroad. A staunch Pan-Africanist, Dr. Clarke was very concerned and involved with the African Liberation Struggle!

Dr. James McIntosh and Sister Betty Dopson, co-Chairs of **CEMOTAP** orchestrated a program in which the moderators introduced a number of enlightened individuals who simply not only extolled Dr. Clarke but indicated how his humanity and compassion had elevated and encouraged their transition and vision along this path strewn with challenges and pitfalls. They were quick to point out how his famous statements, pearls of wisdom, had guided their emerging philosophy of nationalistic and human consciousness. Among these 5 people received recognition in awards for their contribution to the realization of Dr. Clarke's vision manifested and operationalized in **Clarke House in Harlem**, a community he loved so much, wrote about and spent many of his cherished years.

Mike Tyson was the first recipient because Dr. Clarke wrote him during his most troubling times pointing not to his involvement but his capabilities as a champion and human being. The beautiful award accompanying this report was next given to sister Viola Plummer of

FREDERICK MONDERSON

the December 12 Movement, now on an international mission to observe the national elections in Zimbabwe. She was cited for her consistent commitment to the emancipation and upliftment of African people regardless of the price she had to pay. In addition, the three others who received recognition for assisting Clarke House were L. Londell McMillan, Esq., The Gil Noble Archives and Madeleine Moore-Burrell.

Black Nationalism 360. Amiri Baraka (Leroy Jones) (left); beside a very distinguished Brother Max Roach (right).

Mr. McMillan spoke of his efforts "To make more options that there be no more failures." Ms. Madeleine Moore-Burrell spoke about her efforts to fundraise and raise the $200,000 to pay for and "Burn the Mortgage for Clarke House." The Gill Noble Archives was recognized for the work its name-sake did and his daughter Lisa Noble, moderator, received it for her father!

BLACK NATIONALISM
ALIVE AND WELL

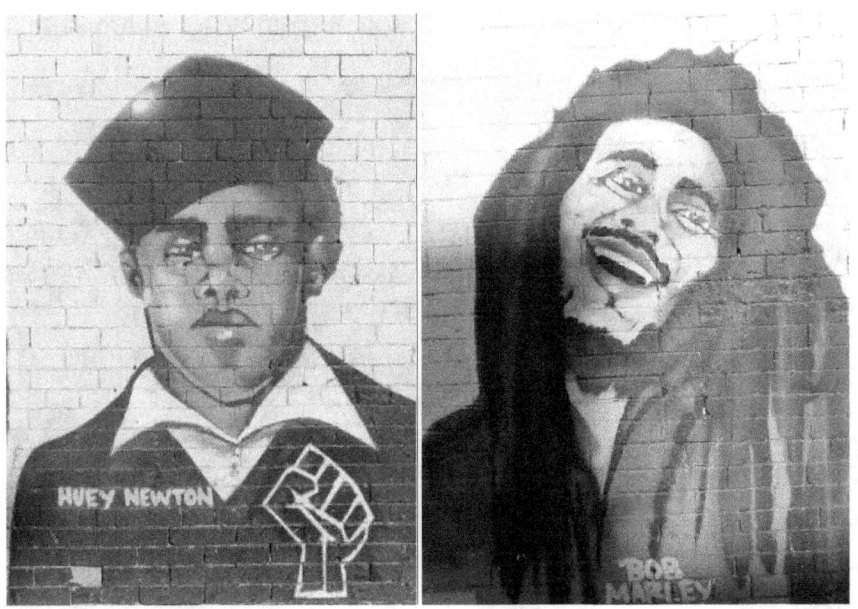

Black Nationalism 361. Revolutionary Huey Newton (left); and singer and entertainer Bob Marley (right).

Addressing the theme, "Failure is not an Option," Gary Byrd began his remarks by quoting one of Dr. Clarke's famous assessments that "History is a clock by which we tell the time of Day." As a student at Hunter College and listening to Dr. Clarke I too also remember so many of his wise sayings, that "The people who preached racism, colonized history" and even further, "When Europe colonized the world, it colonized the word's knowledge." Nevertheless, to open this august ceremony, "Nana Queen Mother" Camille Yarbrough began the libation to bless the proceedings, reminding everyone, "Your first dignity was as the parents of humanity." Echoing what a great teacher Dr. Clarke was, she reminded all, "His teachings are still with us!" Extolling, "We came to praise that ancient seed of the royal line," Sister Yarbrough requested a drum roll-call of ancestral names and got Miriam Francis Ashford, Jitu Weusi, Sonny Carson, Gil Noble, Mitta Monderson, Cherise Preville, Lynton Lawrence, Marcus Garvey, Malcolm X, Asa Hillard, Amos Wilson, Luis Reyes,

FREDERICK MONDERSON

Emmett Till, Michael Jackson, Martin Luther King, Trayvon Martin and John Henrik Clarke who "loved us more than he loved himself."

Black Nationalism 361a. At the Podium Gary Byrd extols Dr. John Clarke as Dr. Adelaide Sanford awaits her turn to give that electrifying speech and J.D. Livingston is there watching their backs!

BLACK NATIONALISM ALIVE AND WELL

Betty Dopson, Co-Chair of **CEMOTAP** and member of the **Board for the Education of People of African Ancestry** (**BEPAA**) housed at **John Henrik Clarke House** located at 286 convent Avenue, New York, New York 10031, next took the podium. The flyer said **BEPAA** has "no affiliation with NYC Government, NYC Board of Education or today's host location Boys and Girls High School, 1700 Fulton Street, Brooklyn, New York 11213." Ms. Dobson opened the program recognizing "Dr. Clarke was a man always available to us." She began discussing Clarke House in Harlem as "a place or institution to celebrate the life and work of a truly great man." Insisting everyone visit Clarke House certainly to admire the wonderful overhead quilt, she mentioned "There is a chair in which no one will sit because his spirit occupies it." Then she thanked Dr. Clarke reminding everyone, "Being African is the most important thing you can be in this world!"

George Edward Taitt, next on the program had not arrived, so Gary Byrd, a poet in his own right filled in by reciting one of his classic pieces that was dedicated to Dr. Clarke and his intellectual associate Dr. A.A. ben-Jochannan and on this day, dedicated to Stevie Wonder, 50 years in the musical business when he was being honored in Harlem for his "Songs in the Key of Life" lyrical message.

FREDERICK MONDERSON

Black Nationalism 362. The "Iron Pipeline" that is killing our young people!

People in attendance this reported recognized included Michael Hooper, Ed Lewis, Co-Founder of **Essence Magazine**, Jeffrey Garrison, Kazembe Butts, Dr. Turner of Cornell fame, Sister Rosina, Ollie McClean, Dr. Jack Felder, David Sanford, Dr. Anthony Brown, Brenda Walker, and Susan Taylor, recognized for her efforts to help young people in and outside the United States.

State Senator Inez Baron, half of that dynamic duo who along with her husband Charles had attended Hunter College, reminded all Dr. Clarke had taught, "Everything that touches your life must be an instrument of your liberation or be thrown into the ash can of history." She insisted we must then capitalize on every situation and always consider "What can we do to better the lot of our people." Taking off on the Trayvon Martin verdict, she emphasized the value of the economic boycott. Praising the stand of Stevie Wonder, Jay-Z, Kanye West, who have agreed not to perform in states where "Stand Your Ground" laws are enforced, she insisted "we boycott Florida. Don't take your conferences there, Don't visit Disneyworld! Pointing to the unending efforts of the Koch Brothers who

BLACK NATIONALISM
ALIVE AND WELL

championed resistance to Barack Obama, has helped pay the bill for George Zimmerman's defense, she asked people not to buy Koch Brothers paper products. Then she enumerated a list of such including "Angel Soft toilet paper, Brawny paper towels, Dixie plates, bowls, napkins, and cups, Madri Gras napkins and paper towels, Quilted Northern toilet paper, Soft and Gentle toilet paper, Sparkle napkins/paper towels, Vanity Fair napkins." She also reminded, we "must not give money to people fighting against us."

Reflecting on a recent march in Brownsville and seeking ideas for the struggle, she noted, a member volunteered, "We should have an economic boycott on the 5th of every month forever and that the 5th is Trayvon's birthday." Even further Ms. Baron expressed, "We might not get anything from the federal level," so we must persevere in struggle. "We must let our young people know they are loved. That they are valued, that they are valuable." Next it was the husband Charles Baron's turn. The articulate and fiery councilman who, at the next election will switch districts with his wife Inez and run for the Assembly seat while she run for the City Council seat he now holds. This is a brilliant strategy first employed by Al Vann and Annette Robinson now Assemblywoman and he Councilman.

FREDERICK MONDERSON

Black Nationalism 363. Judge Bruce Wright, often called "Cut em Loose Bruce" because of his leniency in interpreting the law on bail.

Mr. Baron began by saying "Dr. Clarke was special. He was a kind, nice human being concerned about us. He loved Africans. These things don't just happen. We must question the leadership around us who are simply crisis managers and ask ourselves where do we go from here? We're no better off now in the courts than we were in 1857, referring to the time of Dred Scott and Chief Justice Roger Taney. We need systemic change. Dr. Clarke would say, use these issues as teaching moments to dismantle the capitalist system." He said further, "The one Trayvon Martin defended was unselfish." Then the Councilman spoke of the economic boycott. "Don't go to Florida. Drop Mickey, the Time Share. We are going to win because we refuse to die. Our victory is certain."

BLACK NATIONALISM ALIVE AND WELL

Black Nationalism 364. Sonny Carson (right); Bishop Smallwood (second from left); Prof. Patterson in light suit, in the Brooklyn Navy Yard discussing disposition of the "Bones of the Runaway Samuel Carson."

But who was this intellectual giant so many people came out to hear being praised and pay homage to?

This champion of the sanctity of African womanhood and the virility and creative genius of African manhood, Dr. John H. Clarke was a Professor of African History in Hunter College's Black and Puerto Rican Studies Department. This is the highest intellectual and academic position any black man could aspire to in America.

Dr. Clarke wrote many books, some he edited. He was a poet in his own right, whose first book, back in the day, painted Jesus Black! Then he moved to Harlem during the Depression years from which time is where he lived and died. Dr. ben-Jochannan often reminisced when he and John Clarke were running the streets as young intellectuals and they would stand outside the building of their

FREDERICK MONDERSON

lecture hall and pay people 25 cents to come inside to listen to their lectures! From that first book of poetry, *Rebellion in Rhyme*, Dr. Clarke also wrote *Harlem: A Community in Transition, The Slave Trade and Slavery, My Life in Search of Africa, Who's Betraying the African Revolution* and co-authored with Dr. ben-Jochannan, *New Dimensions in African History* and several others. A sought after lecturer, even after he lost his sight, Dr. Clarke reminded, books were being written even as he spoke.

Black Nationalism 365. Supreme Court Judge Thurgood Marshall (left); and lawyer, scholar, activist Paul Robeson (right).

On a personal note, I was in Egypt with Dr. Clarke and Dr. Ben in 1990 along with Dr. Leonard Monroe and others from Michigan. Dr. Clarke lectured at Aswan and the group visited the Tomb of Seti I in the Valley of the Kings at Luxor. In the "well" beside the sarcophagus, we stayed longer than most and this annoyed the some three thousand visitors who could not enter the tomb through the narrow passageway and so sweltered in the hot sun outside. When we got to Cairo and prepared to return, Dr. Monroe instructed I stay with Dr. Clarke, Sister Sybil Williams Clarke was on the trip, and escort him on board when everyone else was settled. As the plane

BLACK NATIONALISM ALIVE AND WELL

took off it bust a tire and developed hydraulic trouble and fell back on the runway and we had an aborted takeoff as I sat near Dr. Clarke. It was not our time then! Otherwise we would all have been ancestors and I walking beside the intellectual giant!

Black Nationalism 366. "Old Boys High School" in Bed-Stuy, Brooklyn.

Black Nationalism 367. "We the People" (left); and "How would you want to be remembered?" (right).

FREDERICK MONDERSON

Next Ras Baraka, who is running for mayor of in the city of Newark, New Jersey began by saying, "It is always a pleasure to be in New York. Dr. Clarke had early said 'Free your African mind' and "The worse strategy" our oppressors used "was not only to colonize us but they colonized information. These people controlled our thinking, progress, struggle, development. They made us worship them." He believed, "To kill a black boy is not a crime. Our job as leaders is to uphold our lives." He insisted, "We must develop a system that would help us protect ourselves. We must train our own lawyers, judges, doctors, teachers. This is the only way, to make sure we survive in a system designed for our destruction."

Manuel Gilyard, President of the Malcolm X Commemoration Committee in Harlem at 800 Riverside Drive demonstrated how many hats he wore and that, "We're all political prisoners from the time we were taken from the continent!"

Black Nationalism 368. Former Congresswoman Shirley Chisholm (on yellow horse) leads a woman's charge as a "catalyst for change!"

Reverend Herbert Oliver at 88 years young, pointed out, "Dr. Clarke was an immaculate and supreme scholar." Then he spoke of the

BLACK NATIONALISM ALIVE AND WELL

power of the economic boycott in the city of Birmingham that was nicknamed "Bombingham," where he was born and grew up. He said, Birmingham "Died as a shopping mall town" because of the economic boycott. He advised, "Stay out of downtown Brooklyn. Start something to redeem our young people. Mothers let them stand up as men and mothers stay out of downtown Brooklyn."

Sister Yaa Asantewaa, insisting on Black Power! Said, "We must fast from consumerism. Withhold our dollars. I'm not pointing a finger at White people; I'm looking in the mirror."
+
Revolutionary progressivism is what Omowale Clay is all about. He believed, "It is important to honor our history. None can be more honored than Dr. Clarke. Sekou Sundiata and Amiri Baraka believed this." In the making of the movie **Malcolm X** Dr. Clarke made the Director realize, "Malcolm X is not a Spike Lee joint. Dr. Clarke sat Spike Lee down and pulled his coat. Dr. Clarke was someone who not only taught history but how to live history." His autobiography, *A Long and Mighty Walk*, was filmed by Wesley Snipes and should be seen by all."

A sister representing Political Prisoners Defense Committee reminded all, "We are people who never forget. Failure is not an option. Denmark Vesey, Nat Turner, Malcolm X, Sekou Odinga, my husband, was and all are freedom fighters. Until all of us are free, none of us are free!"

Regent Emeriti Adelaide Sanford, who as principal took a school that was at the bottom of the reading list and moved it to the top of the reading chart, was associated with schools from Brooklyn College to Wellesley. She began by addressing the gathering as "Beloved because you are not taught often that you are beloved. The first people, as parents of the universe, you are beloved. Feel it! Believe it! Embrace it! Dr. Clarke was a transformational person. You must understand your intrinsic worth!" She recommended his book, *My Life in Search of Africa* as worthy reading. The she

FREDERICK MONDERSON

addressed the Trayvon verdict, what she called the *Trayvon Phenomenon*.

Black Nationalism 369. Two beautiful and powerful freedom fighters, Myrlie Evers and Coretta Scott King, wives of Medgar Evers and Dr. Martin Luther King.

In this, Dr. Sanford explained, "Dr. Clarke would not be surprised by the verdict. Disappointed but not surprised. We are judged by people who know nothing about us. The world they live in is simultaneously demeaning them." She then addressed how the Burning of the Mortgage" at Clarke house came about. Dr. Clarke often said, "Buy more houses. Don't sell. Buy property. Build factories. Make the things we use. Build a paper factory. Build our economic base. We often said, 'No Justice, No Peace.' Now we only say Peace. Justice has been lost." We must, "create some industry that supplies the needs of our people." Next Dr. Sandford reminded the audience, "You are beautiful. Until we get involved in those systems that define us, we will have problems. The totality of our issues demands action. The Trayvon Phenomenon is an American Phenomenon. We have not taught them we are one people."

BLACK NATIONALISM
ALIVE AND WELL

Again Dr. Sanford reminded the gathering, "Beloved, precious, special, exceptional, resilient, you are beloved!"

Black Nationalism 370. Young people facing choices, "Piece or Peace!"

Black Nationalism 371. Showing Respect for our Community!

FREDERICK MONDERSON

Black Nationalism 372. Congressman Major Owens greeting young people whom he has often expressed great confidence in.

48. MAJOR OWENS: A Reflection
By
Dr. Fred Monderson

Reverend Clarence Norman, Sr., of **First Baptist Church of Crown Heights** in Brooklyn, began the beginning of the end of the service '**Celebration of Life for Hon. Major R. Owens**,' with a familiar verse "It is well with my soul," and that, "Once again we stand on the shore and watch a ship sail" into the mist of the future. This time, however, those in attendance came "to celebrate the life, times and contributions of Major Owens" and to "comfort his family." Telling the family, "God will take care of you," Rev. Norman called Major a "quiet, gentle person who was effective, dynamic and changed the life of so many." In fact, the Congressman was "a servant of god, who was called home, but he will always live" in the hearts, minds and motifs of the people.

Not many people have had the indubitable distinction of having a US Congressman in their living room to discuss the dynamics of a local library, as I did. But then again, not only was Major Odell Owens a

BLACK NATIONALISM ALIVE AND WELL

man of the people, but the only librarian ever elected to the US Congress! As a journalist I covered several Town Hall meetings Mr. Owens held at PS 167 on Eastern Parkway during the Giuliani years. These were in Major's efforts to create economic and political empowerment for his constituency. At an event regarding Panamanian politics and international peace, hosted by Dr. Waldaba Steward at the Eastern Parkway and Bedford Avenue venue, with Carlos Russell in attendance, Congressman Owens discussed the utility of the Congressional Black Caucus by saying, "People often question why we're there. It is not so much the legislation we sponsor, but those we block. So much frivolous legislation is introduced onto the floor of the US House of Congress, if we are not there to block such, it would be disastrous for black and poor people." Nevertheless, while Major was a tireless champion of Civil Rights and an advocate for funding of Black Colleges, his singular legislative accomplishment was the **Americans with Disabilities Act**, of which beneficiaries Agnes Abraham, Peter Jones and Dorothy Williams-Pereira were there to say thank you and sing praises to a remarkable man.

Black Nationalism 373. Albert Vann (left); and Major Owens (right); receiving awards.

FREDERICK MONDERSON

In his **Prayer of Comfort**, Reverend Daryl Bloodsaw said "Major Owens understood the power of words. He was a champion of education who bore the scars of battle of long campaigns against worthy opponents." An admirer of Rosa Parks, Martin Luther King, Jr., Mahatma Gandhi and Mother Theresa, and as an Adjunct Professor at Medgar Evers College, he inspired the youth. In fact, he wrote poems extolling the virtues of young people. His oldest brother, Ezekiel, Jr., described him, "On the floor of the House of Representatives he was 'the little man from Brooklyn,'" this "Rapping Congressman," who "Was ready to put on his long white robes."

Black Nationalism 373a. Major Owens is surrounded by Senator Velmanette Montgomery (left); and Sonny Carson to explain why the Congressional Hearings were needed because of the rampant police killings in New York, with no accountability and no recourse for the community.

Dr. Rudy Crew, former Chancellor of the New York City Board of Education and now President of Medgar Evers College, spoke of the many people whose lives have been touched by this man. His story at Medgar was "one of truth, justice and honor." He said they met in 1995 when Rudy Crew was Chancellor of the New York City School

BLACK NATIONALISM
ALIVE AND WELL

System. Then they had a conversation about the Mayor! Major said, "'Son you're new, be careful. If you're grounded you'll be all right. Stay strong.'" "After all the hoopla and accolades, I was fired in 2000 and on my way out of town I met major who said, "I read there's a problem. Don't worry. Time will come." He was "very gracious, very kind, very spiritual." His very "kindness, strength, character made sense to me." He reassured me, 'Don't worry son, you'll be alright.' In 2008, he became an Adjunct Professor at Medgar Evers College and was loved and revered by students and faculty alike. "He had so much pride in himself. In July 2013 I became President of Medgar Evers College.

Black Nationalism 374. A Tuskegee Airman in a boastful moment!

In an auditorium appearance he looked into the audience and saw a man who liked like his father. It was Major Owens. Then he looked into the faces of Major's children and said, "Your daddy looked just like my father. I felt so much better. It's Ok now. Not because I'm here but because he was here." Major told him, 'This is a good school. This is a good place. This is a good, earnest place. Just do right!' He later said, 'Stay strong, don't worry, I'm here. Do right!'

FREDERICK MONDERSON

Then Dr. Crew, turned to the Owens family and confessed, "We're better in our lives because your daddy did right."

Black Nationalism 375. Harriet Tubman as her image is preserved in the Museum of African American History in Washington, DC.

Councilman Albert Vann, began by asking for a standing roll-call of those who came to pay tribute to Major, in which in a crowded church 6 Congressmen, 9 City Council persons, 9 State officials, 7 Citywide persons, the Brooklyn County Leader, 20 Clergy members and even Carl McCall, all stood up. They came to commemorate the life and work of a former State Senator and Commissioner of Community Development Agency after serving as Bronxville Community Development Executive Director.

First, the Councilman admitted, "This is a humbling experience. Dying is a humbling experience. Honorable Major Owens, May peace be upon him!" The Councilman further explained, "Those who knew or knew of Major Owens respected him. He was an extraordinary, intelligent man who demanded respect and got respect." Second, speaking of Major, he stated "He had an

BLACK NATIONALISM ALIVE AND WELL

unbelievable work ethic. He had endless, boundless energy dedicated to seeking solutions of community problems. Multi-talented, he was a thinker, writer, community organizer." He was also a poet. Third, major Owens was a man of integrity who maintained a high standard of moral authority. Fourth, he chose to identify with the masses and empower the poor through economic and political empowerment initiatives, particularly through his anti-poverty programs. Fifth, Medgar Evers students were blessed to have Major Owens. The foundations of Medgar Evers were made stronger because of Major Owens." Finally, he admonished, "Take your seat dear brother, your job was well done."

Black Nationalism 376. Congressman Major Owens (left); in a joyous mood and about to introduce the architect of "The Algebra Project," Robert Moses (right).

Next, the Civil Rights icon Congressman John Lewis, affirming, "You can tell a Morehouse man, but you can't tell him much," and insisting we "Never forget God is good," quoted the Roman philosopher and Senator Seneca, who said, "Nothing but nothing stops a good man doing what is good and honorable." He likened such to the efforts of Major Owens, who, like himself, served the nation and the world."

FREDERICK MONDERSON

Finally, quoting **Acts** 13: 36 Reverend Norman believed Major Owens came or was born for a specific purpose. He said, "When a man has completed his work, god calls him home! Only the other day we announced the Congressman has passed. Immediately people began asking 'How did he die?' The Reverend iterated, "We should not ask how he died, but how he lived!" He was a dedicated servant of god. A man of the people. We're here to leave this world better than we found it. Ours must be a life of service, to be concerned about people." One aspect of this dedication is the founding of the Martin Luther King Jr. Commission emphasizing and encouraging young people to "Strive for Excellence."

Black Nationalism 377. Two beautiful stalwarts for the cause!

Reverend Norman praised Major Owens as one "who stood up, he never forgot the poor." He believed, 'Education is a great equalizer.' "He was a decent, kind, compassionate, honest, wise, respectful individual with a sharp mind." The Reverend confessed, "I feel more than lucky. I feel blessed to have Major Owens as a friend." The Congressman consistently insisted, 'to bring change people should be bold, be courageous, find a way to make some noise. Don't get lost in a sea of despair.'

BLACK NATIONALISM ALIVE AND WELL

All were in agreement, this Congressional Warrior for Justice should, "Sleep, sleep well, take your seat. We'll see you in the morning. May God bless you! It is well with my soul!"

Black Nationalism 378. Close-up of the architect of "The Algebra Project," Robert Moses

49. SURPRISE: THEY'RE DISRESPECTING THE PRESIDENT
By
Dr. Fred Monderson

The President's team described Republican behavior in the shut-down and debt-ceiling fiasco as those of "extremists," "terrorists." All of a sudden, in response, these "big boys" began crying the President was playing foul! Remember when tough guys would enter a bar and order a "Double Scotch on the Rocks." Today, they say, "Can I have a water, please!"

The **Oxford American dictionary** defines Extremist as "A person who holds extreme or fanatical political or religious views."

FREDERICK MONDERSON

The **Oxford American Dictionary** also defines terrorist as "A person who uses or favors violent and intimidating methods of coercing a government or community."

The New York Times article of October 6, 2013, which is turning out to be the clearest conduit into the Anti-Obamites minds-eye view and working has enlightened us to their "By Any Means Necessary" modus operandi. This "Bull-in-A-China-shop" recklessness has led the nation down a strategy that "could not, would not and did not work," according to the Senate Republican leader Mitch McConnell. It is generally acknowledged leaders set examples and standards their followers or members must adhere to or are called to answer. After all, from day one, McConnell, DeMint and many others have admirably demonstrated the most toxic attitude and behavior toward Mr. Obama. So, it is not surprising Republican rank and file have worn well their coat of disrespect as it relates to challenges to the President of the United States whom the American people have unanimously chosen twice to represent them.

The fundamental reason why the "Tea Party Tail" wags the "Republican Dog" is because that movement was born out of a cauldron of racial hatred fed and perpetrated by a conservative heritage and legacy falsely believing in the inequality of man dictated by skin color. The story is told of a "White Guy who married a Black woman." All his friends got on his case, asking "Why did you marry this Black Woman?" He simply replied, because "Black don't crack!"

BLACK NATIONALISM
ALIVE AND WELL

Black Nationalism 379. Erik Monderson with camera on the Capital Building grounds.

The fact is, none in Republican leadership had the gumption to say, "Sure we are ideologically and politically opposed to the President and his political party, but our efforts must still be bolstered by high moral and ethical standards" That is to say, for example, while we may dislike Mr. Obama for whatever reason, we respect the office he holds and *ipso facto*, we respect him. Comparatively speaking, it's like we tell our citizens, respect the police officer's uniform more so than the man! I'm not saying don't respect the man! We respect and give way to an emergency vehicle's flashing light or the siren of an ambulance whether we know there is a patient within. Unfortunately this civility is alien to Republican behavior towards President Obama.

FREDERICK MONDERSON

Black Nationalism 380. The "Mountain of Despair" from which Dr. Martin Luther King's "Stone of Hope" has been hewn.

Perhaps a more global example may suffice. At the height of the French Revolution, when the movement had turned against itself, the Englishman Edmund Burke in his book *Reflections on the Revolution in France* (1792) wrote, "The only thing necessary for evil to triumph is for good men to say nothing." Thus, as the "Tea Party Movement's" tail began to grow towards initially wagging the Republican dog, their leaders of substance turned a "blind eye and ear" to this behavior. In the movie **Matrix**, when one of the main actors or characters Neo finally reached "Machine City" and "faced the face," he boldly stated, "The program Smith has grown out of control and you can't stop him. Only my efforts can do so!"

It is so with the conundrum facing the Republican Party's mantle, the Tea Party members have lashed out left and right and are now threatening their own members, its leadership and rank and file, who no longer dance to their music. Well, if they could unleash such "friendly fire," imagine the enmity they have consistently spewed towards President Obama. Of course, good Americans have said we will not accept this disrespect of our President and the office he holds. However, in the highly unlikely probability that "Tea Partiers"

BLACK NATIONALISM ALIVE AND WELL

succeed to the Presidency, having sullied the office, so much, one wonders do they have any shame left and how will they clean the shamefully stained environment.

1.   A commentator recently said after Congressman Joe Wilson told the President "You lie" during the State of the Union Address in the House Chamber, he raised one million dollars donation the next day. Naturally when called to the mat for this disrespect of the President, Mr. Joe Wilson wanted to meet personally with Mr. Obama to deliver his apology. Who knows if he wanted to further insult the President to his face? Mr. Obama said, "No, send the apology in the mail." Even more important even though Mr. Wilson was "sorry" in all probability he did not return the million dollars in contributions.

2.   Coming out as a shiny new penny, as she did in the 2008 Presidential Campaign, Sarah Palin was very visible in the first wave of Tea Partiers whose vile criticism of Mr. Obama was cause for astonishment. Today, the time has toll for this faded political glory who sought to be a factor in New Jersey's recent Special Election to fill Senator Lautenberg's vacant seat. The result is history.

3.   A study in contrast pits youth and age. On the one hand, Megan McCain has repeatedly said, "I like President Obama. I'm praying for him" to succeed! On the other hand, in the initial Health Care Reform brough-ha-ha, former South Carolina Senator Jim DeMint, had said on CNN, "I like the President but he has faulty numbers. If we stop him, it will be his Waterloo." Well, he didn't and so left the Senate to head the Heritage Foundation. Under his leadership this organization was mentioned among the treasonous conspirators after the 2012 election of President Obama. In all probability, the team of recycled actors and organizations mentioned in the article were also at work after the 2008 election. Given Senator DeMint's Health Care backlash of the President, it is inconceivable to divorce him from his associate Senate Minority Leader and highest ranking Republican McConnell who made this

FREDERICK MONDERSON

blatantly racist, "I intend to make Barak Obama a one-term president" statement. In many respects both senators who failed in their quest more than likely can be numbered among the 2008 treasonous conspirators from whence they received their marching orders.

Black Nationalism 381. Dr. King's "Stone of Hope" hewn from the "Mountain of Despair."

4. It is interesting that Donald Trump did not "fire" the "Birther Queen" who led him on the humiliating "fool's errand." Then again, as a "circus crier" Mr. Trump as an entertainer relished in noise making fanfare but knows the House does not always win! His most disrespectful feat, having failed the Birth Certificate test, he asked to see the President's school transcript. How low can you go! It is thus fitting for citizens to ask to see Mr. Trump's birth certificate and school transcript.

These are just a few samples of persons disrespecting the President of the United States. Some have argued this demeaning behavior is because Mr. Obama is Black!

BLACK NATIONALISM ALIVE AND WELL

Black Nationalism 382. A small shrine of farewell prepared for Nelson Mandela outside the Apollo Theater in Harlem.

Madiba Nelson Mandela, "The Scarlet Pimpernel!"

50. PRESIDENT OBAMA'S MANDELA ADDRESS – A TRIBUTE

To Graça Machel and the Mandela family; to President Zuma and members of the government; to heads of state and government, past and present; distinguished guests - it is a singular honor to be with you today, to celebrate a life unlike any other. To the people of South Africa - people of every race and walk of life - the world

FREDERICK MONDERSON

thanks you for sharing Nelson Mandela with us. His struggle was your struggle. His triumph was your triumph. Your dignity and hope found expression in his life, and your freedom, your democracy is his cherished legacy.

It is hard to eulogize any man - to capture in words not just the facts and the dates that make a life, but the essential truth of a person - their private joys and sorrows; the quiet moments and unique qualities that illuminate someone's soul. How much harder to do so for a giant of history, who moved a nation toward justice, and in the process moved billions around the world.

Black Nationalism 383. What shall it be, "Peace, Respect, Love or Guns?"

BLACK NATIONALISM ALIVE AND WELL

Black Nationalism 384. Dorothy Height, President of the **National Council of Negro Women**, in full and regal splendor.

Born during World War I, far from the corridors of power, a boy raised herding cattle and tutored by elders of his Thembu tribe - Madiba would emerge as the last great liberator of the 20th Century. Like Gandhi, he would lead a resistance movement - a movement

FREDERICK MONDERSON

that at its start held little prospect of success. Like King, he would give potent voice to the claims of the oppressed, and the moral necessity of racial justice. He would endure a brutal imprisonment that began in the time of Kennedy and Khrushchev, and reached the final days of the Cold War. Emerging from prison, without force of arms, he would - like Lincoln - hold his country together when it threatened to break apart. Like America's founding fathers, he would erect a constitutional order to preserve freedom for future generations - a commitment to democracy and rule of law ratified not only by his election, but by his willingness to step down from power.

Given the sweep of his life, and the adoration that he so rightly earned, it is tempting then to remember Nelson Mandela as an icon, smiling and serene, detached from the tawdry affairs of lesser men. But Madiba himself strongly resisted such a lifeless portrait. Instead, he insisted on sharing with us his doubts and fears; his miscalculations along with his victories. "I'm not a saint," he said, "unless you think of a saint as a sinner who keeps on trying."

It was precisely because he could admit to imperfection - because he could be so full of good humor, even mischief, despite the heavy burdens he carried - that we loved him so. He was not a bust made of marble; he was a man of flesh and blood - a son and husband, a father and a friend. That is why we learned so much from him; that is why we can learn from him still. For nothing he achieved was inevitable. In the arc of his life, we see a man who earned his place in history through struggle and shrewdness; persistence and faith. He tells us what's possible not just in the pages of dusty history books, but in our own lives as well.

Mandela showed us the power of action; of taking risks on behalf of our ideals. Perhaps Madiba was right that he inherited, "a proud rebelliousness, a stubborn sense of fairness" from his father. Certainly he shared with millions of black and colored South Africans the anger born of, "a thousand slights, a thousand indignities, a thousand unremembered moments ... a desire to fight the system that imprisoned my people."

BLACK NATIONALISM ALIVE AND WELL

Black Nationalism 385. Personal expression of sympathy beside the small shrine erected to pay tribute to Nelson Mandela outside the Apollo Theater in Harlem.

But like other early giants of the **ANC** - the Sisulus and Tambos - Madiba disciplined his anger; and channeled his desire to fight into organization, and platforms, and strategies for action, so men and women could stand-up for their dignity. Moreover, he accepted the consequences of his actions, knowing that standing up to powerful interests and injustice carries a price. "I have fought against white domination and I have fought against black domination," he said at his 1964 trial. "I've cherished the ideal of a democratic and free society in which all persons live together in harmony and with equal opportunities. It is an ideal which I hope to live for and to achieve. But if needs be, it is an ideal for which I am prepared to die."

FREDERICK MONDERSON

Black Nationalism 386. Rosa Parks, "Queen of Civil Rights Protest," in a pensive mood.

Mandela demonstrated that action and ideas are not enough; no matter how right, they must be chiseled into laws and institutions. He was practical, testing his beliefs against the hard surface of circumstance and history. On core principles he was unyielding, which is why he could rebuff offers of conditional release, reminding the Apartheid regime that, "prisoners cannot enter into contracts." But as he showed in painstaking negotiations to transfer power and draft new laws, he was not afraid to compromise for the sake of a larger goal. And because he was not only a leader of a movement, but a skillful politician, the Constitution that emerged

BLACK NATIONALISM
ALIVE AND WELL

was worthy of this multiracial democracy; true to his vision of laws that protect minority as well as majority rights, and the precious freedoms of every South African.

Black Nationalism 387. The "First Black Boro President of Brooklyn," Abdul Hafiz, formerly Minister Kevin Mohammed.

Finally, Mandela understood the ties that bind the human spirit. There is a word in South Africa- Ubuntu - that describes his greatest gift: his recognition that we are all bound together in ways that can be invisible to the eye; that there is a oneness to humanity; that we achieve ourselves by sharing ourselves with others, and caring for those around us. We can never know how much of this was innate in him, or how much of was shaped and burnished in a dark, solitary cell. But we remember the gestures, large and small - introducing his jailors as honored guests at his inauguration; taking the pitch in a Springbok uniform; turning his family's heartbreak into a call to confront HIV/AIDS - that revealed the depth of his empathy and understanding. He not only embodied Ubuntu; he taught millions to find that truth within themselves. It took a man like Madiba to free not just the prisoner, but the jailor as well; to show that you must trust others so that they may trust you; to teach that reconciliation is not a matter of ignoring a cruel past, but a means of confronting it

FREDERICK MONDERSON

with inclusion, generosity and truth. He changed laws, but also hearts.

Mandela showed us the power of action; of taking risks on behalf of our ideals. Perhaps Madiba was right that he inherited, "a proud rebelliousness, a stubborn sense of fairness" from his father. Certainly he shared with millions of black and colored South Africans the anger born of, "a thousand slights, a thousand indignities, a thousand unremembered moments…a desire to fight the system that imprisoned my people."

Black Nationalism 388. Grandma and the Youth. We must talk to them.

But like other early giants of the ANC - the Sisulus and Tambos - Madiba disciplined his anger; and channeled his desire to fight into organization, and platforms, and strategies for action, so men and women could stand-up for their dignity. Moreover, he accepted the consequences of his actions, knowing that standing up to powerful interests and injustice carries a price. "I have fought against white domination and I have fought against black domination," he said at his 1964 trial. "I've cherished the ideal of a democratic and free society in which all persons live together in harmony and with equal

BLACK NATIONALISM
ALIVE AND WELL

opportunities. It is an ideal which I hope to live for and to achieve. But if needs be, it is an ideal for which I am prepared to die."

Mandela taught us the power of action, but also ideas; the importance of reason and arguments; the need to study not only those you agree with, but those who you don't. He understood that ideas cannot be contained by prison walls, or extinguished by a sniper's bullet. He turned his trial into an indictment of apartheid because of his eloquence and passion, but also his training as an advocate. He used decades in prison to sharpen his arguments, but also to spread his thirst for knowledge to others in the movement. And he learned the language and customs of his oppressor so that one day he might better convey to them how their own freedom depended upon his.

Mandela demonstrated that action and ideas are not enough; no matter how right, they must be chiseled into laws and institutions. He was practical, testing his beliefs against the hard surface of circumstance and history. On core principles he was unyielding, which is why he could rebuff offers of conditional release, reminding the Apartheid regime that, "prisoners cannot enter into contracts." But as he showed in painstaking negotiations to transfer power and draft new laws, he was not afraid to compromise for the sake of a larger goal. And because he was not only a leader of a movement, but a skillful politician, the Constitution that emerged was worthy of this multiracial democracy; true to his vision of laws that protect minority as well as majority rights, and the precious freedoms of every South African.

FREDERICK MONDERSON

Black Nationalism 389. "The Iron Pipeline" that is killing our young!

Finally, Mandela understood the ties that bind the human spirit. There is a word in South Africa - Ubuntu - that describes his greatest gift: his recognition that we are all bound together in ways that can be invisible to the eye; that there is a oneness to humanity; that we achieve ourselves by sharing ourselves with others, and caring for those around us. We can never know how much of this was innate in him, or how much of was shaped and burnished in a dark, solitary cell. But we remember the gestures, large and small - introducing his jailors as honored guests at his inauguration; taking the pitch in a Springbok uniform; turning his family's heartbreak into a call to confront HIV/AIDS - that revealed the depth of his empathy and understanding. He not only embodied Ubuntu; he taught millions to find that truth within themselves. It took a man like Madiba to free not just the prisoner, but the jailor as well; to show that you must trust others so that they may trust you; to teach that reconciliation is not a matter of ignoring a cruel past, but a means of confronting it with inclusion, generosity and truth. He changed laws, but also hearts.

BLACK NATIONALISM ALIVE AND WELL

51.   "SOUTHERN SHERIFFS"

BY
DR. FRED MONDERSON

Whether it was Rod Steiger or Archie Bunker who played Sheriff Gillespie as the lawman in the movie *In the Heat of the Night*, the Black detective had to enlighten him about the intricacies and perspectives of coming to correct conclusions regarding police work. This time two contemporary sheriffs from South Carolina and Georgia are in the news not simply for exceptional performance of their jobs but for statements that many consider controversial with other implications. There is another sheriff from Arizona, who earlier also came under scrutiny because of statements and the degree with which he executed his responsibilities as they relate to immigration and whether persons were legal residents or not. However, this latter official is not the focus of this essay; his case has been known, scrutinized and settled, sort of.

The South Carolina Sheriff recently questioned President Obama ordering the American flag lowered in honor of the passing of Nelson Mandela, one of the great leaders of the 20th Century. It is interesting, at the memorial Service in South Africa in which President Obama and First Lady Michelle Obama represented this nation, he was accompanied by an American star power delegation including Presidents Jimmy Carter, William "Bill" Clinton, and George W. Bush. First Ladies Rosalind, Hillary and Laura respectively, accompanied their husband. Chelsea Clinton was also in attendance accompanying her parents. Mr. Mandela's wife Graca Machel and his former wife Winnie Madikizela-Mandela were there for their man.

FREDERICK MONDERSON

Black Nationalism 390. Gun Shows require No ID to purchase firearms.

Nearly 100 world leaders, active and retired, came to pay their respect to a man whose life was like no other; a unique figure in history; who inspired the world through political and personal forgiveness. Released from prison in 1990 he succeeded F.W. De Klerk who headed the white racist government, becoming the nation's first Black president four years later. Calling for reconciliation, he effectuated the power of unification in a land torn apart by the crimes of apartheid and standing on the precipice of a destructive race war. In anticipation of this gathering and the solemn nature of the occasion, the President's action was prudent policy.

The other Sheriff from Valdosta, Georgia, pronounced the death of a very athletically active teen-ager, Kendrick Johnson ("KJ"), as a tragic accident claiming the young man climbed into an enormous rolled up floor mat in the gymnasium of his school. There, searching for his shoe, he ostensibly suffocated. An autopsy was performed and the family notified about the cause of death. Not satisfied with "the official version," for nearly a year, six days per week, the family staged a demonstration outside a local courthouse, bringing attention to the case and demanding more satisfactory answers. Finally attention focused on their plight and a new interest ensued in efforts to get to the bottom of things.

Listening to the "Steve Harvey Morning Show" in New York on December 10, 2013, an attorney for the family; a Mr. Crum who was

BLACK NATIONALISM
ALIVE AND WELL

the Trayvon Martin family attorney in that tragedy; informed on some troubling developments in the Johnson case. Mr. Crum explained High School gymnasium area was under video coverage and in several angles the view was crystal clear where Mr. Johnson was clearly identified taking part in gym activities. However, the video covering that part of the gym where the potential "foul play" may have happened, where Mr. Johnson supposedly climbed into the rolled-up mat to retrieve his sneakers, that part of the film is very cloudy, essentially unidentifiable, useless. More important, however, when the family rejected the official report on cause of death and insisted on a more detailed report on the examination of the body, it turned out there was traces of blood, whose ownership the attorney did not specify. Additionally, examination exhumed body revealed the internal organs of Mr. Johnson were missing and his insides was stuffed with newspapers. Even more significant, Mr. Johnson's nails at the fingertips were all cut deep as if to remove all traces, potentially, of blood ostensibly indicating perhaps there was a struggle, he scratched someone and blood remained. Cutting off the fingertips was designed to get rid of potential DNA evidence.

Black Nationalism 391. City Councilwoman and now State Assemblywoman, Annette Robinson (right) receives an award.

FREDERICK MONDERSON

Now, we know in the case of suspicious death and not from natural causes, law-enforcement conducts extensive investigations to determine the true cause or death. In the case of this very healthy teenager who played baseball, football and basketball, it stands to reason he did not die of natural causes! Given that law enforcement investigates and the now coming to light revelations regarding Mr. Johnson's end, it challenges the Sheriff's firm declaration as to the actual cause of death. It raises a question as to why he never became suspicious given the now revealed facts of the case; thus, one would wonder whether he is willing to stake his career on his official cause of death declaration? Is there a cover-up? Was the Sheriff ever suspicious of events? In this day and age, how could he believe the family would accept that coca mammy story? How did he determine the kid crawled up into the folded-up mat? Again, given that law enforcement investigates, did the Sheriff put two and two together to arrive at 300? Does this sloppiness call into question other "causes of death" officials reports of his office? All this forces us to wonder about the behaviors of Southern Sheriffs and others whose behaviors can certainly use some scrutiny.

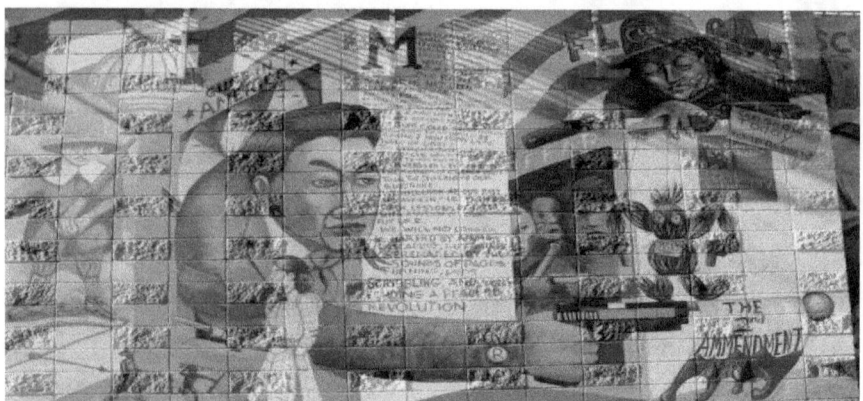

Black Nationalism 392. Forked tongues of the Devil and much more.

Well, in terms of the South Carolina Sheriff who questioned the President of the United States' decision to fly the Stars and Stripes at half-mast, did he know the US has done so since 1957 for world leaders? Does this "porgy" trying to swim in "whale waters" realize

BLACK NATIONALISM
ALIVE AND WELL

such pronouncements are above his "pay grade?" Given such, is his pronouncement that the flag should only be flown at half-mast for Americans is actually an anti-Obama statement. Also, given South Carolina's history as home of the virulent anti-Obama former Senator DeMint; uncensored "You lie" Congressman Joe Wilson; and as Jessie Jackson exclaimed a few years ago, "South Carolina has 36 state prisons and 1 state college." In a stretch of the imagination, the Sheriff could easily fit in this "cabal."

These associations, notwithstanding, the Sheriff is so wrong! The United States lowered the flag for Winston Churchill, Pope Paul II and several other deserving world leaders. The interesting this is, President Obama is a very intelligent visionary whose every action, decision has been questioned, challenged, some say even sabotaged by persons acting in a "treasonous" manner and all because the President is a Black man; all a part of the virulent Republican opposition designed to make his administration a failure. After all, Republican Senator Mitch McConnell expressly stated his goal "to make Barack Obama a one term President." However, unable to prevent the President's re-election in 2012, Mr. McConnell never renounced his goal and *The New York Times* of October 6, 2013 expressly maintained and named individuals who met and planned to sabotage the President's every legislative and otherwise action on behalf of the American people! While this occurred after the 2012 election, every reason suggests the plot was instituted after the 2008 election and all the principal players remained involved and were named in the later revelation.

Fast forward to the sorrowful passing of the South African leader and statesman and recognizing the personal strength of Mr. Mandela, as his health began to decline; President Obama instituted plans for a high level American delegation to attend the funeral. This show of American Presidential star power consistent with lowering the flag was not simply above the South Carolina Sheriff's intellectual comprehension and pay grade, but as a stroke of genius the President put America on the right side of history recognizing and tributing as

FREDERICK MONDERSON

he called Mr. Mandela, "the last great liberator of the 20th Century." Here then was a man who "earned his place in history through struggle."

Black Nationalism 393. Attorney and Black Panther freedom fighter Malik Zulu Shabazz holds *The New Black Panther* newspaper announcing the "Million Man March Strikes Black!!!"

After the enormous suffering of South Africans for much of the 20th Century; Mr. Mandela's trials and tribulations; his lengthy prison incarceration until global activism in its many ramifications forced the racist South African government to free this long-serving prisoner. Upon is release he held no recriminations, urged his people to peacefully accept the transfer of power and exercise the long-sought after franchise. To set the record straight he established a Truth and Reconciliation Commission under the leadership of Bishop Desmond Tutu and the Afrikaner Reverend Byers Naude, a long time critic of Apartheid.

BLACK NATIONALISM ALIVE AND WELL

Black Nationalism 394. The role of Grandparents is crucial in influencing young people and being there for them.

Black Nationalism 395. Brooklyn Pride involves Community and is courageous, full of respect, truly full of family love, honor, honesty and relishes in culture.

When all is said and done, Mr. Obama has always provided excellent leadership despite the enormous efforts expended to sabotage his presidency. Mr. Obama always led in the best interest of the American people and nation. History has always been the best judge of leaders and their tenures, and as it has judged Mr. Mandela, so too it will judge Mr. Obama and the Southern Sheriffs, those mentioned here and others whose performance will ultimately become public record.

FREDERICK MONDERSON

52. MR. MANDELA'S LONG WALK
By
Dr. Fred Monderson

When Jesus hung on the cross it was reported, one of the Centurions uttered, "What manner of man is this?" When activist Sonny Carson died, this writer called a friend to inform him of such and he replied, "Sonny Carson dead, God help us!" When Nelson Mandela passed on to his historical and heavenly glory, the world felt its moral compass shift and the terrain below its feet shutter. Whether the parallels may be appropriate or not; the life, times and passing of "Maida" Nelson Mandela are like a dashing comet plunging into the deep abyss of the universe, never to be seen again in many lifetimes. But this personal experience is part of the reason the world mourns the loss of this man of courage, endurance, resilience while also possessing unifying, ethical, moral and philosophic rectitude embodied in a bright mind, a gentle soul, a universal champion of freedom, humility and equality. Even more astonishing, this preacher of reconciliation was blest with a funny side that in totality makes him tremendously human though many think him divine. Having ascended the world stage as a great ambassador of South Africa, his principal aspirations achieved, this towering figure of world history, like Cincinnatus, he stepped down from power after a single term as President.

Black Nationalism 397. Good advice: "Never Give Up on Yourself."

BLACK NATIONALISM ALIVE AND WELL

Black Nationalism 396. Nelson Mandela as he exits the plane on his first visit to the United States invited by David Dinkins, Mayor of New York City, where his first stop was Brooklyn, Fulton Street, Boys and Girls High School, which will be renamed in his honor!

When the "Powers" of this world show their true selves in their magnanimous tributes to Mr. Mandela, this giant of history, it says much of the man, his tenacity, ability to stand as a pillar for his principles and the tremendous influence he has and will continue to exert on many over the past and decades to come. He is without question the embodiment of one man becoming a majority because he stood for and laid it all down for principles of his ideal, universal franchise of one man, one vote! Recognizing the "moral necessity of racial justice" in his beloved land, he sought and achieved the abolition of the vicious system of Apartheid. Now the world, even

FREDERICK MONDERSON

his enemies have come around to recognize he was right from inception and his lack of recrimination, reconciling black and white, inspired untold millions around the globe, and especially those at home.

While the word enemy is a harsh term, it also embodies the state of an unalterable opposition evolved from the arrogance of an imperial onslaught that manufactured the intractable and challenging reality of racism and discrimination molded in the false belief that some persons are of an inferior/superior nature because of the color of their skin. This falsity has failed to recognize that Osiris was Black! Jesus was Black! Isaiah and Jeremiah were Black and many other religious and spiritual minds and souls who enlightened humanity were also Black. It's acknowledged, no one race is responsible for the total progress of this world, and not forgetting science confirms the earliest humans were Africans. Somewhat strange but even the concrete sidewalk in an urban environment can give birth to and nurture a beautiful flower.

The legacy of imperialism and colonialism in Africa created the lasting conditions that gave birth to the needs of a person, revolutionary savior, a Mandela, to address and correct the situation, requiring both wisdom and humility.

It is also interesting, when persons, institutions, even heads of states are allowed the view the awesomeness of the shadows they cast, when they finally come around, sometimes they question "How could we have gotten away with it?" But, unlike many such individuals, Mr. Mandela mastered the art of success and succeeded by studying not simply his history but that of his enemies so he could communicate and negotiate with them on a level they could understand. He was fluent in Afrikaans, the language of the oppressor.

BLACK NATIONALISM ALIVE AND WELL

Black Nationalism 398. Will Allen, ready in service to "The People!"

For centuries, the rapaciousness of the European mindset unleashed in Africa laid the foundation for thievery, racialism and resource exploitation and brutality visited upon that continent and its people. The resultant appalling "rape of Africa," exile of her sons and daughters beyond her shores, and theft of her real estate and wealth are phenomena as wide as a solar system, philosophically speaking, and as dangerous as the dynamics of a black hole! As an example, at the 1981 Oxford University International Summer School held at Exeter College, an English Tutor exclaimed, "If we knew how wealthy Africa was in 1900 there would have been no decolonization and independence after World War II."

It is, however, amazing that the year 1900 was the time of the Boer War between Britain and its South Africa Cape Colony peopled by British expatriates, Africans, "colored" and Dutch Boers. The land at the southern tip of Africa, that Bartholomew Diaz and Vasco Da Gama in 1898 praised its pilots for helping them navigate the Cape, would later attract the Boers in 1652. They settled there to escape the

FREDERICK MONDERSON

horrors of the religious reformation and would in turn visit similar brutality on Africans. These religious zealots would later falsely claim upon their arrival the land was devoid of Africans, when in fact Blacks occupied that area for hundreds of thousands, if not millions, of years. We know, for sure, Africans were mining hematite, an iron ore, in South Africa as early as 41,000 years Before Christ. In 2011, *The New York Times* newspaper reported discovery of a paint pot still containing red paint with a mixing device inside probably used as a stirrer and paint brush, carbon-dated to 107,000 years. Such evidence settles the argument as to who came first!

Black Nationalism 399. Mr. Mandela gives his famous salute!

After 1814, when the British annexed the Cape of Good Hope and forced the Boers inland to begin their "Great Trek," they encountered the Zulu Chieftain Shaka expanding his territory and organizing his nation. The Boers bribed and tricked his brother Mpande offering promises he would become chief. He then stabbed Shaka in the back. With the great African general removed from the scene, this paved the way for the "Great Trek" to move further inland with little or no resistance. In no time these Dutch Boers had

BLACK NATIONALISM
ALIVE AND WELL

seized much of the land, beginning to consign the Africans to being landless menials in their place of birth. Still, a number of Zulu leaders including Cetewayo began struggles against the whites whose firearms ensured victory against the poorly armed Africans. In aftermath of the many clashes, Moshesh, an astute African leader, gathered many strands of Africans fleeing both Zulu and Boer explosiveness and formed the Basuto nation on a high Veld in South Africa. As events unfolded, before he died, he entrusted his land to the British as a protectorate to be defended against the Boer encroachment and the small enclave became Swaziland in the South African balkanizing scheme of things.

By 1870 gold and diamonds were discovered in South Africa and after the enormous mayhem of competing European and American miners laying claims, the Africans were sidelined. Cecil Rhodes and big conglomerates prevailed in consolidating claims to the fields and so began the systematic exploitation of the nation's wealth. Elsewhere, this was also a time of developing "spheres of influence" as "precursors" to the Partition of Africa ultimately set the stage for colonial control. The wealth of South Africa encouraged expropriation, rape and pillage of the land and the evolution of a mindset that by the turn of the century had initiated the genesis of the evil system later called apartheid, becoming "legal" in 1948 under Paul Kruger, the "father of Apartheid." His disciples among the Afrikaner nationalists were Malan, Vorster and Botha, succeeded by De Klerk, the last white ruler. However, from 1872 to the start of the Boer War in 1898, discovery of precious metals of unimaginable reservoirs tremendously increase world supplies. This "outpost of the British Empire" found itself fighting with the "Mother Country" for control of the wealth and this led to the Boer War (1899-1902). Soon after, the two parties "kissed and made up." Then they agreed on a mechanism to extract the resources for export mainly to Britain, advantageously rewarding whites and disadvantageously exploiting Blacks. In 1910, with Jan Christian Smuts playing a significant role, Britain acceded to the creation of the Union of South Africa

FREDERICK MONDERSON

comprising Transvaal, Pretoria, the Orange Free State and Cape Coast Colony.

Black Nationalism 400. A beautiful couple in aid of the cause of "Our People!"

Moving quickly, from 1910 to 1931, a number of draconian laws were enacted to further restrict and control the movement of Africans, and also to consolidate white control of the nation. All this Britain acceded to, because South Africa was part of the British Commonwealth and she wanted access to the nation's mineral wealth.

BLACK NATIONALISM ALIVE AND WELL

Black Nationalism 401. Mr. Mandela being introduced to various guests at an affair.

Essentially, from 1910 to 1948, spanning World War I and World War II, South Africa mercilessly exploited the resources of that part of the African continent with Britain benefitting enormously from handling the gold and diamonds and enjoying the enormous benefit of being principal and favored trading partner. They supplied the newly declared nation's major industrial equipment and other trading items. However, in response to Britain recognizing establishment of the Union of South Africa in 1910, the African National Congress (ANC) was also formed in 1910 to advance the status of Africans in the land of their birth. Eight years later, in 1918, Nelson Rolihlahla Mandela was born in Qunu in the Eastern Cape Province, w here he spoke the Xosha language.

At the conclusion of World War II, the 5th Pan African Congress was held at Manchester, England. There, W.E.B. DuBois ceded leadership of the Pan-African Movement to the Chairman of the Conference, Kwame Nkrumah, who accepted a mandate to organize and decolonize Africa. Along with Namdi Azikwi of Nigeria; Julius

FREDERICK MONDERSON

Nyerere of Tanzania; Jomo Kenyatta of Kenya; and Sekou Toure of Guinea, these African leaders vowed to wrest control of Africa from white rule and they ultimately succeeded in freeing the continent.

On March 6, 1957 Ghana became the first African country to gain independence and a whole slew of others followed suit by the mid-1960s. However, white control in South Africa was more entrenched from being buttressed first by German then Anglo-South Africa control of Namibia; by the Portuguese in Angola and Mozambique; and the British in ill-gotten Rhodesia, essentially under rule by Ian Smith and his predecessors from whom Robert Mugabe ultimately wrestled power. The struggle for South Africa was thus much more difficult than what transpired across the other parts of the continent.

After Manchester, within three years in 1948, the system of Apartheid became a reality as a result of white control of the legislative process in South Africa. In a work entitled The *United States and Africa* by the American Assembly at Columbia University (1958L 149-150) the authors write regarding "The South African Racial System."

Black Nationalism 402. Another great warrior for the cause!

"The system of race relations in the Union of South Africa is a product of history, not merely the creation of a Malan or Strijdom. It has developed over the past three hundred years." This behemoth,

BLACK NATIONALISM ALIVE AND WELL

global pariah, then, is what Mr. Mandela sought to overthrow, and to do it he had to become a martyr and convert his enemies into friends. Sort of, "Kill them with kindness."

Accordingly, "The two crucial features of the system are separation and subordination. Separation (or apartheid) means keeping non-Europeans (particularly Africans) apart from Europeans in housing, education, religion, public amenities, conveyances, recreation, and social life. Subordination means the consistent placement of Africans (and other non-Europeans) in an inferior position in all their relationships with Europeans. The system is rationalized by a complex ideology, rooted in the conviction that the non-European is not only different but inferior. In addition to the sanctions of custom, the system is enforced by an elaborate body of statutory laws designed to exclude Africans and other non-Europeans from social and political life, control their movements (the pass laws), and regulate their activities (the **Riotous Assemblies Act** and the **Suppression of Communism Act**, for example). In practice the system does not work perfectly; apartheid is only partial, and subordination is not invariably prevalent. Non-Europeans do occasionally share aspects of European life and exercise (extremely limited) influence on government; and not all Europeans accept the prevailing theologies about Africans."

More significant, however, is the need to reinforce separateness and inferiority coupled with the need to earn cash to fend for one's families and still be in white areas where such could be earned. "Apartheid is the best-publicized feature of the system. It is an Afrikaans expression meaning "separation" or "separate development." It symbolized the ultimate objective of the Nationalists (who came into power in 1948) to separate the races in all spheres of life: residential, economic, sexual, social, educational, religious and political. Ideologically, the emphasis is on differentiation of the races, not assimilation or integration. This objective is expressed in a large body of laws passed since 1948 such as the **Group Areas Act** (1950) designed to enforce residential

FREDERICK MONDERSON

segregation in urban areas; the **Mixed Marriage Act** (1949) and the **Immorality Amendment Act** (1950) which makes intermarriage illegal and interracial sexual intimacies a crime; the **Reservation of Separate Amenities Act** (1953) reinforcing existing segregation patterns in transportation and public places; the **Bantu Education Act** (1953) which strengthens the traditional system of separate education and gives the central government greater control over African education; the **Separate University Education Bill** (proposed in 1957 but not yet law) designed to provide separate universities for the races and to debar non-Europeans from the two "open universities" which they may not attend; and other laws which aim to restrict or eliminate all contact between Africans and Europeans."

Black Nationalism 403. Rev. Timothy Mitchell, "Can I get an Amen!" on that!

Subordination is in some respects a more basic feature of race relations in South Africa that is separation. Subordination, not separation of the total apartheid variety, characterizes the economic relationships. In theory, and largely in practice, the African is consigned to lower-level jobs while positions requiring skills,

BLACK NATIONALISM ALIVE AND WELL

management, and direction are assigned to Europeans. This policy has been operative in the great mining industry, is reflected in the **White Civilized Labor Policy** dating back to 1924, and is expressed in the determination of the present government to secure the skilled and more highly paid jobs for Europeans in the clothing and secondary industries where the color bar was less rigid in the past. Thus, despite protests from industry, the Minister of Labor (under the authority of the revised **Industrial Conciliation Act**, 1957) intends to proceed with his plan to reserve for Europeans certain occupations in the clothing industry. The Minister was apparently unmoved by the claim of leading industrialists that, if this policy was extended, thousands of non-Europeans would lose their jobs and the development of industry in South Africa would be greatly hampered.

Complete separation is not actually possible. It neither existed in the past nor exists now. Subordination of the non-European in all relationships is easier to enforce and at the same time serves the major objective of the Europeans: to maintain their prestige and supremacy."

This system then instituted and enforced a system of Pass Laws that not simply separated the races, black and white, by creating white areas and consigning blacks to what became regulated black areas called "Bantustans." These were essentially economic backwaters with nothing, only providing enormous numbers of Africans who could be hired as laborers in white areas. To get from the "Bantustans" (Black towns) or "nations within a nation," Black Africans needed a Pass Book that essentially contained every bit of information about the holder. As the system became more and more enforced, Africans were reduced to contract laborers who had no rights and needed permission to be in white areas. They could be accosted by anyone, must produce their Passbook on demand, and if not correct in all aspects they could be arrested, fined or sent packing back to the "Bantustans."

FREDERICK MONDERSON

Black Nationalism 404. Mural at Maggie Walker Middle School in Brooklyn, where several members of this writer's family received a quality education, in praise of Public Schools.

Under the pretext of a practicing democratic system upheld through laws, the white minority of South Africa viciously discriminated against and oppressed the Black majority through the Pass Law mechanism   enforced under a brutally oppressive system of imprisonment, murder, banishment and fines. Persons were also banned. Both Mr. Mandela and his wife Winnie were separately banned.

First and foremost, the law required every Black person to have a Pass Book. This was not a requirement for whites! The Pass Book was more than a passport, it re counted one's entire life history, from birth to the time it was demanded by a white person or law enforcement agent.   Even more important, the Blacks were oppressed through a system of taxation that required them to work. To work and earn cash to support their families and to pay taxes, they had to be in white areas. In white areas they needed to have a valid pass and authority to perform contract labor. At the expiration of the contract, the African had to vacate the white area or face arrest. Once arrested for "trespassing" in their country of birth, it was stamped into the passbook and visible to anyone who demanded to

BLACK NATIONALISM ALIVE AND WELL

see it, which meant it was more difficult to secure employment the second time around.

Now, as the society expanded, the demands for labor increased and a system of "influx control" regulated the movement of Blacks. This impacted where they came from, whether from Bantustans, the impoverished and over-crowded areas to which Blacks were consigned and from which pools of labor were contracted; or from outside the country in neighboring lands. Whether to work in the mines, to work on farms and to perform all forms of menial labor within South Africa, Blacks were contracted on an annual basis and upon completion of the contract, they had three days, sometimes 24-hours to return to their place of origin. Because of the society's demands for laborers were more than the Bantustans could provide, neighboring states such as Rhodesia and Mozambique and as far as Malawi were contracted to supply workers whose wages were remitted directly to their home governments, themselves glad to earn the badly needed foreign exchange. In turn they paid the family of the worker in local currency.

Black Nationalism 405. We all need to be reminded, Children are our future!

FREDERICK MONDERSON

Black Nationalism 406. The Steps to Success!

This is the South Africa Nelson Mandela came of age in, became educated as a lawyer and activist having joined the African National Congress in 1946 as one of its political operatives. It was also the age of continental African agitation and organization of decolonization strategy. What British Prime Minister Harold McMillan called "the winds of change" sweeping the British Empire and the world at the start of the 1960s decade, forced the South African government under its system of apartheid, to become harsher in treatment of Blacks and enforcement of the draconian laws in hope to forestall majority rule in that wealthy country, of untold poor Blacks. Economically speaking whites would work and be entitled to insurance, health and dental care and otherwise, even receive unemployment benefits which were practically non-existent since whites had full-employment form completion of school to retirement upon which time they were entitled to a pension. All these amenities were denied the Blacks who left their families in the Bantustans and eking out a wage, were not entitled to anything when either unemployed or in old age unable to provide the back-breaking labor.

BLACK NATIONALISM
ALIVE AND WELL

This inequity was still endured because they had to provide for their families.

Since only males could work in the mines and farms they were housed in oftentimes substandard dwellings whether in urban hostels or on farms. In hostels especially, the most unsanitary and unhealthy conditions predominated, encouraging homosexuality and sickness. Such conditions Blacks were consigned to had the most deleterious effect on their psyche and on families back home in the Bantustans where the government and private enterprise further cultivated fresh crops of strong young men to replace the worn out ones "on point."

These conditions are what Nelson Mandela and the African National Congress actively sought to change. By the mid 1950s, Mr. Mandela was constantly monitored, finally arrested he was charged with treason, a trial that lasted for several years. For the duration he was "banned." This was a form of punishing prohibition in which a person was prevented from having contact with more than one person at a time and restricting his movement. Though Mandela and his colleagues were found not guilty at first, by 1960, they were forced to go underground and on the run.

Some two years later he was again arrested and charged with subversion, for publicly burning his Pass Book in defiance of the system and accused of trying to overthrow the South African government. Finally convicted, sentenced to life in prison, he was sent to Robben Island, one of the most draconian prisons in the country where he spent 18 years and another 9 in a variety of prisons.

FREDERICK MONDERSON

Black Nationalism 406a. The ongoing struggle between **"Mother Africa"** and forces of oppression constantly seeking to divide to conquer Africans at home and in the Diaspora.

While Nelson Mandela managed his prison sentence, his wife Winnie Mandela kept up the struggle through her own activism. She too became a "banned" person who could only be in touch with a few people at any one time. She was constantly harassed and her home monitored. Winnie, however, would not be silenced. She

BLACK NATIONALISM ALIVE AND WELL

traveled abroad, coming to the United States but could not speak as condition for her visa. Nevertheless, many spoke for her as she stood firm as a symbol of opposition to apartheid and as a pillar of what African womanhood stood for. In America and elsewhere she was regarded as a Queen of the Black World. Queen Mother Moore took her under her wings and the world loved and adored this beautiful fighter for freedom and justice. One particular and later front page of the New York *Afro Times* featured a picture of Minister Louis Farrakhan beside a seated Winnie Mandela and below words on the beginning of a series on **Thebes**, the city of Ancient Egypt, begun by Fred Monderson.

All the while in prison Nelson Mandela's image continued to enlarge. He became the first and only global icon of the 20th Century. Michael Jackson was known for his music but people demonstrated, held sit-ins, wrote, acted and demanded an end to Apartheid and freedom for Nelson Mandela.

As more African states became independent, attention began to focus on the plight of South Africans. Before his imprisonment, Mandela, had launched the armed wing of the **ANC**, called the "Spear of the Nation" and empowered it to wage an armed struggle against the government. Secretly he left the country, perhaps for guerilla training. Surreptitiously African governments and others began to train and supply the **ANC** with arms and the wherewithal to continue to struggle to Free South Africa. Libya under Mohmar Khadafy provided training-grounds, arms and money; so too did Fidel Castro of Cuba; even Yasser Arafat of the **PLO** aided the African cause. A most significant development occurred in the 1970s. For more than a century Germans, French, Italians, Belgians and British had deployed soldiers to Africa. In 1974 when Fidel Castro deployed Cuban troops to aid Angola under threat from Jonas Savimbi acting in concert with the marauding South African Army threatening liberation movements in Mozambique, Rhodesia,

FREDERICK MONDERSON

Namibia and Angola, the pariah Apartheid state's "Achilles heel" became evident. This signaled the final push to rid the continent of the white settle minority regimes in South-West Africa (Namibia) and South Africa (Azania).

Across the globe young and old people, from college campuses to local government, began to demand divestment from investment in the apartheid state. Professors taught classes and demanded term papers on "Apartheid," "Nelson Mandela" and the "History of South Africa." Movements sprang up and began targeting any and all American institutions that invested funds, whether for business, unions, pension funds, insurance companies and insisted that American technical know-how must be withdrawn. The Free South Africa Movement gained steam in Europe and everywhere. The "Fight Apartheid" and "Free Nelson Mandela" buttons appeared everywhere. The might of South Africa was threatened.

Western nations that depended on mineral resources which South Africa had in abundance were caught in a dilemma having to satisfy their citizens' insistence that ties to Apartheid be cut. The world was awaked to the evils of apartheid and Nelson Mandela became a symbol of the opposition to the racism and brutality practiced in that country. As this movement escalated, divestment, protest, calls to end ties, sports boycott, etc., world leaders of major nations such as Margaret Thatcher and Ronald Reagan were caught in a bind. Ronald Reagan, as President of the United States, a nation whose citizens, in many respects, lead the fight, pursued a policy of "constructive engagement" with the pariah state. The "Iron Lady" stalled on sanctions but the Commonwealth of Nations forced her hand. Importantly, persons such as Rev. Leon Sullivan began to be more vocal in efforts to squeeze and bring down the government. The image of Nelson Mandela grew further. Hugh Masekela sang a song "Bring Mandela home to Soweto."

BLACK NATIONALISM
ALIVE AND WELL

Black Nationalism 407. Reverend Daughtry and Charles Barron at the House of the Lord Church.

South Africans such as Walter Sisulu and Oliver Tambo were active in the country. Young Steve Biko, an activist was arrested and killed mercilessly by South African Security Forces. Donald Woods, a white friend of Biko was hounded and had to leave the country. In this Country, such nationalists as Jitu Weusi and Sonny Carson certainly were engaged in raising the conscience of their brothers and sisters. Harry Belafonte continued to organize on-going protests

FREDERICK MONDERSON

Black Nationalism 408. Reverend Herbert Daughtry, Pastor of **The House of the Lord Church** on Atlantic Avenue in Brooklyn.

in front of the South African Embassy that resulted in Major Owens, Walter Fauntroy, Mrs. Effie Barry and Reverend Herbert Daughtry, pastor of the House of the Lord Church which became the epicenter

BLACK NATIONALISM ALIVE AND WELL

of the Anti-apartheid Movement. An Anti-Apartheid organizer at Hunter College, Charles Barron was married to his wife Inez at the Church. Here too was centered Sisters Against South African Apartheid (**SAASA**) of which Barbara Emanuel was a member who also coordinated this through the Maurice Gumbs political campaign for School Board 17 and later the 21st State Senate, with Cherise Maloney and Fern Greenberg as operatives. Conrad Worrill of Chicago was an ardent anti-Apartheid proponent. Rev. Jessie Jackson, Randall Robinson of Trans-Africa, Cleveland Robinson and Jim Bell, union leaders, galvanized unions across the nation and world to protest that workers of South Africa had no representation. In churches, on college campuses, especially in Brooklyn at Medgar Evers College, as student Emanuel noted, "Everybody was working!"

As the pot boiled, the racist South African regime that slaughtered untold numbers at Sharpsville in 1962 did the same thing on June 16, 1976 in Soweto as the youth took to the street to protest the evil system. All this aroused the conscience of the world that apartheid must go. More and more Mandela's release from prison became a top priority as the sanctions against South Africa escalated; squeezing the nation; the system began to crack from the pressures without and within. In response, the government sought an escape from the vicious and debilitating web they had wove. Prime Minister Pieta Botha tried to bribe Mandela with early release from prison if he would renounce the armed struggle he initiated under *Umkhonto we Sizwe* or "Spear of the Nation." This offer was rejected, according to Mandela because prisoners cannot negotiate.

The Free Nelson Mandela Movement saw the revered leader released in 1990, a day the world sang praises in triumph against the evils of apartheid. By that time, David Dinkins had been elected Mayor of New York City and along with other operatives as New York Secretary of State Basil Patterson, radio personality David Lampel and others, including El Hombre Brath and members of the

FREDERICK MONDERSON

American Committee on Africa all welcomed Mr. Mandela to this city and nation. Bill Lynch, a Deputy Mayor in the David Dinkins administration orchestrated a parade for Mr. Mandela within the "Canyon of Heroes" in down-town Manhattan. Betty Shabazz, wife of Malcolm X was given a rousing embrace by Winnie Mandela as they stood on the podium in Harlem. Mandela visited Boys and Girls High School in Bedford-Stuyvesant and he gave speeches. Appearing on Television, when asked by Ted Koppel of **Nightline**, 'Why did he associate with and invite to his Inauguration such persons as Khadafy, Castro, Arafat, Mugabe, Farrakhan,' he replied, "These people helped us when apartheid oppressed us" as the west only extracted and benefitted from the wealth. And so many felt proud of being part of something greater than themselves!

Black Nationalism 409. Council Member Charles Barron and his wife Assemblywoman Inez Barron, with an unknown person (left).

While Jesse Jackson pointed out Mr. Mandela's vision and outlook was shaped by persecution, the world praised him for seeking reconciliation in the best interest of the nation. Along with F.W. De

BLACK NATIONALISM
ALIVE AND WELL

Klerk, the last white ruler of the apartheid state, Mr. Mandela was awarded the Noble Peace Prize in 1993. After serving as the nation's first Black President, he was succeeded by his Vice President Thabo Mbeki, followed by Jacob Zuma who announced Mr. Mandela's death at 8:15 p, December 5, 2013.

Black Nationalism 410. A quintessential Black Nationalist, Dr. Marimba Ani, formerly of Hunter College of the City University of New York.

FREDERICK MONDERSON

Mr. Mandela's legacy, besides the dissolution of apartheid was relentless against **AIDS**, poverty and African educational upliftment. He was against the US invasion of Iraq. However, while many have praised his conciliatory gestures towards the perpetrators of the crimes of apartheid, others have pointed out, he may have been conciliatory but he never forgot his experiences and the revelations of the Truth and Reconciliatory Committee that chronicled the brutality the South African government prosecuted against its citizens.

"Nelson Mandela, giant," Editorial *New York Daily News* Friday, December 6, 2013, p. 30.

It is true, all true. Nelson Mandela led the fight against an evil, racist regime; went to jail for a quarter-century; emerged from that dark place a stronger, wiser man; and, with quiet strength, led his nation toward peace, democracy and prosperity. His story is a rousing personal journey that conveys the boundless potential in every life, no matter how battered. It affirms the moral power that a single extraordinary person can exert on history by being better than his oppressors, by ultimately embracing reconciliation over revenge.

In 1964, on the eve of prison, he gave one of the century's greatest speeches, concluding: 'I have cherished the ideal of a democratic and free society in which all persons live in harmony and with equal opportunities. It is an ideal which I hope to live for and to achieve. But if needs be, it is an ideal for which I am prepared to die.'"

That he did – expanding health care to children, Radically improving education, protecting workers, lifting people out of desperate poverty and settling thousands of land claims. This hero of history has his flaws. All men, great and small, do. They are of no moment. Today, brought short by his death, we revere Mandela for saving a nation's soul and for galvanizing the global conscience of as a beacon for the proposition that all people are created equal."

BLACK NATIONALISM
ALIVE AND WELL

Black Nationalism 411. Xavier Bost lays it all out for Mr. Mandela.

"A true hero passes into history," *New York Daily News*, Voice of the People. Saturday, December 7, 2013, p. 21.

Brooklyn: We cherish the stars – actors, athletes, etc. – and mourn their death when we know nothing about them. Nelson Mandela was a man – yes, a real man – who never showed bitterness or hatred for the 27 years he spent in prison. He won the presidency of a country where there were no gray areas, only black and white. Yet he did everything to bring his nation together. He is a true inspiration. Mandela has my ultimate respect, and my sympathy goes out to his family and friends. A true hero has passed away. David J. Gushue.

Bronx: Nelson Mandela was a good and great man who became revered by freedom-loving people throughout the world. His refusal to be broken by the vile apartheid government of South Africa will serve as an inspiration for generations to come. What a great voice he was, as opposed to those hucksters and hustlers, Al Sharpton and Charles Barron. They could learn a lot from Mandela's example. Kim Theobald.

Black Nationalism 412. Mr. Bob Law addresses his audience in Tribute to Nelson Mandela.

53. BOB LAW'S TRIBUTE TO MANDELA
By
Dr. Fred Monderson

Incomparable Bob Law of "Night Talk" fame sponsored another of his tremendously informative Forums at historic **Church of God in Christ** on Kingston Avenue in Brooklyn, December 17, 2013,

BLACK NATIONALISM
ALIVE AND WELL

7:00 – 10:00 pm, in tribute to Nelson Mandela. After Bob Law had laid the foundation for comprehensive understanding of Mandela's passing, Dr. Leonard Jeffries provided a scintillating analysis and synthesis for the some 100 persons who braved the inclement weather to see beyond the outward appearance of global, even South African, tribute to the fallen leader, icon and freedom fighter. Both Mr. Law and Dr. Jeffries painstakingly turned on its head much of Mandela's tribute from world leaders and Western media by focusing not on the man as a mountain, but as a "tree" in a forest of freedom fighters.

This was elucidated in "Mandela and the Unfinished Freedom Struggle" *Daily Challenge*, 12/17/13, p. 5, where Ron Daniels wrote, "Mandela was the 'tallest tree' in a forest that included many movements and stellar leaders, e.g., the Pan African Congress, Black Consciousness Movement, Mass Democratic Movement, Steve Biko, Bishop Desmond Tutu, Allan Boesak, Cyril Ramaphosa, Albertina and Walter Sisulu and Oliver Tambo to mention a few. This is an important note because there is a tendency to cast successful movements as the result of the acts of a solitary heroic figure." We should also include the Afrikaner cleric Byers Naude.

Many attributes of Mr. Mandela were demonstrated in loyalty to his tribal heritage, his education and profession as a lawyer, his activism and daring; and his role as student, husband and family man. These men who conceptualize so readily and well, were quick to point out the cliché, he went from "Prisoner to President" and his steadfast "commitment to reconciliation;" do not tell the full story that he was forced into armed struggle; convicted and while in prison those 27 years became a symbol, an icon; yet, the struggle continued to be waged by others suffering at the hands of the oppressive and repressive regime that banned, tortured and killed many.

FREDERICK MONDERSON

Black Nationalism 413. Mr. Law shares a humorous moment in Tribute to Nelson Mandela.

It's universally recognized, the Afrikaners who perpetrated the racist, evil system of apartheid, did not suddenly have an epiphany and decided to free Nelson Mandela. Like Ian Smith of Rhodesia, they hoped to rule for another 1000 years, though in 1000 days power was wrestled from Smith by "the boys in the bush." In the case of South Africa, it was the insistence, commitment and unrelenting struggle of the women, the young people, the African National Congress cadre and the global mobilization for divestment to rid the world of the evil system that apartheid represented, despite President Reagan and Chester Crocker's policy of "constructive engagement," and many Americans both black and white, who supported apartheid and considered Mandela a terrorist, the people's efforts are what contributed to successes of Mandela's and South Africa's freedom struggle. This is what forced the half-hearted offer by President Pieter Botha's offer to free or release Mandela in 1988. Such release, however, was dictated only if he would renounce violence! clearly, if Mr. Mandela did accept an early release under those conditions it would have undermined everything he stood for, what he spent those many years incarcerated to achieve, and he would have lost the respect of the South African people whom he

BLACK NATIONALISM
ALIVE AND WELL

represented as well as the people of the world who stood with him and pressured change agents demanding his release.

Black Nationalism 414. Craig Crawford creates sweet horn music for Mr. Mandela.

It's also acknowledged; globally Africans see the world differently because of their shared racist imperial and colonial experience. That is why Mr. Law wanted his audience to understand the continuity of that experience. That is why, "We not let others tell the story," for when they do it's with a twist that actually distorts the experience. The "Prison to President" cliché is thus not correct! He did not

FREDERICK MONDERSON

commit a crime; yet, as a man of principle, he was willing to forgive all the wickedness of the apartheid regime and this demonstrated his humanity was of a higher standard.

Black Nationalism 415. Xavier Bost sings one of her two songs, "A Hero Lies in You."

Though he was called a terrorist, he was actually a freedom fighter who became President! Prison was only a step on the way! In the horrendous experience, there was a long history of struggle against the murderous, vicious racists who stole the best land confining Africans to "black spots," then removing them into balkanized and barren reserves called "Bantustans." These were supposed independent nations, yet dependent on South Africa, of course, with the whites in control, politically and economically. This and more forced the African National Congress to pick up the gun. These Africans actually pressed into armed struggle amidst hopelessness and dehumanization instituted through fear and intimidation and use of "stooges" as the Inkatha Movement of Chief Buthelezi. That's why Mr. Mandela insisted Xhosa, Sotho, Zulus, all Africans, are one people suffering under the same oppressive system. The racists fermented a blood bath between the Africans before they could fight

BLACK NATIONALISM ALIVE AND WELL

the white man! Yet, Mr. Mandela would say, "Let us forgive these wicked people who have oppressed us for so long!" Importantly, nobody went behind his back seeking vengeance! No one sought to assassinate or injure those who perpetrated the system. Much more significant, because Mr. Mandela refused to compromise his principles, his liberation was real! This behavior demonstrated tremendous patience of African people while "superior white folks" were stealing their land and its riches. Showing magnanimity, in his uncompromising stance, he also denounced violence from both black and white elements. This is because Madiba understood the potency of violence and its impact on the people, nation in its policy, infrastructure and views of the world.

Naturally, most people never really or fully understood Mr. Mandela or his strategy. It can be assumed Mr. Mandela went to prison an angry man after his trial and conviction, but he was still a proud man! Observe his walk into prison! He probably never expected to be freed one day. In that "Long Walk," he experienced much and had the time to reflect, think and strategize. He said he matured! He knew he represented the people; he had them on his side. He also studied his enemy! He learned Afrikaans, the language of the oppressor, so he better understood their history and culture relative to the Africans and this was important in his negotiations to end apartheid.

In reflecting, Madiba probably thought "We may be able to kill some whites but Africans would suffer more in any bloodbath." The nation would also suffer from the unleashed carnage. The Afrikaners knew he was coming and expected riotous behavior, so they stockpiled their armaments. They strategized and erected their forts and barriers, their "Alamos" to create their "Amritsars." Madiba outfoxed the devils! He said no recrimination! "Africans, let us forgive the white citizens of our nation." Thus, their arms were useless, ineffective, their barriers yet showed their thinking and bunker mentality! As Sun Tzu advised, "Win the battle before taking the field!" This Mandela did! To recall, even more, Nkrumah had

FREDERICK MONDERSON

said, "Seek ye first the political kingdom." In the South African system, whites controlled economics and politics. Mandela realized he could not dislodge them from economic control. By virtue of the Black majority and to keep democracy alive, he chose the democratic way to political power. Ron Daniels said it best. Mandela theorized through political power the African people will whittle away at the preponderance of white economic dominance.

One African lady explained why she loved Mandela in part; Soweto had no electricity, the night belonged to whites! Now they have electricity and she has a fridge and TV. The muddy roads are now paved. Houses are being built but poverty also lingers. These were government efforts initiated by Mandela. Unrelenting political effort over time will economically empower Africans much further!

Mr. Mandela's humanity pulled the mask off the white racists and he exposed their true selves. Much more significantly, he was well versed in his historical responsibility, coming as he did from a community with a royal duty to the people of his land. That is what we must seek to fully understand in putting him in proper perspective. The Western and American media does not tell or focus on Mr. Mandela's and the **ANC's** true role in total liberation of African people and their struggles of pushing back colonialism as well as the significance of true elimination of the immoral system of apartheid. In reality, it's who he forgave rather than what he forgave them for is really the issue and this forces another look at the Afrikaner Boers, South Africa and Mr. Mandela. The role of women in all this is certainly important.

In one of the features run in the media recently about an Afrikaner Museum, a young woman visiting boasted of her need to know her history! It is clear the museum would not recount the brutality, the killing, the betrayal, the African humiliation, the wrongs, so that is why the Africans must know and tell their story to get a more balanced view for historical recounting. Mandela's insistence on the **Truth and Reconciliation Commission** was a masterful stroke! In the many confessions it gave the "monsters" a chance to

BLACK NATIONALISM ALIVE AND WELL

reveal their mechanism of repression and control for the world to realize how right they were in insisting that apartheid must go!

Changing pace, in a musical interlude Craig Crawford played a beautiful jazz rendition of a tribute and he followed this up with another really great song. Also, Xavier Bost sang two wonderful pieces, "Shattered but not Broken" and "A Hero Lies in You." Bob Law then praised the musicians and audience for being *"Credoso Africans"* who were "strong and resilient." He even tied this trait to the tenacity of braving the weather to attend the event, insisting more such forums are planned.

Not discounting Mr. Mandela was a good man; they however, pointed out, but he was not unique as a freedom fighter! Mr. Law expressed, "We came from a long line of freedom fighters who fought courageously in liberation struggles." This is why he insisted, "It is important that we claim our own history." At that point he mentioned African leaders of Mr. Mandela's stature such as Ghana's Kwame Nkrumah, Guinea's Sekou Toure, and Congo's Patrice Lumumba who liberated their country and gave their all in its cause. These leaders were uncompromising liberation fighters. Of course, Mr. Machel of Mozambique must also be numbered in this lot. At this point Mr. law waxed philosophical by telling the audience, "When you celebrate Mr. Mandela, you celebrate yourself; you celebrate the African liberation struggle." He spoke of "something on the inside that is so strong, Holy Spirit, Holy Ghost," that cannot be touched or conquered that contributed to his and the African people's successes. Then he reflected on an old African liberation saying, "The higher they build the barriers, the taller you will rise." Even further, "To celebrate Mr. Mandela, let every leader be a Mandela" who refused to hate, was uncompromising, principled, and a man of great integrity. Despite his circumstances, he continued to fight which showed his character. He fought for what was right and would not compromise. This is what his enemies had to recognize. He fought against poverty and against inhumanity of man to man. He recognized gay rights and praised education.

FREDERICK MONDERSON

Black Nationalism 416. Dr. Jeffries stands tall in explaining Mandela's role in African liberation.

Bob Law insisted; we must guard against "People who will come to confuse us, who will betray us." Because Mr. Mandela would not compromise, would not back down, Mr. Law quoted biblical wisdom to reflect his strong, principled personality, for "No weapon formed against me will prosper." Even more philosophical and spiritual, he offered, "You think you are doing it on your own," but divinely

BLACK NATIONALISM ALIVE AND WELL

guided forces are at play in guiding your every move! To explain where Mr. Mandela got his strength poses a profound proposition; for Mr. Law quotes Isaiah, the prophet, who wrote, "They that wait on the Lord shall renew their strength, they shall mount up with wings of eagles; they shall run and not be weary; they shall walk and not faint." This strength, this life in commitment to struggle, is a reminder of how great as a people the audience really is! This again is why we must not let them separate Madiba Mandela from the continuity of the history of his people.

Bob Law used analogies to get his point across. He asked the audience to **Google** two interviews between Malcolm X and Mike Wallace and Farrakhan and Wallace on "The Hate that Hate Produced." He veered off to speak on the disrespect Blacks receive, especially when shopping at high-end stores such as Barney's. He spoke of the young lady at Barney's who "Was not arrested for shoplifting but for spending too much" when she bought the $2500.00 ladies bag! He also talked about new and upcoming ventures of the church in addressing the suffering of families, families of loved ones in prisons. People never really understand the hurt they put their families through when they commit a crime and go to prison. The family, the mothers, brothers and sisters, sons and daughters, also *do the time* on the outside. This suffering is what the church will now address.

Next it was Leonard Jeffries' turn, late as he always is! Jokingly Mr. Law referred to the keynote speaker as "The Late Dr. Jeffries." Pulling no punches, he focused not just on Nelson Mandela but the moment of African Liberation. While the focus today is on Mr. Mandela, Dr. Jeffries insisted, for 27 years he was only a symbol! At the funeral Winnie and Graca demonstrated the strength of the black woman. These women were the wind that powered their husbands' sails!

FREDERICK MONDERSON

There were many similarities in the struggles of the **ANC** (1910) and the **NAACP** (1912) who sought to restore African humanity in a world of white rapaciousness and ugly wrongs. In South Africa it was the **African National Congress**, the **Pan-African Congress**, the **Student Movemen**t that gave us Steve Biko and of course the church, in close association with the **World Council of Churches** under the leadership of Dr. Philip Potter in which Dr. Jeffries and Professor Scobie, in Geneva, were lending assistance to coordinate activities in the South African struggle. From this vantage position he realized and stated emphatically, "The most devastating destruction of the Black man was in South Africa."

In that horrific experience was the 1962 Sharpsville massacre and response to the June 16, 1976 student uprising in Soweto that demonstrated the viciousness of the white minority regime. However, efforts to brain-wash the students in demands that they learn Afrikaans was "more than a bridge too far," it was a tremendous miscalculation! The Africans suffered but the move failed!

First, in laying out his presentation, Dr. Leonard Jeffries reminded the audience, the Boers comprised Dutch, German and French elements from Europe mingled with Britons. With the discovery of the gold and diamond wealth of South Africa in late 19th Century, his "3 Rs," were not reading, 'riting and 'rithmetic, but Rothschild, Rhodes and Rockefeller who conglomerated to exploit the riches. A secret society called the **Broderbund** of some 20,000 was created. These men swore to maintain power no matter what. This is what Mandela challenged! Thus, "If there is a place for Reparations it is South Africa." The Boers fostered unity among Europeans and divisions among Africans. They used the Zulu Mpande to kill his brother Shaka in 1835. The same way they "encouraged" Chief Buthelezi of ferment violence among Africans in 1975. This created a universal moral crisis. In their grab, that minority took 85 percent of the best land. However, despite Mandela's victory, "We won the

BLACK NATIONALISM
ALIVE AND WELL

battle but they won the war," by remaining in control of the nation's economics.

Black Nationalism 417. Dr. Leonard Jeffries makes a point in his Tribute to Nelson Mandela.

Dr. Jeffries also shed light on Afrikaner examination of the role of the church in the struggle. They studied Archbishop Tutu's many speeches, dissecting the many times he mentioned the **ANC**. They realized they were fighting the church on the inside and the freedom fighters on the outside. They entrapped and neutralized Rev. Boesak rendering him ineffective as a voice in liberation theology.

FREDERICK MONDERSON

Black Nationalism 418. The Message is clear! **DC STATEHOOD NOW!**

Dr. Jeffries explained further, "Politics is what you do to control your economics." His synthesis depicted a triangle compromising economics, politics and culture, the mind values, he called it. Importantly, he pointed out, the 1948 election victory of the Nationalist Party "set in motion the dehumanization process of Africans." This resulted in "The African people suffering from a shattered consciousness and a fractured identity." Again, emphasizing the need to organize economics, politics and culture, as well as the role of women – Winnie Mandela; children – Steve Biko; church – Archbishop Desmond Tutu and Rev Allan Boesak, Dr.

BLACK NATIONALISM
ALIVE AND WELL

Jeffries insisted, "To serve the people, the curriculum of inclusion is not sufficient, we need a curriculum of liberation."

Black Nationalism 419. The Black Institute. Org.

Black Nationalism 419a. Dr. Michael Erik Dyson at Rev. Al Sharpton's 2014 Convention.

FREDERICK MONDERSON

Black Nationalism 419b. The "Fireman" Hodari, who mastered the craft of "Eating Fire" and practiced on many an occasion.

Black Nationalism 419c. Kwaku, Santina and Adwoa Payton and Santina's brother Kofi Brown in white shirt and sunglasses, at the International African Arts Festival.

BLACK NATIONALISM ALIVE AND WELL

Black Nationalism 420. Erik Monderson walks with the Children at the 50th Anniversary March on Washington.

54.   KWANZAA AT CEMOTAP
By
Dr. Fred Monderson

In a packed house full of gifts on December 28, 2013, Dr. James McIntosh and Sister Betty Dopson, Co-Chairs of **CEMOTAP** welcomed young and old citizens to celebrate this year's **Kwanzaa Festival** which was tremendously interactive with the young people performing African Dances to the beat of the young drummer Naim Blake. The adults and elders sat attentively, clapped their hands, applauded and enjoyed themselves. Everyone recited the **Nguzu Saba, 7 Principles of Kwanza**.

1. **Umoja** - Unity
2. **Kuji Chakagulia** - Self Determination
3. **Ujima** - Collective Work and Responsibility
4. **Ujamaa** - Cooperative Economics
5. **Nia** - Purpose

FREDERICK MONDERSON

6. **Kuumba** - Creativity
7. **Imani** – Faith

Black Nationalism 420a. Portrait of Rev. Al Sharpton unveiled at the 2014 **National Action Network** Convention.

Not only did the full-house joyfully recite the **Principles**, but they also did vigorous **Harambes** after the **7th Principle**. How apropos, in this storehouse of intellectual fortitude and a reservoir of

BLACK NATIONALISM ALIVE AND WELL

cultural and historical motifs, a prominently displayed *Class Magazine* of 1989 Black History Month Cover featured a photograph and lead article entitled"

Black Nationalism 421. Rev. Charles Norris of Bethesda Missionary Baptist Church and "Spiritual" head of **CEMOTAP** among the audience celebrating Kwanzaa.

FREE NELSON MANDELA, FREE SOUTH AFRICA and it also mentioned **WINNIE MANDELA**.

Sister Ilene Edwards did a display and short talk explaining the meaning and significance of **Adinkra Symbols**. She pointed out, much of the "Iron Works" concepts we see fronting and decorating the entrance to buildings are actually imitations of **African Adinkra Symbols**.

Because the **Keynote Speaker Prof. James Blake** was running late, **Dr. McIntosh** decided to feed the attendees as we waited. In a specially choreographed exercise Dr. McIntosh was able

FREDERICK MONDERSON

to fit the entire audience in the dining hall where a wonderful and delicious meal of some 10-courses of food including sweet potato, potato salad, chili, egg parmesan, shrimp, cabbage, chicken, macaroni shells, Mac and Cheese, Mac and vegetable with tuna, topped with juice, pound-cake and a still wider assortment of desert satisfied the "sweet tooth." With stomachs filled we sat back to enjoy **Dr. Blake's Kwanzaa Message**.

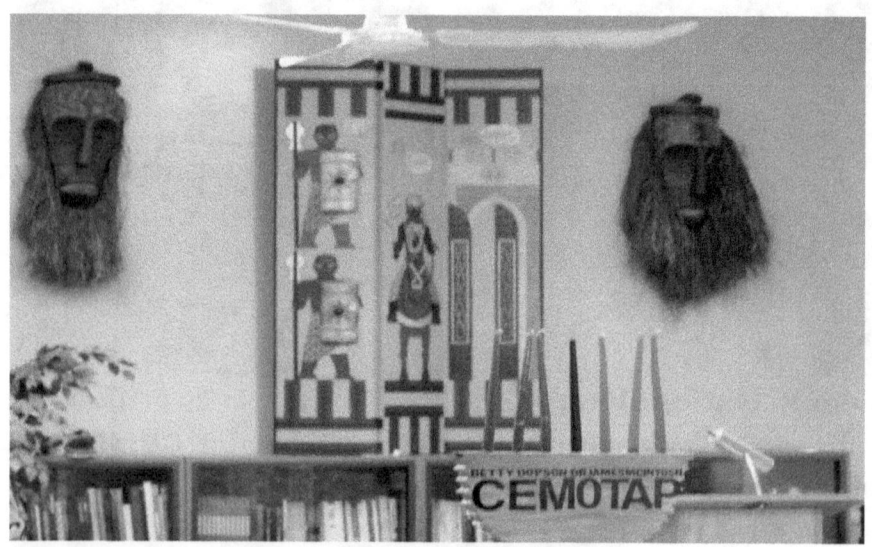

Black Nationalism 422. CEMOTAP and, Betty Dopson and Dr. James McIntosh display the **Kwanzaa** symbol while paving the way and keeping alive the tradition.

Prof. Blake's Theme centered on the **"Million Man March,"** a topic not much talked about these days, said the Chairman of the Million Man Coordinating Committee of Queens and currently a Professor at the Borough of Manhattan Community College. Beginning with the Muslim greeting of "Salaam Wali Kom" "Salaam," he asked if everyone ate and then focused on the third principle of the **Nguzu Saba**, celebrated this Saturday, **Ujima** which is "Collective Work and Responsibility."

BLACK NATIONALISM ALIVE AND WELL

Emphasizing "We're in this together," Prof. Blake insisted, "We must build and maintain and keep our committee together. If we don't, no one else will!" Further, "We must make our sisters and brothers' problems our own and work to make them better. We have to solve each others' problems and take inventories of what we have accomplished." Insisting that media negatively portrays and does not serve our people, Prof. Blake said we must do "self-criticisms" and will realize, "We have achieved a lot in our community. We must celebrate our accomplishments." Then he gave a partial listing of things accomplished while emphasizing their impact and why we must work together in the same fashion.

Black Nationalism 423. Prof. James Blake and Sister Betty Dopson, clearly in a joyous festive mood.

FREDERICK MONDERSON

Black Nationalism 424. Dr. James McIntosh, Co-Founder and Co-Chairman of **CEMOTAP**, clearly "fighting the good fight," with results.

1. The "Million Man March" was "The greatest assemblage of Black men in the world. The numbers varied but there were more than one, maybe two, million men who gathered in Washington, DC on October 16, 1995. These men were a group. A group has purpose, aims and goals. It is like a contract, an agreement."

BLACK NATIONALISM ALIVE AND WELL

2. We must not focus on differences; we must only focus on what unites us. We must realize; liberation is not something you will get easy. Collective Work and Responsibility was crucial on the March. We have to always be aware of individuals who want to destroy or to betray the collective effort! We came home from the March with goals in mind.

3. We agreed to keep the local Organizing Committee together and plan a series of activities to benefit our community. We created the Historic Black College Tour and took 500 youths to Historic Black Colleges. They visited Howard University, Fisk, Morgan State, Tennessee, Spellman, North Carolina Central, Virginia State and Morehouse College. Some mothers praised our efforts saying, "When my child came home he or she said I want to go to this or that college. Several have already graduated."

4. We organized the first "Father and Son March" on Merrick Boulevard and into Roy Wilkins Park. We created a chant:

> "What do we want?"
> "Fathers!"
> "How do we want them?"
> "Strong!"

This "Father and Son March was peaceful!" Rosa Parks was our Grand Marshal! She came out just to be with us!

5. We created an "Annual Youth Day" with committees divided into Youth, Social Justice and Economic Development, etc.

6. The legendary lawyer Johnny Cochran came to speak to our young people. Here at **CEMOTAP** we engaged in Collective Work and Responsibility. It is amazing what we can do when we work together. We must 'Look for the good and praise it.'"

7. Dr. Blake further informed, they "Created a VIP Youth Committee." Between 1999 and today they prepared young people

FREDERICK MONDERSON

and secured 8,000 jobs. The Committee has some terrific sisters such as Zinga and Rosa. Sister Henrique is a jewel who sits on the Board. There are 50 parents in the group. Sister Erica did all the hotel arrangements for the Black College Tour." He continued further, "They are building prisons faster than they are building schools or colleges. Today prisons are a profit making enterprise and the statistics are frightening. The people in prison look a lot like us."

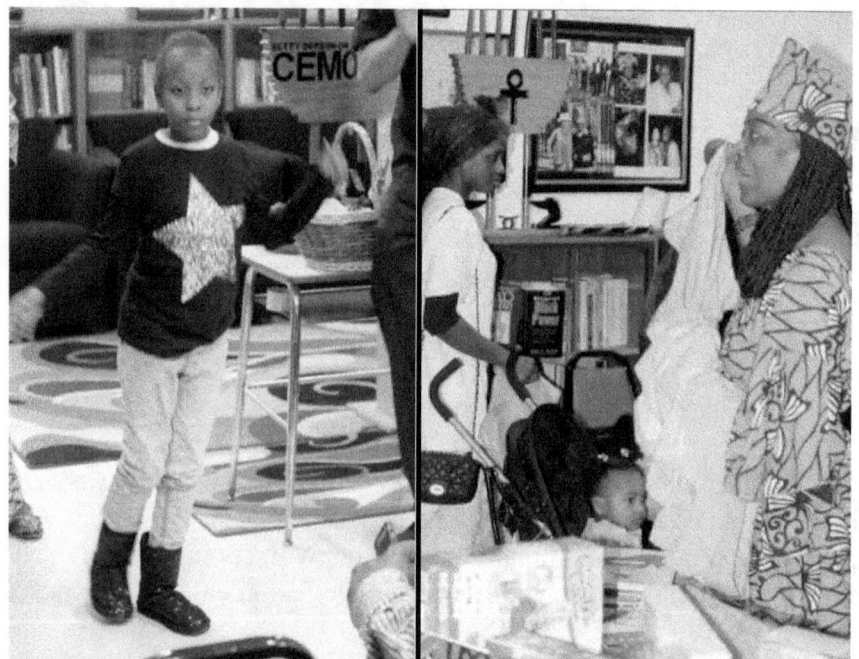

Black Nationalism 425. An African Dancer and Sister Dopson among the children!

BLACK NATIONALISM
ALIVE AND WELL

Black Nationalism 426. Another African Dancer beside Sister Dopson and Dr. McIntosh.

With that, it was time to share out the gifts and the young people lined up. Everyone was to take a gift and return to the end of the line and repeat this until all the gifts were gone. Some young people got as many as four or five gifts and so they really had a happy Kwanza!

Black Nationalism 427. Rev. Charles Norris and a family attending.

FREDERICK MONDERSON

Black Nationalism 428. The Drummer Naim Blake and Prof. James Blake.

Black Nationalism 429. Brother Vincent Emanuel, very much a **Pan-African Black Nationalist** who can boast of being very much African and been part of many struggles on part of African Liberation.

BLACK NATIONALISM ALIVE AND WELL

Black Nationalism 430. On a wall, **Kwanzaa** book advertising.

55. DR. KARENGA ON KWANZAA
By
Dr. Fred Monderson

Dr. Maulana Karenga, the founder and theorist of Kwanzaa celebrated this year's festival by giving his traditional annual speech in Brooklyn, not at Boys and Girls High School on Fulton Street, its customary venue, but at PS 35 on McDonough Street. His appearance this year was also not on the First Day, 26th of December (**Umoja** - Unity) either, but on the Second Day, (Friday) 27th of December, the day of **Kuji Chakagulia** (Self Determination). Nevertheless, his message was just as clear and resounding that "We must Create, Celebrate and Sustain Kwanzaa" and in so doing, "bring good into the world!" In this celebration of the **Nguzu**

FREDERICK MONDERSON

Saba, the **7-Principles of Kwanzaa**, we must never see this as a practice simply to be celebrated, only during the festive season but as a creative and lived way of life celebrated the entire year. Seeming just as creatively forceful and on message as when he first started celebrating the **7 Principles of Kwanzaa** 47 years ago, Dr. Karenga laid out his message of bringing good into the world, while even taking jabs at "the oppressor" and those who "confuse and betray" the movement. In this he decried, "The dog is man's best friend" refrain as germane to the "oppressor," and insisted the African's best friend must be a human being, his sister or brother, father, mother or some relative but not a dog! He even exclaimed and demanded, "We do not speak anything bad about African people this Kwanza season."

Black Nationalism 430a. The **Kwanzaa** Candles backed by the "First Fruits of the Festival."

After an invigorating **Habari Gani** to a resounding **Kuji Chakagulia** response, Dr. Karenga began dealing straight from the shoulder asking those in attendance to "do justice and walk in the way of life!" He praised John Branch who recently passed into the "blessedness of being a revered ancestor." More, importantly Mr. Branch did a great deal in founding the **African Poetry Theater** in Queens! He founded the **African Trade and**

BLACK NATIONALISM
ALIVE AND WELL

Business Assistance (ABTA) group and helped establish the **World African Diasporian Union**. Mr. Branch was an active member of the New York chapter of the **National Association of Kawaida Organizations (NAKO)** and a staunch Pan-Africanist, Black Nationalist, community organizer and more. This cultural leader, organizer, activist and entrepreneur now take his earned and rightful place among the great ancestors of the Black Pantheon.

After this, Dr. Karenga moved to point out, "Each season is a reaffirmation of our condition, harvesting the fruits planted by the African people." Insisting as we "Create, Celebrate and Sustain good in the world," we must also "focus on good as the central process and practice of Kwanzaa." Since Kwanzaa is about embracing ethical views and values, we must concentrate on "remaking the world so that the good of the world would be shared by us and everybody. In this Kwanzaa becomes a celebration of ourselves as an African people, our families and culture."

Poking fun, he truthfully pointed out, "When other people celebrate Kwanzaa they are not asking for the African, Native American, Asian or Palestinian cause." So many have asked, "Can we accept white people practicing Kwanzaa?" No, the question should be, "Can white people celebrate blackness?" Can they celebrate Black people? Celebrate Black culture? What we object to is people walking in, taking over and diluting what we created and stands for? Then they tell us, how to do it! You can care for a people and still not respect them. This is what we object to!" Even further he insisted, "To respect someone's history you must see them as a people and treat them as such."

FREDERICK MONDERSON

Black Nationalism 431. Dr. Maulana Karenga sits beside his wife awaiting his turn on the Dais.

Kwanzaa is a reaffirmation of our African-ness. We must first celebrate ourselves. There must be a reaffirmation of our Africanness and social justice tradition. We must celebrate ourselves without explanation, without justification but with edification and gratification. It's like history says, then what? If we don't do it who will?"

Kwanza must be a celebration of ourselves, celebration of life and all the goodness in the world, fruit and flower, field and forest, beast and bird, rock and river, water and mountain and the magnificence and mystery of the earth."

The **Nguzu Saba**, **7 Principles of Kwanza** are:

1. **Umoja** - Unity
2. **Kuji Chakagulia** - Self Determination
3. **Ujima** - Collective Work and Responsibility
4. **Ujamaa** - Cooperative Economics
5. **Nia** - Purpose

BLACK NATIONALISM ALIVE AND WELL

6. **Kuumba** - Creativity
7. **Imani** – Faith

These principles of the **Nguzu Saba** were created, conceived and constructed in the midst of the Black freedom movement. It reflects the movement's emphasis on culture groundings, self determination, social justice, liberation and struggle. This cultural nationalist philosophy called **Kawaida** is a synthesis of the best in African thought and practice in constant interaction and exchange rooted in thought and practice.

The thought and practice is rooted in fundamental propositions of which culture is primary.

Culture – To free oneself, it must be rooted in self-consciousness. The defining feature of any people or nation is its culture. For a people to be itself and free itself it must be self-conscious, self deterring and rooted in its own culture. The quality and life of a people and the success of its generations of culture must be waged by the Cultural Revolution within and the political revolution without. There must be a radical transformation of self, society and utterly humanity. This celebration of Kwanzaa thing gives us an opportunity not only to celebrate the goodness in the world but to meditate on the meaning and being African in the world."

Maulana, as some oftentimes address this titan, insisted, no matter what, "We not lose our social and moral identity as a people, while the world uses our winning freedom strategy as a model for their liberation. We have to stay in Kwanzaa remembering who we are, the elders of humanity. We are the people who spoke the first language and established the first basic principles of human knowledge."

He rightly pointed out, "We were wounded, but we have the capacity to heal ourselves, and in process heal the world. We have to

FREDERICK MONDERSON

celebrate us. Let the world know we are here but we will remain and we will not go quietly! In 2013, we are celebrating and living Kwanzaa, sowing seeds of good."

Black Nationalism 432. African dancers doing their thing in the cultural show before Dr. Karenga spoke.

We are living and harvesting the seeds of good while reminding and reinforcing our obligation to the ancient African to sow and bring good into the world. To build upon the harvesting of sowing seeds of good of necessity, we must practice the **7-Principles** which are the **Nguzu Saba**. We must practice them throughout the year seeing that Kwanza is a living and lived tradition. We must practice them every day. We must practice them in our lives, in our relationships with each other. We must teach them to ourselves and to our children. Teachers must not only teach but they must remain students. We must study ourselves. The first book you must read thoroughly from beginning to end is your life. You will be surprised by the instruction of richness in your life. But you can't read it without the right vocabulary; otherwise you will indict yourself without truly understanding yourself.

BLACK NATIONALISM ALIVE AND WELL

Dr. Karenga rightly recognized the deficiencies of Corporate Media then railed against Social Media, seeing "we are a world historical people; so, can we, after you put up your picture on Social Media, can we engage in conversation without shameless self-exposure? Can we talk about the people in Haiti, the struggle in South Sudan, Congo, Palestine, the rest of the world?"

"We must see ourselves in world encompassing ways. If we don't do that, then our enemies, our oppressors have taught us to appreciate the diminishing segment of ourselves. So we must practice Principles every day. Kwanza is a firm foundation and overarching framework of how we understand ourselves as an African people, living and expressing African ways in the world. It is how we ground ourselves, build relationships, wage our struggle and direct our lives towards good." He keeps reiterating practice of the 7-Principles and sowing seeds of good. He says, "For each good deed done is a seed of good sown. Anytime good seeds are sown they will ultimately bear fruit. A good soul promises and produces good deeds and good seeds. Every good deed done reinforces the belief that we are one in the world."

FREDERICK MONDERSON

Black Nationalism 433. Luis Daniel, one of the young people attending the **Kwanzaa** show in which Dr. Karenga delivered his outstanding lecture on this important festive day.

"Doing good is not difficult. In fact, just speaking good is a compliment to others." In fact, doing good is a manifestation of yourself for if you're goods, you would do good. **The Husia** teaches us, "You are not doing good for someone else, you are sowing good for yourself and this must eventually bear fruit. The **Nguzu Saba** sets out a clear way toward and struggle in the world as African people."

We must establish common ground which we call Communitarian. "We come into being, develop and flourish in relationships. We exist through relationships. The **Ubuntu da Buntu** says, I am a

BLACK NATIONALISM ALIVE AND WELL

person because of other persons." The **7-Principles of Kwanzaa** are thus:

1. **UMJOA** – Unity. The oneness of life. Common interest of our people everywhere. For every principle to be real it must be transformed into a living practice. In striving and maintaining good, we must think of ourselves in world encompassing ways. We are entitled to live our lives, to enjoy rights and responsiblities, to experience a full measure of justice in our time!

Black Nationalism 434. Dr. Segun Shabaka introduces Dr. Karenga.

2. **KUJI CHAKAGULIA** – Self-determination. To strive for and maintain unity in our families, nation and the world. This carries responsibilities without denying other people similar rights. Whatever we claim for ourselves as righteous, we claim for other people. We have the right to define ourselves, to name ourselves, to create for ourselves. If we don't do it, who will?

3. **UJIMA** – Collective work and responsibilities. Shared responsibilities in building a good family, society and world we want

FREDERICK MONDERSON

to live in. We must be concerned about the well-being of the world. To relentlessly resist evil and injustice and to constantly seek common ground is our responsibility. Common good. What can we do together given that we are surrounded on all sides? If you run out of friendships, let's talk about other possibilities.

You must be groundedin culture. Culture is a fundamental way of being human in the world. One of the most useful tools of the oppressor over oppressed people is to make them think like him nad believe they are thinking like themselves.

4.   **UJAMAA** – Cooperative Economics. Teaches us the essence of shared work and shared wealth; a just and equitable share of the goods in the world. Teaches us to struggle to establish policies and practices which aid and empower the poor. To protect and preserve the environment. To a life of dignity and decency for everyone which creates the condition conducive to a life of dignity. Only the oppressor thinks otherwise.

Black Nationalism 435. Part of the entertainment on this Kwanza Day!

5.   **NIA** – Purpose. Given to us in sacred texts to bring good into the world. We are all chosen. This text makes everybody chosen not over anybody but to do one thing, to constantly bring good into the world. Whenever we claim we will do good in the world, we must

BLACK NATIONALISM ALIVE AND WELL

remember it requires work, sacrifice, service. Service is about giving yourself, your mind, and heart, your time and effort. Harriet Tubman, Frederidck Douglass, Malcolm X, the Messenger Mohammed, Ms. Cooper, Nelson Mandela, Robert Sobukwe, Yaa Asantewaa; they all gave themselves in an unselfish manner.

6. **KUUMBA** – Creativity. We must heal, prepare and remake the world into a beautifu and beneficial heritage. These were the instructions of the ancestors. We must ask ourselves, what shall I leave? How can I remake myself in the most beautiful and beneficial way? We must never forget, our fundamental task is to remake the world.

The 3 fundamental principles of white supremacy are domination, depredation and degradation and this is manifested in segregation, Jim Crow and apartheid, where 10 percent of the people control 80 percent of the wealth. They try to control every movement you make. They strive to control your body and mind, even your breathing. They engage in depravation of your sense of dignity. Degration of your blackness. If blackness means nothing, let me have it! They know who we are. We know who we are. Sometimes we forget it.

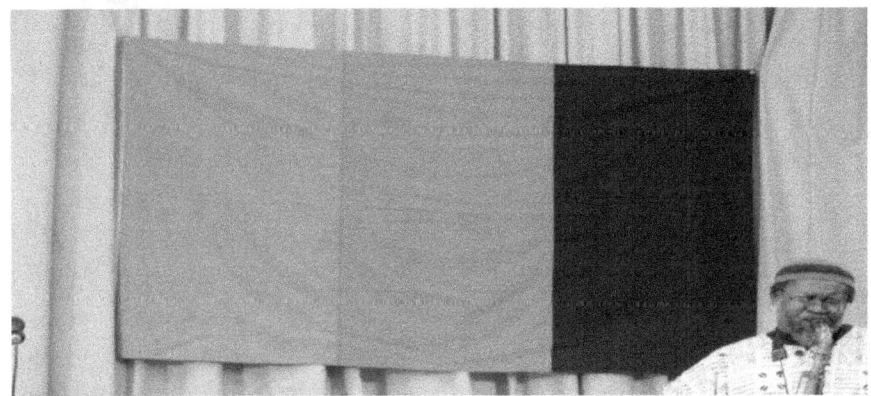

Black Nationalism 436. Before the **Kwanzaa** flag, a saxophonist gives his all for this significant cultural festival.

FREDERICK MONDERSON

Some of us are brainwashed into believing, "If we stop being so much of ourselves, they will let us alone. Ask Obama! He turned every way he could. When people hate you no matter what you do, they will never give you credit."

We must see ourselves as principal in our capacity to heal ourselves. In this we have the capacity to heal the world.

7.   **IMANI** – Faith. Without unity there is no family, friendship, bond, marriage. There is nothing but chaos. We must start with unity.

We must recognize doing good all over the world has its downside. Some people will not thank you . Some will not recognize what you do. However, no good is ever wasted. "I do good for myself. If I don't do good I can't call myself good!" When I do good I am aiding myself, mys community, society and te world!

Black Nationalism 437. Dr. Karenga sits beside his wife on the Dais before the Black Nationalist **Kwanzaa** flag of Green, Red and Black.

BLACK NATIONALISM
ALIVE AND WELL

Black Nationalism 437a. Mteteaji O. Mlimwengu (A.K.A. "Wakili") with the Red, Black and Green on Black Solidarity Day in Brooklyn.

Black Nationalism 438. A mother who brought her daughter to the Unveiling of the new US Postage Stamp in honor of Congresswoman Shirley Chisholm, a fighter for justice and equality.

FREDERICK MONDERSON

On January 31, 2014, the USPS unveiled a postage stamp at Boro Hall in Brooklyn, New York, honoring Congresswoman Shirley Chisholm. Ms. Chisholm, the first Black Woman elected to the United States Congress and the first Black and woman to run for the Presidency, was instrumental in being a "catalyst for change" and paving the way for Blacks especially, and women, who sought political and other forms of empowerment. Many of those in attendance spoke in praise of the visionary from Brooklyn extolling her strength, resolve, commitment and unwavering devotion to children, women's rights and equality, and political and economic empowerment for people of color, women and the poor. Many confessed of the impact the Congresswoman had on their lives. This was particularly so of Rev. Al Sharpton who spoke of his association with Ms. Chisholm from the time he was a 13-year old activist and preacher.

Black Nationalism 438a. Brooklyn Boro President Eric Adams spoke on behalf of Shirley Chisholm, in her role in paving the way for many including this former NYC Police Captain and State Senator to become the leader of the Boro.

BLACK NATIONALISM
ALIVE AND WELL

Black Nationalism 438b. Legendary TV Newscaster Bill McCreary, Brooklyn Boro President Eric Adams and Assistant Post-Master General who unveiled the stamp in honor of Shirley Chisholm.

Black Nationalism 438c. Rev. Al Sharpton spoke on behalf of Ms. Chisholm, praising her influence on him as a young activist.

FREDERICK MONDERSON

Black Nationalism 438d. Congresswoman Yvette Clarke spoke on the influence and impact of Shirley Chisholm in furthering an agenda that championed women, children, jobs, end to poverty and how this "fighter for justice" paved the way as "A Catalyst for Change," for herself and mother Una Clarke who both became New York City Councilwomen.

Black Nationalism 438e. Before the unveiling! All are gathered in anticipation!

BLACK NATIONALISM ALIVE AND WELL

Black Nationalism 438f. The Unveiling of **Black Heritage series US Postal Service Stamp** in honor of Congresswoman Shirley Chisholm.

Black Nationalism 438g. Councilwoman Darlene Mealy, Councilman Robert Cornegy, Boro President Eric Adams, Councilwoman Inez Baron, the Postmaster General, the MC for the program, Rev. Al Sharpton, Congresswoman Yvette Clarke and Congressman Charlie Rangel.

FREDERICK MONDERSON

Black Nationalism 438h. Time to reflect, Caucus and look to the future with a serious eye on the past!

Black Nationalism 438i. Shirley Chisholm, "Catalyst for Change," gets her due recognition; for it is said, if the United States Postal Service recognizes your work and value then it's a significant honor; but more importantly, it represents recognition of a tremendous life of service undergirded by integrity, daring, intellectuality and an unwavering commitment to aid and speak for people, without a voice or power, across a wide spectrum of the nation who benefitted tremendously from the Congresswoman's unselfish efforts.

www.ingramcontent.com/pod-product-compliance
Lightning Source LLC
Chambersburg PA
CBHW050319020526
44117CB00031B/1245